Academic Films
for the Classroom

Academic Films for the Classroom
A History

GEOFF ALEXANDER

Foreword by Rick Prelinger

McFarland & Company, Inc., Publishers
Jefferson, North Carolina, and London

Frontispiece: Encyclopædia Britannica's Tom Smith makes a new friend (Isidore Mankofsky, A.S.C.).

LIBRARY OF CONGRESS CATALOGUING-IN-PUBLICATION DATA

Alexander, Geoff, 1952–
Academic films for the classroom : a history /
Geoff Alexander ; foreword by Rick Prelinger.
    p.   cm.
Includes bibliographical references and index.

ISBN 978-0-7864-5870-7

1. Motion pictures in education — History.
2. Educational films — History. I. Title.
LB1044.A535   2010   371.33'523 — dc22   2010025348

British Library cataloguing data are available

©2010 Geoff Alexander. All rights reserved

No part of this book may be reproduced or transmitted in any form or by any means, electronic or mechanical, including photocopying or recording, or by any information storage and retrieval system, without permission in writing from the publisher.

Front cover: the "on screen" shot has CRM's Steve Katten (left) and Larry Logan filming in a California poppy field (courtesy Peter Jordan, CRM); classroom scene ©2010 Shutterstock

Manufactured in the United States of America

*McFarland & Company, Inc., Publishers
Box 611, Jefferson, North Carolina 28640
www.mcfarlandpub.com*

To the memory of John Barnes,
who fought intellectually and passionately
to forge a standard for cognitive and affective
excellence in the academic educational film.

Table of Contents

Acknowledgments ix
Foreword by Rick Prelinger 1
Preface 3
List of Abbreviations 11

One   The Formative Years of Educational Film: 1900–1960   13
Two   A Cold War Funds a Hot Medium: The Progressive Era, 1961–1985   38
Three   Writing a New Cookbook: How Academic Films Were Funded, Made, Bought, and Sold in the Progressive Era   47
Four   The Companies That Made the Films and the People Behind Them   62
Five   Immortal Longings: The Life and Films of John Barnes   139
Six   Profiles of 34 Significant Academic Filmmakers   157
Seven   Final Takes: The Denouement of the Academic Film in Classrooms and Its Resurgence on the Internet   194

Appendix A: 36 Films in This Book Currently Available for Free Viewing Online   201
Appendix B: Milestones in Academic Film   204
Appendix C: Requiem   206
Chapter Notes   209
Bibliography   219
Index   223

Acknowledgments

This book would not have been possible without the cooperation of more than 150 producers, directors, executives, cinematographers, writers, subject experts, and librarians, many of whom are no longer with us. They helped to create and elevate the world of the academic educational film in North America and consented to be interviewed for this book.

Several of these individuals went well beyond the call of duty. In particular, Charles Benton was exceptionally generous in providing not only his opinions, but his time in reviewing the early draft and in helping me weave though the important areas of public law and corporate lobbying. Learning Corporation of America's Bill Deneen was exceedingly gracious in providing constant support for the project, and courageously provided access to his correspondence. I am indebted to Martha Gonzalez, who embodies the heart and passion that makes academic film an endlessly fascinating discovery. John Barnes generously opened his personal archive of letters and contracts before he passed away, and I thank Jeanne Barnes for giving me access to these. Isidore Mankofsky, Bill Pierce, Lois Siegel, and Encyclopædia Britannica's Bill Bowe all enthusiastically gave me access to important photo archives.

I thank Marti Gorman, who spent hours on the book on her own dime simply because she loved the project and encouraged me to do away with my reliance on and love for the subordinate clause. Barinda Samra was with me when I acquired my first film and was at my side when I founded the Academic Film Archive of North America. I want to thank the AFA staff, including Robert Emmett and Kirsten McGlynn, Michael Selic, Margie Newman, Dave Peters, Scott Edmonson, Dan Greenbank, and Bruce Wakayama. They have put more volunteer hours into preserving and documenting academic classroom films than I can count. Without Alida Bray and her team at History San Jose, we would not have had the space to archive our films. Rick Prelinger has been a longtime supporter of my research, and generously agreed to write the Foreword. A very special personal thanks to Dr. Gary Steinberg and the team at Stanford University Hospital. And without the timely assistance of Iris Shimada during a medical crisis, I would not have been around to finish this book.

The following individuals cannot be adequately thanked for the time they took to discuss their involvement with academic film, and there are many more who I cannot list for reasons of space. My deepest appreciation and heartfelt thanks to them all: Lynn and Denise Adams, Johanna Alemann, Bill Ambrose, Don Barr, Frank Batavick, Myrna Berlet, Peter Boulton, Judith Bronowski, Sam Bryan, Nick Charney, Peter Chermayeff, Bruce and Katharine Cornwell, Nadine Covert, Stan Croner, Tom Daly, Carson Davidson, Jack & Fran Davidson, Gene Deitch, Peter Dow, Gwynne Dyer, Gary Evans, Warren Everote, Clifton

Fadiman, Chuck Finance, Virginia Garner, Robert Geller, Stephanie Glidden, Linda Gottlieb, Leo Handel, Milan & Shanta Herzog, Bruce Hoffman, Don Hoffman, Preston Holdner, George Holland, John Hoskyns-Abrahall, Barry Howells, Patterson Hume, Grace Garland Janisz, Piers Jessop, D.B. Jones, Emily Jones, Becky Jordan, Peter Jordan, Harry Joy, George Kaczender, David Kennard, Wolf Koenig, Bob Kohl, Richard Leacock, Richard Lukin, Elaine Mason, John Matoian, David McCallum, Gerald McDermott, Jay McMullen, Ib Melchior, Ken Middleham, Wayne Mitchell, Donald Moffat, Peter Morris, Russ Mosser, Bill O'Farrell, Jerry Olk, Stephen Parr, Ted Peshak, Sidney Platt, Alan Root, Bruce Russell, Sheldon Sachs, Paul Saltzman, Bert Salzman, Morton Schindel, Brian Sellstrom, Wynn "Biff" Sherman, J.G. Secondari, Tom Smith, Marion Sloan, Mike Solin, Philip Stapp & Johnny Bass, Ann Stevenson, Phyllis Stanton, Phil Stockton, George Stoney, Patricia Harvey-Thompson, Bert Van Bork, Richard Von Busack, Tina Viljoen, Frank Visco, Amos and Marcia Vogel, Mel Waskin, Hal Weiner, Clifford & Bente West, David Wexler, Bernard Wilets, Jon & Nancy Wilkman, Donald Winkler, Art Wolf, Mike Wright, Robert M. Young, Larry and Clara Yust.

Foreword
by Rick Prelinger

For the past twenty years, Geoff Alexander has been the lead investigator of a rich body of film production where many have labored but few are remembered. Today he combines the diverse threads from his career as collector, archivist, critic, exhibitor, annotator and advocate into a book that transmits a message likely to surprise those of us who consider ourselves knowledgeable about film: cinema history is not what we thought it was.

While most cinema students concentrate on feature films, documentaries and those examples of independent, avant-garde and experimental work that have survived the scholarly canonization process, few have ventured to examine the far greater number of films produced for educational purposes. Aside from contemporary coverage and sporadic reviews in now-defunct educational film journals, there is almost no critical or historical assessment of a body of work that comprises well over one hundred thousand films. What little has been written tends to concentrate on low-hanging fruit (social guidance films, safety training and driver education films), and focuses more on the films' (often unconsciously) entertaining qualities and their subject matter than on how the films actually functioned as films. And while numerous scholarly works have addressed the history, production and house styles of the major Hollywood studios, almost no one has done similar work on educational film companies, some of which (like Encyclopædia Britannica) produced thousands of films.

Alexander's book therefore addresses a substantial gap in our understanding of film history. Focusing on a genre that he himself has identified and named — the academic film — he traces the history of knowledge dissemination in film from the silent era through the 1980s, when film finally gave way to video-based and digital media. The films he describes aren't campy guidance titles that litter late-night television; rather, they're sophisticated productions that represent the work of hundreds of skilled and thoughtful makers. Many were made with a sense that they were works of cinematic art, and many represent the ideas, discoveries and narratives of eminent artists, writers, musicians, scholars and scientists. In this sense it seems highly ironic that films that aimed so much higher than studio-produced mass entertainment have been implicitly less valued by scholars. While nothing seems more out of date than an old textbook, these films still evoke immense power, embodying vivid evidence of a longtime campaign to infuse education with drama, emotional intensity, and innovative representational styles and strategies.

There is much here that illuminates areas where few have ventured before. The interaction of pedagogies with corporate cultures and budgets always piques the interest of educational film viewers, but has not received detailed treatment before Alexander's study of

Encyclopædia Britannica Films. Alexander also traces the complex history of federal government-funded educational initiatives, some enacted as a direct result of the Soviet space challenge, and shows how political and legislative exigencies shaped film content and reach. Addressing many commonly asked questions about the production and distribution of educational films, his "Cookbook" chapter clarifies issues that cannot easily be gleaned from simple viewing. His detailed profiles of large and small production companies and key makers, many created as an adjunct to his pioneer efforts to exhibit academic films to public audiences, are definitive references that will inform every scholar in this field. Finally, his profile of John Barnes establishes Barnes's place as a key auteur in an underappreciated field and sets the stage for deep study of his unjustly neglected works.

Along with fans, independent scholars are often the first to identify and analyze bodies of cultural work that have been overlooked or ignored by the institutionally affiliated, and film history is an area where individuals outside the academy play a key role. As if to recognize this, in recent years the vector from independent study to peer-reviewed scholarship has dramatically shortened. As students seeking to work in uncharted territories begin to take notice of tens of thousands of meritorious academic films that now await discovery and analysis, I believe we will see the contours of cinema studies begin to expand in the same way they are now opening to other ephemeral and orphaned genres, such as sponsored films and home movies.

John Barnes on the set of *Shaw vs. Shakespeare* (1970) (Bill Pierce).

While this book pulls together the fruits of Alexander's pioneering work, perhaps its most lasting contribution will be to serve as a point of departure for all who seek to understand, appreciate and theorize the lost art of the academic film. Full of discoveries, it also points toward the many discoveries yet to be made. I very much hope that *Academic Films for the Classroom* will inspire a new generation of scholars (and audiences) to turn their attention towards these films — their artistic, cultural and historical value necessitates their immediate rescue from jeopardy and obscurity.

RICK PRELINGER *is an archivist, writer and filmmaker in San Francisco. His collection of over 60,000 educational, advertising and amateur films was acquired by the Library of Congress in 2002.*

Preface

Everything that moves on the screen is cinema. I often hear people say: "A very interesting film, no doubt, but not cinema." I don't know why the use of pictures that move should be restricted to traditional melodrama or farcical comedy. A geographical film is cinema just as much as Ben Hur. *A film designed to teach children the alphabet has as much claim to be considered cinema as a grandiose production with psychological pretensions.*[1] — Jean Renoir

What do a world-renowned architect, the special effects genius behind *Star Wars*, a World War II spy for the OSS, a secretive man whose final effects were sold on the floor of a gun dealer's, and a pilot who crafted a secret compartment in his plane to carry cinematic contraband have in common? They all participated in making classroom academic films, and they spied, smuggled, shot, or spanked (*that* story doesn't make it into the book, sorry) their way into an industry that created many of the most visually compelling and intellectually stimulating films of the 20th century.

That historically significant, culturally valuable, and artistically prolific film movement very nearly disappeared before our eyes, however. Yet how could it? After all, millions of us saw hundreds of academic educational films while we were in school. Part of the reason is that this revolution in film, education, and culture has very little formal written history to date and has, up until very recently, been pretty much ignored by scholars. The 16mm classroom academic film is a phenomenon that's not old enough to be *antique*, but just old enough to be seen as *moldy*. Reason enough for a scholarly vacuum.

The good news is that academic films are beginning to be more popular on the Internet, where anyone with Internet access can view them. And people *are* viewing them. Millions are viewing them today on computers and hand-held devices, everyone from Baby Boomers to retro fanatics to independent film producers. The bad news is that many original 16mm prints are still being thrown away, and are in danger of becoming lost forever. The book you're reading is the first to define Academic Film as a genre. It offers a number of solutions, but asks a number of critical questions as well. What, exactly, were these films? Why, for whom, and by whom were they created? What objectives did they hope to accomplish? Why should academic films be documented and saved? What will be lost if they're not saved? This book is also your guide to some of the finest academic films ever made. That begs another question: what makes them worthy of the appellation "finest"? From the catbird seat of the future, we can now see that the best of them stand the test of time remarkably well. And from a sobering perspective, there is an unmistaken urgency to this book, which seeks nothing less than to save a great many classroom educational films from oblivion.

Cinematic Archaeology: The Quest to Uncover a Hidden Past

Before I define what Academic films are, I want to tell you why I think they're important, and why I've taken a few years out of my life to interview the principals, watch the films, and write this book.

My passion for these films was formed in the mid 1970s, when, as an instructional aide for the Santa Clara County Office of Education, I used academic films in the classroom. I used to review the films the evening before the lesson by taking them and a projector home, shining the beam against the apartment across the alley, and inviting friends to watch as well. In 1992, long after I'd stopped teaching, the local public library began selling off its 16mm films. I bought what I could carry at $25 per title to show in my backyard to friends on warm summer nights. They were terrific, so I contacted my old school film library and found out that the collection would soon be coming up for sale as well. I bought the entire collection for several thousand dollars, and I suddenly owned an educational film library. It quickly took over my entire basement, much of the house, and the backyard potting shed.

As I watched more and more of these films, I was exceptionally surprised at the cinematic quality of many of them. I began to wonder about the people who had made them: many appeared to be cinematic *auteurs* who had their own style and panache. I did some research to find out who they were, and found nothing. As it turned out, very little had been written about them other than a few magazine articles here and there, and a fine but nearly forgotten body of work generated over the years by the Educational Film Library Association, of which I was unaware at the time. It was as though the films I had acquired never existed beyond a brief moment in historic time, headstoned by a credit line on a film header. I then looked up some of the companies that made these films. They were mostly gone, too.

I couldn't really believe that what appeared to be a significant movement in film had vanished so quickly and so completely, so I began making phone calls. At Encyclopædia Britannica, I found Phil Stockton, who led me to John Barnes, who pointed me to Larry Yust. Soon, I found myself in a race against time, as many of the filmmakers and film executives were getting on in years. I followed leads, conducted interviews, and documented the stories about a forgotten film movement. Getting their stories before they vanished became a compelling mission.

In 1996, I began showing these films to small groups of invited guests on occasional Saturday nights in the backyard of my home. A cranky neighbor, perplexed by this amateur film event, called the San Jose police with a noise complaint, and three squad cars showed up in riot gear with a demand to break up the party. My backyard cinema was out of business, but it gave me the idea that perhaps a more traditional public venue would expose more people to these films. I then began holding free public cinema events in a bar beneath the streets of San Jose. And thus was born ciné16, a bohemian environment in which attendees were free to smoke, drink, and watch these amazing films. I was helped tremendously by volunteers (and later Academic Film Archive of North America officers) Barinda Samra, Mike Selic, and Robert Emmett McGlynn. In 1997, I began the manuscript which has become this book.

Between 1996 and 2004, we held 412 events at which more than 1,500 films were shown. The filmnotes for these shows are posted on www.afana.org. Documentarian Richard Leacock, who made several academic films, was among the many filmmakers who traveled to join our salons and discuss their films.

As I viewed thousands of films and conducted hundreds of interviews, it became apparent that a formal research center was necessary if the history of this film genre were to survive. In 2001, I founded the Academic Film Archive of North America (AFA) as a non-profit organization dedicated to "acquiring, preserving, documenting, and promoting academic film by providing an archive, resource, and forum for continuing scholarly advancement and public exhibition." Big words, and an even bigger job.

Defining Academic Film

Although it's nearly impossible to determine the exact number, an estimated 100,000 16mm films were distributed for educational purposes to North American schools from the early part of this century through approximately 1987.[2] It became apparent to me that in reality two sub-genres, *academic* and *guidance* films, made up the Educational film world, each with different educational objectives and made by different groups of filmmakers.

For many, the term "educational film" evokes thoughts of school bus safety, hygiene, and teen dating films. To be more precise, these are examples of the *guidance* film sub-genre which, although they provide high entertainment and social history value for today's viewers, make up only a part of the world of educational film. *Academic* films, which were designed to enhance the learning experience in the humanities and sciences, make up the other significant element. While guidance films have enjoyed something of a resurgence in art houses and micro-cinemas, Academic films have been all but lost. They simply don't receive high enough marks on the prevailing camp, kitsch, and socio-historic relevancy scale.

What are the significant differences between guidance and academic films? Guidance films had the prime objective of inculcating a certain form of behavior, or promoting behavioral change. They were largely dependent on the social values of a specific era, and thus could become quickly dated as fashions, mores, and tastes evolved. Today, many of them serve primarily as historical markers indicating societal change. The prime objective of academic films, on the other hand, was to disseminate knowledge. The vast majority of academic films featured a scholar as a content expert. Although knowledge itself is in a constant state of evolution, the content of many academic films remains fresh, interesting, topical, and powerful 20 to 50 years after their initial distribution. The cinematic treatments given academic films by their creators are often remarkable, and play a large role in the academic film story. This book emphatically focuses on the academic film as an independent and important film sub-genre of the 16mm educational film world, worthy of renewed study and interest. Considering the fact that they are rapidly being deaccessioned from film libraries the world over, this book promotes their salvation.

What kind of people specialized in making academic films? The finest of these films were made by exceptional technicians who excelled in the craft of telling compelling stories, even when shackled by the relatively low budgets imposed by often penurious educational film companies. Some of the fascinating people who made these films started as war cinematographers, others as documentarians, and still others as teachers who, after acting as advising scholars for other filmmakers, began making their own films. Their talent was in the art of telling a story in a period of time short enough to allow for classroom discussion afterward, often in just 20 to 30 minutes. Academic filmmakers' place in cinema is analogous to that of short story writers in literature who, unlike their novel-writing colleagues, must delight, challenge, and intrigue the reader in a single sitting. Some were recognized by

Academy Award nominations and Oscars (John Barnes, Bert Salzman, Bert Van Bork, for example), while others went on to brilliant careers as documentary filmmakers (like Richard Leacock and Bob Young), or made feature films (such as George Kaczender and Larry Yust). Most, however, remained exclusively in the academic film world, perhaps occasionally venturing out to make a sponsored institutional film for a corporate client to put a little bit of extra bread on the table. While business films might not have been as interesting to make as Academic films, the renumeration was greater, even if gaining it meant commiserating with people the filmmaker might occasionally have found distasteful on a personal level. Academic filmmakers were never very well paid. Many have admitted that they were supported by working spouses and family loans as they pursued their craft.

Why are their films important today? In addition to the fact that many were exceptional works of cinema in their own right, these films tell us a little about who we are as people and, more than occasionally, show how we got here. Academic films shown to us as children helped shape our evolving opinions and future actions. *Science* films encouraged us to understand the importance of ecosystems to global well-being, and showed us the colorful, fascinating world of micro-organisms found in a drop of lake water. *Literature* films made Shakespeare a little more accessible and graphically displayed the horror of tales such as Shirley Jackson's short story *The Lottery*. *Social studies* films instilled in many of us the desire to build and maintain a racially diverse and integrated society, and introduced us to the beauties of—and challenges faced by—nations and cultures in an ever-shrinking world. *History* films, while bringing to life the drama of events such as the Constitutional Convention of 1787, also perhaps propagandized a generation into being willing fighters in at least one costly and, many would argue, unproductive war.

If, as many educational theorists believe, classroom discussions facilitate learning more effectively than lessons involving only non-interactive lectures and reading, then academic films may have been an important spark that lit the flame of our own youthful opinions as we tested them out on our parents, teachers and fellow students.

Because of their pervasiveness in the classroom, most of us probably saw more academic films as children and adolescents than we did feature films during our formative years. Yet, with very few exceptions, these films have passed from our conscious memories, lying as artifacts buried under increasing layers of informational silt, while the knowledge they conveyed, to a greater or a lesser degree depending on the film, has remained.

If classroom academic films are so important within the overall context of North American cinema, why are they ignored by scholars and film historians alike? This question can be answered by understanding two contextual elements that reflect little on the absolute quality of the films, but bear heavily on their perception: the classroom as the original screening venue, and the adolescent age of the viewer.

When we first saw these films as youths, we classified them as schoolwork, warily filling out mimeographed work sheets with one eye as we attempted to view the film with the other. Unlike other arts that were accessible in books commonly found in libraries, the classic feature and documentary films that many of us needed to see to develop an appreciation for the cinematic form were not available until, as young adults, we spent hard-earned dollars in art and repertory houses catching up on *nouvelle-vague*, *neo-realism*, and *film noir*. By that time, the academic films we saw in school, often steeped in these same cinematic traditions, were just a dim memory or forgotten completely.

The most engaging films of this genre were intellectually stimulating, engaging, and often multicultural. The greatest Academic filmmakers occupied a rarefied stratum, producing films on history, ethno-cultural subjects, the arts, humanities, and the sciences that stand the test of time, culture, and age. They provoke a certain wonder that inspired cinema such as this could have been for the most part buried in school libraries, out of the public eye for so long.

A Call for Survival and Preservation

Sixteen-millimeter academic film as a discrete medium is pretty much lost, and understanding the reasons for its demise is an important element in recognizing the need for its preservation. Funding issues related to a changing political climate and shifts in technology are to blame, probably the same two main reasons that most art movements eventually fall out of fashion. Although academic films are increasingly becoming available for viewing on the Internet, it's a bit too early to fully rejoice.

What made these films go away? Public funding for classroom films, much of it initiated by the political fear engendered by the Soviet launch of Sputnik in October 1957, was dramatically curtailed as the perception of Russia as a global threat diminished. The leap — and some, with a perspective on quality of resolution, would call it a descent — of school media libraries into the video era was ushered in by the high cost of films (generally $195 to $900 per title), the difficulty of using and maintaining film projectors, and the labor costs associated with film maintenance. Film companies, in rushing to service this new lower-cost-per-unit video medium, refused to transfer films to video that they considered old, outdated, or which appealed to too small a segment of the market.

By 1985, the wholesale destruction of the 16mm classroom academic film world was already underway, as venerated academic film companies were already in the process of leaving the business. Important historical ephemera, such as records, letters, publicity stills and production photographs, were thrown into dumpsters by corporate survivors, descendants of filmmakers, or even filmmakers themselves, convinced that their work was no longer valued. Written records of their philosophies, goals, objectives, and ideas have been scattered on the winds of time, and have finally settled, becoming another stripe of sediment in the humus of our culture. The entire film libraries of some smaller companies vanished as principals passed away, their descendants uninterested in the remnants of a legacy consisting of heavy, dusty cans of film that they believed no longer had any commercial value.

More tragic yet, the filmmakers themselves are also disappearing. Possessors of a unique history, they can relate the story from the perspective of those who created it in a quest that was often life-long, whether or not they had originally intended it to be such. It is critical to document this history while as many of the filmmakers as possible are still living and able to discern omissions and correct any errors. Academic films must be recognized as a significant part of North American film history so that those that remain are not destroyed and forgotten. There is still time to put a stake in the ground and make a case for cataloguing, preserving, and yes, even showing 16mm academic films in contemporary cinematic venues.

Today, many media libraries are contributing to the disappearance of important academic film content as they sell off films to the highest bidder (who is often mining for the lucrative gold of high-camp Guidance films from the 1950s, to be sold in online auctions) or by literally throwing them into dumpsters, sealing the destruction of these collections, which originally cost hundreds of thousands of public dollars to create.[3]

Very much like the sudden end of the silent film era, in which the historical value of the genre went unrecognized until decades after its passing, 16mm classroom academic films are rapidly disappearing. Film historian Penelope Houston points out the danger of recognizing the value of film genres too late in the game, estimating that 80 percent of all silent films have been irretrievably lost.[4] Academic film has been in decline for more than 20 years, and it is high time to recognize the value of this hidden corner of North American cinema and take steps to ensure that extant prints are salvaged.

It is critical to take a fresh look at this little-understood star in the film firmament before its history erodes completely. All but a very few of the film companies specializing in academic film have changed hands or disappeared entirely. Prints of many important academic films are increasingly difficult or impossible to find, and even when individual prints have survived, there is no guarantee that pre-print cinematic materials from which future prints can be made are still in existence.

What's in This Book?

Approximately 7,000 academic films from the collections of roughly 200 school and public libraries were viewed during the process of writing this book. I have mentioned those that I consider to be among the most engaging and relevant from the perspective of effectiveness of treatment, cinematography, writing, and editing. This book is a reference manual that describes the history, philosophy, and economic realities that provided the structure around which these films were created.

In writing this book, while a fairly straight chronological reading of classroom film history made sense when describing the relatively static pre–1960 years, it didn't when describing the massive upheaval that characterized the post–1960 era. Growth during that later era was chaotic, like a series of Venn diagrams that evolved into yet more Venn diagrams. The post–1960 years, therefore, are most effectively told as the histories of individual filmmakers and film companies. If it seems as though that post–1960 era was metaphorically the Big Bang theory as classroom film history, it's because it was, with the Elementary and Secondary Educational Act (discussed in Chapter Two) at its core.

Many of the most compelling academic films were produced between 1960 and 1985. The significance of this progressive era can best be understood by looking at what preceded it. Chapter One describes the earlier, pre–1960s era of educational film, the advent of the 16mm film format, the emergence of the military training film, and some of the significant people and companies participating in its development. The better known of these include Western Electric's Educational Research Products Inc. (ERPI) films, and later, William Benton's Encyclopædia Britannica Films, Coronet Films (founded by David Smart of *Esquire* magazine), and the early efforts of John Grierson at the National Film Board of Canada.

Chapter Two begins by examining the massive changes in the educational film world brought on by the launch of the Soviet satellite Sputnik, essential to the understanding of how many of the most memorable films of the genre were funded and produced. The world of academic film was heavily influenced by public laws such as the Elementary and Secondary Educational Act (ESEA), and the Civil Rights Act of 1964. The films that were made as a direct result of laws such as these form a significant part of the history of education in the United States. This chapter looks at the ways various Acts of Congress helped shape subject matter, film treatment, curriculum, and classroom diversity.

In addition to being a foundation of curriculum and an important vehicle for filmmakers to develop and create new ideas, classroom films were also a *business*. Chapter Three unveils how films were budgeted, planned, produced, sold, and how school districts and film libraries acquired film.

The history of the "golden era" of educational film from 1961 to 1985 is to a great extent the history of educational film companies, the people who ran them, and the filmmakers who worked for and with them. Chapter Four introduces many of the most significant academic film companies and principals, shares the joy of their successes, the tears of their divestitures, and at times, the agony of their failures. This chapter also looks at films produced by television networks, which, via distribution by classroom film companies, were also a big part of the academic film picture.

Through vision, craft, and creativity, the most resourceful academic filmmakers overcame the obstacles of low budgets and curmudgeonly management, often creating outstanding works of cinematic art in spite of inadequate sets, costumes, and personnel. The work of John Barnes stands out as exceptional in its artistic quality, breadth of subject matter, and timelessness. The profile of Barnes in Chapter Five describes a filmmaker who many consider the exemplification of an uncompromising director. The chapter devoted to his life and work captures the milieu familiar to every filmmaker who worked in (and, as one might expect, occasionally fought to escape from) the world of 16mm educational film. The dialogues, battles, and negotiations with his film company as detailed in this chapter are echoed by scores of his colleagues.

Barnes, of course, was not the only exceptional filmmaker noted for making Academic films. Chapter Six introduces many of the most significant filmmakers of the era, including Bruce Russell, Paul Saltzman, Bert Salzman, Bert Van Bork, Bernard Wilets, and Larry Yust. These are just a few whose work will stand the test of time as informative, entertaining, and exciting according to the cinematic standards of any era.

Chapter Seven provides optimistic suggestions for the survival of the academic film. By virtue of the fact that you're reading this book, you are part of the solution. I hope that as you turn these pages, you will want to know more about various films and filmmakers, and will also want to seek out physical and cyberspace venues that show them.

Also included are three appendices. More and more academic films are becoming available for free viewing on the Internet, including many of those mentioned in this book. Appendix A provides a list of 35 films mentioned in the text that are available free to view on the Internet, along with their URLs. Such films are indicated in the text of the book by an "*" before the year of release (e.g., *1971). Appendix B, is a thumbnail history of some of the critical landmarks discussed in this book. I have also included, as Appendix C, a Requiem for academic film filmmakers and principals who contributed their thoughts to this book, and died before they could see the finished copy. They would have appreciated knowing that their work was not forgotten.

Why This Book?

This book serves a threefold purpose. It introduces (or perhaps re-introduces) important academic films to viewers who saw them in school or came along later to view them in the Internet age. Today's viewers are intrigued and interested in the films, and are searching for context that is found here. The book describes the history of the film companies and filmmakers associated with this genre, and, before they slip away from us, issues an urgent call for the cinematic re-evaluation and preservation of their important contributions to North American cinema. It is also a lodestar for scholars and media historians seeking to contribute to the literature. There are many jumping off points for them, among which are foreign language instruction and primary school and children's films. While such films are not the prime focus of this book, they are but two of the many research areas available to scholars that are deserving of further investigation.

Preserving the 16mm academic film genre is the soul of the book, and the appreciation of the makers of these films is its heart. Many of the filmmakers were, and are, exceptional craftspeople, storytellers, and visionaries. Filmmakers working in the educational realm are among the most underrated stars in the film galaxy. Viewing their work now, we are beginning to see a nebula of film unfolding that we somehow missed as budding secondary school students. These filmmakers are undeniably among the last undiscovered film geniuses of the 20th century. This book attempts to bring them and their work to wider acclaim as perhaps the most powerful argument to save these films from destruction and oblivion.

A Note on the Research

After seeing and documenting over 7,000 of these films, talking with scores of filmmakers and others associated with the making of these films, and reading through quite a bit of literature, I realize I still only have part of the story. As I mentioned before, many of the people who could provide a great amount of detail are now gone. Many of those remaining have the admittedly spotty memories of many people in their advanced years (although I'm continually amazed at what they do remember, and how often these memories are corroborated by others). There are still stories out there, yet unknown to me, that I wish I could have uncovered, but didn't. I know where these fallow acres lie, but I think I'll let you discover them by troweling on your own. The information you have in this book is the best I've been able to accumulate to date. You'll pick up on my biases, occasionally (annoying music on soundtracks? Oh yeah!). I formed a lot of opinions in watching these films, and I'm comfortable with them, as well as owning up to any errors herein that future scholars uncover. They're mine. That's one of the beauties of scholarship, so I throw down the gauntlet to today's cinema studies and history scholars: go after my opinions and find new and heretofore buried knowledge on academic film.

List of Abbreviations

AFA	Academic Film Archive of North America
AGC	Altschul Group Corporation
AGI	American Geological Institute
BBC	British Broadcasting Corp.
BFA	Bailey/Film Associates
CBC	Canadian Broadcasting Corp.
CRM	a film company whose name was an acronym derived from the last names of its founders, Nicolas Charney, George Reynolds, and Winslow Marston
EBEC	Encyclopædia Britannica Educational Corporation
EBF	Encyclopædia Britannica Films
EFLA	Educational Film Library Association
ERPI	Educational Research Products Inc.
ESEA	Elementary and Secondary Education Act
ESI	Educational Services, Inc
IFB	International Film Bureau
IFF	International Film Foundation
FWU	Institut für Film und Bild in Wissenschaft und Unterricht (Institute for Film and Picture, in Science and Instruction, abbreviated to FWU)
LCA	Learning Corporation of America
MACOS	Man: A Course of Study
MIS	Moody Institute of Science
NDEA	National Defense Education Act
NET	National educational Television
NFBC	National Film Board of Canada
NGEO	National Geographic
NSF	National Science Foundation
PSSC	Physical Science Study Committee
SND	Screen News Digest
SSR	Science Screen Report

CHAPTER ONE

The Formative Years of Educational Film: 1900–1960

In order to fully comprehend the dramatic evolution that took place in the 1960s in terms of the overall cinematic quality and educational effectiveness of academic film, it's important to understand the formative years of the educational film movement. Early contributions by Thomas Edison and others, the decisions made by the Hollywood studios, the role of military training films, and the beginning years of companies that specialized in educational film, all played critical roles in the development of 16mm academic film.

The larger-than-life personalities of the owners of these emerging educational film companies were particularly influential, and helped determine the overall philosophy and direction of the medium. William Benton's alliances with the intelligentsia at Encyclopædia Britannica and the University of Chicago, David Smart and Jack Abraham's "lean and mean" policies at Coronet, Julien Bryan's multicultural emphasis at the International Film Foundation, and John Grierson's insistence on detail at the National Film Board of Canada constituted perhaps four of the most influential philosophical paradigms that shaped the world of academic film. In discussing their contributions, we can clearly see how they influenced the trends and revolutions that formed the base upon which the progressive era of post 1960 academic film was built.

Like many other books on aspects of cinematic history, this one is heavily laden with judgment and opinion. Prior to jumping into the history of the early years, I'd like to discuss qualitative issues surrounding the concept of "quality" as it relates to academic film.

A Qualitative Assessment of Academic Film Through Bloom's Taxonomy

In compiling a historical record of the world of the educational classroom film, one invariably begins to form qualitative judgments about the films themselves. A researcher who views thousands of these films chooses favorites, loves certain films, film companies, and directors, and forms negative opinions about others. One tries to be objective, then realizes that objectivity is an elusive construct. Therefore, a word or two is in order here regarding the approach I've found useful in judging the efficacy of a film. I found it to be of value to view academic films from two perspectives, those of overall cinematic quality, and of educational value. Of the former, professional standards of cinematography, directing,

An Educational Research Products Inc. crew filming in Africa (courtesy Encyclopædia Britannica, Inc.).

acting, graphics, and set design are just as important as in any other form of cinema. There is no reason for the scholar, critic, or viewer to judge academic films differently than any feature film or documentary.

There are many ways to judge the educational value of a film, but there may be none better than the taxonomy initially developed by Benjamin Bloom. Bloom's Taxonomy was introduced by the University of Chicago educational psychologist in 1956, and consists of three learning domains: *psychomotor*, *cognitive*, and *affective*. The latter two are extremely applicable to gauging the value of an academic film.[1]

In terms of the *cognitive* domain, we can ascertain if the material is relevant to the subject, presented in an easy-to-understand manner, and topically appropriate to the stated or implied learning objective(s). Learning objectives are often stated in the first minute or so of the film, and are commonly found listed on a study guide found in the film can itself, either glued inside the lid, or inserted as a stand-alone document.[2]

Much of the "art and craft" particular to academic film can be associated with the *affective* domain. Distilling the 200 or so pages of *Handbook II: Affective Domain*[3] into its simplest form, one must determine if, after seeing the film, the viewer has expressed an interest in learning more about the subject, is enthusiastic about its presentation, or perhaps even wants to see the film again. The "wow" factor is implicit in characterizing a film as being affectively successful or not. In viewing thousands of academic films, there have been many cases in which, as an educator, programmer, or archivist, I've prioritized viewing an entire film series (Bruce Russell's *Biological Sciences* series comes immediately to mind) or the work of a particular filmmaker (for example, Bert Van Bork) based on the affective qualities of a single film. I therefore use the term *affective* liberally throughout the text to indicate films that, in my opinion, are superior academic films that rise above the mundane and ordinary, and stand the test of time as interesting, even exciting, decades after their initial distribution.

One also must be cognizant of the original educational objective of the film. I've found it of value to determine if, even when viewed decades after its initial distribution date, the film can still enthuse and instruct viewers, thereby achieving its learning objective in an affective fashion years later. I call this *latent objective value*. One reason for considering this concept is that I believe film companies that today hold these old film properties will eventually consider using them in repackaged form to serve again as valid educational tools. Some film companies clearly understood the value of presenting a topic in a form that would, to a certain degree, stand the test of time. At Encyclopædia Britannica, for instance, a certain degree of care was taken to see that students would not make fun of a film. Under the leadership of president Maurice Mitchell, music was eschewed for a number of reasons, one being that music could become quickly dated, and students would then relate to the film as being hokey, content and all. This issue of content verisimilitude prioritized the value of presentation in all of its facets, including writing, acting direction, and sets, in part by trying to anticipate the potential criticisms of student-viewers and teachers. Dating from William Benton's days as president of EB Films, when he changed the company's newly acquired film entity from the name ERPI because he'd once heard a student refer to it as "burpy," the company had a thin skin when it came to laughter at the expense of any of its films.

With an eye to the future and a sense of some of the concepts behind what constitutes an educationally effective academic film, let's look at the important foundations of the academic film movement.

The Early Years of Educational Film: A Foundation for the Future

Instructional films made prior to World War I were predominantly culled and edited from 35mm theatrical, industrial, welfare, or government films,[3] made by a small number of companies, among them Bell and Howell, Atlas (heavily funded by Henry Ford), and Thomas Edison.

The first use of smaller gauge film made specifically for educational purposes appears to have occurred at the 1912 National Educational Association meeting in Chicago, with a film shown on an 1897 Edison Home Kinetoscope projector. Thomas Edison was an early and enthusiastic educational film booster, stating that "books will soon be obsolete in the schools ... our school system will be completely changed in ten years."[4] His own involvement was hindered by two catastrophic fires in April and December of 1914, in which many of the Edison Film Library negatives were destroyed. These events were a prime reason for the discontinuation of the manufacture of the Kinetoscope projector as well as the practical end of Edison's foray into educational film, although some Edison prints continued to circulate in George Kleine's catalogues as late as 1929.[5]

In addition to the appearance of the Kinetoscope in Chicago, 1912 also marks the year that Swedish inventor and magician Alexander F. Victor introduced the first 16mm spring-driven camera and the first 16mm projector, soon patented and marketed by the Victor Animatograph Corporation. This heralded the standardization of the specific gauge that would ultimately achieve primacy over the other small gauge film stocks of the era.

Progressive educators were soon taking enthusiastic notice of the new technology. One of the earliest instructors to make extensive use of multimedia educational tools was M.I. Smith of Duluth, Minnesota, who, as a student accompanying a lecturing professor in 1914, traveled throughout the state of Wisconsin operating a 3" × 4" lantern projector. Smith soon acquired a film projector, often using the battery of his automobile to power the unit if electricity was unavailable.[6]

Ambitious film programs sponsored by public agencies became popular as well. In 1917, the North Carolina Board of Education, with $25,000 in legislative funding to improve educational and social conditions in rural communities, initiated a program of distribution which ultimately resulted in 20 counties hosting 400 monthly community educational film nights, with an average attendance of approximately 100. Many in these audiences had never before seen a motion picture and some would "walk for either eight or ten miles to attend a meeting."[7] To participate, a community would agree to pay two-thirds of the cost of film, projector, and projectionist (recouped through a small admission charge), while the state covered the remaining third.

Several key companies soon began preparing for this emerging market. In 1922 Eastman Kodak, jointly with Bell & Howell and Victor Animatograph, began selling 16mm film cellulose-acetate fireproof safety film, cameras, and projectors, creating the 16mm standard film format.[8] Soon, filmmakers were making films with new lightweight camera equipment, enabling them to film in far-flung venues that had heretofore been impractical. Among the earliest genres of film to become popular due to the advent of lightweight camera was the travelogue. The trouble and expense of shooting large rolls of 35mm film in heavy cameras under arduous conditions had made travelogues difficult to produce. Projectors were becoming more portable as well and, unlike 35mm units, 16mm projectors could use the electrical voltage found in virtually any school, library, or community center. However, the requirement that classrooms be fitted with fireproof projection booths to store and project the volatile cellulose-nitrate films prevented many schools from showing any films at all. The advent of Safety film allowed public institutions to take advantage of the comparatively easy-to-project 16mm film gauge, and schools, libraries, and community centers across the nation soon began to transform themselves into instant theatres.

Film executives at that time were not ignorant of the fact that school districts were quickly becoming large potential customers, and Kodak and AT&T (then a manufacturer of 16mm projectors through its subsidiary, Western Electric) desperately wanted to profit from this emerging market. The coming of talking pictures alerted schools to the possibility of audio-visual education, and educational institutions began seeking funding for the purchase of sound projectors. In 1928, Western Electric stepped in to fill the talking educational picture film void by starting a subsidiary of its own, Electrical Research Products, Incorporated, known as "ERPI," the first organization to produce educational sound films.[9] The introduction of sound films for education was not achieved without difficulty, however. At an educational convention in St. Louis, an Eastman Kodak representative challenged ERPI's research director, Clyde Arnspiger, to an alley fight, believing that the economic fate of Kodak's 300-some odd silent titles would be put in jeopardy.[10]

Journals specializing in the critical analysis of individual educational films appeared as early as 1918, with *Reel and Slide*, edited by Lynne Matcalfe. While many educators in the 1920s viewed film as a valuable educational resource, quantifiable data confirming its efficacy didn't arrive until the following decade, with the publication of books such as *The Educational Talking Picture* by ERPI's Colonel Frederick Devereux, which cited studies that quantified the educational outcomes of the use of film in classrooms.[11]

In 1932, in a meeting that started a chain of events that would eventually lead to the formation of Encyclopædia Britannica Films, Frederick Devereaux of ERPI, believing that the films would gain much needed credibility with the cooperation of educational subject matter experts, entered into an agreement with the University of Chicago with the help of Beardsley Ruml, dean of Social Sciences at the University.[12] ERPI would now produce films with University-contributed scholars and curriculum. The imprimatur of a respected institution of higher learning gave ERPI the scholastic cachet needed to sell films to educational institutions, state boards of education, and school districts throughout North America.

By 1937, the surging success of ERPI had raised eyebrows within the Federal Communications Commission, which requested that Western Electric divest itself of some of its ERPI activities, including the division which licensed the use of sound equipment.[13] ERPI's triumphs had also been noted in Hollywood, where studios were already formulating ideas on ways to make money on the educational market from sequences in their feature films, mining the trinity of idle footage, splicing blocks, and educational consultants.

Educational Film and the Motion Picture Studios

Major film studios had been indirectly involved in the process of making educational films edited from major motion pictures since 1929. Formal attempts to address this market didn't begin until 1934, however, when censorship czar Will Hays convened a group of consultants to investigate enlisting the aid of the studios to make edited feature films available for school use. One of the outcomes of these meetings was the formation in 1939 of Teaching Film Custodians, Inc. (TFC), a non-profit organization whose review committee of 50 educators viewed more than 1,800 theatrical films, culling 360 of them to be edited for school use and transferred to 16mm format.[14]

While educational film companies were mostly on hiatus during World War II, TFC continued to pump out abridged studio material, much of which today appears to be of dubious artistic and educational value. A typical product was *Story of an Immigrant* (1944, Teaching Film Custodians), edited from an MGM feature called *An American Romance*, featuring unaccomplished actors sporting woeful attempts at foreign accents, acting out a mediocre tale of farcical love, and having only a superficial connection with its supposed thematic interpretation of immigration issues, multiculturalism, and international politics. Such films enjoyed truly amazing longevity: *Immigrant* was still available for classroom viewing in one large school system as late as 1995.[15]

From Classroom to Quonset Hut: The Educational Film Goes to War

Perhaps Hollywood's greatest contribution to classroom films derived from the efforts of its crews, pressed into service in World War II, to help create the largest educational film project ever conceived up to that time, to educate soldiers, sailors, fliers, and civilians to fight the most extensive war the world had ever seen.

Training millions of American men and women to engage in war required educational materials that would stress not only *how* to fight the war, but also inculcate the *desire* to fight, by emphasizing the reasons that North American forces chose to engage in battle.[16] Taking separate but similar paths, the U.S. and Canadian governments developed training and propaganda films for civilian and military personnel alike.

In the U.S., using motion pictures to train soldiers dated back to the last few months of World War I, when 63 films were produced by commercial film companies under private contract for the U.S. Army. The Army eventually began making its own films in 1930, when the non-profit Research Council of the Academy of Motion Picture Arts and Sciences initiated cinematic training for officers of the Army Signal Corps. Initially, the output of the Signal Corps was meager, consisting of roughly 20 titles per year prior to 1938. But it was also efficient, considering that its entire film staff was made up of just three enlisted men, an officer, and a civilian.[17] The Signal Corps film unit grew, and was influential: in the decades to follow, many academic filmmakers cited the Army Signal Corps as their primary source for training in the craft of filmmaking. The Navy, on the other hand, utilized independent film contractors exclusively, a policy it would continue throughout World War II.

The passage of the Draft Act in 1940, combined with the bombing of Pearl Harbor on December 7, 1941, resulted in many from the Hollywood community joining the war effort in a cinematic capacity, including 1,500 members of the Screen Actors Guild, 48 executives and producers, 132 members of the Screen Directors Guild (including Lt. Colonel Darryl Zanuck and Major Frank Capra), 230 members of the Screen Writers Guild, 40 cameramen, 75 electricians and sound technicians, 453 film technicians and 80 machinists.[18]

Films made for military audiences encompassed at least one of the following objectives:

- To describe the moral purposes of the war, characteristics of allies and enemies, and the part played by individual military components
- To impart self-control and proper conduct of the individual soldier
- To describe military progress on all fronts
- To instruct in skills[19]

By the end of World War II, more than 9,000 training film titles were available to U.S. Marines, Navy, and Coast Guard personnel and several thousand more were used by the Army Air Force.[20] Like civilian training films, many of the military titles featured first-person narration and visual perspective, reflecting an upbeat "can-do" philosophy. *Castaway* (1944, unknown director), for example, was a 50-minute sea-crash recovery film made by Willard Pictures for the U.S. Bureau of Aeronautics, a first-person drama portraying the travails of an allied pilot shot down in the Pacific. In first person narrative, the flier illustrates the use of the inflatable life raft and ancillary items and makes it to the shore of an island. Encountering a native in traditional dress, the flier avoids harming the individual by reminding himself: "Remember, he's just as scared of you as you are of him." Ultimately, the flier is rescued, but before he departs, he makes a gift of a knife to the native who befriended him.

This overt advocacy of inter-cultural understanding was uncommon in contemporaneous academic films. Other than Julien Bryan's International Film Foundation, educational film companies tended to explore and celebrate the exotic and primitive aspects of the inhabitants of developing nations instead of discussing common elements of the human condition that cross all borders and cultures.[21] One therefore wonders about the process by which the U.S. Navy would approve a film such as *Castaway*. Might there have been a pacifist or conscientious objector element within the Navy's approval unit, working with filmmakers at companies such as Willard to embed humanitarian acts within such films? Or, as was indicated by the post-war work of General George Marshall (whose office hired animator Philip Stapp to assist the French in reconstructing their animation industry), might that philosophy been a stated one, sanctioned at the highest level?

War training films were not only made for military personnel. In January 1941, the U.S. Office of Education formed the Division of Visual Aids for War Training, chartered to develop instructional material for civilians and led by Floyde E. Brooker, who had spent many years promoting educational film as associate director of the American Council on Education.[22] In his new job, Brooker would advocate film as a preferred training tool, securing millions of federal dollars to train industrial workers to make the materiel of war. Since previous research had suggested that people responded better to an "I" perspective than to "you," the elements of first-person narration and point-of-view camera shooting from the eyes of the learner became the preferred treatment. Between its inception in 1941 and June 1945, the Division made more than 450 films. During one two-year period, more than 4 million showings were estimated to have occurred in the U.S. alone.[23]

Although numerous prints were made of each civilian and military title, careful storage of film in temperature and humidity-controlled environments was hardly a priority for the military during the war, so a great many prints of World War II training films were eventually destroyed by the "vinegar syndrome." This syndrome is a result of storage in adverse temperature and humidity conditions, accelerating a chemical reaction within the film itself, and causing the base layer to separate from the emulsion. This process produces the telltale odor of acetic acid as well as visible warping, resulting in the film's sprocket holes missing the projector's claw, causing jams and rendering the film virtually unshowable. Insidiously, this acid travels well in its gaseous state, becomes airborne, and corrodes adjacent metal reels and film cans, making it necessary to remove infected prints from the vicinity of those not yet experiencing symptoms. Unfortunately, many of the remaining prints of these important films from World War II have fallen victim to this condition.

Some of the military training films of greatest interest to the general public were the 17 films in the *Why We Fight* series produced by Frank Capra to provide military personnel and civilians with the historical, cultural, and moral reasons for U.S. involvement in World War II. To the north, the *Canada Carries On* series was developed to accomplish the same objective, narrated by CBC newsman Lorne Greene, whose bombastic delivery eventually wearied the ears of National Film Board of Canada commissioner Sydney Newman, who subsequently fired him.[24] In titles such as *Guards of the North* (1941, dir. Raymond Spottiswoode), which described the task and importance of defending Iceland, the approximately 62 films in the series made from 1940 through 1945 were uniquely Canadian in approach and perspective, furthering the Film Board tradition of defining Canada to its citizens and to the world at large. After the war, the Film Board expanded the series to include peacetime subjects, adding 138 more films by the series' end in 1960.

How effective were military training films? Researchers Charles Hoban and Edward van Ormer compared more than 200 efficacy studies made over 30 years, many of which were conducted during the war years. While most studies were inconclusive, providing insufficient quantifiable data to prove the supremacy of film over other training media, indicators seemed to point to the value of film as an important and essential element in the learning matrix.[25]

Perhaps the greatest contribution of World War II military training films to the business of education was to reinforce the increasing feeling among educators that the medium had survived its infancy and grown into a powerfully effective and accepted means of delivering information. As Floyde Brooker noted, films had gone from being an "educational luxury" to a necessity.[26] Hundreds of filmmakers who were soon to become significant players in the 16mm educational film business either returned to or entered the world of classroom film directly from the military.

The training film's ubiquity in the military had influenced its viewers, too. As researcher Kenneth Kaye notes:

> [Fifteen million] men returned home after the war with a keen sense of what instructional films could do — and some of them had also been trained in their use. Many of these veterans became teachers. Others were active parents, school administrators, state legislators, even Congressmen. They did not need to be convinced that films were a good way to learn.... As these men grew to hold positions of responsibility in American education, the audio-visual movement gradually acquired permanence and acceptability everywhere.[27]

Hollywood, the military, and educational film companies themselves were the three most significant entities engaged in instructional film prior to 1950. Hollywood's failure to provide intellectually stimulating films for the classrooms of America was primarily due to a conflict in mission. It was, after all, in the business of entertainment at a profit, not in meeting the educational objectives of a generation of students. The military, in teaching young filmmakers how to make and test the learning objectives of educational film, had successfully delivered on its ultimate goal of using the outcome of film to achieve success in a global conflict. It would now be left to companies specializing in the business of educational film to take what it had learned from pre-war experimentation and wartime refinement to craft an industry that would augment and create curriculum, and dispense factual information in a way that would inspire the learner to continue his or her own internalized educational process. Four of the best known companies to serve the immediate post-war educational film market were Encyclopædia Britannica Films (EBF), Coronet Films, the International Film Foundation (IFF), and the National Film Board of Canada (NFBC). A brief overview of their respective histories will help illustrate the foundations of many of the elements that would define educational film prior to the progressive era of the 1960s.

A Quest for Excellence: The Early Years of Encyclopædia Britannica Films

The discussions between ERPI's Colonel Devereaux and the University of Chicago's Beardsley Ruml that began in 1932 had borne productive results by 1936. The ERPI–University of Chicago cooperative effort produced no fewer than 36 science films geared toward first- and second-year college students, also shown in high schools and elementary schools. When a test group of schoolchildren exposed to a film curriculum scored higher on exams than control groups not seeing these films, Robert Maynard Hutchins, the noted educator who had become president of the University of Chicago in 1929 at the age of 30, declared

Executive meetings at EB Films often included noted scholars as well as EB execs. From a meeting circa 1963, front row (L to R): Helen (Mrs. William) Benton, Robert Hutchins (EB Board member), William Benton (EB Chairman), Maurice Mitchell (EB President), Unidentified man. Back row: Orton Hicks (VP, Dartmouth College), George Stoddard (President, NYU), Paul Hoffman (EB Board member), Charles Benton, Laurence Fitzsimmons (EBF Treasurer), Warren Everote (President, EB Films) (Bill Deneen).

that films would revolutionize learning to much the same extent as had the printing press or the textbook.[28]

However, there were already rumblings of discontent in the ERPI world. Although 1,000 schools had purchased projectors by 1936, AT&T had just discovered that a procedural error had invalidated its patents on existing units. Having failed by that time to set up adequate distribution channels, the corporation decided that selling motion picture projectors — and therefore film — was too far from its core line of products to make long-term financial sense. In addition, schools that did have sound projectors had begun to request films on the social sciences as well as the hard sciences and, in a theme that was to reverberate throughout the educational film world for the next four decades, the company feared that such films would be controversial and viewed as social propaganda, thereby leading to adverse publicity for the company. It can be surmised that some of the concern might have been around racial lines. It wasn't until the early 1950s that EBF's Gordon Weisenborn–John Barnes film, *People Along the Mississippi* (*1952) became what was perhaps the first classroom film to show children of different races playing interactively.

Perhaps the single most far-reaching personnel decision for the fledgling 16mm educational market took place in 1937 when Robert Hutchins hired William Benton to serve as the vice president of the University of Chicago. Benton was formerly the head of the prestigious Benton & Bowles Advertising Agency, and a disciple of National Cash Register magnate John Henry Patterson's "scientific selling" process.[29] On Benton's first day on the job, Hutchins asked him to review a report commissioned by brothers Nelson and Laurance

Rockefeller on the feasibility of the purchase of ERPI by the Rockefeller Foundation, an idea soon vetoed by father John D. Rockefeller, Jr. Advancing the progress of educational film in the U.S. so intrigued Benton that, on the heels of the Rockefeller disappointment, he attempted to convince his friend, *Life* magazine publisher Henry Luce, to add educational films to his publishing empire. Luce's treasurer, however, generated a report stating that educational films were a "dead end," abruptly terminating the discussion. Undaunted, Benton refused to let his passion for educational film disappear.

Benton and Hutchins formed a close working relationship with General Robert E. Wood, World War I hero and chairman of the board of Sears, Roebuck and Company, among whose properties was the venerated Encyclopædia Britannica. First issued by a private society in Scotland in 1768, the Encyclopædia was assisted financially by Sears in the early part of the twentieth century, and was ultimately acquired outright by the Chicago-based firm in 1929. Although profitable, it was apparent by 1941 that the Encyclopædia was badly in need of an update. Discussions began in earnest as the retailing giant and powerhouse university began to forge an agreement for a massive academic revision. Benton, however, had an even more aggressive plan in mind.

Over lunch at the Chicago Club on December 9, 1941, Benton asked General Wood if, rather than paying a hefty tax bill resulting from a year of formidable profits, he might be willing instead to donate the Encyclopædia outright to the University as a tax write-off. The General took more than two long, silent minutes to respond to Benton's "closing" question, during which time he got up from the table, put on his coat, walked down the winding staircase, got in his car, smiled, and finally said: "All right, Bill, I'll give you the Britannica."[30] Benton's patience during those two minutes of silence while Wood deliberated ultimately resulted in the acquisition of the Encyclopædia by the University, but it would take almost a year to ratify this transaction with the trustees of the University and would also require $100,000 of Benton's own money in working capital, which Benton traded for two-thirds of the stock of the venture. The University retained the option of buying one-third back from Benton for $50,000 at any time during the ensuing 17 months, which, if exercised, would have allowed it to regain control of the operation. When he formally took over the publication on February 1, 1943, Benton also acquired the services of Walter Yust, editor of the Encyclopædia since 1930, whose son, Larry, would eventually become one of the most significant director/producers of the dramatic academic film, and creator of EB Film's most controversial film, *The Lottery* (1969).[31]

Shortly after acquiring the Encyclopedia for the University, Benton learned that AT&T was once again trying to unload ERPI. He began talks with Walter Page of AT&T and Kennedy Stevenson of Western Electric which culminated in the sale in November 1943 of the film company to EB for $1 million to be paid over a decade. One of Benton's first acts was to change the name ERPI (he had once heard a child refer to it as "burpy") to Encyclopædia Britannica Films.[32]

Although its annual sales had averaged only $300,000, ERPI was still the leader in the educational film market when it was acquired by the University of Chicago. Benton then put $1.5 million into building a greater inventory and developing sales and marketing channels. Recognizing that its own silent educational films would be no match for Benton's growing educational talking film organization, Eastman Kodak divested itself of its educational cinema enterprise by donating its library of three hundred titles to the University of Chicago for Benton's Encyclopædia Britannica Film company.[33] To further solidify the academic credentials and professional reputation of his venture, Benton gathered an impressive board of directors that included Robert Hutchins, Illinois governor Adlai Stevenson, George Shuster, president of the University of Illinois, and University of Chicago professors Robert Tyler and Mortimer Adler.[34] Later, literary critic, editor and lecturer Clifton "Kip" Fadiman, who later hosted many of the films in the company's *Humanities* series, would also join the board.

By mid–1944, the University had decided not to exercise its option to acquire half of Benton's stock, thus relinquishing the rights to future ownership. The reason was simple: Benton was running the company profitably enough that the university had already realized $300,000 in royalties, and thus saw the probability of increasingly greater payments if it left well enough alone.[35] It was clear that Benton had correctly identified a trend. In 1936, only 6,500 16mm projectors had been sold, but this figure had risen to 150,000 by 1946, and the production run for 1947 alone was estimated at 50,000. While Benton himself took a sabbatical from EB Films in 1946 to accept his appointment to the post of Assistant Secretary of State for Public affairs to President Harry S Truman, the company under the direction of close associate and friend Beardsley Ruml continued to flourish, as did the educational media market in general. Educational films were now being made at such a rate that some 3,800 educational titles were listed in H.W. Wilson's 1948 edition of the *Educational Film Guide*.[36]

Film cleaning lab at Encyclopædia Britannica Films (courtesy Encyclopædia Britannica, Inc.).

William Benton was appointed to the Senate in 1949 by Connecticut governor Chester Bowles, his former partner at Benton & Bowles. Benton was perhaps most noted for being the first well-known politician to take on Senator Joseph McCarthy, who rebutted by accusing Benton of "knowing Communists" and collecting lewd works of art.[37] Benton lost his bid for re-election in 1952 in the Eisenhower landslide, and soon returned to EB.

Benton believed in hiring high-powered business executives to the EB staff, including Cyril Scott Fletcher (whose tenure as president of EB Films ended in 1951 when he left to head the Ford Fund for Adult Education, a seminal educational television group), and his successor, Walter Colmes from Republic Films. The appointment of Colmes, who had a reputation for adhering to tight shooting schedules, proved ultimately disappointing.[38]

The course of EB films changed dramatically when Colmes was replaced by Maurice Mitchell, recruited from Benton's Muzak company in 1953.[39] Maurice Mitchell has been cited by many EB personnel as the most powerful unifying force behind EBF's great leap forward in terms of film quality and content, as well as its most effective political spokesperson. To many academics, Mitchell may have appeared to be an unlikely choice to head educational film's most prestigious company. In 1959, *The Saturday Evening Post* characterized him as follows:

> He calls himself "the most unqualified guy in the world for my job." Although he heads a company loaded with Ph.D.s and turns out classroom films relying heavily on color and music for their themes, he has no college degree, has never been otherwise connected with education, has never made a movie, is tone-deaf, and partially color-blind. [He] previously had been successful as an advertising salesman for *The New York Times*, a country editor, a promotion manager for a newspaper chain, and manager of radio station WTOP in Washington, D.C.[40]

By the end of his fifth year on the job, Mitchell had doubled the company's business to nearly $4,500,000.[41] Under his guidance, the well written, photographed, and edited EB Film titles in the mid-to-late 1950s began slowly evolving cinematically beyond those of competitive companies.

In 1958, Mitchell traveled to Washington to appear before the Senate Committee on Labor and Public Welfare, in its second session on Science and Education for National Defense. Armed with small excerpts from a number of EBF films, he made an impassioned and effective argument for additional government matching funds to be made available to schools for films and projectors. In the hearing, Mitchell displayed the salesperson's cageyness when asked about the price of film and equipment (in 1958, a typical 30-minute academic title might cost $350):

> SENATOR ALLOTT: What would be the cost of film to the ordinary school?
>
> MR. MITCHELL: The ordinary school has access to the film through a variety of ways. In the State of Georgia, the cost would be practically zero, because in Georgia there is a tremendous State film library, centrally operated by the State, which makes these films available to schools on the payment of a nominal fee once a year and sends them to the school, postage paid both ways. In the State of Wisconsin, the school could obtain the film from the audiovisual library for a rental fee of about $1.90.[42]
>
> THE CHAIRMAN: What would be the cost of a projector, the sound box, and the screen?
>
> MR. MITCHELL: Let me say that for $350 you can get the equipment in a school building to show films.[43]

Mitchell, it can be surmised, did not want to scare the Senate at that delicate moment, refusing to suggest the scaled-up, realistic amounts of money it would cost to adequately outfit every school and school district with films and equipment. Convincing them of the need came first. He and his colleagues continued to work diligently to advocate legislation that successfully freed millions of dollars in public funds for school film libraries. One significant result of this largesse would be an increase in the number of young filmmakers who would soon help create a revolution in academic film.

Mitchell habitually referred to "the unique contribution" of film to classroom curriculum, arguing that through techniques such as time-lapse photography, photomicrography, color, and enlargement, film could show students a world inaccessible through textbooks alone. He also pointedly differentiated EB Films from those made by its chief competitor, Coronet, which, Mitchell maintained, preferred films that correlated curriculum to textbooks, rather than creating superior films that stood on their own as educational materials. Mitchell even appeared as host in a film that served as a vehicle explaining his philosophical approach to the medium, *Unique Contribution* (*1959, uncredited director, EB), saying:

EB's John Barnes directing *Magna Carta* (1959) at Runnymede (John Barnes).

You get some idea of the vexing nature of the teacher's problem when you realize that some everyday things just aren't easy to explain. We tell a child, for example, that a caterpillar turns into a butterfly. When the teacher asks him on the quiz next Friday, he'll repeat that a caterpillar turns into a butterfly, but the chances are he won't know what he's saying and won't really understand the process. This is where the educational film maker frequently gets in his best licks. He uses the magic of time-lapse photography, filming action that takes hours and days, weeks and months, and compressing it into a dramatic few moments, as we did in the *Monarch Butterfly Story*. He uses animation and extreme close-up and photomicrography and he turns an event that can't have meaning — unless you personally participate in it and observe it yourself — into one that has deep educational significance.

The *Unique Contribution* film showcased the work of director John Barnes (*The Pilgrims*, 1954) and well-known still and movie photographer Roman Vishniac, who had made *Protozoa* (1954), a science film for EB using close-up and time-lapse cinematography. Perhaps the best gauge of the veracity of Mitchell's comments is to compare the work EB was doing in the sciences, featuring the work of exceptional cinematographers such as Bert Van Bork, Isidore Mankofsky, and Vishniac, with films on similar subjects made by its competitors in roughly the same time period.

In terms of camera technique, EB was ahead of its time. Even into the 1960s, films produced by competitive companies such as McGraw-Hill (e.g., *Higher Fungi* and *Lower Fungi*, both 1961, uncredited director), by contrast, make precious little use of time-lapse and micro-cinematography. McGraw's *Fungi* films, for example, concentrated most of the footage on a canned lecture by Duke University's Dr. T.W. Johnson, Jr., whose graphics of choice are rough animated figures and labels located on easels. Each of the McGraw films is a half hour in length, exemplifying what viewers came to characterize as "boring educational films." In truth, the McGraw *Fungi* films were no better or worse than many of the non–EBF science films of the era, and quite possibly might have been of value to students already interested in the subject. What they often did not do — and what EBF films of the era *did* — was to capture the visual interest of those who wouldn't ordinarily express an interest in fungal fruiting bodies.

EBF drew primarily on the talents of its own in-house directors and producers such as John Barnes. Through films such as *Roger Williams: Founder of Rhode Island* and *Sir Francis Drake: Rise of English Sea Power* (both made in 1957), Barnes was perhaps the only educational filmmaker of the era to explore the rights of religious and racial minorities. In its quest for authenticity, EBF would, when possible, shoot its historical films on location, as with Barnes' *Magna Carta* (1959), filmed at Runnymede. EBF also occasionally licensed outstanding foreign material from filmmakers such as Arne Sucksdorff (*Gray Gull the Hunter*, 1955).

In the latter part of the 1950s, EBF embarked on several lengthy series of films dedicated to subject areas in Science and the Humanities. The first, *Physics: the Complete Introductory Course*, wasn't considered a success, due in part to the lack of camera presence of host Harvey White (e.g., *Algebra and the Powers of Ten*, 1957). The second series, the *Chemistry Introductory Course*, was affectively superior. This massive series consisted of 162 half-hour films, produced by David W. Ridgway, hosted by University of Florida professor John F. Baxter, and photographed by Isidore Mankofsky.[44] The genesis of the series was a conversation between Alvin C. Eurich, executive director of Ford Foundation's Education Division, and EBF Vice President of Production Warren Everote.[45] The Ford Foundation had already agreed to fund the Physical Science Study Committee (PSSC) series, a project intended to

Dave Ridgway (left, wearing a tie), John Baxter (right foreground), Isidore Mankofsky (cameraman at right), and crew shoot one of the *Chemistry Introductory Course* films (1958) (Isidore Mankofsky).

replace EB's physics series, but one which had been turned down by EBF president Maurice Mitchell because of a disagreement with PSSC developer Dr. Jerrold Zacharias. This time, EBF agreed to do the chemistry project. Although a success educationally, EB found that sales were poor, as few schools could afford to buy each of the 160 PSSC films. Instead, the series was mostly bought at the district level, and the films were loaned round-robin to individual schools. When ESEA funding became available to schools in the mid–1960s, schools now had money for the series, but it had already been superseded by the Ford Foundation-funded *CHEM Study* series begun in 1960, developed by Nobel Prize-winning chemist Glenn Seaborg.[46] *CHEM Study* films were made by companies such as Davidson Films and Wexler Films, and were distributed by the University of California. Seaborg had preceded EB vice president Warren Everote in the Chemistry department at UCLA by one year, and although they were good friends, Everote joked that Seaborg had "stolen" producer Dave Ridgway from him, as Ridgway had left EBF to become the new *CHEM Study* producer.[47] While *CHEM Study* films were commonly found in educational film libraries as late as the 1990s, the earlier *Chemistry Introductory Course* films were not, having been replaced by the latter series, or never having been ordered in the first place. Today, films in the earlier EB series are nearly impossible to find.

Although sales figures were disappointing, the Ford Foundation was impressed sufficiently with EB's chemistry series to fund EB's *Humanities* series of the mid–1960s as a follow-on project. Focusing on Western Classical Civilization, the later series featured high-powered scholars such as Mortimer Adler, Clifton Fadiman, Bernard Knox, Maynard Mack, and Gilbert Highet, all of whom eventually appeared as hosts in EB films.

EBF's instructional materials ultimately extended well beyond academic films to include books, filmstrips and learning aids such as the *Study Print* series, consisting of packs of 18" × 12" cards suitable for display in classrooms. These materials paralleled the content of EBF Films and enhanced the learning experience. EBF also founded a school in the Chicago area which standardized on EBF learning materials and offered educational "perks" to employees, as well.[48] After five years with the company, a worker was eligible to choose either a full set of the *Encyclopædia Britannica*, or a set of the 54 (later to be 60) volume *Great Books of the Western World* series, a Benton-Hutchins-Adler anthology of 443 writings by 74 authors. After another ten years, the employee was given the other set.[49]

EBF's brain trust often took public advocacy positions, generating political support for mediated instruction. EBF's leaders also commented on social policy. A good example of the latter is Maurice Mitchell's article in the 1958 *Britannica Book of the Year*, which predicted the proliferation of technology in the home via film-on-demand, microwave ovens, and instant communication devices. An advocate of the right of privacy, he was also prescient enough to sound a warning that the proliferation of instantly accessible mass communications could well be a Trojan horse. In reading Mitchell's advisory which follows, it's interesting to note that it was written over 50 years ago, well before the age in which there was a computer and mobile phone/PDA in millions of North American homes:

> To some extent, we have already become the slaves of our new communications media. They are growing faster and developing and spreading more rapidly than the apparent skills of the general public in living with them, handling them and mastering them. Many believe that this is the greatest single challenge of the communications revolution. Just as the machine in the early days of the industrial revolution threatened to make slaves out of the millions of workers who were tied to it, so does the communications instrument of the world of electronic miracles loom as a great threat to man's mastery of his environment.
>
> Under the control of the public, and working at its bidding, the science of communications can open unlimited doors to wider enjoyment in and satisfaction with the world in which we live. Out of public control and in the hands of a limited group of specialists in the art of communications devices, it can become a monster far more devastating than any atom-splitting devices that man is likely to create.
>
> The average person senses that only through joint action and the exercise of great effort can he bring resources to bear that will keep the atom and other great physical forces under control. It is an interesting phenomenon, however, that the far greater force and power of the mass of communications devices that are spreading across the length and breadth of our civilization can be individually controlled by the average man with nothing more than the flick of a finger or the turn of a knob.
>
> To this extent, he can at any instant disconnect himself from the whole mass of communications apparatus that seeks to invade his privacy, that clamours for his attention, for his ears and his eyes, for his subconscious mind. The great challenge to modern man is to learn when and how to flick the switch and turn the knob, and the extent to which he develops this discrimination will determine the kind of world he makes for himself when the communications revolution has run its course.[50]

William Benton had rejoined Encyclopædia Britannica as chairman following his battle against Joseph McCarthy and losing his bid for re-election. He spearheaded efforts to form the National Defense Education Act of 1958, and steered the company successfully into the 1960s. A rumor persists that MGM entered into discussions to buy EBF during this time, with Benton slated to become the major stockholder and chairman of the new company. Benton is the one, it is reported, who turned the deal down.[51]

EB film editor Grace Garland Janisz (Grace Garland Janisz).

Expediency at the Expense of Illumination? Coronet Films Makes Its Mark

Born in 1892, Coronet's David Smart was noted for being dapper, mercurial, and flashy.[52] He had already made and lost a fortune in the sugar market prior to founding the *Esquire* magazine empire. Smart had acquired a showman's eye for promotion and publicity (he would later introduce the Petty and Varga pin-up girl illustrations to the American magazine reader) and, on a trip to Germany in the early 1930s, immediately recognized the educational-propagandistic potential of films being made by the Nazis. Returning home to Chicago, he and his brothers Alfred (who died in 1951) and John launched Coronet Films in 1934.

Smart built what became the largest privately-owned studio east of Hollywood on his estate in Glenview, Illinois. Temporarily stalled in his mission to fill America's classrooms with Coronet titles, he aided the U.S. Navy by providing his studio for its use to develop training films for World War II. Some Coronet films of the late 1940s are compelling. *Forests and Conservation* (1946, filmmaker unknown) is a landmark conservation film, detailing the work of an unnamed (Zellerbach?) paper products company in progressive nursery and reforestation programs. When government funding declined at the end of the war, Smart hired Jack Abraham, noted for his financial expertise at Paramount Studios, to take over responsibility for the company as general manager.

The low-budget "crank 'em out fast" philosophy promulgated by the irascible magazine publisher and led by Abraham had the goal of producing a film every 4.2 days.[53] The Coronet catalogue consisted primarily of short film dramas on social guidance topics, historical subjects, nature and science, and travelogue-based cultural titles. Coronet's philosophy, unlike EBF's, was to strictly correlate films to existing textbook curriculum rather than create new takes on subject matter. They were often didactic, formulaic, and unexciting, devoid of filmmaker credits while always crediting scholars.[54] Typical of films in the Coronet catalogue was *Labor Movement: Beginning & Growth in America* (1959) in which stills of documents and broadsides are interspersed with short dramatizations of incidents involving an actor playing labor organizer Samuel Gompers. As is the case with many pre–1970s Coronet titles, the acting is mediocre, the actors aren't on microphone, and the voice-over narration is dry. This results in a dull treatment of an otherwise interesting historical subject, particularly when contrasted with the well-acted and finely scripted work John Barnes (*Industrial Revolution in England*, 1957) was doing for rival EB Films at the same time. Exciting, dynamic, compelling Coronet films from this era are not easy to find.

The abysmal overall quality of Coronet films of the era wasn't lost on its chief competitor, EB Films, whose chairman, Senator William Benton, was a stickler for both verisimilitude and quality. As EB's Warren Everote recounts:

> At an EBF Advisory Board meeting in 1959, Senator Benton requests that I bring to the next meeting several competitive films for screening. This kind of check on the quality of films from other companies should prove interesting. I call Hal Kopel, our former producer, who now heads Coronet, and ask him to send several of its films that he feels represent the best they have to offer. At our next Advisory Board meeting I explain to our members where the films are from and that Kopel states they are examples of Coronet's best products. We are watching the second film of the collection when the Senator explodes.
>
> In essence he loudly proclaims that I obviously selected the worst competitive films I could find to make our films look good. He adds that he cannot waste his time on any more of this trash and leaves the meeting.[55]

In 1957, a Special Productions unit for Coronet was formed under the leadership of Bob Kohl and Tom Riha, which contracted with independent producers to provide primarily geography and history films. Kohl and Riha were able to acquire properties, such as a series of three 400-foot (ten minute) reels made in 1956, *India's History*, a beautifully photographed and written explanation of the sub-continent from early civilization to independence, apparently shot by an uncredited British cinematographer who was guaranteed anonymity by Abraham's strict edict that filmmakers not be credited (one guess is that this was presumably to prevent "star directors" from asking for more money).[56]

In 1952, David Smart, so germ-phobic that he always used handkerchiefs on doorknobs when traveling from car to car on trains, passed away, a victim of exploratory surgery. Smart had ordered a minor intestinal polyp operation against his doctors' advice, and one surgeon is reported to have stated that he died of "mental suicide."[57] The company was left in the hands of Jack Abraham and John Smart, who, in 1955, closed the studio in response to mounting pressures to unionize. Some directors such as Ted Peshak left to form their own companies, which continued to provide films to the Kohl/Riha team on an ad hoc basis. Coronet was led by Abraham until the early 1970s.

In summation, perhaps, Coronet's early academic film output can be characterized as a large number of titles that provided a livelihood for amateur actors and fledgling directors, nearly all of whom will forever remain uncredited. Coronet in the pre–1970s era never strived to be a company overly creative in its themes or treatments.[58]

Promoting World Cultures: Julien Bryan and the International Film Foundation

The International Film Foundation (IFF) was founded by photographer, writer, and cameraman Julien Hequembourg Bryan in 1945. Born in Titusville, Pennsylvania, in 1899, this son of an elder in the Presbyterian church became fascinated with stories told of other lands by traveling missionaries. At age 17, right out of high school, he joined the American Field Service for the French Army in World War I. He drove an ambulance in Verdun and the Argonne and wrote *Ambulance 464,* a book made up of excerpts from his diaries and illustrated by his photographs.[59] After the war, Bryan graduated from Princeton and attended the Union Theological Seminary but chose not to be ordained as a minister. He instead directed programs at the YMCA in Brooklyn, New York.

Bryan's passion for film began in 1923, when he first shot vacation footage in 28mm. He converted to 16mm gauge in 1930, and then to 35mm in 1932. When he returned from Russia in 1932 with film records of the peoples of the Soviet Union, he began a series of lecture tours throughout North America. Critics have occasionally maligned Bryan for "sugar-coating" the Soviet existence, suggesting that the store shelves shown in Bryan's films were fully stocked by Communist officials as a propagandistic ruse (son Sam Bryan today emphatically denies that this was the case). As one of the few foreign filmmakers allowed relatively free reign by the authorities, he celebrated the ethnic diversity of the country and emphasized the complexity of the evolution of a nation from a feudal state to a modern one, focusing on its human element in the process (*Peoples of the Soviet Union*, 1946).

In 1939, Bryan found himself to

Ambulance Driver Julien Bryan in the Argonne Forest, World War I (Sam Bryan).

be the only neutral-country reporter left in Warsaw when the Nazis began their brutal three-week Blitzkrieg attack on the city. Finding himself with 6,000 feet of unexposed film left after a trip to Switzerland and Holland, Bryan documented the fighting, misery, and courage of the population of the city. This eventually resulted in a book and documentary film of the same title (*Siege*, *1940). Nominated for an Academy Award, *Siege* lost on the technicality that it had not yet been shown in public theatres.

In August 1940, Franklin Delano Roosevelt created the Office of Coordinator of Inter-American Affairs (CIAA) to foster social understanding in the western hemisphere. Nelson Rockefeller led the CIAA and hired Bryan to make a series of what would become 23 films on Latin American culture and customs. These films were shown in schools throughout the United States during the war years, and their success led the State Department to contract with Bryan to make five films on similar aspects of the U.S. which, in turn, were translated into 40 languages for foreign distribution. This latter group of films was brought to the attention of David and Ella Mills, whose New Jersey-based Davella Mills Foundation was seeking to fund an educational project to combat international aggression. In 1945, they gave Bryan a three-year grant of $300,000 to start a non-profit film foundation for the purpose of creating greater understanding among the peoples of the world.[60] Joining the filmmaker on a freelance basis in 1947 was Philip Stapp, an outstanding animator and filmmaker (*Boundary Lines*, 1947) whose contributions to IFF would continue for two more decades.

Throughout the late 1940s and 1950s, the IFF produced ethnographic and world documentary films (e.g., *Sampan Family*, dir. William James, 1949) notable in their respect and appreciation for cultures differing economically and socially from that of many of the schoolroom viewers in North America. Bryan was as noted for his showmanship as for his films, giving dozens of film-enhanced lectures across the U.S. Bryan was a master publicist, never shirking from occasional sleight-of-hand. For instance, before traveling to a foreign country, he meticulously hand-wrote letters and cards to his many customers, sporting *bon mots* such as "Wish you were here" or "Greetings from Budapest." Once off the plane in the appropriate country, Bryan would instruct his team to run down to the post office to buy interesting postage stamps, then hold a mailing party to stuff and mail envelopes back to the States, postmarked and containing the letters and cards he'd created originally in his New York City office.

Bryan's films did not objectify his subjects, emphasizing instead the similarities of peoples rather than their differences. When addressing dissimilarities, Bryan tended to embrace rather than criticize them, contrary to the common practice of other film companies dealing in similar subject matter. IFF made films well into the 1970s, eventually led by Bryan's son and fellow filmmaker, Sam Bryan.

Julien Bryan's filmmaking philosophy of embracing cultural diversity was to a great extent shared by the National Film Board of Canada, which also made many of the more effective multicultural films of the 1940–1960 era. The Film Board's accomplishments were not in any way diminished by its films' relative lack of distribution in the U.S. during the early years, and its story is a significant one in the history of North American academic film.

Canadian Sunrise: Presenting the National Film Board

Whereas the educational film movement in the U.S. was largely driven by ERPI and the efforts of EB Films and the University of Chicago, the enormous contribution to the

North American educational film genre made by the National Film Board of Canada (NFBC) is due largely to the documentarist philosophy espoused by its founder, John Grierson (1898–1972). Film Board documentaries such as *Universe* (1959, dir. Roman Kroitor and Colin Low) and *City of Gold* (1957, dir. Colin Low and Wolf Koenig) were commonly used in schools in both the U.S. and Canada, and represent some of the most engaging academic films of the era.

Soon after graduating from Glasgow University in 1923, John Grierson spent three years in the United States on a Rockefeller grant, studying for a short time under Walter Lippmann at the University of Chicago, investigating ways to improve voter education in a world rife with increasingly complex issues.[61] While in the U.S, he also helped prepare Sergei Eisenstein's feature film *Potemkin* (1925) for theatrical release, and encountered Robert Flaherty, whose proto-documentary *Nanook of the North* (1922) Grierson had seen in Scotland.

Stanley Jackson, the "voice" of the National Film Board of Canada (Lois Siegel).

As befit two of the more opinionated philosophers of the documentary form, the Flaherty-Grierson friendship was a stormy one that would span decades.

Returning to England after his stay in the U.S., by 1935 Grierson had created and directed both the Empire Marketing Board and the General Post Office Film Units, which were responsible for many of Britain's finest documentaries. A stern taskmaster and superb organizer, Grierson's view of public support for film was strongly grounded in his philosophy that "the greatest single discovery in the development of the documentary came with the realization that its logical sponsorship lay with the governments and other bodies conscious of their public responsibilities."[62]

In 1938, Grierson was invited by the Canadian government to visit Canada, investigate the state of its national cinema, and deliver a report on his findings. His report criticized the Canadian film industry, and recommended a publicly-funded bureau that would use cinema to interpret Canada to Canadians and non–Canadians alike, operating independently from any individual governmental department. He was invited back to Canada in November to implement the report's recommendations, and drafted a bill proposing an organization called the National Film Board of Canada, responsible for administrating the production of films, rather than producing, which was instead perceived as the responsibility of free enterprise. The resulting National Film Act was passed by parliament on March 17, 1939.

In September 1939, Canada, Britain, and Australia found themselves involved in World War II, and Grierson was torn between staying in Britain, accepting an offer to initiate a film board in Australia, or accepting Canadian prime minister MacKenzie King's offer to head the newly chartered National Film Board of Canada. Unbeknownst to everyone except the necessary few, Grierson had taken a role within British Military Intelligence, had discussed the Canadian offer, and was encouraged to accept it by his superiors, who felt the position would be the perfect guise for an intelligence official. For the remainder of the war, Grierson operated in a dual role: that of the Commissioner of the National Film Board, and as the head of M.I.6, British Military Intelligence in Canada.[63]

Grierson's two areas of responsibility are perhaps best illustrated by his disagreements with commissioner Frank Badgely, originally recommended by Grierson to lead the Bureau. Upon seeing Nazi propaganda films, Grierson felt the need to begin producing a series that could be used by Canada to similar ends. Badgely, who felt that the Film Board was supposed to function solely in an advisory capacity and not compete with commercial production companies, strongly objected. Grierson quickly cut through the bureaucracy and brought over the young British producer Stuart Legg in 1940. Legg soon began producing the country's first significant documentary series, *Canada Carries On*, describing Canada's goals and successes in the war effort.

National Film Board documentaries had a reputation for being well thought-out and generally sympathetic to the subject, and they attempted to cover all geographic areas and peoples in that vast country. To ensure that as many Canadians as possible saw the films, traveling teams of mobile projectionists set up shop weekly in community centers in populous as well as remote areas, often leading film-related discussion groups after showings. NFBC films do not appear to have been widely distributed to U.S. school film libraries prior to the late 1950s, with several notable exceptions, including Norman McLaren's animated films (e.g., *Fiddle-De-Dee*, 1947, and *Neighbours*, 1952). Other NFBC films from the pre–1955 years that were commonly found in the U.S. include the important early work of "Unit B" (discussed below), and several ethnographic subjects, one of which was Douglas Wilkinson's exceptional 1952 Inuit portrait of a year on Baffin Island, *Land of the Long Day*. Filmed on Baffin Island under extreme conditions, *Long Day* chronicles the life of the Inuit through Idlouk, a hunter who took his own life shortly after this remarkable film was made.

Many NFBC films documented a world that was rapidly passing from existence: Tim Wilson's *Chairmaker & the Boys* (1959) is an idyllic film from another era, in which Ernest Hart of Cape Breton Island's Margaree Valley served as both chairmaker and blacksmith. His grandson nearly drowns while playing in his water-powered woodshop, as the current surges through a dangerous penstock. Having ignored Grandpa Ernest's admonitions, the boy earned a whack on his behind.

The films made by a loosely-knit group of disparate individuals who came together in the early 1950s to form a group called "Unit B" epitomize the "look and feel" of many of the best known films distributed by the National Film Board of Canada. Launched in 1948, Unit B was chartered to make cultural, scientific, animated, and sponsored films.[64] It was led by executive producer Tom Daly, who arrived at the Film Board as a junior researcher and eventually became the associate producer of the war series *Canada Carries On*. By the mid–1950s, Daly had assembled a crew that included cameraman Wolf Koenig, Colin Low and Robert Verrall (who had originally been trained as animators), talented writer and narrator Stanley Jackson, and a newer recruit, Roman Kroitor. In addition, the ill-fated Hugh O'Connor arrived to head the science film subject group within the Unit.[67] During its most productive decade, from 1954 through its demise in 1964, this stellar group of contributors made more than 100 films. Unit B included a wide diversity of personalities, the most challenging of which to manage, according to writer D.B. Jones, were Kroitor and Jackson:

> Kroitor originally had come to the Film Board as a summer intern. Now he was a full-time employee, but still a trainee unassigned to a specific unit. He had done work for Unit B, and Daly thought him immensely talented. But Kroitor had annoyed the administration when he took an extra week of Christmas holidays without permission, and other filmmakers and producers disliked him. "Roman," Daly recalls, "had incensed almost everyone with his direct comments and criticisms — the more so because they were often so close to the bone. [Director of Production Donald] Mulholland knew I had been using Roman on some projects, and he came to me one day and said he was afraid he'd have to let Roman go. None of the other producers wanted to work with him. I thought quickly, and said that I didn't find him a problem to work with, and that his contribution to *our* unit was fine. And then I asked him, 'If I can keep him fully and usefully occupied for the whole [fiscal] year, do you have any objection to keeping him in my unit?' Mulholland accepted that."[66]
>
> [Stanley] Jackson was beloved in Unit B. He was a bachelor and apparently had no close relatives. Unit B was his family. For two years he paid the private school tuition fee for Roman Kroitor's son. He was also a gifted raconteur. [Colin] Low recalls, "I was often under the table, doubled up with laughter. He was funny largely because he laughed at himself a lot."... He was [eccentric] in his work habits, whether writing commentary or recording it. "...I knew," sighs Daly, "that Stanley was irreplaceable in the commentary field. Even if you 'fired' him, you couldn't get another to compose anything like the same quality and effectiveness of commentary. And even if you got another narrator to read Stanley's commentary, it never came off with anything like the convincing effect of Stanley's own voice ... so in our own ways, we each realized we had to suffer whatever was necessary to get the real stuff out of Stanley.... In budgeting a film, Daly "would ask Stanley carefully how much *time at the most* he felt he needed for his commentary to work. Then I'd double it without telling him.... It was rarely, if ever, enough."[67]

NFBC's Unit B Executive Producer Tom Daly (Lois Siegel).

Things at Unit B didn't go smoothly at first, as Daly's early management style tended toward gentle but emphatic criticism. An early attempt by Verrall, Low, Kroitor, and Koenig to have him removed failed, as Mulholland recognized the value of the team as a whole, which now included, informally, composer Eldon Rathburn. The magic created by Unit B was due to its collaborative and insular nature:

> If they possessed the requisite drive and imagination ... Unit B provided them with an appropriately nourishing environment. It insulated its members somewhat from the bureaucratic imperatives and tendencies that could suppress creative daring in even the freest of government filmmaking organizations. And, in Eldon Rathburn, Stanley Jackson, and, especially, Daly, the unit provided an essential structuring discipline to balance and bring into harmony the wilder impulses of its younger members.

This balance between innovation and structure is a common feature among the six films that probably remain Unit B's best-loved works and best display the range of Unit B's documentary achievement. The films are *Corral* (1954), *Paul Tomkowicz: Street-railway Switchman* (1954), *City Of Gold* (1957), *Universe* (1960), *Circle of the Sun* (1961), and *Lonely Boy* (1961), and they were primarily the work of the group who had met at Daly's apartment to discuss his style of leadership. Low directed *Corral*; Koenig shot it. Kroitor directed *Paul Tomkowicz*. Low and Koenig co-directed *City of Gold*. Kroitor provided a story-line and technical innovation, and he contributed to the editing. Low directed *Circle of the Sun*. Kroitor and Low co-directed *Universe*. Koenig and Kroitor jointly made *Lonely Boy*. As head of Unit B, Daly was of course executive producer for all six, but he also edited all but *Paul Tomkowicz* and *Lonely Boy*. Others made essential contributions; among those who contributed significantly to more than one of the films were Jackson, a writer for four and adviser on all, and Rathburn, who created original music for all but *Paul Tomkowicz* and *Lonely Boy*.[68]

While *Corral* is the first Film Board documentary to be produced without narration, *City of Gold*, the yesterday-today story of a small Klondike boom town, appears to be the first documentary made anywhere to make use of pans, zooms, and tilts across still photographs, thanks to a tracking device invented by Kroitor.

Tom Daly's description of the editing sequence in *City of Gold* describes not only the transition between live-action and still photography, but also something of the humanist element, an important aspect of each Unit B production:

> [At] the beginning of the film, after we had shown the live present day activity we gradually shifted the attention to the houses behind them which were full of broken windows and empty doorways and boarded up areas. Then we moved away to old locomotives in the forest and decaying ferries aground and then to a ship's rope that was thrown down carelessly and left rotting on the gangway. Without seeing him, you feel the presence of the person who once threw it there. Then we take you to the crosses in the cemetery, with the grass grown up around the graves. Again you feel the individuals of those days in their numbers though, of course, you do not expect them to move ever again. You know they are dead. So even the unconscious expectation of their moving is already ruled out by the order of the images up to this point in the picture. The next time you see these people they are appropriately still, forming a line wending its way into the Yukon.[69]

By 1954, many in the Unit B team, including Koenig, Kroitor, and Terence Macartney-Filgate were becoming increasingly interested in ways to achieve a greater level of intimacy with their documentary subjects. Along with cinematographers Michel Brault and John Spotton, among others, they sought ways to shorten the physical distance between subject and camera, which would, in theory, lessen the psychological/emotional barriers between subject and viewer. Their expectations came to fruition within the next several years with the introduction of a series of lightweight cameras and synchronized sound tape recorders, used in the Unit B-produced television series *Candid Eye*. Several months prior to making *Eye*, Unit B's cameraman Michel Brault and soundman Marcel Carrière had begun making films for the French unit at the Film Board, utilizing mobile sight and sound for films such as *Les Raquetteurs* (1958), documenting a meeting of snowshoers. These techniques, known as *direct cinema*, or *cinéma vérité*, would become increasingly common in documentary, feature, and educational film.[70]

By the end of the 1950s, the Film Board had established itself as a force in documentary film, and NFBC films had become staples in Canadian classrooms. Soon, they would become important educational elements in United States classrooms as well, through distribution arrangements with companies such as the international Film Foundation and Learning Corporation of America. The Film Board's post–1960 activities in academic film will be addressed in Chapter Four.

The End of an Era

The remainder of the history of academic classroom film in North America in this early pre–1960s era is filled with primarily smaller companies and organizations acting as producers and/or distributors, as well as several larger corporate players. Among them were Bailey/Film Associates, who will be discussed in Chapter Four.

In retrospect, many of the films of that early era are little more than cinematic lectures framing poor acting and uninspired writing. Subject matter and treatment, particularly in films relating to social issues, were all too often dictated by the relative social perspective of the white, male psychographic of the people who owned and managed most educational film companies, and who ran the school organizations that bought the films. Films on the diverse social and ethnic structure of North American society in the pre–1960s era are exceedingly difficult to find. The few that were produced — the Gordon Weisenborn–John Barnes production of *People Along the Mississippi* (*1952, EB) being a prime example — are exciting in their rarity and vision.

As we close on the early era of educational film, we find much of what constitutes the educational film business stuck in a creative tar pit. Who would have guessed that, in much the same way that an attack on a remote U.S. port gave a new spark to the creatively moribund educational film industry in the 1940s, a new threat from still another foreign nation would provide the financial impetus for a renaissance in educational film that would last a quarter century? That threat and the U.S. government's financial response to it provided North American academic filmmakers with the means to produce some of the finest short films ever made.

CHAPTER TWO

A Cold War Funds a Hot Medium: The Progressive Era, 1961–1985

From a cinematic perspective, an important outcome of the aftermath of World War II was the influx of military-trained filmmakers moving into the educational film world. Effective educational filmmaking, however, encompasses more than technique. As was discussed in the last chapter, the majority of academic films of the 1950s, from a content perspective, were merely didactic mirrors of what was found in textbooks. It took another major world event to provoke the educational film world to provide more engaging, creative content from a cognitive, affective, and socially conscious perspective. The catalyst was Sputnik. And if you don't think Sputnik was big, just ask anybody who was an elementary school kid in the era: for many of us, the toys *du jour* were the tiny Sputniks we were all making out of Tinker Toys. In that critical time and for the next few years that followed, it was a common occurrence for our dads to drag us to home fairs where we could see prototype fallout shelters that we could build in our own backyards. The world had changed.

This chapter explains why academic films made during the three decades following the Soviet launch of Sputnik were less didactic, broader in scope socially and intellectually, and frankly more enjoyable to watch than their predecessors. They were propelled by important Congressional acts that funneled funds from public coffers directly to schools, and indirectly to educational film companies and a new generation of filmmakers.

While the money needed to produce great academic films eventually flowed mightily, it didn't come easily at first. This chapter describes the dramatic battle that took place on a federal level to allocate funds for a new revolution in mediated technology. It changed the way educational films were made, how curriculum was taught, and, it can be argued, evolved the social climate in classrooms as well. It was nothing less than a teaching and learning revolution, prompting perhaps the most significant educational movement in the 20th century as far as classroom education was concerned. From an instructional technology perspective, its ramifications are still being felt today. To begin, it is necessary to travel back to that autumn day in October 1957.

The Launch of Sputnik and the Renaissance of Academic Film

The Soviet launch of the first Sputnik satellite on October 4, 1957, created a climate in Washington that would soon bring dramatic changes to American school curriculum. Politicians became increasingly fearful that Russian students might have eclipsed their U.S.

counterparts in mathematics, the sciences, technology, and foreign languages. Influential individuals such as Admiral Hyman Rickover soon were making well-publicized statements about the importance of changing the way Americans thought about education.[1]

In 1958, influenced by testimony from Encyclopædia Britannica Film's William Benton, former FCC chairman Newt Minow, Anna Rosenberg Hoffman, and Adlai Stevenson (who would become chairman of the EBF Board of Directors the following year), Congress passed Public Law 85–864, the National Defense Education Act (NDEA). NDEA authorized the government to distribute $480 million in matching funds to assist educational institutions in developing curricula, programs, and learning aids, including film and audio-visual equipment.[2] Under Title VII of the Act, a New Educational Media program was established to conduct, assist, and foster research and experimentation for mediated instruction, with grants to educational institutions administered by an advisory committee. Essentially, the federal government provided 50 percent of the funding for math, science, and foreign language instructional materials, as well as support for local education leaders who wished to promote innovative instruction. The government also funded subject matter–based instruction, such as the Physical Science Study Committee (PSSC) curriculum, which received funding from the National Science Foundation.

Many of the projects conducted by researchers funded by Title VII resulted in quantifiable data that would eventually be used by educational film companies to prove the efficacy of educational film in the classroom. This provided the impetus for further federal programs that would pump ever greater amounts of money into educational film companies primarily via school media purchasing departments. An example of a grant for just such a research project on the efficacy of educational film shows the painstaking process taken by researchers to compile data:

> 132. PREPARATION AND EVALUATION IN USE OF A SERIES OF BRIEF FILMS OF SELECTED DEMONSTRATIONS FROM THE INTRODUCTORY COLLEGE PHYSICS COURSE (13 & up) (PBS)
> Description: Study will compare the effectiveness of short film recordings of selected lecture demonstrations with "live" demonstrations, in an introductory college physics course for engineering students.
> Evaluation will be as follows: (1) Four hundred students will be randomly assigned in 2 groups. One group will receive filmed demonstrations; the other will receive live demonstrations. The same professor will lecture to both groups. The achievement of the 2 groups will be assessed by several quizzes, a mid-semester and a final examination. Analysis of covariance will be used. (2) Students will be randomly assigned to several sections of the lecture ball for each of the 2 Instructional methods. Scores on achievement tests will be analyzed to assess the effects of viewing distance, instructional method and possible interactions between the 2 conditions. (3) Students will be encouraged to review the filmed demonstrations on an optional basis out of class. A study will be made of the amount of attendance and characteristics of student attenders. (4) The long range effects of the 2 methods will be studied over a period of 2 years using as criteria withdrawal rates, cumulative grade point averages, and changes of academic major.
> Beginning and Ending Dates: July 1, 1959 to August 31, 1961
> OE Grant: $71,184
> Grantee: Purdue Research Foundation, Lafayette, Ind.
> Principal Investigator: D. J. Tendam, Associate Professor of Physics[3]

Educators had consistently tried to secure federal funding for educational programs prior to the Sputnik era, but experienced only marginal success. In 1950, major federal school funding legislation had failed because of congressional fears that such an act would take power away from local schools, and the *Brown v. Board of Education* decision of 1954 fueled the fears of local politicians and school administrators that any financial ties with federal entities would result in unwanted judicial meddling.

Much of the resistance came from rural communities, particularly in Southern states. Many politicians were concerned that, upon receiving federal aid, local schools would be forced to follow federal desegregation policies.[4] At the core of the federal funding vs. local schools debate was the intense distrust by politicians and local school board members alike of the "intellectual elite," loosely defined as any group of scholars who might, through writings, testimony, and political affiliation, force unwelcome curricular material on local schools, an attitude well-defined by Peter Dow, project editor for the ill-fated *Man: A Course of Study (MACOS)* program in the mid–1970s:

> Too much education, many Americans still think, tends to set people apart from the crowd, makes them leave home, gives them an inflated view of their capabilities, weakens family ties, and destroys religion. Our provincialism and our belief in equality make us uncertain about how much learning we really want to have take place in our schools. Unlike most other nations, we remain suspicious of intellectuals, and continue to revere nonacademic routes to success and power. After all, some of our most celebrated national heroes have made it without formal education. Somewhere deep in the American consciousness we probably still shelter a profound distrust of too much schooling.[5]

The launch of Sputnik accelerated Congressional action in response to the perceived threat from the other side of Churchill's Iron Curtain. Because the impetus for the NDEA was driven in a large part by the need to train more engineers to counter Soviet technology, initial funds were earmarked for mathematics, science, and foreign language curricula.[6]

Many in the academic world believed film to be an essential element of learning, particularly in the sciences. Peter Dow writes of the discussions occurring at an academic retreat held at M.I.T.'s Endicott House in Dedham, Massachusetts, in June 1962:

> Some thought that students could be introduced to the romance of the academic disciplines by watching specialists at work on the screen — archaeologists digging up ancient artifacts, anthropologists studying preliterate peoples, historians uncovering ancient records, and so forth. The idea here was to try to give the students a sense of the speculative quality of scholarship and to expose them to the way in which scholars derive inferences from often fragmentary evidence. Film, they thought, was the best medium to establish communication between scholar and student, for it could bring remote material to the classroom in a vivid form, and it could make the academic specialist more human by showing him "in his shirtsleeves."[7]

In 1965, Title III of the NDEA was expanded to include funding for industrial arts, economics, English, reading, and geography, thereby continuing a number of federal programs which, by proxy, funded the work of a generation of filmmakers, in essence creating an informal government-sponsored public film consortia grander in scale than that of any other country. Educational film companies, long used to producing films with meager production budgets, began to improve the overall technical quality of the product, providing a significant amount of work to filmmakers who increasingly found it more lucrative to remain in the 16mm educational film world than to risk battling it out with hundreds of others competing in the 35mm feature film maelstrom of Hollywood.

In addition to NDEA, several more federal programs provided either funding to educational film projects or influenced curricula that led to appropriate films being developed and sold to schools. Curriculum and instruction related to desegregation, racial, and multicultural issues was increasingly being emphasized. Chronologically, these programs included:

- **Civil Rights Act of 1964**
  This 18,000-word document was signed by President Lyndon Johnson on July 2, 1964, with noted civil rights leaders Martin Luther King, Jr. and Roy Wilkins of the NAACP in attendance. This new law was empowered by an edict that denied federal funds to schools engaged in policies of segregation, and consisted of regulations addressing several areas of concern, the most significant element of which was, from a curriculum and film perspective, Title VI, which banned discrimination based on race, color, or national origin in any federally assisted program. Policed by the Department of Health, Education and Welfare, school districts could not receive federal funds unless they provided documented proof that desegregation programs were either completed, or quantifiably underway. To a very large extent, this act encouraged educational film companies to make films depicting students of different ethnicities, with content appropriate for use in classes where diversity issues were taught and discussed.

- **Elementary and Secondary Education Act of 1965 (ESEA)**
  ESEA was signed by President Johnson on April 11, 1965 outside the one-room Texas schoolhouse where he once attended classes. It consisted of five titles, the most significant of which, from a film perspective, were Title II, authorizing $100 million for library resources, and Title III, which allocated $100 million for use in several areas including audio-visual aids and programmed materials. Subsequently, additional titles and funding were added to ESEA, an Act which educational historian James Teller called "probably the most significant federal aid to education program ever enacted by the Congress."[8] ESEA created a climate in which progressive educators could create extensive new curricula, with the government paying half the cost. The impact of this Act on the educational film community was astounding. EB Films' revenues reportedly increased from $10 million to $30 million during the first year of ESEA funding.[9] Weston Woods Films' Morton Schindel recalls paying more money in taxes after the first year of ESEA funding than the company had *made* during the previous ten years.[10]

- **National Foundation on the Arts and Humanities Act of 1965**
  Many educators felt that, in the race for technological superiority over the Soviet Union, the arts and humanities were being increasingly ignored in favor of mathematics and science. To emphasize the importance of these areas, Congress passed this important act, stating that: "A high civilization must not limit its efforts to science and technology alone but must give full value and support to the other great branches of man's scholarly and cultural activity ... that democracy ... foster and support a form of education designed to make men masters of their technology and not its unthinking servant ... it is necessary and appropriate for the Federal Government to help create and sustain not only a climate encouraging freedom of thought, imagination, and inquiry but also the material conditions facilitating the release of this creative talent." The Act established separate National Endowments for the Arts and the Humanities, each of which received $5 million from 1966 to 1968. Funding for the latter included support for fostering the "understanding and appreciation of the humanities," which theoretically might include the purchase and distribution of films. In addition, the Office of Education was authorized to distribute $500,000 annually in loans to elementary and secondary schools to purchase equipment and do minor remodeling, and $500,000 to train teachers to deliver arts and humanities curriculum. Under this Act, schools were able to purchase film projectors, screens, and film repair equipment.

- **Environmental Education Act of 1970**
  Designed to bring greater attention to ecological issues and threats to the environment, the Act initially authorized $5 million annually to be used in programs including mediated instruction, allowing for an increase of up to $25 million by 1973.

- **Ethnic Heritage Program of 1972**
  An additional title added to ESEA, this program authorized $15 million in 1973 for the planning, development, and operation of ethnic studies programs, including the necessary curricular materials (e.g., film) needed to implement the instruction.

The fact that these programs were instrumental in the direct funding of the purchase of educational films, or promoting their use to meet new educational objectives, was no accident. To the chagrin of textbook companies that for years had maintained a choke-hold on federal instructional materials funding, film companies had been actively engaged in lobbying activities and testifying before congressional committees, reinforced by quantifiable data attesting to the value of educational film gathered from educational research projects. Perhaps the most significant evidence of the viability of film in the classroom was brought about by *Project Discovery*.

The Proof Is in the Projector: Introducing Project Discovery

Project Discovery was launched in 1964 to determine the impact on classroom education were audio-visual equipment and films to become as permanent, readily available, and plentiful as textbooks. The project involved four school sites, 220 teachers, and more than 5,000 students. It was influential in rewording ESEA to allow some of the funds from that Act to be used by schools to buy educational films in addition to textbooks. Initially, the American Association of Publishers (AAP), a textbook industry lobbying organization, had so heavily influenced the ESEA task force chaired by John Gardner, that schools would have been unable to purchase mediated instruction under the terms of the proposed legislation as written by the Department of Education. EBF's Charles Benton noted, "The AAP's line was that 'the audio visual business got help from the National Defense Education Act (NDEA); now it's our turn.'"[11]

Charles Benton was able to obtain a draft of the ESEA bill, and his team (consisting, among others, of Arnold & Porter lawyer Jim Fitzpatrick and lobbyist Maurice Rosenblatt) began engaging in their own lobbying efforts to change the minds of the task force members and Congress, arguing that choice of instructional materials should be determined at the local rather than the national level.

Benton, who considers *Project Discovery* to be "probably the single most important thing I've contributed to the growth of the field," described the sequence of events that led to its development:

> When I was a traveling salesman in downstate Illinois for EB Films, I met an outstanding head of the State Audio Visual Service in Springfield, a man named Wayne Howell with a PhD in Educational Media from Western Illinois University. Wayne and I became good friends and it was his dream to develop a demonstration project that would remove all of the logistical constraints in the use of audio visual materials so that the major tools of that time would be close to the teachers and students and in fact located within the school building itself. Thus, the idea developed of picking a number of schools across the country that represented different socio-economic communities and that, taken together, would be a good cross section geographically, economically, and professionally of American education. The first community we picked was Shaker Heights, Ohio, a suburb of Cleveland, because we had an entrée and close relationship with the Superintendent of Schools. The rural community of Terrell, Texas was a natural because our Texas rep was from that school district and really had an inside track (we placed the media into each of the 3 elementary and 1 middle schools in Terrell); we chose Daly City, California as the blue-collar West Coast part of the mix; and, of course Washington DC as the urban component for the obvious reason of being in close proximity with our government in the nation's capital.
>
> After two years of being top salesman in the field serving downstate Illinois, I was then appointed as National Sales Manager in 1963 and one of my first hires was to bring Wayne in

as Director of Research and Development for EB Films. Even before Kennedy's assassination, we were exploring the *Project Discovery* idea with the largest manufacturer of audio visual equipment, Bell & Howell, and this was accelerated when we heard of President Johnson's education task force that was working on new education legislation. The research idea came into the picture fairly late in the game and again was driven by Wayne, growing out of his training in media research. This led to Egon Guba at Ohio State University, the leading practitioner of what one might call "inductive research." Guba felt strongly that the traditional research approach of having an experimental group on the one hand and a control group on the other was deeply flawed, and believed instead in the idea of organizing research as an observational tool to describe and measure changes in behavior as the result of the introduction of new elements into the teaching/learning process. His approach seemed ideal to us in our efforts to "discover" what changes in teaching and learning would take place with a rich abundance of new AV tools for teachers and kids close at hand.

The upshot is that the research team led by Guba was awarded a $125,000 grant from the U.S. Department of Education to study *Project Discovery* and evaluate its impact on teaching and learning. With at least one graduate student in each of the 4 locations of the project, the study focused on the learning outcomes of classrooms having unlimited access to 500 films and 1000 filmstrips (provided by EBF), and a 16mm autoload and sound filmstrip projector for each classroom (provided by Bell & Howell). Perhaps the most persuasive advocate of the value of films in the study was Matt Dixon, the principal of Scott Montgomery School in Washington DC (a *Project Discovery* school), in his congressional testimony during hearings for the Elementary and Secondary Education Act (ESEA). He testified successfully before the House Education Committee, using clips from Britannica Films (that) his teachers were using in the classroom, and to speak in favor of allowing schools to select their preferred forms of curriculum and media under the revised provisions of the proposed legislation. This was EB Films at its best in lobbying the government for the entire audio visual business.[12]

To document what was happening in *Project Discovery*, EB Films produced a film (*Project Discovery: A Demonstration in Education*, *1965, dir. Irving Rusinow), primarily for educators, describing how films were currently being used at Mercer Elementary School in Shaker Heights, Ohio. The film demonstrates how teachers used films for instruction as well as how easy projectors were to operate, showing the facility at which second-graders operated Bell and Howell projectors in the classroom and in their own student-centered media labs. At several points, students and teachers noted that instant availability of films through their own film libraries was preferable to the delays experienced when ordering films from a distant archive, promulgating the not-so-subtle message that global access was the key to pedagogical success (and, to be sure, also increased sales for film companies). The prime audience for the *Project Discovery* film consisted of education leaders at all levels in the governance of schools, including school board members, administrators and others involved in resource allocation decision making. The goal was to maximize the visibility of this important project to demonstrate the potential contributions of visual media for improved teaching and learning.

Striving to Create a Better Academic Film

An immediate outcome of ESEA funding was the loosening of the production purse-strings by educational film companies. Better photography (particularly in science films in which color photomicography would play a key role, and in theatrical/literature films, which could now utilize more than one camera, provide better sets, and pay professional actors and more engaging hosts) was one immediate and far-reaching improvement. Filmmakers had the luxury of more robust shooting ratios in the quest to provide a more professional product.[13] Many academic film companies were now open to a new world of creativity: EBF would offer ten-minute *"Discussions Of"* films to accompany titles in their dramatic series, with hosts such as the once-infamous quiz show expert Charles Van Doren, who discussed themes developed in Yust's film interpretation of Joseph Conrad's *Secret Sharer* (1973, dir. Larry Yust). EBF also offered similar ten-minute digests for filmmaking students, such as John Barnes' *Story into Film* (1977) in which the director discussed his decision making process in choosing or rejecting various parts of Walter van Tilburg-Clark's short story for his final film, *The Portable Phonograph* (1977).

ESEA not only provided tools for progressive educators, but allowed many educational filmmakers the freedom to make films more in keeping with their own personal philosophies. Prior to this important Act, educational film companies practiced an unwritten code of developing films that were careful not to offend state and local school administrations, the majority of which were run by white, conservative — and often fundamentalist — males. Pre–1960s guidance films, for example, featured primarily white actors, on social themes relating to dating, health, and civics issues orbiting around the nuclear family. Academic films on historical themes focused primarily on Euro-centric civilizations.[14]

Filmmaker Tom Smith recalls the ways educational film companies, including the otherwise progressive EBF, produced and sold films in this monocultural environment:

> Until the 1960s, no school district was asking for blacks to be included in the films while many gave it as a reason for rejecting a film ... old timers at EBF told me that if you put an African American (they used "Negro") in a film, it would kill sales in the south. Remember at that time the south was segregated and most schools were either black or white. So "Negroes" were not shown in educational films, at least not at EBF. If they were filming in a classroom and there were a couple black children in the room, they'd just frame the other way. If they had to choose several kids to be featured and the black kids were taller than the rest they'd ask for the shorter children. The class room was all white at EBF 'til the 60s. I was about to shoot a scene for *Food From The Sun* (1966) in Evanston, Illinois, a town that has a minority population and integrated schools. I was cautioned NOT to include "Negroes." I couldn't understand this so I mentioned this to Charlie Benton, the new president of EBF (and son of Encyclopædia in Britannica Films' William Benton). Benton, who was about my age, was — and still is — an active liberal. He marched for

Charles Van Doren on the set of Larry Yust's *Secret Sharer* (1973) (Isidore Mankofsky, A.S.C.).

integration. He didn't understand or like the policy. He told me he wanted minorities in the film. He thought all film should include a mixture of races. So it was that *Food from the Sun* was one of the first EBF films with black children in it. After that, because the federal government was subsidizing sales, all films not only included minorities, they required them. Sometimes it was difficult to include them where they were not naturally available where we were filming but we always tried ... it is clear to me why EBF excluded black children from the educational screen until the mid 1960s though it seems silly to us now. Silly isn't the right word here. It is yet another reminder of our national shame. EBF was not a pioneer in racial integration, they simply followed the demands of the culture to whom they were selling.[15]

As mentioned earlier, John Barnes of EB Films had been involved in the making of films prior to 1960 that depicted interaction between peers of different races: *People Along the Mississippi* (1951, dir. Gordon Weisenborn, written and photographed by Barnes), and *Sir Francis Drake: Rise of English Sea Power* (1957, dir. John Barnes). He had also offered a revisionist perspective on the history of the Native American in *Roger Williams: Founder of Rhode Island* (1957), but such ideas didn't appear to have influenced the brain trust at headquarters significantly enough to encourage them to produce more material promoting similar social outcomes. Instead, EBF management seemed content to allow only Barnes, residing in England, Italy, or New York, and existing outside of EB's political and procedural dog-

Bert Salzman's *Geronimo Jones* (1970) explored inter-generational conflict in Native American culture (Bill Deneen, Learning Corporation of America).

matic corral in Chicago, to explore such themes. In effect, prior to the Civil Rights Act of 1964, EB appeared to have one set of rules for Barnes and another for everyone else.[16]

In spite of its limited approach to addressing racial issues through film, EBF was denigrated by many in the generally conservative educational film industry for its executive pedigree of progressive politics, embodied by men such as William Benton and Adlai Stevenson. Charles Benton was at the March on Washington in 1963 with Martin Luther King, Jr., and his wife Marjorie had been jailed in Chicago for sitting in Superintendent of Schools Ben Willis' chair in a public school desegregation protest. Rival Coronet Films jumped on the opportunity with southern conservative film buyers and branded the younger Benton an agitator, an act which led to Coronet's loss of their valuable promotions guru, John Field, who was married to an Asian American and, offended by his own company's archaic social attitudes, left to join EBF in the same capacity.[17]

From the mid–1960s onward, a time teeming with a new awareness of the politics of segregation, racial injustice, women's issues, concerns of the aged, multiculturalism, and changing family structures, the "face" of educational film changed rapidly. Due to the involvement of the federal government, films now more frequently addressed previously marginalized students that heretofore rarely saw people who lived, acted, thought, or looked like themselves. Prototypical people could now be non-white, might live in nicely maintained project housing, have two working parents (or even a sole working parent), and have friends of several different ethnicities. Historical elements important to U.S. history would now include positive contributions made by Asians, Blacks, Latinos, and Native Americans. LCA's Bert Salzman, for example, made a series of films on Americans of different ethnicities (*Geronimo Jones*, *1970) and stations in life (*Shopping Bag Lady*, *1975) that had been almost completely ignored in the pre–Sputnik days. Films now broached societal taboos as deep-seated within American culture as interracial dating, in films such as Noel Black's *Reflections* (1975, Pyramid) and Seth Pinsker's *Overture — Linh from Vietnam* (1980, LCA). While it's difficult to say how much of the educational film status-quo of the 1950s would have still been maintained if Richard Nixon had won the 1960 election, it is inarguable that educational film flourished in an era of progressive politics combined with federal capital fueled by Cold War fear, and remained strong enough to maintain its new charter of inclusion through the mid 1980s.

As we have seen, this renaissance in academic film didn't happen overnight. It was an evolution that occurred in fits and starts and required film executives to alter their 1950s-era mindsets regarding production, distribution, and sales. The significant infusion of capital to school libraries for mediated instruction attributable to Congressional acts such as ESEA provided a financial motivation for film companies to evolve the cinematic curriculum to mirror a society in a state of transition. This evolution changed the course of the way students were taught about their world, as evidenced by the dramatic new films produced by academic film companies. These companies, and the people behind them, are discussed in Chapter 4.

The changes brought by the laws described in this chapter dramatically altered the *business* of educational film, and how these films were produced, bought, sold, and promoted, as will be seen in the next chapter.

CHAPTER THREE

Writing a New Cookbook: How Academic Films Were Funded, Made, Bought, and Sold in the Progressive Era

Fueled by new laws and a changing political climate, educational film companies were now in a situation where they had to essentially relearn their business. Simply maintaining status quo and making films in the old way wouldn't support much of the new curriculum that resulted from the Congressional Acts that were changing the face of education. An emerging generation of young filmmakers, with new ideas and attitudes often rebellious to old ways of thinking, made for a difference as well. As young adults to the 1960s, they could be unafraid to openly challenge corporate edicts with which they disagreed, and it behooved film execs to listen, as there were plenty of other companies in need of good young filmmakers disenchanted with their current employers. A filmmaker could easily make films as an independent as well, and find a more established company to distribute them. Publicity organizations were aware of these changes too, and embraced them. One of the most important elements in promoting films and filmmakers was the Educational Film Library Association (EFLA), whose publications and film festivals provided a critical factor in promoting educational film to educators and even the public at large. Its influence was significant. The "cookbook" for funding, making, and promoting educational films was in the process of being rewritten, made possible because of the funding revolution that created a larger market and greater profits.

Profits by the Numbers

Just how profitable was the educational film business coming on the heels of this new legislation? Approximately 3,000 public and private schools and libraries comprised the total available market.[1] Sales statistics from film companies are never easy to come by, but a rule of thumb used by one company specializing in elementary films suggested that during the "life" of a successful film, 300–500 copies of a given title might be sold, with more popular titles achieving sales of 2,000 or more.[2] Although prices continually rose, by 1970 standards a four-hundred foot (ten minute) film might be sold for approximately $150, with 1200-foot (half-hour) releases fetching approximately $450. A production budget of $15–50,000 would be set for most films made during the 1965–1985 era, so it can be extrapolated that a typical half-hour film selling for $450 would find 500 buyers, producing gross receipts of $225,000.[3]

NFBC's Co Hoedeman arranges the set for an animated film (Lois Siegel).

Many executives believed that the length of a film could be used to judge its potential profit: films of ten minutes in duration typically sold ten times as well as a thirty-minute title on the same subject, with twenty-minute long films selling twice as many as thirty-minute versions.[4] From the gross profit, production costs and royalties to filmmakers or independent production companies (approximately 5 percent of gross) would be deducted to realize a net profit figure. And that's not the best of it: many educational films were revised as curricula and social mores changed. New revisions could now be sold to replace older editions, the older footage re-edited, music re-scored and voice re-narrated. This revised title cost far less than a new film, and often sold for a higher price than the previous edition. Filmmaker and producer Paul Hoefler, on the other hand, had a different tack: by not inserting the date of production in the credits, he was able to sell the same aging titles to school districts for years and years and years.

There was a burgeoning film market for overseas schools as well. Companies such as EBF would sell to distributors in foreign countries, providing both an internegative and a magnetic soundtrack without narration to a distributor, who would then dub the narration in the native tongue. In this fashion, EBF sold over 400 titles in Spanish (dubbed in Mexico), 300 in Italian, 300 in Portuguese, 400 in Levantine Arabic, and countless others in Hindi.[5]

Although film companies were now reaping the financial rewards brought on by greater access to government funds via sales to school districts, they still maintained strong fiscal discipline when dealing with filmmakers. Educational filmmakers fought continual battles for budget, and generally worked on a compensation plan that gave them a fixed amount for the initial finished film, followed by royalties based on sales. Financially astute filmmakers would often bring the film in under budget in order to realize some immediate profit for themselves, but not all film companies were very good at releasing the sales statistics filmmakers needed to ensure they were getting a fair shake on royalties. The secrecy surrounding actual sales remains a major reason why today adequate statistics cannot be derived regarding the number of films sold by a given company, or the "best sellers" of any era or sub-genre.[6]

To better understand the world of the educational filmmaker, it's of some value to break down the process by which a film was planned, developed, made, distributed, and promoted. The best stories involve those of struggle, as this brave new world of filmmaking sought to redefine itself.

Reel Mechanics: Planning and Developing an Academic Film

To begin a film project, the idea and treatment would be proposed by a director or producer — their roles were often interchangeable — or an executive producer (who would typically be responsible for doling out funds to a series of line producers or directors). To judge potential sales demand, the opinions of one or more educators would be elicited as

EBF's Bert Van Bork (far left) and Milan Herzog (seated far right) on the set of *Art in the Western World* (Bert Van Bork).

to whether a film produced on a given topic would have sufficient curricular value. It was also common to poll members of the in-house sales team to judge how a film would sell in certain areas of the country. If the answers elicited a "go," the filmmaker and/or executive producer, rarely being subject matter experts themselves, would ascertain whether sufficient authoritative research had been done on the topic to warrant a film. If approved, a budget would be allocated, a script would be developed, and the filmmaker would go about choosing a crew, actors, a host/narrator, and music, if necessary. If not already chosen prior to the scripting phase, an educational consultant was selected, usually by the film company, to provide a cursory review of the script, in order to establish educational credibility. This subject matter expert would typically also serve as the educational advisor to the film, an engagement often stipulated by public film funding guidelines. In many cases, however, the scholar was rarely consulted, or, when so, was virtually ignored, an approach labeled "rent-a-scholar" by writer Jay Ruby.[7]

Filmmaker Tom Smith confirms that consultants were often such in name only:

[Academic/educational] Collaborators at EB were a strange thing. In most cases they had nothing to do with the production except to review the script and look at the finished film. They represented the academic seal of approval for the film and were usually paid $200 for lending their names. In the case of a science film they'd be very helpful in making sure we got it right but on a "Social Studies" film such as (my) farm films, there really wasn't much they could contribute.[8]

Educational film credits in general were not what we see on TV or in features. We'd often make films with actors and not give them or the narrator a credit. The credit "Producer" often meant Produced, written and directed by: _____. Most film credits had less than 20 names. For years EBF did not allow ANY credits as they said these films were educational tools, not entertainment.[9]

Some companies, to their credit, took painstaking care in making sure that the finished film did pass scholarly muster.[10] Many films were sold with study guides written by scholars either inserted inside, or glued directly to the underside top of the film can. Such guides suggested discussion topics, review questions, and educational objectives for the lesson plan. John Matoian's instructor notes, glued to the inside of the film can for a number of Learning Corporation of America (LCA) films, occasionally suggested that teachers remove students from their comfort zones by challenging them to ask pointed questions of their parents, then report the results the next day in class.[11] Probably the most professional and comprehensive study guide ever released was EBF's 8½" × 11", glossy 26-pager for John Barnes' *Shaw vs. Shakespeare* series, complete with filmmaker bio, production notes, and dialogue, which in some ways resembled a well-made and researched symphonic program booklet.

Focusing on Film Crews

With the exception of the relatively few productions requiring a large crew and actors, academic films were typically made by small crews consisting of a director and camera and sound professionals. They weren't, as a rule, extremely well paid, and often looked on the process of making educational films as a way to hone their craft prior to moving on to feature films.[12] A number of exceptional cinematographers worked in educational film, many of whom, such as EBF's Isidore Mankofsky, went on to achieve future success in feature films (his telescoping shot depicting the protagonist's travel through time in the feature film

EBF's Isidore Mankofsky preparing to shoot a burning building scene in *Mayor* (1966) (Isidore Mankofsky, A.S.C.).

Somewhere In Time (1980, dir. Jeannot Szwar) has become famous, and is discussed in film schools). Some of the more exceptional camerawork often appeared in science films, where time-lapse and photomicrographic sequences were filmed by people such as Peter Boulton (Boulton-Hawker), Ken Middleham (Stanton), Bruce Russell (BioMEDIA/Coronet), Georg Schimanski (FWU), and Bert Van Bork (EB). Van Bork's own aerial camerawork on films such as *Mesa Verde: Mystery of the Silent Cities* (1975, EBF) rivaled that of any feature cameraman, and his close-up shots of volcanic activity were exceptional, and risky to obtain.[13] Richard Leacock, a developer of the "cinéma vérité" technique, proudly admits that his work in educational film was influential to his later films.[14]

Shooting educational films was often challenging, given the financial and time constraints dictated by film companies. The sometimes uneasy relationship between executives chartered with holding to the bottom line and filmmakers concerned with product quality are elucidated by two letters, detailing concerns and discussions among cameraman Isidore Mankofsky, VP of Production Milan Herzog, EBF exec Gene Feldman, directors Stan Croner and Larry Yust, and President Warren Everote of EBF, describing some bizarre and frustrating events occurring during the shooting of a science film in the early 1960s. The letters not only illustrate the financial give-and-take between management and film crews, but describe the arduous climactic conditions under which crews sometimes had to work. The matter at hand is the breaking down of the field film unit's Travelall vehicle, used to transport equipment and personnel, under trying desert conditions:

18 July 1961
To: Stan Croner, Gene Feldman, Izzy Mankofsky, Larry Yust
From: Warren Everote

The recent virtual destruction of the Travelall has raised anew some serious problems and led to some firm determinations about future action pertaining to our vehicles. As some general information, you should know it cost the Company $1100 in book value to lose this vehicle under those circumstances. Further, it cost us Izzy's down time in Tucson and miscellaneous expenses such as long distance calls.... In the past, there has been the cry here that Production people have, on occasion, misused Company vehicles in terms of excessive speed, indifference to proper maintenance procedures and overloading.... Without knowing any details pertaining to the recent experience, my guess is that it was avoidable if careful maintenance and attention to the recording instruments on the dash were practiced and if the car were operated at normal speed end under designed-for loads. If I'm wrong, I'd like to hear the rebuttal in the written report of details that I am asking for from Izzy.

Now we have a new wagon. While it is on the Coast, I want Larry Yust to be specifically in charge of its maintenance and use. He of course will delegate his authority as required. Whoever drives it is to be requested to have tires, oil and water periodically checked (one oil change a mouth is refunded by Emkay), necessary repairs arranged for and greasing done every 2,000 miles. Excessive overloading simply has to be avoided end extra transportation arranged for by other means...

What I'm saying gentlemen, is that in our setup, the car problem is part of the job. Maybe other companies can provide chauffeurs and maintenance people. We can't! So those in Production must maintain the vehicles they use and they must give them better care than I think has been generally true of our past performance... In any case, Izzy, please send me a full report on the recent incident. I'm on the pan but good. If evidence exists to cool the temperature, I need it.

— Warren Everote

July 24, 1961
Dear Warren,

There is no one as unhappy as I am with over the recent trouble I had with the Travelall, but let's face it. Anyone unfortunate enough to be driving the truck at that time would have had the same thing happen to him. As it was, I was not driving, Paul Leimbach was. Of all the people who have driven the Travelall Paul is the most conscientious. At time we were driving across the Arizona Desert and the temperature in the shade was 115 degrees. We had been driving for 11 hours with stops for gas, water, and food. Twenty minutes before our trouble started we had stopped for gas and water and oil check. Up 'til this time there was no sign of the truck over-heating. In fact, that was one of the strong points of this truck, it never over-heated because of the oversized cooling system. We were 30 miles from Tucson when Paul told me the truck was showing signs of overheating. I told him to stop and by the time we had gotten the truck stopped it was too late. That is how fast it happened. We never had a chance and neither would anyone else. Our speed at the time was 60 miles per hour.

I repeat — we had plenty of oil and water. The mechanic explained what happened this way. He said we had blown a head gasket and this had caused backpressure in the water jacket, which had prevented the water from circulating. This could have happened to anyone at any time and was not caused by speed or carelessness of any kind. I was in extreme mental torment during the whole incident and would have given anything to have prevented it.

To answer your other charges pertaining to the truck: anyone who has ever driven the Travelall would know that it is virtually impossible to speed in it because once you had the truck past sixty miles an hour the vibration noise made it almost impossible to maintain an excessive speed. I cannot answer for other EBF employees but as long as I had the Travelall in my charge it has had meticulous maintenance. If anyone would care to check the bills, they would find that this is true. The truck has been overloaded on many occasions and this has not been my choice but because of necessity. At the time of the trouble the Travelall was not overloaded. This vehicle was a bomb from the day we got it, and it has proved to be a bad luck vehicle ever since.

The new station wagon is a dandy, but not at all suited to our needs. For instance, I had an extremely light load for the Travelall on my last trip, consisting of cameras, reflectors, and other necessary gear. Yet, when this load was transferred to the station wagon the rear springs were hitting bottom. The only way I could make it back to L.A. was by putting 1500 lb. Overload springs on the rear of the wagon. I did this for a cost of $22.00

Sincerely, Isidore Mankofsky

Some filmmakers avoided the realities of big-company economics by serving as their own one-person crews, as was the case with filmmakers such as Wayne Mitchell and Norman Bean. Bernard Wilets was probably unique in terms of the control he had over his films, retaining all rights, which allowed him to distribute his films through several companies simultaneously.[15]

Class Act: Character Portrayal in Educational Films

Even with the bigger profits resulting from the funding avalanche in the 1960s, educational film companies still had to produce a product that was affordable to schools, and financially competitive with films made by their counterparts. Since the comparatively low budgets of educational film dictated like economies of scale in terms of actor compensation, filmmakers either had to be financially creative in hiring acting talent, or risk producing an inferior product. Some filmmakers, such as John Barnes, elected to do much of their work overseas, where fine actors could be found who wouldn't have to be paid based on U.S. pay scales. EBF, wishing to stay on a high professional level, worked out an agreement with the Screen Actors Guild (SAG) that allowed for the use of SAG talent, limiting the distribution to classrooms.[16] Bernard Wilets arrived at a verbal agreement with SAG, who, wanting to find work for its large unemployed talent pool, agreed to allow the producer to use its actors provided that they went uncredited, a practice ultimately frustrating for the film researcher wanting to credit any of the number of exceptional actors appearing in Wilets' films.[17]

Filmmakers not able to afford SAG scale often resorted to the film-school practice of using their friends, resulting in films such as *Democracy: Role of Dissent* (1970, uncredited director, New Document Productions/Coronet), a film notable for being among the most amateurish educational films ever made. This film, sporting an ancient crew of non-actors, is highlighted by a motley protest march, in which wandering, distracted participants are repeatedly redirected back to the area covered by the camera lens. Quixote-like, they valiantly attempt to keep aloft their protest signs, lettered by the same hand that painted the logo on the side of the building belonging to the company being picketed. One suspects that they were drawn to participating in the film by a free lunch, common remuneration for those participating in low-budget films.

The "Voice" of Education: Narration Styles and Perspectives

From the advent of the sound era through the late 1950s, academic films were typically narrated by "omniscient" male voices in one of two vocal treatments, which I characterize as the "lecture" and the "stentorian" styles. The curt, sharply-clipped "lecture" style was delivered in monotone, emotionally distant from the subject matter, as epitomized by Jim Brill, whose career as in-house narrator of EB Films lasted several decades prior to his retirement in the early 1950s. The stentorian, reporter-like newsreel commentator style was personified by Alexander Scourby at its most definitive, or the National Film Board's Lorne Greene in its most bombastic. Declamatory in nature, even the interrogative points in the script were articulated as commands, rather than as thought-provoking questions. Scourby's narration was commonly featured in television documentaries of the 1950s and 1960s, and many school libraries owned a number of his narrated films, from the legendary documentary on Nazi Germany, *Twisted Cross* (1956, prod. Henry Salomon, NBC) to Nicolas Noxon's well-written *Dr. Leakey and the Dawn of Man* (1966, *National Geographic*). Greene wasn't the first of the "heroic" narrators to infuse content with emotion, but he may have been a most pervasive. In the wartime series *Canada Carries On*, Greene seems to be playing the part of the carnival barker in one of the more overwrought military propaganda films of the era (e.g., *Guards of the North*, 1941, dir. Raymond Spottiswoode).

Occasionally, individual producers would come up with something completely out the norm in terms of narration. John Barnes, for example, in films such as *Magna Carta* (1959, EBF), created an effective narrative style by interspersing his own voice with that of the formal narrator, probably an effect that derived from his days as a producer of radio programs.

One of the more intriguing methods of classifying different narrative styles has been suggested by professor of communication Richard Campbell, who defines several distinct "actor" roles that a reporter/narrator may adopt, any of which may define a discrete viewpoint, and can shift within each film or episode as the story evolves.[18] While Campbell defined them in order to explain an element of the overall treatment of a popular television documentary series, such terms may also have value in assessing differing narrative perspectives in the academic film as well, applicable to both on-screen hosts and off-screen narrators. They, with appropriate examples from the academic film world, are:

- Detective: the narrator describes a mystery, then attempts to solve it, sometimes successfully, sometimes not. [Example: Lloyd Bochner, in *The Jean Richard* (1963, dir. René Bonnière, Crawley), describing the building of a "goélette" flat-bottomed boat outdoors, in the dead of winter.]

- Tourist: the narrator takes the viewer to distant destinations, guiding the viewer through scientific, cultural, political, or historical aspects. [Notable examples include Nick Pennell, who acts as a tour guide to 14th century Europe in Piers Jessop's *Middle Ages: A Wanderer's Guide to Life and Letters* (1970, LCA), and Phillip Morrison, in *Powers of Ten: A Rough Sketch* (1968, dir. Judith Bronowski, Pyramid), describing the universe from cosmology to atomic theory, by moving away from, then approaching, a man napping after a picnic.]

Nicholas Pennell as the host and narrator of Piers Jessop's *Middle Ages: a Wanderer's Guide to Life and Letters* (1970) (Bill Deneen, Learning Corporation of America).

- Social critic: the narrator investigates a societal problem, typically one without overt criminal or negligent activity. [Example: Mortimer Adler, in *Emperor and Slave* (1965, dir. John Barnes, EBF), in describing the philosophy of stoicism and its impact on Roman life.]

- Historian: the narrator describes historical events in expository form. [Example: Ed Stoddard, *Background of the Declaration of Independence* (1985, dir. Paul Burnford, Media Guild).]

- Prosecutor: the narrator uncovers destructive, negligent or illegal activity, and takes an active, accusatory or remedial posture. [Example: Harry Shearer in *Modoc* (1980, dir. Peter Winograd, Educational Media), in describing the events leading to the famed Indian war of 1873, mentions that the white settlers "brought smallpox, whiskey, and Christianity."]

- Therapist: the narrator elicits information from the subjects, and takes on the role of a healer. [Example: R.H. Thompson in *Mozambique: Building a Future* (1987, dir. Charles Konowal, NFBC) in describing the crisis in which every dentist (all of whom were white) left the nation of Mozambique after the revolution, and Canada's role in training an entire new young corps of native Mozambican dentists to quickly fill the void.]

- Referee: the narrator takes the dialectical approach, presenting two or more sides to an argument or discussion. [Example: the uncredited narrator in *From Where I Sit: Foreign Policy* (1967, prod. Harry Strauss. U.S. State Department), in describing fishing rights as viewed from the perspectives of opposing nations.]

As academic film evolved into the 1960s, the formal narrative styles of the 1950s gave way to a "friendlier" approach to the viewer. Where 1950s-style narration dictated, 1960s-style narration patiently educated, even cajoled. Often, film companies would revise a film, keeping much of the footage from the old format, adding a few shots, and re-narrating. A most impressive example of this reworking and redistribution was BFA's *Bees, Backyard Science*, directed by Norman Bean. In the first edition of 1967, stilted narration (decidedly a holdover for the 1950s era) and a pedantic music score detract somewhat from Bean's compelling close-up insect photography. In the revised edition of 1978, the music has been redone, and the narrator, while using the same text, seems more mellifluent, excited, and engaged in telling the story.

In ethnographic subjects, narration styles changed dramatically, from the native English speakers in the 1950s, to voice-overs from native speakers, as exemplified by mellifluous West African Athmani Magoma in Gerald McDermott's well-made animated films for IFF (e.g., *Magic Tree*, 1970) or the native speakers used by Paul Saltzman in his *World Cultures & Youth* series (e.g., *Slima the Dhowmaker*, 1978). In a category all its own is Bill Deneen's *Japanese Boy: the Story of Taro* (1963, EBF), self-narrated by Deneen utilizing a Japanese accent.

A Few Notes on Music

To a great extent, musical accompaniment to educational films slavishly mirrored the popular commercial music of a given era, from the lavish orchestral "elevator-music" of the 1950s, to the meandering piano tinklings which emerged in the mid–1980s. In the most egregious of cases, music was overly loud in the sound mix, drowning the narrator in a sea of musical mediocrity (e.g., *Halley's Comet*, 1985, prod. Terence Murtagh, York Films/EBF). Much of the music used in different sub-categories of educational film was formulaic and predictable. Some common examples would include American historical films and patriotic orchestral arrangements, animal films and Disney-inspired "mickey-mousing" music (in which instruments imitated physical movements of animals). Films on Latin American culture often featured Flamenco guitar music scores (oops, wrong continent!)

Some companies, fearing that the inclusion of music would introduce an unwanted "entertainment" component to academic films, eschewed it altogether. Many executives at EBF, for example, had firm opinions on keeping music

Slima the Dhowmaker, from Paul Saltzman's *World Cultures & Youth* series, distributed by Coronet (Paul Saltzman).

out of films. Some EB films of the 1950s, such as William A. Anderson's *Life in the Desert* (1954), with its mickey-mousing musical score, justified this concern. In retrospect, as musical fads and tastes have changed, a cogent argument can be made in favor of the exclusion of music as a necessary element in keeping a given film "current" for as long as possible. EBF wasn't completely at odds with sound enhancement, however. Although it's not exactly an experiment in *musique-concrète*, several of EBF's *American Geological Institute* (AGI) series of films feature the pleasant drone of a light aircraft accompanying spectacular geological aerial shots, creating a marvelous ethereal ambience that music would not have enhanced. Noted documentarian Richard Leacock, who eschewed music in his academic films, also preferred ambient sound, and the tremendously loud generator in his immortal *Physical Science Study Committee (PSSC)* series film *Magnet Laboratory* (*1959, Modern Talking Picture Service) would, one could guess, leave today's industrial music fans drooling.

Some of the more intriguing music in academic films was generally subdued and original, the worst overbearing and jarring. Michael Fano & Jacqueline Lecompte's electro-acoustic accompaniment to Robin Lehman's *Nightlife* (1975, Opus/Phoenix), and *Undercurrents* (1973, Opus/Phoenix) was interesting in itself as a soundscape. Occasionally, academic film music actually contributed materially to the content of the film. Director Paul Burnford utilized contemporary experimental music by composers such as Ruth White (*Railroad Rhythms*, 1954) and Werner Bracher (*Art and Motion*, 1952) to emphasize abstract elements in his films.

Coming into fashion in the 1960s was didactic "message" music, with preachy lyrics, most often accompanying sociodramas and social documentaries. Author Stephen Mamber addressed the problem in describing Frederick Wiseman's use of the song "Sitting By the Dock of the Bay" in his film *High School* (1969):

> Music ... employed in this fashion is akin to narration, and the direct expression of filmmaker attitude regarding his material by these means goes against the filming method. Above all, although the song may be thematically relevant ... it is structurally irrelevant. If one agrees that the song relates to other elements of the film, then one already sees "what actually happened" in this case, and there is no need to press it further through the use of the song ... when it is used, the filmmaker is in essence rejecting the complexity of his own material.[19]

Wiseman certainly didn't invent the artifice of using thematically-based musical material to unnecessarily underscore visual content. At least one educational film series was seriously marred by a never-ending concert of folk tunes written and sung by folksinger Stan Davis. *Exploring: the Story of America* was an 18-part series produced in 1965 by Ed Scherer of NBC and hosted by Dr. Albert Hibbs. Davis had been hired as the musical director and elected to create and sing a number of folksongs on historical themes. Rhyming "butter" with "Sutter," stretching syllables to their breaking point or cramming them into what was left of a stanza, and whistling off-key were all in a day's work for this folksinger whose intrusive music continually interrupted the cognitive momentum built up by host Albert Hibbs. Unlike other NBC series that appeared in virtually every school film library (e.g., *NBC White Paper*), the author could only find *Exploring* remaining in one.[20]

Influenced by the message music trend that had infiltrated documentaries, some educational filmmakers took the plunge and adopted schmaltzy songs to use in their own films. Among the more egregious of these was paraplegic mountain climber Rick Leavenworth's heartfelt musical ode to his girlfriend in Lee Stanley's guidance film *Mountain Tops* (1980,

Pyramid), a film that compounded this sin by offering the double-whammy of additionally subjecting the viewer to religious "praise music."

Thematic music, however, could occasionally be quite effective when integrated directly into the story line. George Kaczender's exceptional sociodrama *You're No Good* (1966, NFBC), on the subject of teen angst, was enhanced tremendously by an original soundtrack performed by the Mersey Brothers. Several films for elementary students cleverly integrated music into the subject matter, among the most notable of which were films in the *Multiplication Rock* series (e.g., *The Good Eleven*, *1974, prod. Tom Yohe, Xerox/ABC), featuring music and clever lyrics by people such as noted jazz singer Bobby Dorough.

Perhaps feeling that country music, blues, or jazz would somehow narrow the breadth of distribution of a given film, many educational film companies seemed to prefer the blandness of pop, middle-of-the-road, folk, or orchestral music, ignoring the richness of regional musical forms. Notable exceptions included EBF's Paul Buchbinder, who used a country string band as a backdrop to his animated tales (*Three Fox Fables, 2nd edition*, 1984), and the street-poetry group Rant/Chant to his film on the properties of sound (*Wondering About Sound, 2nd edition*, 1968).

Jazz soundtracks were relatively uncommon, although companies such as California-based Churchill Films would from time to time utilize soundtracks written and performed by jazzmen such as West Coast "Third Stream" jazz stalwarts Fred Katz and Buddy Collette (*Land of Immigrants*, 1981, prod. Robert Churchill). Filmmakers Bruce and Katherine Cornwell brought mathematics films to a high art form, combining computer animation and Bach-based Third Stream jazz in films such as *Congruent Triangles* (*1976). Occasionally even jazz-rock musicians, such as Colosseum's Jon Hiseman, would be hired to compose and perform soundtracks (*The Chinese Word For Horse*, 1986, dir. Richard Callanan, Thames/Media Guild).

Profits to the Principals: Promoting and Selling the Academic Film

In the immediate post–Sputnik era, film companies often had to sell their school prospects on the concept of using mediated instruction — rather than textbooks alone — prior to being able to sell their films.[21] Sales strategies used by film companies included both "push" (field-based salespeople) and "pull" (catalogue) sales strategies. Larger film companies such as EBF had the luxury of fielding field-based sales staffs that, often aided by curriculum experts such as EBF Humanities consultant Marion Sloan, would make presentations at districts, conferences, and seminars. Smaller companies that couldn't take on the expense of a field-based sales department would take different approaches. Morton Schindel, for example, sent complimentary films to teaching colleges, where, in the classic "pull" marketing strategy, professors would introduce future teachers to films in the Weston Woods catalogue. They would, it was anticipated, recommend them to the schools that would eventually hire them.

Distributed free of charge to thousands of institutional buyers, educational film catalogues are especially important and somewhat rare today, providing important content and production documentation. Some were visually striking, notably designer Elaine Mason's opulent hard-cover catalogues for Learning Corporation of America.

It is believed that the first educational film catalogue, the *Catalogue of Educational*

Motion Pictures, was produced in 1910 by George Kleine. It encompassed 330 pages, 1,065 selected titles, and thirty main topic areas.[22] In 1936, screenwriter Lorraine Noble and the U.S. Office of Education, in conjunction with publisher H.W. Wilson Company, printed Wilson's first *Educational Film Catalog*, listing eighteen hundred sources, describing the 1,175 educational films known to exist at the time, and classified under the Dewey system. Decades later, R. R. Bowker's massive *Educational Film Resource Locator* (1978, 1st edition) rolled off the presses, featuring descriptions of some 37,000 film titles selected from 50 university libraries.

Public and school film libraries also published annotated catalogues. Today, such catalogues are among the best sources for descriptions of forgotten films, as well as being valuable artifacts in themselves, detailing the collecting philosophies of film librarians, who often saw themselves as curators as much as cataloguers. Classifying and describing such films was no mean feat, as the massive 627-page Santa Clara County (California) Multimedia Catalogue for 1994, for example, attests, with its library of approximately 11,000 films classified into 51 main and 267 sub-categories.

While widely disseminated, the information contained in guides, books, and catalogues was disparate and often contradictory. An objective public forum was needed to act as a clearinghouse for information related to recently released films, sources of funding for film acquisition, and collegial sharing of ideas. In 1943, such an organization was formed, and, surviving several early twists in its mission as well as its funding, the Educational Film Library Association soon became the most significant informational source for educational film in North America.

The Influence of EFLA: Promotion and Critique Through the Educational Film Library Association

The achievements of the Educational Film Library Association in documenting, promoting, and serving as a discussion forum for educational film were critical to the financial well-being of educational film filmmakers and companies, and were of vital importance to educators. Although founded in 1943, EFLA's biggest impact on media buyers arguably occurred in the 1960s through 1980s, with publications such as *Sightlines* magazine, *EFLA Evaluations*, and the *EFLA Bulletin*. Its annual American Film Festival awarded ribbons to many of the finest educational films each year, and occasionally made the award winning films available as a package to film libraries on a routing basis.[23]

EFLA had been founded with support from the American Film Center, a Rockefeller Foundation project, and had its first office in Rockefeller Center, with Elizabeth Harding "Bee" Flory serving as its first executive secretary. Documentary filmmaker Emily Jones became the new executive secretary in 1946, and soon faced her first crisis: the American Film Center had gone bankrupt, and Rockefeller had withdrawn all support, leaving EFLA with $250 in the bank. Julien Bryan of the International Film Foundation came to the rescue by donating office space at IFF and guaranteeing Jones' salary for the first year. Jones' priorities were increasing the membership of the organization and publishing evaluations of educational films, a necessary motivator for prospective members. Her efforts proved a success, as EFLA's reputation as a prime resource for information on films, mediated educational practices, and business issues related to buying practices was stellar. In 1959, EFLA's first American Film Festival was launched.[24]

In 1959, with the involvement of people such as Contemporary Films' Leo Dratfield, EFLA's annual American Film Festival began its twenty-year run as the top showcase for educational film in the United States. The categories, judges, and criteria tended to change from year to year, as did the members of the pre-screening committee. Subject categories evolved to the point that there were an astonishing 112 separate categories by the 33rd festival held in 1991. Neither judges nor committee members were paid, in keeping with EFLA's philosophy of being as objective as possible in the reviewing process. Blue and red ribbons were awarded in each category, and final results were published in a document distributed to the membership, which at its height reached approximately 1500 dues-paying (at $50 annually) members. Afterward, public film libraries could rent a special "Blue Ribbon" or "Red Ribbon" package that would be sent by EFLA on a circuit around the United States, in order to expose library and school patrons to the best the art form had to offer in a given year.

EFLA's critiques and reviews were well-written and comprehensive, and make great reading today. They represented some of the finest writing on the subject of educational film, and were the most valuable resource available to school and library film buyers available.

Emily Jones, needing a change after 24 years at the helm of EFLA, left the directorship in 1970 to join Stelios Roccos at ACI Films as executive manager.[25] Esmé Dick served in the executive director's capacity until 1972, when Nadine Covert, formerly the assistant film librarian at the Donnell Library (New York Public Library) began her tenure. Covert left in 1984 become a project manager, then executive director of the Program for Art on Film, which began as a joint venture of the J. Paul Getty Trust and The Metropolitan Museum of Art. Marilyn Levin then led the organization for two years, followed by Ron McIntyre until 1993 when the organization, then called the American Film and Video Association, went out of business due to declining subscriptions and the overall financial decline of the educational media industry in general.[26]

In addition to its directors, numerous individuals, including longtime *Sightlines* editor Judy Trojan, were involved in making EFLA the most important and influential educational media organization of the era. EFLA clearly deserves more attention than history has given it. It is impossible to overestimate the importance of this organization from the perspective of film criticism alone. Its reviewers clearly understood that the affective element was just as critical as the cognitive aspect in the pedagogical success of an academic film. Today, if it were available, a compendium of category winners from the first American Film Festival to the last (thought to be the 34th festival, in 1992) would be a document essential in understanding the breadth of excellence in the American educational film.[27]

Regional Politics and Localized Films

In some areas of the country more than others, feedback from school administrators to company salespeople could change the content of a film, in ways not always beneficial to the students. In addition to the common practice of "hiding" non-whites in films, prevalent in the pre–Civil Rights Act of 1964 era discussed earlier, companies were increasingly being held to task when encountering religious dogma emanating from certain school districts. Community sexual mores were always of concern to conservative school superintendents, afraid that the sexual revolution of the late 1960s would arrive in the Trojan Horse of a school film. One such situation is remembered by EB filmmaker Tom Smith, whose story of the distribution of *VD: The Hidden Epidemic* (1973) is an interesting study of the manner in which regional politics and religion affected the making, distribution, and sale of a school film during an era otherwise generally regarded as socially progressive:

> In 1973, I made a film on venereal disease — *VD: the Hidden Epidemic*. It is still on my list of best personal films. But there are two versions of that film out there (if any are still out there). The film was very frank and clearly showed the history, the symptoms of syphilis and gonorrhea and the cultural reason for it. (This was before we knew about AIDS.) There was nothing sexual about the film, no intercourse and all clearly clinical. We also advocated the use of a condom and in some cases of repeated infection suggested antibiotics as prophylaxes.
>
> When the film as shown to EBF management they applauded it and prints were struck. We thought we had a hit. But when it hit the market, salesmen in the field (particularly in the Bible belt) complained that we could not show genitalia and certainly could not advocate the use of a condom or antibiotic prophylaxes. The condom demonstration was done by a doctor in the film. He simply spoke of the advantages of its use and fitted one on two fingers. So the VP of the EBF science department flew to California and went through the film with me on an editing machine. Though personally embarrassed by his task, he showed me each part of the film that had to be incised. In one place we showed a black and white image of a nude woman over which we superimposed an animated interior view of the reproductive organs. The company insisted we should not see her nipples. So that part was cut. All reference to condoms and other forms of prophylaxes were removed.
>
> Meanwhile, the film had been selling like hot cakes around the nation. The City of Santa Monica (where I was living at the time) bought several prints and the head of health education went out of her way to look me up and complement me for making the first honest film about VD she could find. The film had also been entered in several film festivals and was winning awards. Britannica had a dilemma, some insisted it showed too much and others delighted with its honesty and bought it. In the end management decided to sell two versions. I guess we can call them the "R" and "PG" rated versions. This clearly illustrated to me that "closing the sale" trumps "effective truth." Anything that would hurt sales was forbidden. Charlie Benton was no longer with EBF when we had the VD controversy. He might have stood up for the more honest approach....[28]

By 1973, the year of Smith's film, however, the educational film world was beginning to change, and companies such as LCA and CRM were already making films that challenged traditional thinking, concepts, and values. Dozens of new companies were being started, each with a different philosophical approach to making and selling films. Many companies were started by filmmakers themselves. In the next chapter, we'll meet some of most significant companies that emerged or evolved to create new elements of mediated curriculum, influenced by, and contributing to the revolutionary curriculum changes of the 1960s.

CHAPTER FOUR

The Companies That Made the Films and the People Behind Them

Exploring the philosophies and practices of the companies that made and distributed classroom films can be a fascinating experience. Most of the people who ran these companies had big dreams, and managed, to a great extent, to realize them. Their stories are an important element in understanding the genre, and their perspectives are those of businesspeople, educators, and scholars. They had a passion for film as an educational tool as well as a real-world business sense that allowed them to survive in a competitive market, even if that savvy was acquired along the way. (Bob Churchill, 13 years after founding his company, belatedly learned "that to pay for new films, you had to sell the old ones. A wrenching discovery.")[1] I've attempted to include the most common companies of significance in the post–Sputnik era that the academic film researcher, historian, scholar, or collector will encounter when viewing a film. The list is not exhaustive, as literally hundreds of companies produced films, many of them with an output totaling fewer than five titles. Inevitably, as more research is done in this area of film scholarship, more will undoubtedly emerge. This chapter introduces many of the important players in the theatre of academic film, and reveals critical elements in the history of the business of mediated classroom instruction.

It could be estimated that approximately 1,000 different entities were involved in making and distributing academic films to North American classroom in the 1960–1985 time frame, including companies specializing in making school films, television networks, motion picture studios, religious organizations, government-sponsored film units, and corporate entities.[2] Education film companies ranged from large (e.g., EBF) to small, family-run operations (e.g., Berlet Films), and sometimes included units within units (e.g., Perspective Films, a subsidiary of Coronet). Television network series that appeared in classrooms were typically distributed through the classroom distribution divisions of large publishing houses such as Time-Life and McGraw-Hill. These not only includes those made by major U.S. networks, but also encompass those made by the British Broadcasting Corporation (BBC), Canadian Broadcasting Corporation (CBC), and Film Australia, among others.

Two major motion picture studios, Columbia (through Learning Corporation of America division) and Universal were involved in making academic films. Religious organizations found it increasingly difficult to place their films in public school systems due to church-state separation issues, but many district film libraries still somehow managed to have one or more Moody Institute of Science titles in their collections. Corporate-sponsored films were mainly to be found in vocational and health-education classes, but Shell Film Unit's science films were commonly found in most academic film libraries, as were AT&T's ubiq-

CRM's Steve Katten (left) and Larry Logan filming in a California poppy field (Peter Jordan, CRM).

uitous Bell Science films, with their well-recognized host, Dr. Frank Baxter. Government-sponsored film units distributing films to North American schools included not only those found in the United States, but also organizations such as the National Film Board of Canada (distributing its films in the U.S. through the International Film Bureau and LCA, among other firms) and Germany's Institut für Film und Bild (FWU).

A challenge faced by today's historian in attempting to track these disparate entities is that with time, film companies tended to be absorbed into others, sometimes many times over. Many of the individuals who ran these companies are no longer with us or are difficult to find. In the final analysis, a strong case can be made that most films made during the 1960–1985 era are no longer being distributed in any format, thereby presenting researchers with the additional challenge of attempting to determine if a company credit on the film represents the maker, distributor, or both.

In addition to companies specializing in academic film, the films produced and distributed by television networks mentioned above are worthy of discussion. Why are networks an important part of the educational film story? The access to large production budgets and a philosophy that tended to be somewhat less pandering to regional social concerns are two prime reasons. Typically, television could put more money into production than educational film companies could. Some of these network-produced films, particularly those of the 1960–1970, era were exceptional. As was discussed in the previous chapter, educational film companies, to placate the regional social philosophies of many school administrators and buyers, shied away from controversial subject matter, wishing to avoid the costly process of making multiple versions of a given title. Thus, prior to the Civil Rights Act of 1964, practically the entire subject area of race relations and possible solutions was ignored by the educational film world. Television networks had been broaching the subject for years, with public affairs programming and news documentaries. Ultimately it was probably the school distribution of CBS News' executive producer Perry Wolff's *Of Black America* series, distributed by CBS' BFA Films distribution channel in the late 1960s, that pushed many educational film companies to finally make films addressing these issues.

I have broken the entities distributing films into two broad classifications: Educational Film Companies in the post–1960 era, and Television Network Series and Documentaries in the classroom. Companies in the former category are listed alphabetically. In an earlier chapter, I discussed the pre–Sputnik days of Encyclopædia Britannica Films, Coronet, the International Film Foundation, and the National Film Board of Canada. Here, I will continue their stories after 1960, along with those of a number of their most significant competitors. Television Network Series and Documentaries are alphabetized by network, and include Wolper Productions, an independent production company whose films were shown on networks before being distributed to schools.

Notable Educational Film Companies, Organizations, and Corporate Educational Film Divisions in the Post–1960 Era

ACI

After producing the film *The Purple Turtle* in 1962, Stelios Roccos founded ACI in order to distribute his film to schools, largely because the American Crayon Company, which had funded the *Purple* film, didn't want to be in the educational film business. ACI (the initials of which apparently stood for nothing, being attractive to Roccos because they were close to the beginning of the alphabet) went on to distribute some 400 titles, roughly 25 percent of which were produced in-house. Its biggest selling titles were those in the *Rediscovering Art* series, consisting of sixteen elementary-level films on subjects such as crayon, collage, and paper construction. Among the most memorable films distributed by this New York City–based company were those in the *Today and Yesterday: American Lifestyles* series, showcasing families engaged in traditional crafts and ways of living. Of them, *Birch Canoe Builder* (1970, dir. Craig Hinde), is especially notable, showing 80-year-old Bill Hafeman of Big Fork, Minnesota, in the laborious task of building a canoe from scratch. Seventy-two-year-old Sherman Graff is profiled in *Maple Sugar Farmer* (1973, dir. Craig Hinde/Robert E. Davis), shown boiling down 40 gallons of maple water to make one gallon of maple syrup, then 11 pounds of syrup to make 7 pounds of maple sugar. Also in the series were two films by Philip and Gay Courter, who had met and married while working at ACI, *Grist Miller* and *Cider Maker* (both 1975). The Courters had earlier left ACI to work for Hal Weiner's Screenscope Films, but were hired by Roccos as independents to film these two aspects of traditional life with which they had become familiar after moving to northern New Jersey.[3] *Grist Miller* invited the viewer into the home of a Stillwater, New Jersey, family that baked bread ground on the wheel of their mill built in 1844. *Cider Maker* Ellis Apgar, along with wife Ethel & family, displayed the craft of making apple mash, with the film combining old photos of ancestors engaged in the tradition juxtaposed with action shots of this contemporary family enjoying the fruits of their labor.

Notable ACI employees included sales executive Frank Visco (who would later found

Lucerne Media), consultant Emily Jones (former director of the Educational Film Library Association), Daphne Brooke (who later headed the film library at the United Nations), Bert Salzman (whose *Angel and Big Joe,* made for Learning Corporation of America, won an Academy Award), Gay Weisman (later Gay Courter), and director Hal Weiner, who holds fond memories of working with Roccos. Weiner, who later founded Screenscope Films with wife Marilyn, remembers working on a particularly odious project with Roccos, a political propaganda film called *Nixon-Lodge: Champions of Freedom* (196?, unknown director, unknown company), glorifying a presidential candidate respected by neither filmmaker: "I think Roccos really needed the money," recalls Weiner, "and we both cringed when the narrator mentioned that 'FDR sold us down the river at Yalta.'"[4]

The mercurial Roccos, whose own best film effort may have been *Niko: Boy of Greece* (1968, shot on Mykonos, an island he loved), became, according to some reports, increasingly irrational and difficult, and was eventually institutionalized in the late 1970s. Toward the end of the 1970s, the ACI catalogue was sold to Paramount, which soon sold the ACI library to Charles Cahill Associates, which itself was later acquired by AIMS Multimedia. In August 2004, the *AIMS* catalogue was acquired by Discovery Communications' Education division.[5]

After the sale of his company, Roccos embarked on an ambitious and somewhat ill-advised plan to create a huge video distribution center, a project which never came to fruition. He was killed in the crash of his small airplane in Pennsylvania after reportedly refusing to heed a flight control warning not to take off due to extreme icy conditions, leading to some speculation that his last flight may have been suicidal. He apparently had canceled his life insurance policy a short time before the flight, leaving his four children in uncomfortable financial circumstances.[6]

AGC/Journal Films

Gilbert Altschul, formerly head of production at Coronet Films, founded the company (later called Altschul Group Corporation) on April 1, 1954, and incorporated several months later, in partnership with cinematographer Bruce Colling. The company specialized in producing health, safety, and industrial films, but soon began distributing academic films made by other producers, primarily on historical and geographical subjects. Altschul founded Journal Films in late 1959. Under division president Joe Farragher, Journal distributed approximately 877 films, consisting of in-house productions and films made by smaller non–U.S.-based film companies. Two notable independently-produced Journal films included *El Pueblo* (1983, prod. Tristram & Wilson, Juniper Films), a non-narrated and fascinating visit to the small Spanish town of Villaluenga del Rosario, and *Yukon Territory* (1977, dir. Wilf Gray). Journal also distributed a number of science films made by Reinald Werrenrath Productions.

A significant part of the Journal catalogue consisted of films acquired through an arrangement with United Nations' film coordinator Daphne Brooke-Landis, consisting of specially-edited versions of films made by the United Nations, UNESCO, and UNICEF (e.g., *Yemen,* 1976, uncredited director). After Gilbert Altschul's death in 1982, the company, under sons Joel and David, began an aggressive program of acquiring other film companies. By 1996, fifteen were under the AGC banner, including Beacon Films (founded by Bob and Jane Vale, and bought by AGC in 1988), Wombat Films (founded by Gene Feldman, bought in 1990), and Film Fair (founded by Gus Jekel, bought in 1992). Eventually, David Altschul left for Will Vinton Productions, eventually becoming its president. In 2003, AGC's 4,000-title catalogue, consisting primarily of health, safety, and industrial education films, was acquired by Discovery Communications' Education division.

AIMS Media

The story of AIMS Media begins in 1957, when Charles Cahill founded Charles Cahill Associates to distribute his traffic safety and law enforcement training films. Soon, he acquired approximately 400 educational film titles from Paramount Pictures. He also distributed films made by other producers, specializing in civics films, animation, and international short subjects (e.g., *Dream of Wild Horses*, 1960, dir. Denis Colomb de Daunant). In 1982, the company was purchased by the Audio Visual Group (AVG), comprising Mel Sherman, Bernard Donenfeld, Jason Brent, and William Siegel.[7] The name of the company was soon changed to AIMS Media. Noteworthy *AIMS* films included a ten-part series on the twentieth century in the United States, *American Chronicles* (1986, dir. Barry Clark), Bernard Wilets' exceptional *Man and the State* series, and Wah Chang's clay masterpiece *Dinosaurs: Terrible Lizards* (1971). In 1987, sons Wynn "Biff," Jeff, and Dave Sherman bought Siegel's share, running the day-to-day operations with Siegel remaining on the board. A 1998 company profile noted that its library contained more than 6,000 titles, 25 percent of which were produced and owned outright by the company. In 2001, AIMS acquired Preston Holdner's Media Guild film company. In August 2004, AIMS Multimedia was acquired by Discovery Communications' Education division.

AT&T Bell Labs

American Telephone and Telegraph didn't make all that many educational films. The ones they did make tended to be about proper telephone techniques and manners (e.g., *Telezonia*, 1984, dir. Eric Karson), or the telephony business in general. There were few titles more commonly found in North American school film libraries, however, than AT&T's ubiquitous *Bell Science* series, hosted by Dr. Frank Baxter. These films were originally made for television broadcast, but it's a fair wager that many more individuals saw them in classrooms than on television. They were shown at practically every grade level including high school, although they were originally aimed at a younger audience. And although many remember the characters in the films and Frank Baxter, few seem to recall that several of the films contained overt religious messages. They were included purposefully, ordered as part of the original contract.

Beginning with *Our Mr. Sun*, originally telecast on CBS in 1956, this series consisted of eight one-hour programs and one of one-half hour in length. The final eight programs were broadcast on NBC. The first eight programs in the series were hosted by perhaps the best-remembered individual ever to appear in an educational film, the bald, bespectacled Dr. Frank Baxter, professor of English literature at the University of Southern California.[8] As well-known for his stiff, cardboard-like suits as he was for his glib persona, Baxter had previous on-screen experience as host of two earlier television series, *Shakespeare on TV* and *Now and Then*.

The first four films in the *Bell Science* series were produced by legendary director Frank Capra, who agreed to take the job with the stipulation, as agreed to by AT&T president Cleo F. Craig, that the renowned director would be allowed to embed religious messages in the films.[9] In a posture at odds with the Establishment Clause of the First Amendment, and contrary to the objective sprit of the scientific process, Capra stated to Craig: "If I make a science film, I will have to say that scientific research is just another expression of the Holy Spirit ... I will say that science, in essence, is just another facet of man's quest for God."[10] Capra's religious messages, which would appear at different points in each film, were incongruous to the content, and contrary to the beliefs of teachers and students not of his religious persuasion. *Hemo the Magnificent* (1957, dir. Frank Capra) opens with an on-screen quotation from Leviticus 17: "For the life of the flesh is in the blood," and *Our Mr. Sun* (1956, dir. Frank Capra) begins in similar fashion with a quotation from Psalms, "The heavens declare the glory of God." The religious perspective is taken to extremes in the latter, as Baxter, through the Capra-written script, tells the animated Sun, "Man's greatest source is his mind — God gave him that, not you!," admonishing viewers who would dare to question the causal relationship between solar energy and the divinity. Other dogmatic chestnuts in that particular film include "It's right that you should want to know, or the good Lord wouldn't have given you that driving curiosity," and the memory verse-like "Measure the outside with mathematics, but measure the inside [a still shot of a cross is inserted here for effect] with prayer." These statements are obviously more in keeping with Sunday School classes than what is legally acceptable in public school classrooms, but considering the dates the films were made, it's not surprising that these religious messages in films about science were apparently rarely questioned by school authorities.

In the Capra-produced *Unchained Goddess* (1958, dir. Richard Carlson), we again find Baxter, with director Carlson co-starring as the Fiction Writer, and a host of well-known voices including Mel Blanc and Hans Conreid, depicting animated weather gods led by the sexy goddess Meteora, who ultimately throws a stormy "fit" when Baxter turns down her proposal for marriage at the end of the film. In *Goddess*, Baxter explains weather concepts through footage of meteorologists at work mixed with the standard destructive tornado and hurricane shots. In addition to the typical Capra religious pitch (this time, quotations from the book of Job), the film introduces the viewer to bizarre concepts such as the possibility of "steering" hurricanes away from land by creating bio-hazards such as ocean borne oil-slicks and inducing oil-based ocean fires, about which Baxter notes: "The possibilities are endless, the unanswered questions fascinating! No wonder more and more young students are turning to meteorology."

Unchained Goddess was Capra's final film in the Bell series, after which production was taken over by Jack Warner, who selected veteran producer/director Owen Crump to supervise the next four films in the series, *Gateways to the Mind* (1958, dir. Owen Crump), *Alphabet Conspiracy* (1959, dir. Robert Sinclair), *Thread of Life* (1960, dir. Owen Crump), and *It's About Time* (1962, dir. Owen Crump).[11] The final film in the series, the one-half hour *Restless Sea* (1963, dir. Les Clark), was produced by Walt Disney.

Owen Crump's own history in film is fascinating, and he is notable as being a major player in the largely forgotten but fascinating and ill-fated feature film *Cease Fire!* (1953, Paramount Pictures, dir. Owen Crump). Crump and Jack Warner were hardly strangers. Shortly before the Second World War, U.S. Army Public Relations had contracted with Warner Bros. to make a series of films acquainting the general population with different branches of the military, a project supervised directly by Warner himself. He soon brought along Crump, employed as a writer at the studio, to research and write what became eight Technicolor shorts. After war broke out, Warner was commissioned as a lieutenant colonel in the Army Air Force, chartered with organizing the First Motion Picture Unit of the U.S.

Army Air Force. Crump was commissioned a captain, and eventually became the Picture Unit's production chief. Military historian George Siegel described the first Warner-Crump project of the war:

> Of immediate necessity ... was the demand for a two-reel short subject aimed at speeding up enlistments in the Army Air Force Cadet Training Program. General (Hap) Arnold felt this to be the most urgent need since the Army Air Force, at that time, could not draft men for Cadet Training and was in a position where more than 100,000 young men must enlist voluntarily within a three month period.
>
> Colonel Warner turned over all facilities of Warner Bros. studio to the project. Work was carried out on a twenty-four hour basis. Owen Crump wrote and directed the film. Within fourteen days it was written, photographed, edited, dubbed, scored. Jimmy Stewart, then Lt. Stewart (later to become a Brigadier General Stewart) played the leading role. The picture was promptly released in most of the theaters throughout the United States. Its effect was immediate, intense. More than 150,000 enlistments were directly traced to the effect of the picture, which was called *Winning Your Wings*.[12]

After the war, Crump returned to Warner Bros., but continued to work on military projects, including the Oscar-nominated documentary short *One Who Came Back* (1951, United States Department of Defense). Crump's *Cease Fire!* was purportedly the first feature film showing the fully-integrated U.S. Army, starring the ill-fated Pfc. Ricardo Carrasco. Wishing to tell the story of the Korean War from the soldier's front-line perspective, Crump picked actual soldiers to star in the film, with Carrasco taking the leading role, that of a soldier dying in combat on the final day of the war. All scenes, with the exception of the final death sequence, would be filmed on the battlefield as action occurred. Feeling guilty about leaving his friends to fight the war while he made a movie, Carrasco continually begged Crump to "kill" his character so he could resume fighting. Meanwhile, producer Hal Wallis had screened the rushes in Hollywood, saw the star quality in the 19-year-old private, and ordered Crump to put him under contract with Paramount. When confronted with the news, Carrasco refused to sign the contract, and asked instead that his character be killed two weeks earlier than scheduled to he could return to assist his friends. The final death close-ups were shot on the morning of July 6, 1953, and Carrasco returned to his unit that afternoon. At 11:25 that evening, Carrasco was killed on Pork Chop Hill by a mortar blast. Wishing to save his mother from the agony of seeing her son "die" on screen, Crump hastily re-filmed the death scene using a stand-in in this, the last feature film the Department of Defense would ever allow to be filmed on the front lines of a war zone.[13]

From the perspective of overall cohesion, writing, and set design, Crump's Bell series films are superior to those of Capra. Crump did not overtly proselytize, relied less on animated characters interacting with Dr. Baxter, and utilized the set design as almost a character in itself, as exemplified by William Kuehl's sound-stage set for *Gateways to the Mind*, and his madcap carnival-like set for *Alphabet Conspiracy*.[14] *Gateways* features cameramen, sound technicians, animators, and grips as they prepare to make a film with Baxter. Gaining ever-increasing interest in the subject matter, they relentlessly question Baxter as to the functions of the five senses, which Baxter relates to their own equipment: the camera for the eyes, the mixing board for the ears.

Crump's *The Thread of Life* (1960) featured former Mouseketeer Don Grady (who eventually gained greater fame as "Robbie" in the popular television show *My Three Sons*) as one of the talking heads occupying six contiguous television screens, whose personae fired a battery of questions to Frank Baxter regarding the origin of life. With Capra finally removed from the project, religious messages were now supplanted by healthy skepticism; when asked when life begins, Baxter replies, "We don't know *that*!" a response that probably would not have been written into the script during the Capra days. While the subject matter in *Thread* consists of footage and discussion of genes, chromosomes, heredity, and DNA, the star of the show is, again, the dry and bemused Baxter, whose romantic side appears momentarily when he responds, "And very fashionable!" to a woman who directed his attention to her white forelock.

Alphabet Conspiracy (1959, dir. Robert Sinclair) is the only Bell Science film to explore a subject not specifically related to a traditional "hard science," the study of language. Frustrated by the ambiguity inherent in the English language, the Mad Hatter (Hans Conreid) and Jabberwock attempt to destroy language by lighting an explosive charge under the world's great literature. On a fantastic, enlarged cartoon library set designed by William Kuehl, they convince a young girl to join their conspiracy, when Baxter as "Dr. Linguistics" arrives to illustrate the value of the written and spoken word. Guests range from beat-bantering jazz trumpeter Shorty Rogers to psychologist Keith Hayes, whose research on chimpanzee communication was made with chimp family member and guest Viki.

The final film in the Bell series, *The Restless Sea* (1964, dir. Les Clark), was produced by Walt Disney Productions, and is the shortest of the series at one-half hour in length. Although continuing the Bell tradition of animation mixed with live action, former host Dr. Frank Baxter was nowhere to be found, replaced instead by the voice of actor Sterling Holloway as a water droplet. Its animation, particularly in the surrealist deep sea floor sequences, is superior to that of the Capra films. In its explanation of core samples, wind movement, and composition of water, *Sea* provided a credible if elementary compilation of facts. It was, however, accompanied by the pedantic orchestral music endemic to many Disney films of the era, in contrast to the subtle musical elements of the Crump-era Bell films.

In terms of popular iconography, the Capra and Crump Bell Science films are among the best known and remembered educational films ever made, and enthroning Dr. Frank Baxter as something of a legend as the omniscient king of academic science films hosts.

Atlantis Films

J. Michael Hagopian made over 70 films on the subject of international cultures, most of which were distributed by Atlantis Films, the company he founded. Born in Kharpert-Mezreh, Armenia, in 1913, he emigrated with his parents as a young boy to Fresno, California, and eventually moved to Los Angeles in his teens.

Atlantis Films' J. Michael Hagopian (J. Michael Hagopian).

He graduated from UC Berkeley, did two years of graduate study in the cinema department at the University of Southern California, and received a PhD in international relations at Harvard. He taught political science and economics at UCLA, the American University in Beirut, Benares Hindu University, and Oregon State University. In 1954, dissatisfied with the quality of educational films that were available for use in his classroom, he left his teaching career, began filmmaking, and founded Atlantis Films. Hagopian made films for young learners as well as for secondary school students. His most intellectually stimulating films were those made for the secondary schools market, spanning the world's geographies and cultures, and winners of numerous educational film awards (*Mountain Community of the Himalayas*, 1964).

In 1979, he founded the Armenian Film Foundation. As of this writing, the 96 year old Hagopian remains actively making films, primarily on Armenian historical subjects, and coordinates the Armenian Film Festival.

Bailey/Film Associates (BFA)

BFA resulted from the merger of two smaller, well-known firms, Film Associates and Bailey Films. Film Associates was founded in the mid–1950s by schoolteacher Irwin (Irv) Braun and Paul Burnford, a former director at MGM who had begun his film career making documentary films for John Grierson's Post Office film unit in England.[15] Prior to his tenure at Post Office film, Burnford had been a still photographer at the London Zoo, directed at the time by Sir Julian Huxley. In roughly 1939, Burnford, along with a number of other young British filmmakers, was sent by the British Ministry of Information to the U.S. in order to film short subjects in conjunction with the U.S. Department of Agriculture. Burnford remembered flying over farmlands, making agricultural short films on topics such as crop rotation. He was directed by Huxley to hand-deliver his films to contacts at 1 Rockefeller Center in New York City. Occasionally, he would be requested to return to the U.K. with his raw footage, and deliver them to other contacts, under strict orders to talk to no one — family included — before returning to the U.S.[16] None of this footage was ever, to his knowledge, edited and put to use in classroom film, but years later Burnford realized that, as one of a number of unwitting cinematographer-spies, he had undoubtedly carried microdots surreptitiously embedded into his footage back to the U.K.[17] He was also, in approximately the same time period, engaged in another historical enterprise related to the film world, traveling to Mexico to edit Sergei Eisenstein's footage from the latter's legendary and ill-fated project *Qué Viva México* (shot in 1930), in what would be re-titled *Time in the Sun* (1939).

At Film Associates, Burnford was responsible for the camerawork and editing in the new company, while Braun handled scriptwriting duties. Ann Stevenson, who was with the firm for eighteen years serving in numerous capacities, describes the work environment as being "just like a family. At noon, everyone would stop working and have lunch around a long table."[18] Of special note were the firm's unusual and eye-catching promotional items, including a circa–1965 five-panel, accordion-fold mock Chinese screen, showcasing the social science films of Wayne Mitchell and Bernard Wilets, among others. In 1963, Burnford left the firm in an acrimonious breakup. His more than one hundred self-produced films, such as the remarkable *Caverns & Geysers* (1961), would continue to be distributed by the firm and its successors.

In 1966, Film Associates was purchased by CBS, who at the same time acquired the

Hollywood-based Bailey Films Inc., founded by distributor Al Bailey in the 1950s. (Bailey departed the organization at the time of the purchase, although his name was retained on the masthead.) *Bailey's* catalogue contained fewer titles than did Film Associates,' among them several fine Spanish-language films focusing on the art and culture of Mexico (e.g., *Fabricantes Méxicanas de Ollas* and *Pueblo Méxicano de Pescadores,* *1962, prod. Stuart Roe & Richard Guttman). One of Bailey's most memorable films was the charming *Circus* (1959, dir. Willis Simms), consisting of paintings on paper of circus animals done by Simms' art students at Hughes Junior High School, pixilated by the director, with accompaniment for the film contributed by Hughes' music teacher Robert Clark.

Paul Burnford, co-founder of Film Associates (Zelda Burnford).

Typical BFA budgets were set at $1000 per minute, and royalties were paid to filmmakers only after 10 percent of the budget had been recovered through sales. BFA also used a "loss-leader" marketing approach to boost the sales of films that weren't as popular as others, by including them, at no charge, with larger orders. As royalties were not paid to filmmakers for these free films, a class-action lawsuit on the part of filmmakers resulted.[19] At BFA, filmmakers also received a royalty of 1 percent if they elected to have their film ideas used by other in-house filmmakers.

CBS initially ran the merged BFA company with a hands-off policy, allowing Irv and his wife (Bernice?) Braun to run the company from a refurbished grocery store near their home in Brentwood, California. In 1971, CBS built 20,000 square feet building in Santa Monica to house and expand BFA operations, production, and staff. The Brauns soon hired Lloyd Otterman to assist them in running the expanded operation. George Holland, an English professor teaching drama at the University of Arizona, who had made extensive use of films in his classrooms, was hired in 1973 as the director of products.[20] Filmmakers such as Norman Bean (whose *Backyard Science* series featured stunning close-up insect cinematography), Bernard Wilets (maker of the intellectually stimulating *Man and the State*, *Bill of Rights in Action* and *Discovering Music* series), and Wayne Mitchell contributed scores of films to the catalogue through the decade of the 1970s. The firm distributed several of the exceptional films being produced by John Seabourne in Great Britain (e.g., *Mideast*, 1978, a five-part series on the history and culture of the Middle East, and possibly the first focused attempt in educational film to portray Arab and Islamic cultures in a sympathetic light). BFA also distributed CBS-made network films that were marketed for school use, including the exceptional *Of Black America* series (1968).

In 1975, uncomfortable with the larger role CBS was taking in the company, the Brauns left BFA. Day-to-day management was now the responsibility of Otterman and various executives brought in by CBS, which had now renamed the company BFA Educational Media. In 1981, CBS sold the BFA unit to Phoenix Films; for a time it maintained a small office in southern California, headed by George Holland, VP of production for the BFA brand. Many of the BFA titles today remain in distribution in non–16mm formats, distributed by the Phoenix Learning Group.

Barr Films

Arthur Barr, who served as the audio-visual technician the Pasadena City Schools, founded his company in 1937. Entering the educational film market first through the production of a number of wildlife titles, Barr produced the *Pioneer Life* series prior to World War II, consisting of *Spinning Wheel, Kentucky Rifle, Candlemaking,* and *The Loom.* By 1946, the firm was successful enough for Barr to leave his technician job to devote himself to full-time film production, making films such as *Rocky Mountains: Continental Divide* (1949), a well-made investigation into the flora, fauna, and geography of the area. Son Don Barr returned from military service in 1952 and became a partner in the enterprise, which had by then branched into language arts films as well. In 1958, Bob Earle, who had married daughter Elaine Barr, joined the company as office manager, eventually becoming a one-quarter partner. The 1971 Barr catalogue listed 59 in-house produced films, including oddities such as *Bird Circus* (1956), featuring the carnival act "Dorothy and Her Trained Birds," complete with carnival barker-style narration. One important Barr film was *Indians of California: Food* (1955), in which Josie Atwell, an elderly Native American woman from the small central valley town of Lemoore, helped the film team to reconstruct a village, and was filmed showing how arrows were made and how food was cooked and eaten. Barr-produced historical films of the pre–1972 era were in many ways similar to the fare produced by Coronet, consisting of silent re-enactments of historical events with voice-over narration, featuring actors in period clothing and setting (*Mountain Men,* 1964). Author Hardy Pelham tells a story that, while specific to Barr Films, would probably relate to virtually any of the small companies making educational films with small crews and tiny budgets:

> Don spent a great deal of time helping his father [Arthur] build an elaborate model of a square rigger to be used in their film *Rancho Life* [1949] showing hide trading between Californians and Boston Sea Captains. They wanted a sunset shot of the ship in full sail but could not maneuver this on water. They came up with a creative idea of "sailing" the ship past the setting sun by pulling it along a carefully crafted track in the sand.
> As [Don] recalls, "By careful framing we had a fantastic full frame shot of the model against the sky with the right amount of pitch and roll to make it look like the real thing. When we were ready, we popped on the lens cap to keep the salt spray off the lens and sat back to wait for our sunset. It came, and was beyond all expectations. We ran the film, sailed the ship across the sky ... an incredible shot ... but ... we had failed to remove the lens cap."[21]

After Arthur Barr's retirement in 1971, Barr Films began distributing titles made by other companies and filmmakers, one of the most notable of which was *Taleb & His Lamb* (1975, dir. Amiram Amitai), a fine ethnographic drama which explored Bedouin family traditions in a non-judgmental context. A significant contributor to the Barr catalogue was Ron Casden, who wrote, produced, and directed films specializing in science and nature. In 1981, Barr acquired distribution rights to fifty films made by Bernard Wilets, including the *Bill of Rights* and *Man and the State* series, also distributed by BFA. The same year, the company began selling specialized films to the Management and Training market, resulting in a separate catalogue and additional revenue. In 1985, George Holland, previously of Phoenix Films' BFA division, was hired as EVP of production (Holland remained at Barr until 1996). By 1986, with the addition of selected titles from the United Nations, the National Film Board of Canada, and Holland's emphasis on creating more in-house films, Barr's catalogue had grown to 319 titles, including the exceptionally photographed *Animal Families* series from Video Japonica (e.g., *Firefly* and *Praying Mantis*, 1986). Although exact sales figures are no longer available, the average Barr film sold between 400 and 500 copies over its lifetime. Two of its best-selling titles were *Day in the Life of Bonnie Consolo* (1975, dir. Barry Spinello), the story of a disabled woman, and *You're Not Listening* (1978, prod. Jerry Callner), a series of dramatic vignettes designed to assist the learner to identify and ameliorate poor listening habits.

George Holland, VP of Production for BFA and Barr Films (George Holland).

Amidst the softening of the educational film market in the 1990s, the company experienced a period of upheaval that led to its passing from the educational film scene. Don Barr, who retired in 1994, remains reticent to discuss the painful events surrounding the closing of the family firm.[22] The rights to Barr films are now held by Steve Markoff's A-Mark Entertainment.

Benchmark

Myron (Mike) Solin's small but artistically significant distribution company began in 1967, when he left McGraw-Hill, where he had been editing foreign language films, to found Benchmark. Probably the company's most significant contribution to educational film libraries has been in distributing the spectacular series of African films made by Kenyan filmmaker Alan Root, including *Mysterious Castles of Clay* (1979) and *Baobab: Portrait of a Tree* (1983). Solin also distributed the fascinating *Modern Biology* series, which included titles produced by Boulton-Hawker films of England, and Germany's Institut für film und Bild (FWU), distributor of the remarkable work of master micro-cinematographer Georg Schimanski (*Housefly*, 1982).

Bullfrog Films

Bullfrog was founded in 1973 by producer John Hoskyns-Abrahall and wife Winnie Scherrer.[23] The company specializes in producing and distributing environmental films.

From a catalogue of just under 200 16mm films, Bullfrog added videotapes to make a total of 600 titles by 1999. Hoskyns-Abrahall's favorite film is his own treatment of back-to-the-land advocates Helen and Scott Nearing (*Living the Good Life*, 1977). The Nearings seem to be cranky sorts in the film, and indeed, Helen initially greeted John and Winnie and their infant child at her front door by issuing a disparaging statement as to the meaninglessness of bringing another child into the world. When the filming began, Scott Nearing abruptly moved out of the frame to admonish the filmmaker by saying, "I don't talk about the good life, I DO it!"[24]

Bullfrog's best-selling in-house produced film may have been *Diet For a Small Planet* (dir. Amanda K. and Burton K. Fox, 1973), selling approximately 250 copies, while the top-seller among distributed films at roughly 500 units, was Daniel Hoffman's *Toast* (1974), which, through non-narrated footage, accompanied by the German electronic music duo Kraftwerk, chronicles the exhaustive forms of energy used in making a piece of burnt toast. Of special note is Albert Ihde's exploration of archaeoastronomer Anna Sofaer's investigation of Anasazi solar calendars, *Sun Dagger* (1983), which resulted in what is one of the most comprehensive teaching guides ever to accompany an academic film, a twenty-two page gem written by teacher Don Reid, who, as Hoskyns-Abrahall states, "walked in the door" one day and "announced, then made good on his offer to contribute a guide to a film he loved."

Centron Films

Boyhood friends since their early days in Topeka, Kansas, Arthur Wolf and Russell Mosser found themselves working together for Boeing in different educational capacities during World War II.[25] In 1946, Wolf worked briefly as a director for Calvin Films in Kansas City, while Mosser held the title of Assistant Director of Visual Instruction at Boeing-Wichita. Mosser and Wolf founded Centron in 1947, in Lawrence, Kansas, with Wolf handling production while Mosser took care of business responsibilities, and made their first training films for government and industry that year. The name "Centron" was coined by Wolf, since the company was located in the central United States, and they were entering the electronic age. They soon branched into educational film, making their own as well as distributing titles made by other organizations, including the National Film Board of Canada (Philip Borsos' 1975 film *Cooperage*, an exceptional title focusing on a small barrel-making factory in British Columbia, among them).

Centron's film were also distributed by others, including the six-part *Middle America Regional Geography*, the ten-part *Modern Europe*, and the ten-part *Our Latin American Neighbors* series, distributed by McGraw-Hill. As a rule, Centron's filmmakers were uncredited ("We didn't want teachers to have to look at 30 seconds of screen credits," said Mosser), but the films in the *Middle America* and *Latin American* series were made by a team consisting of Harold A. "Herk" Harvey, cameraman Bob Rose, and writer Peter Schnitzler. Made in the early 1960's, films such as *Colombia*, *Peru*, and *Chile* (all three distributed in 1961) are today remarkable time capsules of family life and working conditions in the era. Herk Harvey and the crew spent 60 days filming in South America, and ran into several snafus, including the Chilean government confiscating the raw stock until Harvey diplomatically suggested that it be returned or Chile would not be included in the series at all. In Mexico, problems occurred with work visa delays, and Harvey, mindful of production deadlines, sent Rose clandestinely to Mexico to film anyway. Eventually, an agreement was reached and Centron agreed to pay a fine in order to continue filming.

Centron's Art Wolf (left) and Russ Mosser, 1966 (Russ Mosser).

Centron's best selling film was *Leo Beuerman* (1969, prod. Arthur Wolf and Russell Mosser), a film about a notable disabled man in Lawrence, which was nominated for an Oscar in 1970. Costing less than $12,000 to produce, over 2300 prints of the film were sold between 1969 and 1981 (the norm then being 300–500 prints per title), grossing over $600,000. Among the better-known filmmakers appearing under the Centron banner were

Karl and Stephen Maslowski, makers of exceptional elementary wildlife films (e.g., *Owls*, 1976, and *Raccoon*,1983).

Centron's catalogue of approximately 250 titles was sold to Esquire, Inc., the corporate parent of Coronet Films, in late 1981. Gulf + Western eventually acquired Esquire, and in 1984 sold the Centron production operation to Coronet's Senior VP of Production Bob Kohl, who then left Coronet and distributed and produced films under the Centron name until 1994. Kohl sold the Centron building and grounds to the University of Kansas in Lawrence for its Department of Theatre and Film in 1991, and Centron's prints, negatives, documents, and equipment were permanently archived in the Kansas Collection, Spencer Research Library, at the university the same year. Several Centron titles are currently being distributed by Phoenix Learning.[26]

Charles Cahill Associates

See AIMS Media.

Churchill Films

Chicago-born Robert Churchill earned a law degree from Harvard University, passed the California bar and studied photography at the Art Center School in Los Angeles.[27] His still photos were published in magazines such as *Vogue*, and he subsequently tried his hand at filmmaking (*Valley Town*) in 1939. During World War II, he made training films for the Army Signal Corps, including a comedy called *Spare Time in the Army*, which was distributed to commercial theaters by Columbia. In a short autobiography he wrote for EFLA's *Sightlines* magazine, he mentions that in 1946 he "wrote screenplays for B-minus pictures at Eagle Lion. Miserable year."[28] In 1948 he co-founded *Churchill-Wexler Film Productions* with Sy Wexler, who had met Churchill while serving as a cameraman for the Signal Corps.[29] Churchill-Wexler produced over 300 films, beginning with *Wonders in Your Own Backyard* (1948), made with a budget of $836. Churchill and Wexler split the company in 1961, with Churchill taking the educational films and Wexler the medical titles, each forming separate companies. Of Churchill's in-house productions, *Un Pueblo de España* (1960, dir. Gunther Fritsch), a beautifully photographed visit to the village of Mijas, Andalucía, and *Soopergoop* (1975, dir. Charles Swenson), a wacky parody on kids'

Wildlife film director Karl Maslowski in his World War II days (Steve Maslowski).

TV commercials, are among the most notable. In-house filmmakers included Pieter Van Deusen, who made approximately 13 films for the company, and George McQuilkin (who eventually became president and took the company into television production). Churchill reportedly resisted 17 offers to purchase his company in 1977.[30]

Churchill was also a distributor of films made by others, including the Oscar-winning *Flight of the Gossamer Condor* (1979, dir. Ben Shedd), and Bobe Cannon's landmark 1950 cartoon *Gerald McBoingBoing*). In 1984, Bob Churchill sold two-thirds of the company to President George McQuilkin and VP of Sales Bob Glore "in anticipation of retirement or death." He continued working with different partners over the years, producing films until 1996. The company was sold to American Educational Products in 1994. Churchill Films' titles eventually passed into the hands of Chicago-based SVE, and then to Discovery Education.

Contemporary Films

This distribution company was originally founded by Charles Cooper, who sold it to former *Brooklyn Eagle* reporter and film booking agent Leo Dratfield, James Britton (who had worked with Dratfield for the RCA/USA Signal Corps in World War II), and Rudy Kamerling, who ran the American Film Center's Bureau of Communication Research.[31] Under the new management team, Dratfield was chiefly responsible for acquiring films and marketing, Britton for finance, and Kamerling, who was best known as a projectionist, for promotional material. Anne Schutzer, who had been retained from Cooper's operation, served as office manager, film scout, and production expert. Contemporary's first significant release was *The Titan: Story of Michelangelo* (1950), a Curt Oertel film made in Germany from 1938 to 1940, and revised in 1949 by Robert Flaherty and Robert Snyder (Schutzer, who had worked for Snyder at one point, was instrumental in obtaining the film). Contemporary's sterling reputation was based on its exceptional selection in art subjects, documentaries, films on societal issues, and foreign and "experimental" work (e.g., Roman Polanski's early student film *Two Men and a Wardrobe* [1958], and Lotte Reiniger's animated silhouette films). By 1968, the Contemporary catalogue contained nearly 1,000 shorts and documentaries, in 16mm and 35mm formats.

In 1972, with Britton retiring and Kamerling devoting more time to his projection service, the decision was made to sell the company to McGraw-Hill, with Dratfield staying on in a management capacity. McGraw, however, was gearing itself more and more to business films, and heavily pared the once-extensive Contemporary catalogue. Dratfield decided to leave in 1973 to assist in the formation of Phoenix Films, and later joined Charles Benton's Films, Incorporated, as head of acquisitions and editor of the *Kaleidoscope Review*, a Public Media Education publication on good new and independent films of special interest to the library market. A revered figure who is renowned today for distributing worthy titles resulting often in minor profits, Dratfield had just begun to work on a book-length history of Contemporary Films when he was terminally stricken with liver cancer.

Coronet Films, post–1960

Jack Abraham's tenure as general manager of Coronet, a division of *Esquire* magazine, lasted until the early 1970s, as the firm continued to produce low-budget films primarily in the areas of guidance, history, science, and the social sciences.[32] Filmmakers remained uncredited, and the films were affectively lackluster when compared with the output of those of Coronet's main competitor, EBF. Creative Director Mel Waskin, who wrote scripts for many Coronet films of that period, recalls that Abraham's approach was "If it's in the textbook, and we cover enough pages, we can sell the film." Overall film quality was not as important as moving "product." In approximately 1972, as Waskin tells it, a "palace revolt" ensued after board member Abe Blinder began to inquire as to why Coronet films were so stodgy and unimaginative. Director of Research and former Encyclopædia Britannica Films producer Hal Kopel reportedly blamed the policies of Abraham.[33] As a result, Abraham was replaced as GM by Kopel, who immediately changed the "no credits" policy enforced by Abraham. For the first time at Coronet, filmmakers were now identified in film credits. Control over scripts and production were given over to Mel Waskin and Bill Walker, respectively. Coronet now began producing films sporting greater creativity, better acting, and improved production values, and began moving almost totally away from making guidance films.[34] Significant strides were notably made in the Science area, where filmmakers such as Bruce Russell created films that rivaled EBF's in terms of cognitive and affective value.

In 1979, John Smart hired Sheldon Sachs, former president of Esquire's successful Scott division of numismatic books, to be the new VP of Education Films, and president of the brand new Perspective Films division.[35] When taking the position, Sachs forthrightly told Smart that the Coronet catalogue, virtually in its entirety, consisted of boring, didactic canned lectures, and that Coronet did not have the infrastructure in place to produce quality films. He insisted that his mission would consist of buying quality films from other producers, and to this end Sachs (whose Perspective Films days are discussed below) began attending numerous festivals and shows for the purpose of obtaining new properties before the competition did.[36] Among the properties acquired by Sachs for distribution were Canadian director/producer Paul Saltzman's *World Culture and Youth* series (known as *Spread Your Wings* in Canada), consisting of extremely engaging ethnographic-oriented dramas showcasing the transference of arts and crafts from generation to generation.

In short order, Coronet began making significant strides in terms of overall film quality, fueled by the direction and philosophy of Kopel, Waskin, Walker, and Sachs, and aided by the work of editor Bob Gronowski and educational designer Ellen Bowen.

In the 1980s, a number of individuals took on the role of general manager, a period in which Coronet was active in selectively updating many of its old films, including *Rise and Decline of the Roman Empire* (revised 1980, uncredited director), featuring a "mod" wah-wah guitar and combo-organ musical soundtrack to accompany the Roman legions. Notable Coronet films of the era would include the remarkable films in Bruce Russell's visually spectacular *Biological Sciences* series (see Bruce Russell's entry in Chapter 6), made from 1981 through approximately 1987.

A series of major changes occurred at Coronet in the first few years of the 1980s. In 1981, Coronet acquired the Lawrence, Kansas, based Centron Films, retaining the production staff and studio in Lawrence. Coronet merged with MTI in 1984, and MTI's Joel Marks became Coronet's VP of production. Almost immediately, Coronet, along with all *Esquire* properties, was purchased by the Paramount/Gulf+Western/Simon & Schuster conglomerate. In late 1984, Coronet's corporate identity was changed to reflect the MTI name, becoming Coronet/MTI. Also in 1984, former Coronet Senior VP Bob Kohl, who had acted as the corporate liaison between Coronet and Centron, bought Centron from Gulf+Western, moved to Lawrence, and ran Centron from that point onward under its own name.

In a fitting and hilarious postscript to the old Coronet guidance films era, Mel Waskin selected and Bob Gronowski edited a number of old Coronet guidance films using the word "swell," and showed the resulting collage at a meeting of Coronet salespeople. Urged by the salespeople to sell the experiment as a full-blown film, Coronet complied, and the hilarious *The Great American Student* (1985) was unleashed on unsuspecting school librarians. This film is difficult to find in extant film libraries, is unique in the genre for its self-deprecating humor, and is a historical masterpiece.

In 1994, Simon & Schuster moved Coronet's film division to New Jersey. Mel Waskin, who had started with Coronet as a freelance writer in 1949, elected to stay in the Chicago area and teach English as a second language, ending one of the longest tenures of any executive within the educational film industry.[37] Distribution rights to the Coronet catalogue were acquired by the Phoenix Learning Group in May 1997.

Crawley Films

Crawley Films Ltd., the quintessential private Canadian film company, was initially funded in 1939 by a $3000 loan provided by the father of the legendary Frank Radford "Budge" Crawley to Budge's young wife Judith.[38] Budge secured another $3000 from the bank, bought a station wagon, camera and equipment, and set the firm up in the attic of

Dorothy Munro and Graham Crabtree working on Crawley Films' *The Loon's Necklace* (1948) (Crawley Films, Ltd.).

his parents' house. Later that year, the National Film Board of Canada was created by an act of Parliament, and soon Film Board founder John Grierson was contracting with Crawley to make war training films for the Canadian Forces. Shortly thereafter, Judith Crawley shot the first Canadian film ever produced in color, *Four Apple Dishes* (1945?), for the Film Board.

Budge Crawley's eccentricities were established at an early age, and soon became the talk of the Canadian film world. Author Barbara Wade Rose has chronicled wonderfully the filmmaker's unconventional approach to making a film:

> Budge climbed church steeples, descended mineshafts, leaned out of windows of airplanes until he had to be hauled back in. Budge lashed himself to a car to film racing chuckwagons as they hurtled out of the starting gate at the Calgary Stampede. His utter lack of self-consciousness caused titters and gossip: when Budge filmed a scene at an airport, he noticed the colour of a worker's overalls detracted from the scene. He asked the worker to change them. The man replied he didn't have any other pants to wear. "Here," said Budge, unzipping his fly, "Take mine." He filmed the scene in his undershorts, unaware of the scene he himself had just created.[39]

Crawley Films was a family company in which each family member played an integral role, although Budge's cavalier use of his own children would be shocking in any era:

> Pat Crawley was six when he watched as younger brother Sandy was given his first major acting role in a film about toilet training. Sandy was generally too happy a child to play believably a two year old engaged in the power struggles inherent in moving beyond diapers. So they improvised. "What you don't see in *The Terrible Twos* (and *Trusting Threes*, both 1951, dir. Judith Crawley)," Pat said, "is that Sandy, who's a pretty smiley little kid, is sitting on the pot during the toilet training part of the stuff." There was a break in the film. On the outtake, "a hand reaches in and whacks him across the face." Then filming resumed. In the finished film, Sandy almost seems to howl on cue. "Of course he fusses," said Pat. "He's just been nailed."[40]

Getting slapped across the face, as it turns out, was child's play:

> Budge made an insurance film about fire safety in the late 1940s that used a condemned house on Waverly Street, close to where Budge had been born, as the chosen film site. "We made a deal with the insurance company to finish burning it down," Budge explained. "We got shots of the firemen in there with gasoline and coal oil, lighting it up again — with fire helmets on! Same safety rules you see repeated now ... get down on the floor, don't leave your room, keep the door shut ... just don't open that door and let the heat in."
>
> As filming progressed, Budge and the crew realized something was needed to make the film come alive. The firemen had to rescue somebody. Someone an audience could tell wasn't acting. Judy was dispatched to pick up her youngest child, Rod, who was a little over a year old. By then it was three o'clock in the morning. He was wakened, put in the car, and driven to Waverly Street. The crew carried Rod, who was already crying, upstairs and put him in the crib. Then the crew members set fire to the room and left.
>
> Rod grew hysterical. He cried "Mama!" over and over in a hiccupping sob, and as the cameras ran a window flew open and a fireman climbed in to "rescue him."
>
> It made for a great film. As for Rod's hysteria, Budge would make light of it in later years. "It was a reckless kind of thing, stick a kid of one or two in a dangerous situation," Budge reflected in 1978. "I tease him every once in a while, I say, 'Rod, that was the making of you.'" Judy never mentioned the incident publicly, and Rod declines to be interviewed about his father altogether. (Daughter) Michal thought the entire episode "appalling." Pat called it "a human sacrifice."[41]

Life at Crawley Films wasn't all terror, though:

> (Budge) bought a Checker cab for work, the beginning of a long series of large cars — mostly Lincolns — he drove throughout his life. The Checker was, at that van-less period of automotive

history, the biggest car on the market, and Budge maintained he needed to be able to carry film equipment that wouldn't fit in an ordinary car.... Budge drove the cab to work, often carrying that bale of hay he needed for the horses. Then he installed a cab meter in the front seat near the dashboard. It wasn't connected to the wheels — it just sort of ticked over — but it looked real. Then he got one of the still photographers at Crawley Films to take his picture. He stuck it in a folder like the ones that cabbies usually carry and hung it over the back side of the driver's seat. His children gave him a cab-driver's cap.

Inevitably, Budge started picking up fares. He swore he never really charged anyone — he usually explained to his customers that the meter was broken and that the ride was therefore free — but he sometimes used it as a test of his clients' sense of humour. An executive from General Electric, along with filmmaker Arthur Rankin, was met by Budge as a taxi driver at the airport — Rankin, aware of the gag, hailed him as he drove up. "Rankin started to take umbrage with me," said Budge, "saying that I was taking them out of there to run up the meter. I said, 'You bastard, you'll pay whatever it is!'" The GE executive leaned over to Rankin and asked him why their cabdriver seemed so furious, but Rankin waved him off. At Crawley Films headquarters, Rankin handed Budge a $10 tip, to the astonishment of the GE executive, and headed into the building. Budge drove the cab to the back of his building, ran up the back stairs, and sat in his office as Rankin brought his guest in to see the president of Crawley Films. "The GE executive," said Budge, "nearly died laughing."[42]

Although the Film Act of 1950 had decreed that all Canadian government films be made by the National Film Board, Crawley moved forward, undaunted, further into the industrial educational film world.[43] By 1952, Crawley was producing 23 percent of all industrial films made in Canada, and had already begun having an impact on the academic film market as well, with its historically most significant film up to that point, *The Loon's Necklace* (*1948, dir. F.R. Crawley). In spite of its didactic narration, this film is thought to have won more awards than any other Canadian film, and was estimated, in 1976, to have been seen by an estimated 33 million people. In this native tale told through masks borrowed from the National Museum in Ottawa, ghost-like figures suddenly appear against a set painted by artist Graham Crabtree, reminiscent of the work of artist Charles Burchfield.

By 1958, when Crawley Films' staff had expanded to roughly 150 people, Crawley made *The Legend of the Raven* (1958, dir. Judith Crawley?), based on an Inuit story from Cape Dorset, Baffin Island. The film is especially notable for its stone sculptures, all from the collection of historian James Houston, who has been credited with developing the craft of stone carving among the Inuit as a means to providing them greater economic stability. In the early 1960s, Crawley was also beginning to have some success with the first Canadian television series to be exported, the 40-episode *Royal Canadian Mounted Police,* eventually syndicated in 100 U.S. cities and several other foreign countries.

One of the highlights of Canadian documentary cinema was Crawley's unforgettable *The Jean-Richard* (1963, dir. René Bonnière). The film portrays a yearly event occurring each winter: the fishermen of Petite Rivières, Québec, gathering together to build a vessel called a goélette. Hewed from trees growing on nearby hills, these large boats were shown being built outdoors in extremely cold weather, using axes, adzes, and steamboxes to shape the timbers. When completed, these flat-bottomed craft traded along the St. Lawrence River, settling on silt at low tide in each village due to the lack of deepwater docking facilities. The film culminates in an all-night accordion-fueled dance party prior to the launching, and is an exceptional film from a number of different perspectives.

By 1965, Crawley had made over 1500 films, six of them features. The remaining years of Crawley film were highlighted by Crawley's first successful feature film, Canadian writer Brian Moore's *The Luck of Ginger Coffey* (dir. Irvin Kirshner). Crawley also produced the documentary *Janis* (1974, dir. Howard Alk & Seaton Findlay) and the amazing story of Yuichiro Miura, *The Man Who Skied Down Everest* (dir. F.R. Crawley) for which Budge won the 1975 Oscar for Best Feature Documentary Film.

In 1979, Judith Crawley was appointed president of the Canadian Film Institute, coinciding with Budge's disastrous investment in a million-dollar wind tunnel for a never-produced film that was to be called *The Strange One*. Soon, debt service on Crawley's loans was estimated to be $80,000 per month, and in 1982, Crawley Films Ltd. was sold to former employee Bill Stevens for $2.00, who agreed to assume $1.2 million in debt and sell Crawley's film collection to the National Archives of Canada, including production files, correspondence, scripts, legal contracts, music and performance clearances, internal memoranda, and press releases. The initial transfer of the collection, consisting of 4000 productions and approximately 30,000 cans of film, was received in 1984, the remainder when the company ceased operation in 1989.

CRM Films

This prototypical and lively 1970s southern California film company specialized in selling its behavioral science, physical science, and biology films to schools, and eventually evolved its marketing model to include organizational development and corporate training films as well.

CRM, an acronym consisting of the last names of its founders, Nicolas Charney, George Reynolds, and Winslow Marston, was a film company begun as an offshoot of *Psychology Today* magazine. Charney had received his PhD in psychology while studying under Reynolds, who was only five years his senior. When Reynolds moved to southern California to become a professor at UC San Diego, Charney soon followed. Along with Charney's childhood friend Marston, they launched *Psychology Today* magazine. Soon, they determined to "revolutionize the textbook industry" by creating textbooks written by scholars, revamped by professional writers, then vetted by the original scholars. Graphics designer Tom Suzuki was hired to design the books with full-color photos, and an aggressive publishing schedule was set at one year from design to distribution. Not wishing to utilize a field-based sales organization, CRM hired a group of outbound-calling inside sales reps who did all the selling over the telephone. CRM's first college textbook was *Psychology Today: an Introduction*. Because describing the name of the company became too time-consuming, the company soon changed its name to Communications/Research/Machines.

CRM's Nicolas Charney (Nick Charney).

When professors began telling Charney that they needed films to augment the textbooks, CRM decided to start a film division. In 1970, John Veronis was brought in as a partner, noted producer Paul Lazarus III was hired as executive producer, and line producers Carole and Bruce Hart (fresh off their successes as Emmy Award winners on the television series *Sesame Street*) and Tom Lazarus were hired. Preston Holdner, who had been at McGraw-Hill films since graduating from college in 1963, was then brought in to become sales manager. CRM mandated a quality approach to filmmaking, and spending, according to CFO Brian Sellstrom, between $100,000 and $125,000 per half-hour film, thought to be the highest production budgets of any academic film company of the era.[44] CRM's films were sold by the telesales team, and a new twist on selling films was added: schools could either buy the films outright, or have a free limited-time rental based on an agreement to buy a specified number of CRM textbooks. As a result of CRM's high film quality, Holdner's sales management expertise, and its engaging team of inside sales reps, CRM's films were to be found in virtually every educational film library of any substance in North America.

CRM was an "out of the box" company socially, cinematically, and business-wise. Management guru Peter Drucker, a friend of partner John Veronis, served on CRM's board of directors. Robert Townsend, a management expert hired by Veronis and Charney as a consultant, left the company to write his best-selling book *Up the Organization*, which he based on his departing memo to CRM staff. The company's on-screen animated logo was designed by film animation pioneer John Whitney.

Located in the sun and surf-bleached California town of Del Mar, CRM was the quintessential laid-back West Coast company of the early 1970s. "Friday afternoon, the whole staff would sit around and drink wine and smoke," recalls Holdner. "Because of the fun atmosphere, it was not uncommon for people to work 60 hours a week instead of 40."[45] The staff photographs on pages 28 and 29 of CRM's 1975 catalogue chronicle the freewheeling era in style, dress, and demeanor, the women wearing sundresses and bell-bottomed pants, with many of the men sporting long hair. The catalogue was reflective of halcyon Californian times, and a particularly insightful photograph documents director Steve Katten and producer Larry Logan kneeling behind an Arriflex camera, shooting in a field of poppies. Stephanie Glidden, who was hired as an administrator in 1971 at the age of 19 and eventually became general manager, recalls what it was like working at CRM:

> Del Mar is an idyllic seaside town and it was heaven to work there. The offices were strung around Del Mar and up the coast in Solana Beach. They would rent little houses on side streets and prime office property, right on Coast Highway. My first office was in an old hotel building from the 1920s — right across the street from the water.... It is true as well that the "girls" would go out at lunch in their bikinis (I was one of them) and get some sun on the lawns of these houses or just walk a few blocks to the beach. Indeed, there was a lot of drinking and carrying on — major carrying on — but it is also true that the people worked really hard. It was a fabulous culture of young people who cared about their work and the work product deeply. The management style was participative and open. I've never experienced anything as exhilarating or engaging since.[46]

CRM's films represent a remarkable body of work, encompassing a wide and interesting breadth of psychological and biological themes. One of CRM's more creative treatments is found in *Information Processing* (1971, prod. Carole Hart), in which a mock cocktail party with animated conversations is observed from a control booth, with comedian David Steinberg as the film's host. Playing a bit role was adult film star Uschi Digard, in what was surely one of the only instances of a "blue" actor appearing in an academic film. CRM's large production budgets allowed them to hire professional talent and create "movies within movies," and other expensive and affectively valuable cinematic legerdemain. *Learning* (1971, dir. Carole Hart), as an example, included a very funny sequence directed by Carl Gottlieb, mocking up a silent film called "How Francis Learns," in which the child develops a rabbit phobia in youth, and recovers as an adult, surrounded by Playboy bunnies. In keeping with Charney's emphasis on high-quality illustrations, CRM films were often visually compelling. Wendy Vanguard's vivid illustrations of muscles and their contractive forces in *Muscle: A Study of Integration* (1972, dir. Tom Lazarus) were exceptional, in this film for which Michael Crichton served as the content consultant.

In 1972, CRM, which was valuated at $19.3 million, was sold to Boise-Cascade, which, after several public relations snafus, was looking to appear to be a kinder, gentler corporation.[47] It soon proved to be a mismatch. In September 1973, Boise-Cascade sold the CRM operation to Ziff-Davis, whose primary aim was to acquire *Psychology Today* magazine. In late 1974, Ziff-Davis soon sold the textbook division to Random House and shut down the CRM film production operation several months later. CFO Brian Sellstrom, who had joined CRM right out of college in 1969 at the age of 23, was asked to build up the profitability of the film division in order to sell it, and shortly thereafter CRM films were sold to McGraw-Hill. The move resulted in a cultural disconnect for both parties. "The McGraw folks would arrive on a corporate jet, and run into staff members leaving in bathing suits carrying surfboards," notes Holdner. "They wore three piece suits, and we wore bathing suits." Preston Holdner left that year to form the Media Guild film company. By this time, CRM had produced approximately 50 films.

McGraw-Hill had elected to keep CRM's Brian Sellstrom as the new GM of the CRM division, and CRM again began making films in 1976, led by Executive Producer Mike Rachmil, Director of Creative Services Kurt Villadsen, and Production Manager Brent Sellstrom, focusing primarily on corporate management and training films. In 1978, McGraw-Hill transferred its film division to the CRM team.

In 1987, McGraw sold CRM to a group consisting of filmmaker Peter Jordan (whose tenure at CRM had begun in 1971 as a production assistant), Stephanie Glidden, and Bechtel Investments. Glidden and Bechtel left the partnership in 1994. The company, now called CRM Learning, remains in the business, focusing on interpersonal skills training media, led by Peter Jordan. Today, most of CRM's exceptional psychology and biology titles, including notable films such as Steve Katten's *Communication: the Nonverbal Agenda* (1974) and Richard Miner's *Memory* (1980), are no longer in general distribution.

Davidson Films

This San Francisco–based company was founded by Jack Davidson in 1955, and specializes in psychology education. Jack was a pre-med student at the University of Illinois, headed a troop entertainment group at Ft. Lewis, Washington, and attended Stanford University on the GI Bill, where he became involved in the audio-visual department, honing his craft as a cameraman. He was soon hired by KPIX-TV in San Francisco, and developed a friendship with scientist and professor George Pimentel at UC Berkeley. Pimentel asked him to shoot a number of films in the *CHEM Study* (Chemical Education Materials Study) chemistry series, and Davidson launched his company in 1955 on Union Street in San Francisco.

Between 1955 and 1975, Davidson Films made well over 100 films, primarily on the sciences, psychology, and child development. One important Davidson effort resulted in

Elementary Mathematics for Teachers and Students, a series of 42 films made for the National Council of Teachers of Mathematics. In films such as *Fractions and Rational Numbers* (1970, prod. Jack Davidson), non-traditional ways of teaching math are explained to teachers by Michigan State professor Lauren G. Woodby, then demonstrated in actual classroom use by San Francisco State University professor Joseph Moray. While such "teacher ed" films were never shown to students, films such as these were important contributors to ongoing teacher learning and curriculum development.

Fran and Jack Davidson, 2005 (Geoff Alexander).

In 1975, Jack Davidson left filmmaking to obtain his medical degree, and production and day-to-day operations were taken over by his wife, Fran Williams Davidson. Fran's background included a degree in history at Stanford and two years in the Peace Corps in Ethiopia. She soon proved to be an outstanding producer, and under her guidance, the company continued to grow. Having made their last 16mm film in 1999, the Davidsons began making digital films, primarily in the area of psychology. Fran continues to produce films, while Jack has become a successful psychiatrist.

Notable Davidson films include *James Wong Howe: Cinematographer* (1973, dir. Arthur M. Kaye), the *Writers on Writing* series, and a number of films featuring educator Jean Piaget.

Disney (Walt Disney)

Disney, through its Buena Vista distribution subsidiary, sold hundreds of film titles to schools, mostly in the subject areas of geography, wildlife and nature, and math and science. Drawing from its extensive library of animated titles, Disney would often include both animation and live action in the same film.

Some Disney films took extraordinary inventive means to capture the attention of their young audiences, with titles such as *Magic and Music* (1957, dir. Hamilton Luske and Jack Kinney), in which a mysterious face, lit from below, provides an introduction to the joys of music that has subtly macabre undertones. The fun Jiminy Cricket *Safety* series (1961) is a series of guidance films providing cartoon gaffes as a means of teaching rudimentary concepts to lower-elementary children, although the endlessly repetitive "I'm No Fool" theme music must have driven teachers to drink. Disney would occasionally promote its "Tomorrowland" view of the future, but not always get it right: *Magic Highway USA* (1961, dir. Ward Kimball) extols super highways as the cure-all for the world's transportation needs by proposing an animated future in which freeways pass within yards of the Taj Mahal and Sphinx. Disney's films on animal subjects are often marred by hokey "imitative" music, where bassoons accompany the lumbering walk of large animals and flutes trill along with the birds. Commonly, Disney animal films appearing in schools were edited versions of the *True Life Adventure* feature films, such as James Algar's *White Wilderness* (1962), from which the factually questionable *Lemmings* sequence derived. In it, the animals appear to be propelled over a cliff into the water by eager wranglers, judging by the number that seem to be running *away* from the precipice while the sequence is being shot.

Disney occasionally produced well-made factual films as well (*Japan Harvests the Sea*, 1958, prod. Ben Sharpsteen, edited from the feature film *Ama Girls*). Today, much of the Disney catalogue from the 1950–1970 era would appear to be little more than thinly-veiled marketing material, aimed at driving visitors to Disneyland and viewers to its popular Sunday night television program. As of this printing, more than 2,000 Disney titles are available to schools in non–16mm formats.

ESI (Educational Services, Inc.)

ESI was founded in 1958 by a consortium of university scholars and researchers, with the goal of creating reforms in the areas of science and math curriculum. Included under ESI's umbrella was the work of filmmakers such as the noted documentarian Richard Leacock. Originally established under the auspices of the Massachusetts Institute of Technology, ESI's first project was the *Physical Science Study Committee (PSSC)* series of films and textbooks, funded by the National Science Foundation and the Ford Foundation, among others. Originally, the Ford Foundation had asked Encyclopædia Britannica Films to produce the series, but a disagreement between project director and MIT professor Jerrold Zacharias and EBF president Maurice Mitchell caused EBF to decline participating in the project.[48] When finally completed by ESI, the PSSC physics course comprised 60 films. In 1962, ESI launched the social science curriculum *Man: A Course of Study (MACOS)*. This one-year course was devised by psychologist Jerome S. Bruner, anthropology professor Irven DeVore, anthropologist Asen Balikci, and Peter Dow of ESI. MACOS encompassed Balickci's important — and soon to be controversial — series of films on the Netsilik Eskimo. In 1968, ESI and the Institute for Educational Innovation merged to form Education Development Center, Inc. (EDC), which continues to produce educational materials.[49] ESI's PSSC and MACOS series are significantly important to the history of academic film, and their respective stories are exemplars of how thematic series were designed, developed, and filmed.

ESI's PSSC series

Perhaps the most significant advance in the push to improved mediated science curriculum actually began in 1956 when a group of MIT scientists, under the leadership of physicist Jerrold Zacharias, formed the Physical Science Study Committee (PSSC). A component of the charter of the committee was to develop a teaching course and a series of films on the physical sciences. It was initially funded by a grant of $303,000 from the National Science Foundation, the NSF's first science curriculum development program ever (soon, the Alfred P. Sloan and Ford Foundations would join NSF to fund the series). Zacharias' educational perspective was to bridge the gap between scholar and teacher by bypassing the administrative establishment, which he felt had badly eroded the needed link between scholarship and curriculum. Although the initial agreement to make the series included Encyclopædia Britannica Films, a clash between Zacharias and EBF president

Maurice Mitchell scotched the deal early on, and ESI took over. The film series eventually comprised 60 films, three textbooks, and inexpensive lab experiments using everyday items. Noted filmmakers such as Quentin Brown, Richard Leacock, and Larry Yust and made PSSC films, which were hosted by noted physicists such as MIT's Francis Bitter, Bell Labs' Alan Holden, and the entertaining Patterson Hume and Donald Ivey from the University of Toronto. Although a number of the films do not emphasize affective elements, several of those that do bear mention, including five made by Richard Leacock.[50]

Leacock's films are interesting enough cinematically that they are notable to individuals that don't have much interest in physics, but that can't be said of many of the other films in the series. Herman Engel's *Definite and Multiple Proportions* (1960), for example, is not nearly as quirky and fun as Leacock's films, and could have possibly been more effective as a teaching tool if half of its thirty minute length were left on the cutting room floor. In another example, *Interference of Protons* (dir. Wallace Worsley, 1959), like many of the other films in the series, suffers from the lack of camera-presence on the part of its host.

Among the significant elements of PSSC films that make them noteworthy is their use of noted scientists as hosts, the fact that an entire curriculum — including textbooks — was created for them, and that they were the first post–Sputnik science series to be sold to schools. To a very large extent, they influenced all other science films series that were to follow.

ESI's Man: A Course of Study (MACOS) series

As science and mathematics films began to make their mark on the post–Sputnik classroom, social scientists as well began looking for ways to explain and introduce the world's cultures through cinema, and many felt that anthropologically-themed films would be an understandable and effective means of conveying key cultural concepts. With input from experts at M.I.T. and Harvard, and funding by the National Science Foundation, ESI launched a social sciences program intended to engage students a multimedia film effort that would occur in 5th grade classrooms.[51] Although several cultures were considered, only one group seemed to meet all the objectives of the scholars, and thus was created the nine-part *Netsilik Eskimo* series.[52] Filming began in 1963 in Pelly Bay, NWT, by director Quentin Brown and cinematographer Douglas Wilkinson (who had filmed the seminal *Land of the Long Day* and *Angotee*, both released by the National Film Board of Canada in 1952), aided by anthropologists Asen Balikci and Guy Marie de Rouselière. Kevin Smith (formerly of CBS television, and who had produced the PSSC series) was brought in as executive producer. The team documented traditional Inuit customs, including seal hunting and komatiq (dog-sled) making, as they were before the coming of the missionaries and the use of rifles, generally understood as having occurred in 1919 or so. Eventually the team, which later included cinematographer Bob Young, shot over 180,000 feet of film. Each film was non-narrated and non-subtitled, utilizing sound dubbed gratis by the National Film Board of Canada, given in return for international distribution rights outside of the U.S. This cooperative venture was intended to make each film in the Netsilik series among the most widely seen anthropological films ever made.[53]

Each film consisted of recreated actions, based on interviews with Inuit who remembered how traditional tasks were performed and games were played, and the writings of Danish-Inuit explorer Knut Rasmussen. Many of the images are memorable: a hunter rolling on the ice to imitate a seal similar to the one he will shortly attempt to kill (*At the Winter*

Sea Ice Camp), another fashioning his freshly caught fish into runners for the sled he has just made out of caribou antlers (*At the Autumn River Camp*). The films are outstanding documents in the non-narrated ethnographic tradition, filmed in conditions as cold as minus 10 degrees Fahrenheit. Probably the most powerful images were taken in the dead of winter, during the bitter cold short days in which food is scarce, and the sharing of warmth, shelter, and sustenance define the essence of nobility in the human character. To aid in the educational objectives of the series, a curriculum for fifth grade students entitled *Man: A Course of Study* (MACOS) was created in 1963, and distributed to over 3000 schools in the United States. With one of its aims being to replace traditional textbooks with diversified media, MACOS materials consisted of "nine teachers guides, thirty children's booklets, sixteen films, four records, five filmstrips, three games, fifty-four artifact cards, two wall-sized maps, a caribou-hunting strategy chart, a kinship chart, a sea ice camp chart, eleven enlarged photographs taken from the Netsilik films, several poster sized murals, and a take-apart seal."[54] Additional films in the curriculum included treatments on the social order of salmon, herring gulls, and baboons (e.g., *Dynamics of Male Bonding in a Baboon Troop*, 1968, prod. Quentin Brown, Educational Services, Inc.).

The films immediately became controversial on several fronts. In the anthropology community, scholars were uncomfortable with the Flaherty-like recreations of events, preferring the content to reflect the present rather than the past. Textbook publishers, used to gaining the lion's share of funding for curriculum, saw this film-based course as yet another potentially alarming trend toward redirecting moneys away from books. There was some resistance in the educational community as well, for what Balikci cagily refers to as "the vicissitudes of the extremely positive stereotypes of the Eskimos held by western peoples."[55] Simply put, many couldn't reconcile the cuddly, ever-smiling, media-bred Eskimo with the realities of survival in a harsh environment, which included infanticide and senilicide as means to controlling population in a food-poor environment. Religious fundamentalists became increasingly concerned that the curriculum preached "secular humanism," which they interpreted as suggesting that environmental pressures, rather than the word of a deity, governed the morals and behavior of human beings.

Finally, there were issues of course distribution and teacher training. Textbook publishers seemed a natural sales channel, but were reluctant to engage in the new process of printing, warehousing, and distributing the unfamiliar medium of film. They were uncomfortable with introducing a radical change to 5th grade instruction, which traditionally taught U.S. history rather than anthropology. Publishers also were having a difficult time with the breadth of materials, which, it was estimated, would cost a district over $8 per pupil, as opposed to $1 per pupil for a standard textbook.[56] Teacher training was another potential headache for publishers, who, while comfortable with writing predictably competent teachers guides for new textbook, would be working in the uncharted seas of "teachers as facilitators" rather than instructors, as necessitated by the MACOS' inductive learning-based supporting materials. Project editor Peter Dow further reflects on the discomfort many teachers experienced at the idea of teaching in a non-traditional format:

> Few elementary teachers in the 1960s had much formal training in anthropology, and most had been educated in a social studies tradition that views Western culture as the most advanced of civilizations. The Netsilik materials, on the other hand, were designed to illustrate that there is no discernible difference between the intellectual and creative capacity of Eskimos leading a traditional hunting way of life in the arctic and contemporary Americans. In MACOS cultural differences were treated as a reflection of environmental circumstances, the availability of infor-

mation, and shared values. To impose the standards and values of one culture upon another, the course suggested, was to deny those people their humanity. This point of view challenged the deeply held belief in the notion of "progress," particularly technological progress, or what is sometimes thought of as the "advancement of civilization," regarded by some as central to understanding the American way of life.[57]

In spite of these challenges, MACOS had been distributed on a small scale to those who had heard about the curriculum by word of mouth and an inexpensive brochure, comprising two hundred classrooms and some 6,000 students. Because the funding agreement from the National Science Foundation mandated that ownership of the program be transferred to a commercial entity, the MACOS principals embarked on an aggressive campaign to engage a distributor. From 1968 to 1969, the MACOS team visited 43 potential publisher/distributors, without success.

Finally, in 1970, Curriculum Development Associates (CDA), led by President Willard Wirtz, a former secretary of labor, was chosen to publish and distribute the program. The relationship had its difficulties, leading to the estrangement of MACOS developers who wanted to continue with program development, whereas CDA wished to utilize its own staff for such purposes. In addition, the MACOS team, having developed and tested a proven regional method for instructing teachers on the use of the program and materials, found itself rebuffed by CDA management, who preferred its own home-grown methods.

Concurrent with these challenges was the acceleration of the influence of religious organizations in public school systems. Initially, the problem centered around the teaching of evolution. As author Dorothy Nelkin notes:

> Pre-Darwinian biologists based their science on theological assumptions. Science was rooted in religion; its purpose was to prove the existence of God, using as evidence the design and purpose in nature. Darwin introduced an explanation of biological change that excluded the necessity of supernatural intervention and incorporated elements of chance and indeterminacy.[58]

In addition, inquiry-based instruction, in which students were encouraged to question what it meant to be human, was anathema to conservative groups, who felt that such instruction would invariably lead to the breakdown of parental authority, and ultimately, of society itself. Nelkin adds:

> For example, in the course of discussing animal behavior, the children are encouraged to ask difficult questions about human society. If salmon can survive without parental protection, why cannot man? What differences do parents make? What do you think are the characteristics of successful parents? What is the value of the group to the survival of its individual members? And what is the value of cooperation as opposed to competition? The course thus assumes a discernible continuity between animals and man that remains difficult for many people to accept.[59]

In 1969, the California State Board of Education, stating that the creation of the world as told in the book of Genesis should have equal value to the teachings of Darwin, mandated that such stories be taught side-by-side with the theory of evolution. In 1970, Don Glenn, a Baptist minister in Lake City, Florida, obtained MACOS materials from his daughter's class, and, claiming that MACOS represented a "hippy-dippy philosophy" composed of sex education, gun control, pornography, evolution and communism, led a campaign that drove out the course in the following school year.[60] In 1975, Arizona Republican congressman John B. Conlan, a representative of the House Committee on Science and Technology, began a protracted campaign to remove MACOS from public schools and to discredit the

National Science Foundation, who he saw as a catalyst for leftist educational programs, in the process.

Political opportunists like Conlan, sensing a good way to pick up evangelical votes, picked a prime time for saber-rattling: author Dorothy Nelkin notes as a contributing factor the tremendous upsurge of membership in fundamentalist Protestant groups such as Southern Baptists and Jehovah's Witnesses during the years 1958 through 1974, amidst the relative decline in membership of the more moderate Methodists and Presbyterians in the same time period.[61]

From its first publication in 1970, through 1974, MACOS had been purchased by roughly 1,700 schools in forty-seven states, with sales at $700,000 per year, but 1975 saw sales declining by 70 percent, a plunge from which it would never recover. The National Science Foundation, which had funded fifty-three projects to the tune of $101,207,000, also fell under scrutiny in this increasingly conservative environment.[62] The Reagan administration was adamantly opposed to federally funded course development, preferring that schools purchase course material developed by the private sector. By 1982, the NSF, which had once employed 125 people, employed only twelve individuals.

MACOS did have its supporters, including Senator Edward Kennedy (MA) and Congressman James Symington (MO), but perhaps ultimately it failed because its developers lacked the political savvy of which its detractors were becoming so rapidly proficient. The finest epitaph for this noble experiment in education may have been voiced by the congressman from Missouri:

> I found the program both fascinating and worthwhile, and I wish my kids had had a chance to see it in their time.... But it would be good for anybody to see.... I remember during the Korean War we had the habit of saying, you know, just some Gooks over there. Kill a few Gooks. Well, the Korean people turned out in later times to have a rather wide variety of characteristics, and personality traits, and strengths and weaknesses, that made them almost seem like the human beings we are ... not so easily dismissed as Gooks. And I would have thought that, had a generation of Americans, prior to that war, been brought up with a chance to see, not just MACOS but other opportunities to review the cultural differences between people world wide, [they] might not be that easily led into such a characterization. I wasn't opposed to our participation there, but even in war respect for humanity should outlast the killing. And I think a great nation like ours should try in every way to use its power and influence to share and revere a respect for humanity.[63]

The controversy surrounding MACOS weighed heavily on the minds of educational film companies, who would tread lightly through the controversial fields of social science and anthropological subjects well into the 1980s. The films — when they can be found today — remain stalwart testaments to the art of anthropological filmmaking. The important study materials which accompanied the series, most of which were discarded by schools in the aftermath of the controversy, would today be valuable historical artifacts. They now appear to be lost.

Encyclopædia Britannica Films, Post–1960

The history of Encyclopædia Britannica Films in the post–Sputnik era takes up a significant part of this chapter. The company made many of the era's most important films, its filmmakers were, taken as a whole, exceptional, and EBF's contributions to the business and the genre are, of all academic film companies, quite probably most worthy of future analysis and scholarship.

The fortunes and vicissitudes of this descendant of ERPI, sibling of the University of Chicago, and stepson of Senator William Benton, could easily be made into a book itself, full of intrigue, internecine battles, and pathos. Heading into the new decade, ex–Muzak wunderkind and president of EBF Maurice Mitchell, supported by ex-senator Benton, maintained his policy of funding the work of important filmmakers such as John Barnes (who had taken up residence in Italy, utilizing European location shooting, actors, and the Cinecittà sound stage), Larry Yust, and Bert Van Bork.[64] Since much of EBF's film production was taking place away from Chicago, a western film unit was begun in Los Angeles, headed up by veteran producer Milan Herzog. EBF augmented its presence in Washington as Hubert H. Humphrey, fresh from his recent loss in the 1968 presidential election, agreed to come on board to preside over the company's board of consultants (as had Adlai Stevenson before him), devoting 25–30 percent of his available time to the company.[65] EBF had always been a company comprising people with strong opinions, and certainly three of the most vocal, from a management perspective, were Charles Benton, Warren Everote, and Bill Deneen.

William Benton's son Charles had begun his tenure with EBF in 1953, acting as an assistant to Milan Herzog.[66] In the summer of 1954, he traveled to London to work with John Barnes as a production assistant, primarily engaged in searching for stock footage for *William Shakespeare* (1955), *The Pilgrims* (1954) and *Captain John Smith: Founder of Virginia* (1955). In 1955, Charles made his only film, *Food and People*, which was screened at the first Flaherty International Film Seminar, which he and his wife, Marjorie, both attended. The documentary tradition of "film as revelation" that he was exposed to at the seminar was in stark contrast to the didactic tradition of ERPI and most early EBF, with which he, as a young filmmaker, wasn't especially comfortable. Thus, when Mitchell offered him the seemingly mundane task of cleaning up EBF's mailing list, by then outdated due to years of neglect, he readily accepted.

Charles Benton, who maintained that because he was the boss's son, he "had to be twice as good to be equal," states that the job of repairing the mailing list became the single most important event in his early career, due to the fact that it entailed visits to school and audio visual buyers in 48 states, encompassing between 3000 and 4000 entities from a total market consisting of 14,000 school districts, including 20,000 high schools, 60,000 elementary schools, and many thousands of public libraries. Benton reviewed all EBF invoices on record for every school, library, and other AV customer and over a four year period coded all schools,

Films Inc. and EB exec Charles Benton (Charles Benton).

school systems, and libraries into a database. This review of files, state education directories, and meetings with key customers by approximately 40 field sales reps was an extraordinary learning experience for Benton detailing the history and realities of the audio visual marketplace.

When this massive market research project was finished, Charles Benton wanted to apply audio-visual instruction in the classroom himself. He soon accepted a job teaching 5th grade at Evanston's Washington Elementary School during the 1959–1960 school year. That level, the grade in which elementary students are introduced to U.S. history, was especially appropriate for Benton, who had majored in American studies at Yale. The following year (1960–61) he became head of marketing at EB's subsidiary Films Inc., where he reorganized their feature film holdings by genre. The next year, Benton returned to EBF and took a film sales position in the territory of "Downstate Illinois," where he became EBF's top salesperson for two years. He was promoted to national sales manager in 1963, and became president of the film company in 1965, replacing former chemistry teacher Warren Everote, who had just been appointed to the role of president of the Encyclopædia Britannica Press.[67]

Everote had joined EB in 1946 as an associate in research and production, fresh from obtaining a Master's in history from UCLA, a Doctorate in science education from Columbia, and wartime experience with the U.S. Naval Reserve as officer-in-charge of still photography and combat motion pictures at the Bureau of Ordnance. Everote wrote the syllabus for EBF's 160-film *Physics: the Complete Introductory Course* and its 162-film *Chemistry Introductory Course*, and also contributed to the seminal *Physical Science Study Committee (PSSC)* project. He became president of EB Films in 1962. Everote had a reputation as a fiscal conservative who insisted that filmmakers and producers strictly adhere to the budgets dictated by Bill Benton and Maurice Mitchell, and investigated expense reports that more than occasionally seemed to be padded.

In November 1965, EBF acquired the Detroit-based William Deneen Productions, a company founded in 1950 by Deneen, a Portland, Maine, native. Bill Deneen had been contributing social studies films to the EBF catalogue for a number of years, and was immediately granted the position of VP for Production Operations. Among the individuals coming to EBF from the Deneen firm were writer-producer Linda Gottlieb.[68]

By the mid–1960s, it was soon apparent that a whirlwind had taken hold of EBF's Chicago headquarters,

Warren Everote, who held several executive titles at EB (Warren Everote).

much it fueled by the brilliant and opinionated Charles Benton. In reviewing various letters and memos from the era in which Charles Benton presided over the film unit, it soon becomes apparent that the younger Benton's aim was to radically change the way properties were developed and acquired, a 180-degree departure from the way EBF, embodied by the senior Benton and Maurice Mitchell, liked to do business. A prime area of conflict centered around Charles' strong advocacy of acquiring films from television networks and other film-related organizations such as Wolper Productions, National Geographic, and the National Film Board of Canada. On November 11, 1965, he wrote a passionate and prescient five-page letter to his father, abridged here to focus on its more salient points, detailing his vision for evolving EBF into what he saw as a stronger company:

> Dad ... let me stress that I vehemently disagree with certain aspects of your and Mitch's stand on "outside product".... The Film Board [National Film Board of Canada] is going increasingly into the production of material specifically for education. They are talking now in terms of devoting one-third of their total budget to educational materials productions. In view of this trend, my point very simply is why should we not try and develop complimentary production programs? Then, we can distribute the Film Board's output in this country to round out our own offerings. After all, we can't produce everything and run everything ourselves. Let me take two specific examples. The Film Board has recently produced three life-science films that fit directly into our basic life-science program. We worked with them on the treatment and scripts of these films. They put up their own capital. These were films we wanted in our program. Now we do not have to produce them. They, in effect, are serving as a sub-contracting agency, taking the materials we want to fit into our program framework in this particular instance.... My ultimate goal over the next two to four years is to develop the kind of relationship with the Canadians whereby they will come to us first on the distribution of any of their product in this country. Ideally, I would like to have a "first refusal" contract with them. We now do not have such a relationship, though I believe we are making progress toward one....
>
> Now let's take the case of NBC. We have learned an enormous amount out of our brief sixteen-months contract with them. We have learned how to cut down and edit television films for educational use. In fact, we have made the first break-through with any network on doing this. Before we tried it, I don't believe it had ever been done. We now know that we can vastly improve products produced for television through re-editing and re-shaping it specifically to the needs of education, as we see them. Also, we have learned to develop really outstanding teachers guides for this kind of material.... We have just decided with Kip Fadiman's enthusiastic concurrence, to include the NBC-produced "The Louvre" as part of our humanities offering. NBC spent over a quarter of a million dollars on this magnificent production and with it won ten Emmy awards. It is undoubtedly the best television film that was produced during last year's television season. We have broken the film down into two parts — one on the Louvre as the "Palace of Kings" (the historical evolution of the building over hundreds of years of French history) and secondly as the "Golden Prison" (the treasury for the greatest collection of arts works in the world). In this particular film Charles Boyer serves as the "film teacher." Ralph Wagner was the person who first suggested this excellent idea and I believe it may result in the sale of as many as 500 prints of this superb film which we never could have afforded to produce as it was actually produced....
>
> Now, what are the implications for EBF of the above? There is one point about which I feel very strongly. I simply cannot go along with the idea that EBF in any way has a monopoly on the top film-production talent in our field. Nor, can we hope to commandeer all this talent directly within our framework. I agree that the *major* emphasis ought to be in the development of our own products. But I feel very strongly that this should not be our *only* emphasis. We can also mobilize the creative forces on the outside to do what we want and thereby help build up our business. I believe we have done this in the cases of the National Film Board of Canada and NBC.

> So the argument is not whether we should take on outside products or work with outside producers, but to what extent we should do this? I don't believe there are any pat answers here. It is a constant problem and one which we are continually struggling with in the company. Of course, the increasing amount of federal funds supporting film production in special areas just helps to further complicate the whole matter. I suspect this is going to be a subject for continuing discussion and controversy over the months and years ahead. It will be a recurring theme during all of our Advisory Board discussions in 1966.
>
> The main purpose of this memo is to urge you please to keep an open mind on the subject. Let us not prematurely lay down any ground rules or arbitrary percentages that we may find it difficult to live with in line with changing circumstances. This year the market has been vastly increased by the new federal funds and I believe one of the ways that EBF should respond to this broader potential, is by being more flexible about these outside products (that meet our quality standards) and talents. This year I think it is imperative that we all explore the opportunities and pitfalls of outside products and talents with a completely open mind. I would prefer not to have to defend our position here, but rather work with you on improving it.

Charles Benton was never able to fully convince William Benton or Maurice Mitchell that there might be value in working to a greater extent with non–EB producers and distributing their films under the EB banner. His father was perhaps his harshest critic, as evidenced by his tone in this memo marked "Confidential," written from the senior Benton to Charles on January 7, 1966:

> As you know, I am exceedingly uneasy about your preoccupation with products which do not carry the EBF imprimatur. I have the feeling that you hope to get something for nothing. I agree this occasionally happens in life, but not often. I share Mitch's great uneasiness about your preoccupation with TV films.... I share his concern about our interest in the Canadian Film Board films.
>
> We are in a powerful position to back our own films under our own imprimatur. This is what we should be doing, in my judgment.... Let us hammer away at developing our own films and our own prestige. Yes, I can imagine occasional exceptions, but not many. My general impression of the correspondence in the last two years is that we have put five to ten times the time and money into the development of films other than our own—films which we have not produced which carry exclusively the EBF label—[than] I think is warranted.[69]

Occasionally, Bill Benton would begrudgingly agree that Charles had a point, as addressed in a letter to Maurice Mitchell and Warren Everote two months later:

> At my weekend with Charles at Arden House, he gave me a very long argument about our thirty movies which we've made with NBC. I must say that he shook me in my previous attitudes and shook me to the point where I have decided to quit arguing about the matter.... Charles has several arguments that make exceedingly good sense ... I have accepted Charles' viewpoint ... there didn't seem to me to be any reasonable choice.... I do not like selling NBC films ... nor do I like to be selling NBC films when (competitor) McGraw-Hill is going to be selling them ... but I have succumbed. Charles has better arguments than I realized. At any rate, seemingly there's no hope for it.[70]

To which Deneen replied, somehow having obtained a copy of the correspondence, to Charles Benton in a pithy, one-sentence letter dated March 25, 1966: "Congratulations on the victory of Arden House!" This series of letters is particularly significant in terms of the subsequent resignations of both Deneen and Charles Benton. In short order, each of them was to form his own successful film company drawing heavily on quality productions from the National Film Board of Canada, television networks, and independent producers (Benton's Films Incorporated, and Deneen's Learning Corporation of America).

By early 1967, the continuing series of battles was starting to wear on Charles Benton. Prior to a Board meeting in early January, he asked Deneen's opinion about a proposed six-month leave of absence he was considering, temporarily handing the reins back to Mitchell. Several days later, Deneen wrote a heartfelt but hard-hitting advisory letter to Charles, which he copied to William Benton:

> You have always treated me with respect, with kindness and generosity, and even affection. This fact and my genuine feeling and admiration for you makes what follows the more difficult.
>
> I have tried to be optimistic over the past year. Tried to feel that we could solve and were solving some of the problems that plagued us. But seeming to follow on the heels of each solution was only too often another problem of suspiciously the same order as the one we thought had just been solved. I have tried to support you though we have found ourselves as often at odds with one another as in accord. I have tried to see your way of looking at things though I find your mode of operation alien to my concept of how a business should be run. I have tried to understand the methods you have wanted employed, though frequently I found little reason in them. Now optimism is a good thing to have if there is cause for it. It can be a delusion if there is not. Based on the experiences of the last year, and on the way you have gone about "reorganizing," I have come to see little cause for optimism because I see little change in the way you think and act, and a president's thinking and action must lie very much at the heart of the success or failure of a business. venture....
>
> The decision making process by which this company lives and grows is, let's face it, still a forbidding quagmire all but defying passage through. I think that recent organizational changes you have made will tend only to aggravate rather than alleviate the problem and then there will have to be more reorganization. These are all old familiar themes. The question is, it seems to me, whether or not you see that problems of a remarkably similar nature have become self-perpetuating perhaps because of something intrinsic to your own nature and quite apart from the rationality of your approach at any given moment.... I have deep sympathy with your cause, Charles, but surely when you find yourself so frequently, so almost constantly at odds with other responsible people in this company, you must ask yourself some questions.
>
> You have many gifts. Wonderful traits that are to be envied and admired. You're honest and loyal, I believe. You're intelligent. You have a depth of kindness and feeling that is rare and fine. You're a great salesman. You can be magnificently persuasive. You're a fighter. You have ideals. You have incredible energy and drive. Your purpose, what you want to do for and in education is laudable. You have imagination: more ideas per hour than anyone I ever knew....
>
> You have much to offer. But must you offer it as the chief operating officer of EBEC? Or are there other ways in which your goals might be achieved? Other areas in which to apply your considerable talents more happily and successfully? You are now at an age when you must seriously inquire how you are going to use the next twenty years, and these are questions you must find right answers to. It is my strong conviction that you cannot and will not find the success and achievement you desire as president of EBEC. I must concur with Bill Edwards, Milan Herzog, and Jack Saunders that you should indeed take a leave of absence to consider other alternatives.
>
> I'm sorry if the foregoing connotes disloyalty because Charles Benton the man has my loyalty, respect, and esteem as a valued friend, and certainly this fact lies among the reasons why you have received this letter.[71]

Three days later, William Benton replied to Deneen:

> I spent a good part of yesterday afternoon and evening with Charles and he showed me the original of your letter to him even before I received the carbon this morning. We had a fine talk about it and he reaffirmed his enthusiasm for you and your leadership. Of course I like the candor of your letter. I applaud such communications among the top executives of a company. This is the way to hammer out differences. It is the road to progress.
>
> A lot of the problems in our company I think have come from growing pains. But others

have developed because all the top executives are new. Still others trace to Charles' own relative inexperience. Mitch and I undoubtedly are responsible for still others. I have every confidence that we shall work out most of our problems, though perhaps it will take some time. Charles is visiting with Mitch over the weekend and then the two of them are coming to New York next week to visit with me. We have some constructive ideas under discussion. However, as I've told Charles, no decision is ever a final decision.[72]

Within a month, however, Benton and Mitchell made the decision to remove Charles as president of the film unit. Mitchell, who had been serving as CEO of EBEC, returned again to head up the film unit as president, with Warren Everote serving as EVP, and VPs Bill Deneen and Milan Herzog reporting directly to Everote. As William Benton reported in a general memo, Charles had resigned to pursue "curriculum reform" and "new technologies" for the company.

Charles Benton now determined that a clean break from EB was what was needed. In short order, he sold company stock to finance his purchase, with his father's blessing, of EB's Films Incorporated division, which had up to that time been involved in distributing 16mm versions of feature films. Charles then acquired properties for distribution for his new company from U.S.-based independent producers and international organizations such as the British Broadcasting Corporation and Germany's Institute für Film und Bild (FWU), a financially and artistically successful venture that enabled Films Incorporated to become a major competitor to EB within a few short years.

In early 1967, Maurice Mitchell was elected chancellor of the University of Denver, beginning his tenure on September 1 of that year, and on June 6, Warren Everote was selected to replace him as president of EBEC. Everote believed in keeping often out-of-control budgets on track, which caused occasional beefs with filmmakers. He was also a firm believer that the use of music detracted from the narrative in academic films. In view of the fact that film music tends to be representative of a given era, the timeless quality of many EB films is underscored by this lack of a musical track.

On July 6, 1967, Bill Deneen tendered his letter of resignation. Deneen had been a strong advocate for increasing production spending since his arrival as a means for attracting (and keeping) talented filmmakers, which often clashed with the views of Everote, who Deneen felt favored a policy of austerity. While generally conciliatory, Deneen's letter to William Benton contains a two-sentence explanation of what he felt were the overwhelming reasons for his departure:

> I believe Warren shares my feeling that perhaps we're better off without each other — that perhaps there is a mismatch that might not lead to the volume of productivity and economy he envisions. In a way, this makes the decision to leave easier and removes whatever feeling I might otherwise have had of "ratting out" when the going got toughest.

Shortly thereafter, Deneen entered into a series of negotiations with Columbia Pictures, which would culminate in the formation of Columbia's Learning Corporation of America division. A series of three letters written to Columbia by Deneen indicates that questions had arisen in reference to Deneen's tenure at EBF, pertinent to his potential choice as head of Columbia's soon-to-be-launched educational film company. Two of the letters were not sent, one of which contains verbiage that is probably closer to Deneen's heart than the more refined letter (below) that was ultimately sent. It offers an admittedly biased, but historically important view of some of the familial and financial conflicts that were the ebb and flow of daily life at EB:

It was very good of you to call re the "trouble area." I'm sorry a problem has arisen but since it has we'd better tackle it with some facts.

I'm quite familiar with the report of "overspending, lavish etc." I've heard it all before ad nauseam from the older Britannica management group and those close to them, and from their point of view there may be some validity.

I suppose it's no secret in the trade that Encyclopædia Britannica Educational Corporation has undergone severe management struggle and turmoil over the last five years. When Charles Benton, the son of the owner, was made president some years ago, the former management was nearly entirely replaced, going off into other Britannica companies. I was a member of the "new" team, and to the older group I suppose we all were considered pretty much inept as managers even though in terms of product and profit the company enjoyed the best years in its history.

Now, Charles Benton and the new team have all left, and the company is back in the hands of its extremely conservative former management with the exception of the chief executive officer, Maurice Mitchell, who resigned about the same time I did. This group, now men in their upper fifties, had best known me as an independent producer, and in this role we had a very good long term relationship.

As head of production at Britannica however, I would guess I did many things to annoy them. I rather radically adjusted what I considered an antiquated salary structure. With the blessings of the owner, I Installed a bonus program that I felt necessary to attract and hold the talent I wanted. I replaced obsolete equipment. I brought in many new people, hired better and more expensive writers, and gained a reputation as a "spender." The company was in serious need of rejuvenation, and I saw this as part of my job as well as the desire of the owner. Production costs did go up though to a figure well within sound limits in relationship to sales. When I left the company our average production cost on films was running about $1050/minute. I can well understand how all of this may have appeared "lavish" to the former management, a group of rather penurious gentlemen, largely ex-school teachers, long accustomed to living themselves on a teacher's pay, and firmly believing that anyone who earned more than $12,000 a year had to be overpaid. The terms under which the Bentons bought out my company and brought me to Britannica came under considerable attack from the deposed group especially since my salary and stock ownership amounted to quite a lot more than that of the president who had been replaced and now returned, and the reputation for being "expensive" was further enhanced.

So, I suppose much depends on who's interpreting what good management is or isn't. You might talk with some of the producers who worked for me at Britannica and hear that Deneen was a tight-fisted bastard. You might chat with some pre–Britannica associates and learn that we had built a reputation on squeezing the last ounce of value out of every dollar. Depends on viewpoint.[73]

Warren Everote left EB in 1971 to pursue a career in the world of consulting. He freely acknowledges that a significant part of his role there was to keep EBF on budget, and also mentions ongoing discussions with Screen Actors Guild representatives, who continually battled for actors in EB films to receive SAG scale wages.[74]

In 1980, EB began converting its catalogue to video, and stopped production of 16mm film altogether in 1985–1986.

In terms of intelligent content, exacting production standards, and overall affective value, EB's overall output in the 1960–1985 era was never equaled on such a mass scale. A book could be written solely on the subject of memorable EB films. Highlights would include films in the *Biology* series, produced by Ralph Buchsbaum, and the *American Geological Institute (AGI)* series, with John Shelton and William Matthews serving as advisors. These films were made by noted EB filmmakers such as Bert Van Bork and Charles L. Finance. EB's *Humanities* series produced extraordinary films on literature and civilization, many of which were made by John Barnes. The films made by Larry Yust in the *Short Story*

Showcase series, including Shirley Jackson's *The Lottery* (1969), are as stimulating and compelling today, forty years later, as they were when originally released. Tom Smith's *The Solar System* (1977) directly influenced the *Star Wars* films, while other EB filmmakers, including but not limited to Stan Croner and Bruce Hoffman, produced top-notch films that are exemplars in the genre of academic film. Many of EB's films were animated by a crack team led by David Alexovich.[75] EB's infrastructure was highly optimized to support distribution, and included people such as administrator Martha Gonzalez and editor-cataloguer Jerry Olk.

With the death of William Benton on March 18, 1973, ownership of the Encyclopædia Britannica and related book divisions has passed to the non-profit Benton Foundation, which in the 1980s also bought the film company from its owners, the Benton children, Charles, Louise, John, and Helen. The Benton Foundation donated all Encyclopædia Britannica properties to the University of Chicago in the late 1980's. In the mid-1990's, the University sold its EB properties to an international group of investors led by Swiss financier Jacob Safra for the sum of $135 million. Under new CEO Don Yannias (a longtime Safra investment advisor), emphasis was changed from video and book publishing to CD-ROM and Internet media. Times were tough at EB as revenues for fiscal year 1997 were $325 million, half that of EB's peak year of 1990. As of this writing, most of the long-time employees who made EBEC the most intellectually interesting film company of its time have left.

Documentation of historical EBF management changes has been challenging to ascertain. The following is an educated guess as to the chronological management changes in EBF presidents and VPs of production from the end of the Maurice Mitchell era (1967) onward:

- Pres. Warren Everote, 1967–71 (Everote had been president of EB Films from 1962 to 1964. He left on temporary assignment for one year to Encyclopædia Britannica Press, and went the following year to EB Ltd. in England. He became president of EBE's Development Division in 1966.)
- Pres. Jim Parton 1971
- Pres. Jack Saunders, temporary president from 1971–1972
- Pres. Ross Sackett 1973 until November, 1977
- Pres. Ralph Wagner (married to Louise Benton), November 1977 until December 1987
- Pres. Joe Elliott (formerly of Coronet), December 1987 through June 1994
- VP of Production Milan Herzog, 1963–1966 (in 1966, Herzog was promoted to Senior VP, where he served until 1970, when he took over EBF's California production facility, serving there until his retirement in 1973.)
- VP of Production William Deneen, 1965–67
- VP of Production Joe Bower, 1967–1970?
- VP of Production Alvin Feldzamen, 1970?–1972?
- VP of Production Tom Goetz (dates unknown)
- VP of Production Robert Buchanan (dates unknown, a tenure of approximately 3 years)
- VP of Production John Montgomery (dates unknown)
- VP of Production Mary-Kay Kickels (dates unknown)
- VP of Production Philip Stockton, 1988–1994 (Stockton also served as Director of Production under the previous four VPs.)
- EVP and General Counsel William Bowe, 1994 to the present

Film Associates

See Bailey/Film Associates.

Films for the Humanities

This company was founded by producer Harold Mantell and his wife Marianne in 1959, but its roots in the humanities can be traced back to 1952, when Marianne Roney (later Marianne Mantell) and Barbara Holdridge founded Caedmon Records. Caedmon specialized in spoken-word recordings, including those of well-known poets such as Robert Frost and Dylan Thomas. ("The proprietors of Caedmon were, in January of 1952, apparently the only two graduate students in New York who had never been at a party with Dylan Thomas," said the liner notes to their first recording, *Dylan Thomas: Reading his Complete Recorded Poetry*.)

Like Caedmon, Films for the Humanities (later to be Films for the Humanities and Sciences) specialized in arts and letters, and was particularly strong in drama films, with many of its titles, including those in the *History of the Drama* series, produced by Harold Mantell. Eventually, the Mantells would seek out dramatic films made in European countries and bring them back to the U.S. for distribution, translated by the multilingual Marianne Mantell. The Mantells were also marketing innovators, as theirs was probably the first academic film company to use direct mail catalogues and mailing lists in an effort to reach hard-to-find buyers, particularly in university departments. Owning their own printing press, they were able to print and mail catalogues specific to different subject areas, for different buyers.

After selling their company to K-III Communications in the early 1990s, the Mantells stayed on board in a management capacity until December 1996. However, they retained the distribution rights to all Mantell-produced films. As of this writing, the approximately 185 titles in the *Films for the Humanities and Sciences* catalogue are available in non–16mm formats from the Films Media Group, owned by Infobase Publishing Company.

Films Incorporated

Originally called Home Film Libraries, this company was founded in 1928 by Orton Hicks, William Benton's (EBF) high school roommate at Shattock School in Minnesota, to take advantage of the new 16mm safety film medium, which became the amateur film standard in the late 1920's. Hicks' idea was to offer major studio-produced shorts to the developing 16mm home market. In 1935, after acquiring the Paramount library in 16mm for distribution to the institutional market, Hicks changed the company's name to Films Incorporated, because the Paramount sales manager disliked the words "home" (not adequately defining the market) and "libraries" (too academic), but retained the word "Film," thus Films Incorporated, or Films Inc. for short. In 1951 the company was sold to Encyclopædia Britannica Films, who wanted to give the EBF sales reps more to sell in the slow summer months when school was out.

By the late 1960's, Films Inc. had acquired 16mm non-theatrical feature film distribution rights from 20th Century–Fox, RKO, MGM, and Disney. With the avalanche of new federal education funds available through the Elementary and Secondary Education Act (ESEA), however, EBF's field sales reps did not have adequate time to rent Films Inc.'s feature films to schools, libraries, and prisons. Thus, after Charles Benton resigned as president of Encyclopædia Britannica Education Corporation in 1967, he was able to acquire Films Inc. in mid-1968 through an exchange of EBEC stock. Since Warren Everote, his successor at EBEC, wanted to emphasize the core curriculum productions that EBF was best known for, Benton was also able to spin off several of EBF's television acquisition contracts into Films, Inc., including those from NBC, David Wolper, and National Geographic.

One of the early initiatives the younger Benton took with Films Inc. was a $100,000 investment to acquire a 50 percent interest in the Visual Education Center (VEC) in Toronto, a newly formed education film company headed up by his friend Grant McLean, the former acting commissioner of the National Film Board of Canada. Together, Films Inc. and the Visual Education Center made up his new holding company, Public Media Inc. (PMI). Several months later, Benton and McLean traveled to Germany where they met with Walter Cappel, the head of the Institut für Film und Bild (FWU), and persuaded him to allow VEC to produce English versions of FWU's films, which would then be distributed in Canada by VEC and to the rest of the English-speaking world through Films Inc. By doing so, they introduced into the North American market English versions from the leading producer of education films in Europe, comprising over 120 titles. These included a major world geography series, *Man and His World*, an elementary language arts series without narration, which they called *See 'n Tell,* and a secondary school physiology series using animation and microphotography, *Exploring the Body.* The blend of McLean's production leadership and Benton's sales and marketing experience at EBF led to the successful packaging and promotion of FWU's films in the market, with the result of millions of dollars in sales volume.

Two of the more important people who came along with the acquisition of Films Inc. from EBF were Gale Livengood, who had been a school teacher and principal in Ohio before joining EBF in the 1950's, and Al Green, who was a lawyer by training, and had been involved in the feature film part of the business for many years. In 1971, Films Inc. made two major hires: Seth Willenson from New Line Cinema, to head up the company's new college division, and Barbara Bryant from the Washington DC Public Library, who became the first national sales director for libraries. Bryant marketed her films with a separate public library-oriented catalog and newsletter, the *Kaleidoscope Review*, edited by Leo Dratfield, formerly president of Contemporary Films.[76]

In 1973, Films Inc., along with the National Film Board of Canada, created the John Grierson Award to be given each year at the American Film Festival, which was then 20 years old, and the major annual event of the Educational Film Library Association (EFLA). Grierson was the founding executive of the National Film Board of Canada and a close friend of VEC's Grant McLean, who eventually persuaded Grierson to join the Public Media, Inc. board of directors during the last three years of his life (1969–1972).

In the early '70's, Benton and Livengood flew to Los Angeles to meet with David Wolper and his lawyer, Erwin Russell, to renew Films Inc.'s non-theatrical distribution agreement. Wolper had sold his company to Metromedia in the 1960s and then went back into the television production business himself, making network TV specials in collaboration with the *American Heritage Magazine*, National Geographic, the Smithsonian Institution, and others. By the time Benton and Livengood arrived on his doorstep, he had completed approximately twenty network documentary and docudrama specials, for which Films Inc. was willing to make a $250,000 minimum guarantee. Wolper also casually mentioned that he was in the process of creating a new series on black history that might also be of interest, comprising thirteen hours of material based on a historical book by a man named Alex

Haley. When *Roots* finally aired on the ABC Network, Films Inc. sold over a million dollars worth of 16mm prints from leads acquired from its television showing.

In 1974, Films Inc./PMI acquired NBC Education Enterprises, which by then had, in turn, also acquired the distribution rights to TV Ontario in Canada. The NBC acquisition included their well-regarded *NBC White Paper* documentaries on major social issues. These included *If Japan Can, Why Can't We?* (prod. Claire Crawford Mason), about the "Japanese Industrial Miracle" based on the business philosophy of W. Edwards Deming. Later in the 1970s, after Mason left NBC, she approached Films Inc. with the idea of producing a whole library of films around the Deming philosophy, featuring Deming as host, which became the basis of a new unit within Films Inc./PMI, the *Business in Government* division.

In 1978, Charles Benton was selected by President Jimmy Carter to become the chairman of the National Commission of Libraries and Information Science (NCLIS). With Benton now spending more time in the capital, he and his Board decided to bring in Mort Broffman as the new president and CEO of PMI. Benton had originally met Broffman as a fellow Board member of the Exchange National Bank in Chicago, and initially Broffman brought the business and financial skills that were needed for the next stage of the company's development.

In 1980, Films Inc. Education launched the Television Licensing Center (TLC), headed by Ivan Bender, formerly with the U.S. Copyright Office, with the initial distribution of Carl Sagan's *Cosmos* series produced by PBS station KCET in Los Angeles. Off-air taping had been introduced technologically in the late 1970's, but there was no legal way for educators to use the material, hence the need for the licensing center. Distribution agreements were soon added for programs originated by WNET (New York), WGBH (Boston), and WETA (Washington, D.C.), all before the creation of PBS Video later in the 1980s.

In 1981, Films Inc./PMI acquired non-theatrical and television distribution rights to films made by the British Broadcasting Corporation (BBC). Competition for the non-theatrical agreement included Bill Deneen's Learning Corporation of America and the previous licensee, Bill Ambrose's Time-Life Non-theatrical Division.

With this new rights base of BBC programs (such as Kenneth Clark's *Civilisation*), Annenberg/CPB programs (like the BBC co-production *The Brain*), and PBS major station programs (WGBH's *Vietnam* series), PMI became a natural partner for the MacArthur Foundation, which was attempting to get high quality non-fiction program series into public libraries as an additional point of pubic access to them. The Foundation guaranteed a minimum purchase of at least 1000 copies per series in public libraries in return for a price reduction of up to 85 percent. This dramatically reduced the prices of video for public libraries, which were becoming institutional points of entry for the home video business, which in turn was eroding the traditional non-theatrical market.

In 1987, PMI went into the home video business with a line of arts programs, marketing the products under the Home Vision brand. With the growth of the home video business in the 1990s and into the next century, the 16mm film business was in decline, as was much of the non-theatrical education business. The Benton family decided to gradually move out of the traditional non-theatrical business and instead focused on building up Home Vision Entertainment under the leadership of their daughter, Adrianne Furniss, who became president and CEO of Home Vision in the late 1990s. With the advent of DVD, the focus of the company moved from high quality arts and documentary programs to classic international and independently produced feature films, building on a long non-theatrical distribution relationship they had with Janus Films and the Criterion Collection. While Charles

Benton kept the education business alive and well in collaboration with Britain's Channel 4 and the BBC, Adrianne Furniss built a successful home video business that was sold to Image Entertainment on August 1, 2005. She continued in the business with a multi-year consulting contract with Image. Charles Benton now remains active as chairman of Public Media Education, LLC, and also serves as chairman of the Benton Foundation in Washington, D.C. He was recently appointed to the Board of Directors of the National Film Preservation Foundation.[77]

Handel Film Corporation

Leo A. Handel's Los Angeles–based company produced approximately 150 titles, primarily in the subject areas of history, science, and art. Born in Vienna, Austria, on March 7, 1914, Handel was educated in France, Germany and England, and obtained degrees in economics and market research. He combined these disciplines to "create my own job" in Audience Research, was hired by David O. Selznick, and soon was the Director of Audience Research at MGM from 1942 to 1951, a stint broken up by two years in U.S. Military Intelligence in 1944–1945, the result of which was a Bronze Medal. He moved to Hollywood in 1950, and soon contacted the Atomic Energy Commission with an idea to produce a short film on the peaceful uses of atomic energy. This resulted in *Magic of the Atom*, a series of thirteen half-hour films for television. He founded the Handel Film Corporation in 1953. His first book, *Hollywood Looks at its Audience*, was published the same year.[78]

Handel's most intriguing films are found in his ten-part *Art in America* series (e.g., *Photography: Beginning of a New Art*, 1981, prod. Leo Handel). Like many other directors of academic films, Handel dabbled in making feature films. He produced, directed, and wrote two feature films, both released in 1961, *Phantom Planet* and *The Case of Patty Smith*. His 1963 book, *A Dog Named Duke: True Stories of German Shepherds at Work with the Law*, was a springboard to a later TV special, as well as a feature film called *Police Dog*, made in 1975.

Handel continued making 16mm academic films through 1990, and dissolved his company in 2004. He passed away on September 8, 2007. As of this writing, Handel's titles are no longer being distributed.

Leo Handel (Leo Handel).

Hoefler (Paul Hoefler Productions)

Paul Hoefler's classroom films on international themes can still be occasionally found in media libraries, although many were discarded in the 1970s, possibly for their perceived cultural biases. Born in Spokane, Washington, in 1893, cameraman Hoefler gained early notoriety when, as a member of the 1925–1926 Denver African Expedition, he returned with what was reportedly the first film footage of Southwest Africa's Kung Bushmen.

He produced the first non-fiction sound film of Africa (*Africa Speaks*, 1929), and his footage was used by the controversial expedition leader and lecturer C. Ernest Cadle in the 1930 film *Wild Men of the Kalahari* (*1930). (In this film, Cadle described the Kung Bushmen as "among the most treacherous creatures on earth," as he "baited them as we would an animal" to gather them for camera shots, and noted their eating habits: "He doesn't chew, but simply swallows like a dog.")[79] In 1936, Hoefler founded Paul L. Hoefler's World Picture Service, a photo library consisting of stills from his travels. After a World War II stint as the Middle East director of public relations for the U.S.

Willard Hahn, cameraman for Paul Hoefler Productions (Carol Hahn Horton).

Air Force, Hoefler moved to southern California, began producing films for the educational market (primarily on geographical subjects such as Monument Valley, Yellowstone Park, Jordan, and the Panama Canal), and became a friend of Walt Disney. Like Disney, many of Hoefler's films on international cultures suffered from the "edu-tainment" malaise which, with their omniscient narration and orchestral music, were more akin to TV travelogues than films with documented educational value. The Disney-Hoefler relationship eventually evolved into an agreement whereby Hoefler distributed Disney titles in South Africa in return for Disney's agreement to distribute Hoefler films in the U.S.

Unlike other educational film companies, Hoefler rarely provided release dates in the film credits, probably because doing so would have hurt sales of older titles to school districts, who would, unwittingly, order from the catalogue, believing them to be current. (By contrast, it was standard practice in other companies to revise films every few years to maintain their educational credibility, or retire outdated films for good.)

Hoefler's African films tended to ignore the excesses of South Africa's apartheid regime. His *South Africa* (2nd ed., 1954) mentions the good living conditions enjoyed by black miners (it's difficult to believe that Hoefler wasn't aware that black workers were housed in small concrete "bins," hundreds of miles away from their families).

Technically, Hoefler's films were often of exceptional visual quality, reflecting on the work of cinematographers such as Jackson Winter and Willard Hahn, but less care was given to the narration and music. In *Death Valley* (2nd edition, c. 1974), the narrator can clearly be heard shuffling his papers, while in *Mexican Village Life* (*1958, dir. Willard C. Hahn), the narrator occasionally forgets his Mexican accent. Leaving actual filming and directing largely to others in the two decades preceding his death in 1989, Hoefler remains an enigma, a producer of travelogues packaged as educational films, whose role as an apparent apologist for the apartheid philosophy has yet to be fully explored or understood.

Sometime after Hoefler's death, the author obtained two pallets of what presumably were the remaining films from Hoefler's private collection, purchased from an arms dealer.

Institut für Film und Bild (FWU)

Primarily due to the logistical issues surrounding the translation of scripts to English, relatively few educational films made in Germany were distributed to North American schools. The state-run *Institut für Film und Bild in Wissenschaft und Unterricht* (Institute for Film and Picture, in Science and Instruction, abbreviated to FWU), located in Grünwald, Germany, produced some of the most artistically successful of them. Begun in 1950, the *Institut* made films in subjects ranging from the sciences to the arts. FWU's first major inroads into distribution in the Americas resulted in an agreement between FWU's Walter Cappel, Charles Benton's Films Inc., and Grant McClain's Visual Education Centre in Toronto, which allowed the firms to acquire distribution rights in return for royalties, rather than FWU's usual policy of charging by footage, a system which distributors often found too expensive. In addition to Films Inc. and VEC, FWU films were distributed by companies such as EBF and the International Film Foundation.

FWU films included the imaginative work of cinematography genius Georg Schimanski, whose *Housefly* (1982, distributed by EBF) was a visually arresting insect film with extreme close-ups that wouldn't be out of place in a terror film. The *Institut* also distributed the exceptional work of ethnographic filmmaker Hermann Schlenker who produced fascinating and exhaustive studies of groups in Mali, Venezuela, Afghanistan, and Melanesia (distributed in the U.S. by the *International Film Foundation*). FWU continues to thrive as of this writing, specializing in mediated education, serving pan–European educational and cultural institutions through consulting as well as the distribution of its approximately 4,800 media and software titles.

International Film Bureau (IFB)

Specializing in the distribution of films made outside of the United States, IFB was founded in 1937 by Wesley Greene, a former professor at the University of Chicago. IFB titles typically concentrated on art, multiculturalism, and animation. Many of the more than 2,000 titles distributed by IFB represent exceptional filmmaking, including work made by Norman McLaren for the National Film Board of Canada, the *Guten Tag* series from Germany, and the Paul Klee–like mathematics films of Bruce and Katharine Cornwell.

Guten Tag consisted of two 26-film German-language instruction series produced by Bayerischen Rundfunk and the Goethe Institut, known as *Guten Tag* (1965) and *Guten Tag wie geht's* (1966). Entertaining, charming, funny, and occasionally thought-provoking, the films contained embedded socio-cultural messages that clashed with prejudices many North Americans harbored toward Germans. In *So ein Zufall* (*Guten Tag* #15, uncredited director), an African student is assisted in compiling her class schedule at a university by a friendly, white fellow student, and is integrated into a fun dormitory party occurring in spite of the continued re-appearance of a crazed trombone player, attempting to foil any sense of order. This zaniness is in keeping with much of this 1965 series, several episodes of which featured introductory sequences taking place in unlikely-sized constructivist set of oversized alarm clocks and other everyday objects.

The *Guten Tag wie geht's* series, filmed a year later, differs from the earlier series in several respects: the story lines are more complex, the series is filmed in color, and credits are always given to film personnel. *Kennen Sie meinen Sohn?* (dir. Rudiger Graf) is a significant film in view of its treatment of cross-generational relationships. In it, music professor Hoffman, upon hearing his son now has long hair and a beard, searches for the residence of his son, who has just obtained an apartment near to the college at which he's enrolled. Hoffman quickly finds himself immersed in Munich counterculture, and engages in drinking and revelry at a psychedelic "hippie bar." The staid-looking professor eventually finds himself with a five o'clock shadow and a new group of friends, then reaffirms that outward appearances have little to do with the person inside. He finds his newly-shaved and barbered son, now shocked at his father's appearance. Bearing in mind that the episode was filmed in 1966, no educational film made in North America up to that time, to my knowledge, had ever embraced these inter-generational commonalties existing in spite of external appearances; nor did they realistically address the beneficial social aspects of the drinking of alcoholic beverages, which generations of Europeans have successfully integrated into family meals and get-togethers.

Clearly, in both *Guten Tag* series, the Goethe Institut had a social agenda that went far beyond creating a simple series of language-instruction films. They are especially worthy of further study. On one hand, they are a successor to the successful propaganda films of pre–World War II Germany; on the other hand, with their recurrent themes of humor and racial and generational co-existence, they strive to portray Germany as a country seeking to redefine itself, internally and externally, as one radically different from that which the executive producers knew North American students would most often otherwise be exposed to in classroom films.

IFB was closed by Wesley Greene's son Roger in 1998.

International Film Foundation (IFF), post–1960

The beginnings of this non-profit foundation, begun by Julien Bryan in 1945, were discussed in Chapter 1. Entering into the 1960s, in an effort to free ethnic subject educational films from being perceived as travelogues, Bryan would begin to move away from narration to a large degree, feeling that extraneous influences — narrators, study guides and ambient light in the classroom included — took away an important part of the magic of the film experience itself, thereby negatively affecting the learning experience. In addition to fine in-house productions (*Amazon Family*, 1961, dir. Francis Thompson, profiling a *serengueiro* rubber gatherer in the Beni River region of Bolivia), one of the most positive outcomes of this philosophy was his decision to distribute the work of German filmmaker Hermann Schlenker. Creator of fascinating glimpses of daily activities in non-urban settings, Schlenker's work included the eleven-part *African Village* series from Mali, including *Building a House: Bozo People* (1967), the five-part *Pacific Island Life* series filmed in Melanesia, eight films of the Makiritare Indians of the Orinoco River, and fourteen shorts made in Badakhstan, Afghanistan. In 1969, fresh from a two-year stint in the Peace Corps, Julien's son Sam Bryan joined IFF and made his first film, *Ancient Africans* (1970), which, in addition to the younger Bryan's fine camera work, featured Philip Stapp's animation and Athmani Magoma's mellifluous narration.

IFF placed a higher value on quality animation than most educational film companies, and artists Philip Stapp and Gerald McDermott were among the finest animators to specialize in the educational genre. Julien Bryan passed away on October 20, 1974. Since that time, the foundation has been operated by Sam Bryan, who teaches film history at the Pratt Institute and continues to sell non–16mm versions of selected IFF titles.

Journal Films

See AGI/Journal Films.

Learning Corporation of America (LCA)

For several reasons, the Learning Corporation of America can be characterized as the quintessential educational film company of the 1970s. Insightful, tender, hard-hitting, and occasionally kooky, the social films produced and distributed by this division of Columbia Pictures in the late 1960s to the mid–1980s served as a bellwether indicative of the massive social changes occurring in the United States, introduced to schools via film libraries funded by public laws such as the Elementary and Secondary Educational Act (ESEA) of 1965. By virtue of its thematic material, the diversity of its staff personnel, and its Madison Avenue–like corporate identity and design orientation, LCA embraced new social and marketing ideas as no educational film company had before.

In 1968, in order to capitalize on the tremendous amount of money being fed by the federal government to educational film production companies, Columbia Pictures hired former EBF filmmaker-executive William F. Deneen to be president of its brand-new educational film division.[80] Deneen immediately brought in screenwriter/producer Linda Gottlieb as senior VP. Deneen and Gottlieb had a working relationship that began fifteen years prior to the founding of LCA, when Deneen hired the young Wellesley grad to work for Deneen Productions.

Included in Learning Corporation of America's high-powered management picture, fresh from McGraw-Hill films, was

LCA's Bill Deneen during his filmmaking days at EB (Bill Deneen).

VP of Marketing Dave Davidson, who fashioned a polished corporate image, visibly displayed on the shiny indigo film can embossed with the LCA logo.[81] Robert McDonald, former partner of designer Perry Ellis, and later president of the clothing firm, became head of Production. A critical part of the team was dynamic advertising and promotion director Elaine Mason, who, for her first LCA catalogue in 1971, produced a handsome hardbound book that set the standard for educational film collateral materials. Mason's second and last hardbound catalogue was published in 1975, a 168-page *tour de force* that detailed not only each of its approximately 250 films, but featured "behind-the-scenes" production photos of many of them. From the combined perspectives of design, presentation, and information, Mason's catalogue has never been equaled in the classroom academic film world. It occasionally was issued Dewey decimal numbers by librarians who treated it more as a book than a marketing tool, and now serves as an important reference point, chronicling much of the important contribution to the academic film world by LCA.

At Learning Corporation of America, Deneen and Gottlieb determined that bigger production budgets could be justified because of the additional revenue accrued by providing LCA films to major television networks in addition to classrooms. The marriage of two strong-minded talents such as Deneen and Gottlieb required a division of duties. One of Deneen's talents lay in managing upward through the Columbia Pictures corporate labyrinth. Columbia execs encouraged Deneen to utilize their assets, including their extensive film library. Deneen created, in the process, successes such as the *Searching for Values* series, an elegantly edited group of non-hosted educational films compiled from some of the feature films in Columbia's catalogue (e.g., *Spaces Between People*, 1972, from *To Sir With Love*, 1967, dir. James Clavell).[82] Linda Gottlieb's emphasis on educational films with social themes was highlighted in her *Learning to be Human* series, producing exceptional work by filmmakers such as Bert Salzman, who won an Oscar for his *Angel and Big Joe* in 1975.

LCA embraced the growing cultural diversity of the United States as did no other company. Its dramatic films featured Americans from a plethora of ethnic backgrounds. Typical LCA subject matter included inter and intra-familial conflict among immigrants (*Siu Mei Wong—Who Shall I Be?*, 1976, dir. Michael Ahnemann), and cultural conflict between people of different ethnicities (*Overture: Linh from Viet Nam*, 1980, dir. Seth Pinsker).

Action in LCA films often occurred in venues not traditionally addressed by other educational film companies, such as an inner-city housing project, where the quality of life was portrayed as supportive to children, and single-parent families were seen not as inherently dysfunctional, but rather as the norm (*Case of the Elevator Duck*, 1974, dir. Joan Micklin Silver).

The dynamic personalities involved in the day-to-day operations of LCA created an atmosphere of competition, and occasional misunderstandings. Filmmaker Bert Salzman remembers the day Bill Deneen questioned whether he had been partaking of controlled substances:

> I think that the reason Bill D. thought I had been smoking pot was that he a had several real nasty run ins with several LCA filmmakers including an almost-fist fight with Peter Watkins who then went down to the executive offices of Columbia Pictures (LCA's parent company) and had a shouting match with several executives.... So here comes Salzman rushing into his office (I was late for a doctor's appt.) and he must have been expecting another row (we had a recent argument over the editing of *Geronimo Jones*). But being who I am (I get over arguments very quickly), I just wanted to thank Bill for making it possible for me to have the opportunity to

make quality films, etc, etc. So I reached across his desk took his hand and shook it vigorously which must have shocked him as he was probably expecting a fist in the face a la Peter Watkins. A strange puzzled smile appeared on his face as I shook his hand and said, "Thanks Bill for making all of this possible ... we've had our differences but they were honest differences, and I've always respected you," etc. Then I quickly dashed out of the door in order not to be too late for my appointment. The next day I was approached by Irwin Rochman, a lawyer and business affairs mgr. for LCA. He asked me if I had been smoking "pot" on the previous day when I'd met with Bill because after I had left, Bill had gone into Irwin's office and asked him whether he had noticed that Bert Salzman had been acting very strange ... etc. I told Irwin that I had not been smoking pot and asked him why he had asked. He told me about Bill's remark, and then said that "for some people being civil (in the film business) is so rare that it is thought to be "strange...."[83]

One of the more outstanding talents at LCA was former school teacher John Matoian, who wrote exceptional study guides to be used by teachers wishing to involve students in post-film discussions.[84] These took the form of either circular sheets of paper glued to the underside of the lid to the film can, or two-sided, 8½ × 11 sheets, loose in the can to facilitate photocopying. Matoian was originally hired as a result of a recommendation by LCA salesperson Lee Owens, who identified his progressive use of films in the classroom. In his new capacity, Matoian's school-tested suggestions for classroom discussion and exercises were thought-provoking, challenging, and could have immediate impact beyond the classroom. In the study guide for *The Seven Wishes of a Rich Kid* (1979, dir. Larry Elikann), for example, two of the suggested exercises are as follows:

> We are introduced to the word "plagiarism." What does that word mean? Answering honestly (and *anonymously*), write about a time that you were guilty of plagiarizing or cheating. How did you feel? Was the risk worth taking? Did you learn from your experience? If you have never plagiarized or cheated, what has prevented you?
>
> Calvin wishes that he could really talk to his father about feelings. How often do you talk to your parents about your inner feelings? Try a two-week experiment: for the first week, *time* your conversations with your parents and *analyze* the topic of conversation. Are you talking with them about feelings or "things"? The second week, initiate conversations with your parents about feelings or opinions. See if you can increase the amount of time you spend talking with them about their feelings and yours.

Hundreds of films were produced or distributed by LCA during its relatively short existence, including some of the most compelling in the genre. The production quality that gave the right "look" to LCA films, however, also resulted in films that could be perceived as "not educational" in the traditional sense (*Electric Grandmother*, 1982, dir. Noel Black). Occasionally, they plunged into unlikely sitcom-like situations (a young boy paints his uncle's black truck with a can of white spray paint in order to win his affection in Richard Marquand's *Big Henry and the Polka Dot Kid*, 1977).

In the early 1980s, as educational film funding began slowly to erode, and as Columbia itself began to face financial difficulties, the firm decided to divest itself of LCA, among other properties. The division was sold to W.F. Hall Printing in Chicago. Shortly thereafter, Hall itself was bought by Mobil Oil, and LCA became a direct subsidiary of the petroleum giant. Soon after the Mobil acquisition, Deneen founded Highgate Pictures to produce films for both television and feature film markets. Highgate soon became commercially successful producing a long stream of TV movies, mini-series, and features. In 1984 Deneen purchased the companies from Mobil in a difficult leveraged buy-out. The LCA/Highgate merger comprised a library of more than five hundred films produced over a period of nearly twenty years.

The numerous changes and resulting tension at LCA eventually eroded the working relationship between Deneen and Gottlieb. Deneen eventually fired Gottlieb, and in the aftermath of this split, Gottlieb published her book *When Smart People Fail,* which carried the message that not only were defeats survivable, but were necessary for continued personal growth.[85] She would eventually move on to become the executive producer of the daytime television series *One Life to Live,* and the feature film *Dirty Dancing* (1987).

In 1987 Bill Deneen sold the Highgate and LCA properties to New World Pictures and, in his own words, "has been sorry ever since." Deneen continues to be among the most interesting and quotable of the many people involved in 16mm classroom film, as witnessed by his response to a request for his filmography: "Here's a list of films on which I'm reasonably sure of what my role was. On so many others I was often writer or director or cameraman or script doctor, or peace keeper or diaper changer etc."

Many of the actors and directors who participated in LCA films were successful in the more commercially viable world of 35mm film, among them directors Carol Micklin Silver, Peter Medak, John Irvin, and Richard Marquand. Just a few of the many well-known actors that appeared in LCA films include Michael Douglas, Anthony Hopkins, Nicolas Pennell, Paul Sorvino, Christian Slater, James Woods, and Butterfly McQueen. As of this writing, LCA's distribution rights have become somewhat diffused. Many of LCA's approximately 570 titles are owned by *20th Century–Fox.* Others are owned by various other distributors. Today, many LCA titles are distributed to the education market by Phoenix Learning Corporation.

McGraw-Hill Films

Fresh from a stint making training films for the military in World War II, Albert Rosenberg founded the film division of McGraw-Hill in 1946, acquiring and distributing films made by other producers on a variety of subjects.[86] Among the more significant titles distributed by McGraw in the 1960–1985 era was Peter Whitehead's riotous poetry documentary *Wholly Communion* (1965). McGraw films commonly found in educational libraries included the Centron-produced *Middle America, Modern Europe,* and *Our Latin American Neighbors* series, David Wolper's *Biography* series, television network news productions such as Fred W. Friendly's *CBS Reports,* and selected European animation films.

In his eight-film *United States Geography* series, produced for McGraw-Hill, director Jon Wilkman revolutionized geographical educational films by telling the tale of the land through the stories of its people, in their own words. Wilkman's human subjects are not always articulate; they embody the real, unpretentious, unrehearsed elements that determine the character of the eight regions the make up the series. In *The Middle Atlantic Region* (1976), for example, a black truck driver tells how racism affects his business, and a satisfied white ad exec who wants her children growing up in New York City is juxtaposed with a struggling single black mother who wants the opposite. In a nasty Philadelphia dump, a supervisor suggests the best alternative to dwindling landfill is to fill northern Pennsylvania strip mines with urban trash, a solution he's confident will work for 40 years. Wilkman's geographical films are among the most powerful ever produced in that sub-genre. Their themes are compelling and timeless.

In 1963, McGraw acquired St. Louis–based Webster Publishing, and brought along its co-founder, Heinz Gelles, who in 1969 would take over McGraw-Hill's film operations as General Manager.[87] In 1971, Gelles moved to Singapore to head the company's Far East operations, leaving film management duties to David Engler, who stayed until 1973. In 1972, McGraw-Hill acquired Leo Dratfield's Contemporary Films, and acquired CRM films from Ziff-Davis in 1975. In 1978, McGraw-Hill transferred its film division to its CRM Films team on the West coast. In 1987, McGraw sold its film holdings to a group consisting of filmmaker Peter Jordan, whose tenure at CRM had begun in 1971 as a production assistant, Stephanie Glidden, and Bechtel Investments. Glidden and Bechtel left the partnership in 1994. The company, now called CRM Learning, remains in the business, focusing on interpersonal skills training media, led by Peter Jordan.

Media Guild

This southern Californian company, launched in early 1975 by Preston Holdner (formerly of McGraw-Hill and CRM), specialized in distributing historical films, many licensed from the U.K.-based *Thames* television organization. Among the more notable Thames films was Richard Callanan's *Chinese Word for Horse* (1986), a fine 14-minute study in calligraphy, adapted from a Thames half-hour television program, featuring an engaging musical soundtrack by British jazz-rock group Colosseum's Jon Hiseman. Eventually, Media Guild's catalogue would encompass more than 200 educational film titles. In 2001, Holdner sold Media Guild to *AIMS Media*.

Mokin Films (Arthur Mokin)

Founding his company in 1966, Arthur Mokin made twelve educational films prior to his retirement in 1985, at which time he sold his company to his son Bill. His best known film, one found in many educational film school libraries, was *Ruth Stout's Garden* (1976, prod. Arthur Mokin), which consisted of a visit with an octogenarian iconoclast who had achieved a degree of fame as a gardener and also a bonne-vivante, storyteller, and authentic American character. The idea for the film, a memorable portrayal of an older person as a lively, contributing member of society, had come from Mokin's wife, who had read a article about Stout in the *New York Times*. Also a filmmaker, Bill Mokin made a groundbreaking film about gender stereotypes, *Happy to be Me*, in 1978. The firm closed its doors in the early 1990s.

Moody Institute of Science

While public school media libraries in general tended to exercise caution when including overtly religious thematic material, many libraries commonly included titles sponsored by the Moody Institute of Science (MIS), a division of Chicago's Moody Bible Institute. MIS was founded in 1945 by California pastor Irwin A. Moon, who promulgated a philosophy of "Sermons for Science."[88]

"Science" was mixed with religion in every MIS film, every one of which had a religious reference, such as, "Here we see a community life of order and harmony. Such artfulness is evidence of God's thoughtful planning and his continual care" (*Bird Community*, 1955). Continual references to "The Master Designer" and "The Creator" are voiced in the films' narrative scripts. MIS films never contained director or cinematographer credits — a shame, because MIS films could be quite compelling, from an affective perspective. *Spider Engineers* (1956) has wonderful close-up shots of a trapdoor spider weaving silk from spinnerets to form edge of its trap door. *Electric Eel* (*1955) features five people holding hands while a smiling professor in a lab coat hooks them up to an eel, who smites them mightily with a jolt, indicating that the eel's "survival mechanism provides new insights into the relationship of science and the word of God."

A natural showman and evangelist, Moon narrated many of the films, also appeared as occasional host, and loved to tell corny science jokes (*Demonstrations with Light*, 1956) and do stunts, such as riding a motorcycle with eyeglasses that made the visual world appear to be upside down (*Sense Perception*, 1960).

Due to their overtly religious orientation, MIS films are best described as religious films that orient certain scientific principles toward religious dogma, rather than pure science films. As early as 1966, the American Civil Liberties Union was complaining about the use of Moody films in Spokane's public school system.[89] Writing on the outside of a can of a Moody film now housed in the AFA film library, one California Academy of Sciences instructor summed the issue up succinctly: "Too many references to God."

The Moody Bible Institute still exists today, apparently intending for its MIS films to be around as long as Methuselah. It continues to sell films on its website, where "You'll find a collection of biblically based, family oriented videos that help build values and faith in your child, with scientific principles that answer those difficult questions children have about the world around them."

National Film Board of Canada, Post-1960

By the beginning of the decade of the 1960s, the National Film Board of Canada (NFBC) had acquired an international reputation for documentary films, many of which were used as classroom academic films all over North America and the English-speaking world. Its prime objective of chronicling the Canadian experience resonated globally, as the themes of community, culture, and society were viewed as thematically universal.

Canadian schoolchildren had access to virtually every title made by the Film Board, through school distribution, libraries, or film circuits. In the United States, distribution was done through educational film companies under license, which included notable firms such as AIMS, Barr, Centron, Contemporary, EBF, International Film Bureau, Films, Inc., Learning Corporation of America, McGraw-Hill, Mokin, Pyramid, and Wombat.

While Stateside students didn't have the benefit of seeing the vast majority of NFBC titles, a number of popular films were distributed in the U.S., and thus, its charter of interpreting Canada to Canadians and non–Canadians alike was, to a certain degree, fulfilled. Given that U.S. History classes routinely ignore any element of Canadian history that occurred after the Revolutionary War, seeing a film with the NFBC logo printed boldly across the screen might have been the only indicator to U.S.-based students that there was a thriving culture going on up there somewhere between Detroit and Juneau.

NFBC films that were critical of the United States were typically seen in Canadian classrooms only. Tina Viljoen's *The Space Between* (1986), a cynical look at the U.S. government's use of Canada as a nuclear buffer zone, hosted by the glib and acerbic Gwynne Dyer, is an example of a film that probably was never shown in a U.S. classroom. A common complaint among Canadians is that people in the U.S. often think of Canada as a "51st state," and are ignorant of Canadian customs and culture. Exposure to films such as this would have given U.S. students the opportunity of understanding some of the differences in political perspectives between the U.S. and her neighbor to the north.

The innovations created by NFBC's Unit B were discussed in the earlier chapter on pre–1960 educational film. Executive Producer Nicholas Balla's Unit C was also responsible for films that gained justifiable recognition, including two by Donald Wilder, *Rallye des Neiges* (1961), and *Nahanni* (1962, edited by George Kaczender). In the former, lightweight Volvos and VW bugs brave the terrific winters of Québec in a zany sports car road rally, accompanied by a terrific post-bop jazz score by Norman Bigras. This film represented a vast departure from the muscle car films produced by General Motors that were most often shown in North American driver's education classes. *Nahanni* introduces crusty septuagenarian gold prospector Albert Faille, who painstakingly motors and portages his way up the mighty MacKenzie River, only to see his dreams dashed yet again when the river runs too dry. He vows to return the following year with the invective, "I'll be dead or drowned before I quit." The explosive teen-and-childhood angst films of Hungarian ex-pat George Kaczender were, from both dramatic and psychological perspectives, among the most progressive of their type ever made, with abstract camera angles underscoring the alienation of the subjects. His films included *Phoebe* (1964), the first half-hour short drama ever made at the Film Board, which soon became its all-time second best selling film, exceeded only by Roman Kroitor and Colin Low's *Universe* (1959).[90]

From an international perspective, possibly the most controversial film produced by Unit C was Donald Brittain's finely-crafted *Bethune* (1964), the biography of Dr. Norman Bethune, legendary Canadian doctor, inventor of the blood bank, and physician to Mao Zedong's revolutionary army. For ten years following its release, this extraordinary film was seen by North American schoolchildren solely in Canada. Distribution of NFBC films to schools within the United States had always been a bit problematic. Up until 1969, distribution was formally handled by Canada's Department of External Affairs, which evidenced something of a protectionist philosophy to determine exactly which elements of "Canada" would be seen south of the border. This reticence to offend U.S. political interests was often clumsy and unnecessary, most notably in the case of *Bethune*, proscribed from distribution in the U.S. by the Canadian Foreign Office, who feared that Bethune's Communist sympathies would cause irreparable harm to U.S.-Canada relations during the Viet Nam era.[91]

With the coming of the early years of the 1960 decade, it was apparent that the successful "system" developed at NFBC during the 1950s was, from an upper management perspective, beginning to lose is luster. Judging the Unit system to be a detriment to the *esprit de corps* of the Film Board in general, all discrete production groups, including Unit B, were disbanded by director of English Production Grant

NFBC's Donald Brittain, director of *Bethune* (1964) (Lois Siegel).

McLean in early 1964, a crushing blow to executive producer Tom Daly. Under the new "pool" system, however, filmmakers could now collaborate freely without being tied to a particular executive producer, which allowed Daly's time to be available to more filmmakers than ever before. His old "B" team left for different and occasionally more lucrative fields. Roman Kroitor soon joined private industry to promote the IMAX technology that the Film Board had pioneered with the film *Labyrinth* (1967, dir. Roman Kroitor, Colin Low, Hugh O'Connor) at Expo 67 in Montréal. Robert Verrall and Wolf Koenig returned to animation, and Colin Low became a strong participant in Executive Producer George Stoney's new *Challenge for Change* series of social films.

NFBC's Roman Kroitor, co-director of *Universe* (1959) (Lois Siegel).

Compared with the films made during the "Unit" era, little of the output of the "pool" films made between 1965 and 1971 has the timeless quality of the earlier films. By 1971, the new system was judged to have been a failure due to lack of managerial control, and the new "Studio" system was developed to replace it.

In discussing the contribution of the NFBC to the classroom academic film, it should not be overlooked that, with the possible exception of sponsored films made for various branches of the Canadian government, educational film projects were avoided as much as possible by NFBC filmmakers who preferred the more professionally-rewarding work in feature and documentary films. One director who clearly enjoyed educational fare was Don Winkler, whose *In Praise of Hands* (1974) showcased the work of folk artisans the world over and whose films on Canadian writers (e.g., *Earle Birney: Portrait of a Poet*, 1981) are timeless as documents of the Canadian literary world and fascinating portraits of iconoclastic individuals.

The 1979 Canadian elections brought Joe Clark's Conservatives into power, who saw the Film Board encroaching on private filmmaking companies by taking the lion's share of Canada's sponsored film business. Such films, they felt, should instead be made by private Canadian film concerns, a position that had been aggressively lobbied for years by Budge Crawley of Crawley Films.

Regardless of which way the political winds were blowing, the Film Board always managed to produce its share of controversy. Paul Cowan's *Democracy on Trial: The Morgentaler Affair* (1984) was a riveting docudrama, featuring the well-known physician and abortion provider, who philosophized that abortion was more about preventing unwanted children than terminating pregnancy.

In terms of overall impact on classrooms in the post–1960 quarter century, the NFBC made scores of well-made, compelling films distributed to English-speaking classrooms around the world, in spite of the occasional "censorship through non-distribution" issues. Among the most memorable was *Cooperage* (1975, dir. Phillip Borsos), which functioned equally well as an industrial, historical, and cultural film, introducing the viewer to the intricate craft of wooden-staved barrel-making at Sweeney's Cooperage in British Columbia.[92] Some of the NFBC's strongest work consisted of portraits of archetypal Canadians. *Whistling Smith* (1975, dir. Michael Scott/Marrin Cannell) is a cinéma-vérité tour with Sgt. Bernie Smith of the Vancouver PD, focusing on the hookers and addicts on his beat, whose idea of street policing consisted of the admonition to "move along now" as his strongest weapon. *Canaries to Clydesdales* (1977, dir. Eugene Boyko) functions as a vocational film, a Western film, a business film, and a "buddy" film, a "day-in-the-life" visit with country veterinarians Vic Demetrick and Reg Maidment as they make their appointed rounds. Students found they needed a strong stomach for this one: castrating a sheep, sawing out a still-born calf, removing porcupine quills from a dog's muzzle, and sticking an arm up a cow's posterior were all in a day's work for these two, and the playful personal interaction between these old friends at work makes this film one of the most endearing, fascinating, and compelling films ever made by the Film Board.

The Film Board more than occasionally sent crews overseas. Taking a one-day break from filming a ceremony in England involving Queen Elizabeth, director Tony Ianzelo's team was sent out to the country to interview Harold Bate, an eccentric inventor of chicken manure-powered automobiles, as documented in the unforgettable *Bate's Car* (1974), a film remembered long after the royal event for which they were originally sent was forgotten.

CIDA (the Canadian International Development Administration) sponsored several exceptional films documenting the Canadian government's efforts to assist developing nations. Two of them were unforgettable. *Not Far from Bolgatanga* (1982 dir. Barrie Howells and Michael Rubbo) described the Canadian government's role in placing of 2500 water wells in Ghana's unforgiving landscape. *Mozambique: Building a Future* (1987, dir. Charles Konowal) addressed the crisis begun with the departure of the Portuguese colonial structure, resulting in the loss of every dentist in the country. To remedy the situation, a new young group of native students, trained by the Canadian government in dentistry, served their internships in Inuit villages, then returned to Africa accompanied by portable field dental kits. In terms of affective value alone, such films were outstanding examples of public service on a global front, offering career alternatives to students beyond many of the extrinsically rewarding occupations often suggested by school counselors.

NFBC's animation unit, led by Norman McLaren, created titles that greatly enhanced its reputation worldwide. Varied animation techniques were utilized, as in Caroline Leaf's oil-on-glass adaptation of Mordechai Richler's *The Street* (1976), and McLaren's own *Pas de Deux* (1967), a dance duet amplified by multiple images created by the optical printer, with each movement exfoliating in successive strobe-like iterations.

Two important series of films appropriate to classrooms were produced by Wolf Koenig. The nine-episode *Discussions of Bioethics* (e.g., *Happy Birthday*, 1985, dir. Jefferson Lewis) was made for college-age students about to enter the medical profession, and suggested difficult issue surrounding life and death. *Wednesday's Children* (e.g., *Jenny*, 1987, dir. Patricia Phillips) was a series of six films portraying the pressures encountered by teenagers at the brink of crisis. Each film in these two series consisted of a short drama with no clear resolution, approximately 15 minutes in length to allow for a significant amount of time for classroom discussion following the showing of the film.

The year 1984 found technology impacting the NFBC to the greatest degree since the advent of hand-held cameras and synch sound in the late 1950s. For the first time, video sales were greater than those of 16mm film. By the last year of the decade of the 1980s, 15,744 videos were sold, as opposed to 1,302 films, at a lower cost point of $79 versus $400 for a typical one-hour title.[93] The trend would thus be set for the eventual fire sale of all 16mm titles from Film Board distribution centers, which were completely devoid of 16mm film by the mid–1990s. Eventually, political infighting, combined with the shifting of governmental funding over to the television-based Canadian Broadcasting Corporation, led to the perceived demise of the NFBC as Canada's national premier media source.

The contribution of the National Film Board of Canada to the North American classroom academic film cannot be overestimated. Many of their exceptional academic films were not distributed in the U.S., and remain to be discovered by Stateside scholars and media historians.

National Geographic

National Geographic (NGEO) films included titles made especially for classrooms, and network specials reformatted for classroom distribution. The National Geographic Society's classroom film division was formed in 1963 under VP Bob Breeden, who also headed up the company's books and filmstrips divisions. Dennis Kane was brought in as director of Television and Educational Films, and independent film editor Sid Platt was hired as executive producer.[94] After the formation of an original team of 15 people, the NGEO staff was pared down to a working team of associate director, production manager, editor, writer, researcher, and secretary. All productions were now outsourced to independent filmmakers and production companies.

To ascertain which curriculum areas most needed to be addressed by film, Kane and Platt sent out a number of questionnaires to teachers and film librarians. The answers resulted in the production of an estimated 15 to 25 academic titles per year. Up to 500 units of each title were printed, with the best sellers being *Man: the Incredible Machine* (1975) and *Exploring Our Solar System* (1990), each of which sold in excess of 1000 units.[95]

Early NGEO films do not include production credits within film titles, a decision reportedly made by Dennis Kane and later reversed by Platt. Although some production personnel of the Kane era were credited in in-can study guides, the guides were often misplaced, making it challenging for today's historian to cobble together filmographies of those early-era NGEO films.

In terms of cognitive and affective academic value, NGEO's earlier classroom-distributed films are decidedly mixed, but improved over time. *Spain: A Journey with Washington Irving* (1973, uncredited director), for example, consisted of file footage accompanied by a narrator who badly flubbed common *Castellano* words and place names, which detracts from its cognitive value. By contrast later titles such as Klaus Unzu's *East Germany* (1987), from NGEO's *Nations of the World* series, and Sidney Platt's *1917: Revolution in Russia* (1988), provide a more satisfactory experience in both the cognitive and affective domains of learning.

A high point in NGEO's film output was its acquisition for distribution of ten films produced by Gerald Thompson of Oxford Films in the U.K. Thompson was an exceptional and innovative close-up cinematographer who specialized in insect and biological subjects, and NGEO sold his films as the *Bio-Science* series. Thompson's *Plankton* (1974), like his other films, features exacting renditions of microscopic subjects, providing superior affective value to viewers.

Many people today remember National Geographic more for their television specials than for their 16mm classroom films. Beginning in 1965, and produced at the rate of four per year, NGEO created television specials on subjects such as anthropology, natural history, exploration, and sociology, aired successively by the CBS, ABC, and PBS networks. Hoping to add to their educational catalogue of independently-produced films, NGEO edited these specials and distributed them for classroom use.

Initially produced by David Wolper's production team, these specials eventually included programs developed by other independent producers. Two of the more compelling of them were *Americans on Everest* (1965, prod. Norman Dyhrenfurth), featuring the first motion picture footage taken from the summit, and *The Great Mojave Desert* (1971, dir. Nicholas Clapp), which followed naturalist Colin Fletcher on foot through Death Valley. The latter film included a fascinating visit to dancer Marta Beckett and her Amargosa Opera House in Death Valley Junction. While effective in their original one-hour formats, the half-hour versions edited for the classroom suffered in terms of content and continuity. In either length, the specials never sold as well as NGEO films made specifically for classrooms, which Sid Platt attributes to their non-synchronization with curriculum. By the 1990s, owing to poor sales figures, National Geographic had stopped selling its classroom films.

Perspective Films

The Perspective Films division of Coronet Films was founded in 1979 by Sheldon Sachs, recently transferred from parent *Esquire Magazine's Scott Catalogue* postage stamp division. Sachs, who served in dual roles as VP of the Education Group for *Coronet* and President of *Perspective*, operated with the charter to find and distribute films made by non–Coronet producers. Perspective rapidly achieved a level of artistic success that put it on a par with any educational film company of its era, with films such as Sparky Greene's *American Shoeshine* (1976) and Carl Jones' *Floating Logging Camp* (1979). In addition to individual films, Sachs obtained exceptional series such as Canadian Paul Saltzman's ethnographic *Spread Your Wings* (which Sachs renamed *World Cultures and Youth*) and Robert Geller's exceptional 17-part *American Short Story*, which featured well-known actors such as James Whitmore, Tommy Lee Jones, and Cleavon Little. An Esquire employee since 1957, Sachs left *Perspective* and *Coronet* when the firm was purchased by Gulf+Western in 1984. Distribution rights to Perspective titles were acquired, along with the entire *Coronet* catalogue, by the Phoenix Learning Group in May 1997.

Phoenix Films

Phoenix Films was founded in 1973 by Heinz Gelles, formerly of McGraw-Hill Text Films, and Barbara Bryant, an ex-librarian who most recently had been at Charles Benton's Films Inc., in charge of marketing its films to libraries. Gelles' story is a fascinating one, important in the context of the films he and Bryant would choose to distribute and eventually produce.[96] Originally from Vienna, Austria, Gelles' immediate family was killed in the Holocaust. An orphaned youth, Gelles was able, through the cooperation of a family friend, to relocate to St. Louis, Missouri, where he began selling newspapers on street corners. His English was dramatically improved when he became first a popcorn seller then an usher at a local cinema, immersing himself in the nuances of a new language through what he heard and saw on the screen. With a burning desire to help to defeat those responsible for the demise of his family and friends, he entered "my war" by joining the Marines, landing at Iwo Jima. After the war, he leveraged the GI Bill to get an education at Yale, where he received a BA in economics and international relations. In 1955, he co-founded educational publishing company Gelles-Widmer, specializing in flash cards, which soon merged with the St. Louis–based Webster Publishing. In 1963, Webster was acquired by McGraw-Hill, where Gelles became a VP, eventually running the firm's film and far–Eastern publishing business, prior to leaving to start *Phoenix* along with Bryant.[97]

Gelles (at *McGraw*) and Bryant (at *Films Inc.*) had been competing against each other since 1969, and hatched the idea for the new company when they met at an educational film festival. Originally, Phoenix was intended to be solely a distributor of films to libraries and museums, due to the fact that libraries ordered often and consistently, whereas schools would generally place only one bulk order per year.

Initially eschewing in-house production, Bryant, who had grown up on the writings of Langston Hughes, soon found a property that she determined would present a strong story, and serve as well to introduce to students the under-represented school of Black writers: Andrew Sugarman's treatment of Hughes' *Thank You Ma'am* (1975). The success of the film encouraged Bryant to continue to produce films that addressed controversial social issues, proudly stating that "there's something to offend someone" in many of them. Bryant cites Shelby Leverington's *The Detour* (1977), in which a dying woman indicates desire for sexual gratification when harassed by a sanctimonious hospital chaplain, and *William's Doll* (1981, dir. Roberto Carlo Chiesa), illustrating that both boys and girls may enjoy playing with toys generally associated with the opposite gender, as films that challenged students, parents, teachers, and administrators to question the basis and value of popularly held social beliefs.[98]

In 1981, Phoenix bought the approximately 1500-title catalogue of Bailey/Film Associates (BFA) from CBS, and hired George Holland to run BFA from California. Phoenix acquired the Coronet Films catalogue in May 1997. Phoenix also obtained distribution rights to the 20th Century–Fox-owned Learning Corporation of America films. Today, renamed the Phoenix Learning Group, the firm continues to produce and distribute classroom films.

Pyramid Films

Pyramid was founded in 1959 as Adams Productions by the husband and wife team of David and Lynn Adams. The company name was changed to Pyramid Films in 1962. Born in Toronto, David Telfer Adams had served a stint with the Royal Canadian Air Force in World War II prior to graduating from art school in Vancouver. He became a high school teacher in North Battleford, Saskatchewan, where he met Lynn, a student.[99]

The Adams' first film, *That They May Live* (1959), was made in Canada, the first in their series of successful medical films. The film's post-production was done in southern California, and they soon moved there to be closer to their customers. In addition to the medical portion of the catalogue, Pyramid became noted for its visually compelling films, many of which were filmed outdoors in challenging environments (e.g., *Sky Dive!* 1979, dir. Carl Boenish, and *Dawn Flight*, 1978, dir. Lawrence Landsburgh). Pyramid also distributed graphically interesting art subjects, including animator-director Ken Rudolph's *Gallery* (1971), a wild 7 minute film consisting of over 2,000 rapid-fire images of many of the world's best known art masterpieces, accompanied by the music of Walter (now Wendy) Carlos. Pyramid distributed several films made by Charles Braverman, including *Make Mine Metric*

(1975), a funny, engaging film that poked fun of, and also made a compelling argument for, the value of the metric system.

One of the more visually compelling of Pyramid's films was *Iran* (*1971, dir. Claude Lelouch), a non-narrated eighteen-minute tour of the country featuring exceptional editing, juxtaposing shots of common themes from past and present. Daily activities of Shah Mohammed Reza Pahlavi's family are shown in the picture, and rumor has it the film was funded by a petroleum company as a gift to the Shah. Accompanied by Francis Lai's musical score prominently featuring a wah-wah guitar, it remains one of the more artistically memorable geographical films ever made.

Pyramid's biggest sellers included Oscar-winner *Why Man Creates* (1968, dir. Saul Bass) and Charles and Ray Eames' legendary *Powers of Ten* (*1978), which was a landmark film that illustrated positive and negative mathematical powers by showing a couple in a park first incrementally telescoped to outer space, then back down again, eventually microscoping to the cellular level. (The film had initially appeared in an earlier 1968 version called *Powers of Ten: a Rough Sketch*, animated by Judith Bronowski.)

For a number of years, Pyramid occupied a building in Santa Monica, California, redesigned by David Adams to include three pyramids, inspired by a trip to Egypt. The company, now called Pyramid Media and run by daughter Denise Adams and Randolph Wright, continues to distribute educational media in several formats.

Scholastic Films

This division of the well-known publishing company distributed over 1,000 films, including titles originally produced by Learning Corporation of America and Weston Woods (Scholastic purchased the latter company in 1996).

Pyramid Films' David Adams (Denise Adams).

One of Scholastic's film offerings, though socially iconoclastic, was mostly unknown except to a number of instructors teaching French language. *Toute La Bande* was an exceptional thirteen-part French language instruction series of 1970, created by language educator Mary Glasgow and produced by Donald Carter.[100] Each film in the series consists of a light drama, sequentially beginning with the arrival of a student from Dakar, Senegal ("Elisabeth," as played by future French voiceover star Marie-Christine "Maik" Darah), into the home of the Ermont family in France. As the series evolves, character development emerges, as crusty brother Victor becomes attracted to Elisabeth, putting his arm around her as they go for a stroll (*Vacances en Bretagne*, dir. Pierre Sisser), and dancing with her in the highly charged discotheque atmosphere of the final film in the series, *Bon Anniversaire!* (dir. Jacques Soumet). Although only hinting at their romantic involvement, the series introduces the concept of interracial dating as a norm, in possibly its earliest portrayal in a classroom academic film distributed in North America. The series is notable for its exceptional directing by Sisset and Soumet, and its fine acting, featuring wonderful stock French actors such as Zappy Max, and future notables, including Emmanuel Dechartre.

Today, Scholastic continues to distribute mediated educational materials, including films the Weston Woods catalogue. The *Toute La Bande* series is no longer in distribution.

Science Screen Report (Allegro Productions)

Science Screen Report (SSR) is a series of sponsored science films produced by Allegro Productions, dedicated to interesting school children in pursuing careers in science. Each film is outstanding on both a cognitive and affective level.

Film editor Jerome "Jerry" Forman left Hearst Metrotone News in 1960 to open Allegro Productions on New York's Seventh Avenue.[101] Allegro specialized in making sponsored films for numerous entities, including Ford Motor Company and Sterling Communications. It merged with Sterling in 1969, then was acquired by Time, Inc., in 1972, who sold it back to Forman in 1974.

Forman had always had an interest in science, and in 1970 developed a series of short science films as a vehicle to encourage students to study science. The programs were remarkable in that their cognitive content was equally interesting for young students as well as adult teachers, while exceptional pictorial content provided superior affective value. An example of the breadth of interesting topics covered in each film can be found in volume I, issue 2, from *SSR*'s first year of 1971. The five topics include *Marine Biology: Shark Control Research*; *Earth Science: Clean Water from Waste*; *Entymology: Control of Insect Diapause*; *Physics: Car Crusher*; and *Space Science: The Lunar Rover*. Each film was approximately 15 minutes in length to allow for more than ½ hour of classroom discussion per film.

Using the model he developed while working at *Screen News Digest*, Forman selected corporate sponsors that were noted for having a strong interest in science.[102] Each sponsoring company would be responsible for distributing the SSR films into the school film libraries of their communities. Sponsors were allowed to include a brief opening and closing sponsorship message, but no commercials.

Son Scott Forman, who today runs the company, stated that the company could well have written a book in the early days called *How to Lose Your Shirt Making Science Films*. "We had a 30 person crew working on the science films," he notes. "We never got caught up on sponsorship dollars, so our other productions paid for the science films. We soon dropped most of our production personnel, hired outside crews when we needed them, and finally began making a profit on the science films when we could lower distribution costs by sending them out on VHS rather than film."[103] Allegro is one of the few companies that has successfully transitioned from the days of 16mm film and has continually produced mediated instructional materials into the 21st century. *Science Screen Report* continues to be distributed free to schools, in an eight-issue yearly volume for older students and a seven-issue *SSR for Kids* version.

Screen News Digest (Hearst Metrotone News)

Initiated by Jerome "Jerry" Forman in 1958, Screen News Digest (SND) was a Hearst periodical 16mm "magazine" that was distributed free of charge to schools. It descended from the old Hearst Metrotone News (HMN), which had debuted as a newsreel in theatres on September 28, 1929. HMN had a then little-known but checkered past. During the Cold War years of the 1950s, as public interest in theatrical newsreels was waning, Hearst, among other companies, accepted covert funding from the CIA in return for placing U.S. Information Agency (USIA) propaganda in newsreels under the code name "Kingfish" when slated for foreign distribution, according to media historians Erik Barnouw and Raymond Fielding.[104] There is, however, no evidence that I've been able to find that indicates any USIA information migrated to SND for distribution to U.S. schoolchildren.

SND's Jerry Forman had come over to Hearst from Telenews, a television footage and newsreel company acquired by Hearst in 1955. For his new company, Forman produced up to ten cinematic "issues" per year. While most films addressed multiple topics, others concentrated on one topic or individual. Each film was sponsored by a corporate entity, which allowed it to insert a brief opening and closing corporate message of sponsorship. Forman was acutely aware of the resistance of schoolteachers to advertising, and so eschewed advertising in favor of the brief sponsorship mention.[105] Early on, some SND films seemed to be in accordance, philosophically, with the Hearst Corporation's conservatism. *We Seek No Wider War* (1965) parroted official U.S. government policy on the war in Vietnam, as discussed by Defense Secretary Robert McNamara. By 1973, however, a more balanced perspective was in evidence with *Vietnam Epilogue: End of the Tunnel*, which chronicled the war from Dien Bien Phu through the 1973 cease fire. *Women in Politics* (1980) offered a historical perspective of women's rights, with footage of Amelia Earhart demanding a greater voice for women, and clips of leaders such as Shirley Chisholm and Margaret Chase Smith. SND's later films were decidedly more engaging from cognitive and affective perspectives than their earlier counterparts, in spite of occasional experimentations gone wrong, as when Hearst added color gels to black and white footage, turning the Hindenburg disaster (*Lighter Than Air*, 1980) into an undersea-like study in blue.

For schools, one of the benefits of acquiring SND films was that they didn't cost anything. The Hearst corporate entity charged each Hearst-run newspaper a fee to help pay for production, and in return each newspaper was responsible for distributing SND to local school libraries. The brief opening and closing sponsorship messages provided Hearst with additional revenue.

Forman, who in 1957 had worked out an arrangement with Hearst to run his own Allegro Productions film company on the side, formally left Hearst in 1960. In 1983 he and Allegro bought Screen News Digest from Hearst, immediately turning it from primarily a social studies series to a science series.[106] Allegro discontinued the Screen News Digest brand in 1987.

Screenscope

Hal and Marilyn Weiner's Washington D.C.–based company is best noted in the academic film world for producing six films in their *Faces of Man* series, exploring the history and culture of El Salvador, France, Germany, India, Japan, and Southeast Asia. Perhaps the Screenscope film having the most affective impact was their restaging of the Berkeley Rep production *Black Girl* (1980, dir. Hal Weiner and Angela Paton). This exceptional film chronicles the travails of a girl with upwardly mobile aspirations, as she attempts to withdraw herself from the attitudes of her unfulfilled sisters, in a fine performance by Michelle Thompson.

Shell Oil Film Unit

Established in 1934 under guidelines suggested by John Grierson, Shell's film division soon initiated production units in several countries. Eventually, over 130 Shell films would be commonly found in educational film libraries, on subjects ranging from flight to geology to science. Several Shell-sponsored films were made by noted Dutch documentarian Bert Haanstra. His *Rival World* (1955) revealed crop destruction caused by insects, including a remarkable sequence in which a pilot purposely flies into a locust cloud 23 miles long by five miles wide, accompanied by the sound of insects smashing against the windshield, a sound made in the studio by dropping peas onto a plastic sheet lying atop the strings of a grand piano.[107] Other significant films made by Shell include George Sluizer's *Holland: Hold Back the Sea* (1967, distributed by EBF), a discussion of the remarkable Delta Project of the early 1950s. Unlike many other corporations sponsoring classroom films, Shell had a corporate policy eschewing overt references to the company within the film itself, and identified itself solely by its logo in beginning and ending credits.

Stanton Films

Thomas Stanton learned his craft as a photographer while employed by the U.S. Air Force in World War II.[108] In 1962, with the assistance of his science teacher-wife Phyllis, he made his first film, *Big Green Caterpillar*. Stanton produced and/or distributed over sixty films, including several featuring the remarkable time-lapse photography by Ken Middleham, an outstanding cinematographer who gained later notoriety for his work in television and feature film.[109] Middleham's *Carnivorous Plants* (an EFLA Blue Ribbon winner in 1979) and *Crystals: Flowers of the Mineral Kingdom* (1983) are remarkable contributions to the art of academic filmmaking, and the equally engaging work in *Slime Molds: Plant, Animal, Or?* (1979) has the extra advantage of showing Middleham at work in his studio, making the film with his specialized equipment and sets. After Thomas Stanton's death, wife Phyllis and son Jim continued to distribute their own films as well as those made by *Handel Films* until the mid- to late 2000s. Their films are no longer in distribution.

Time-Life

It has been difficult to determine the beginning of Time-Life's foray into the educational film market, but it is believed to have begun in approximately 1969 when, under the Andrew Heiskill/James Shepley regime, the media company bought the rights to market *BBC*-produced titles in North America from Peter Robeck. The prime goal of the purchase was to sell multi-part series, such as Kenneth Clarke's *Civilisation* (1970), Alistair Cooke's *America* (1972), and Jacob Bronowski's *The Ascent of Man* (1974), to television networks such as PBS, with schools as a secondary market. Much of the sales success of these films was realized under Bill Ambrose, who began his tenure as regional sales manager in 1974, and eventually became president in 1982. The *America* series was probably its biggest seller, with approximately 1000 units sold. In 1987, Ambrose left Time-Life to form *Ambrose Video*, which continues to distribute video versions of many of the titles previously sold Time-Life.

Other notable film series distributed to schools by Time-Life were Peter Montagnon's splendid *Heart of the Dragon* (1984), consisting of twelve one-hour films on the subject of contemporary life in China, Michael Latham's *Ten Who Dared* (1976, known as *The Explorers* in England) series on notable explorers, James Burke's *Connections* (1978), the *NOVA* science series (a co-production of WGBH and the BBC), and *The Shakespeare Plays* (1980), a 37-part series produced by Time-Life and the BBC over a period of six years, consisting of all of Shakespeare's plays. For more on these series, see the entry on the BBC, below.

Universal Education & Visual Arts

In late 1946, Universal Pictures, wishing to enter the growing school and library film market, launched *United World Films*, headed by former U.S. Army colonel and Eisenhower staff officer James M. Franey.[110] Franey began the enterprise by having theatrical travelogues rescripted by teachers and sold to schools as social studies films. A few months into the enterprise, he purchased the extensive library of 16mm film titles produced by *Castle Films*, founded by Eugene Castle in 1924. He then purchased the exceptional *Earth and its Peoples* series from producer Louis de Rochemont, comprising 36 films shot in various countries. In the de Rochemont series, films such as *Desert Nomads: French Morocco* (1949, dir. John Ferno) were often shot by filmmakers such as Ricky Leacock, who shipped unexposed footage to de Rochemont in the U.S., where it was edited and scripted by others.[111]

In 1965, Franey, now conscious of the need for an original product that could justify the name "Universal," hired Richard Lukin to set up a production facility.[112] Lukin, a recent director of the CBS *Camera Three* arts series, had been working on a National Educational Television series on demography. Unimpressed with Universal's existing films, he spent a month in classrooms, watching teachers struggle with United's titles and the films of other companies, and recognized that Universal's were, for the most part, neither exciting nor relevant. Typical of these films were those such as *Spain: Land of Tradition and Promise* and *France: Fifth Republic* (both 1964, uncredited directors), originally made by Dudley Pictures and distributed by Universal. These reworked travelogues were accompanied by an "elevator music" score of muted brass, woodwinds, and strings, the pedantic narrator taking the viewer on the standard tour of buildings and monuments, and, in the latter film, spending far too much time describing Lourdes and gushing over the miracles attributed to the water.

Lukin set out to produce and acquire better films. He hired enthusiastic young filmmakers who produced work specifically to engage young minds. In short order, Universal's educational films were winning awards at short film festivals, in spite of the fact that Lukin could not acquire the funding he deemed necessary to build a world-class academic film company. Under Franey's otherwise-protective aegis, no requests for help were to be made of the parent company, an inherent contradiction that kept money a crippling problem. While Lukin tried his best to excite his filmmakers with the prospect of making films that would educate and enchant young learners, he was never able to offer even the best-known filmmakers more than $15,000, plus royalties, per film. Compounding the problem were tiny advertising and promotional budgets and limited sales expertise. To Lukin's chagrin, relatively few teachers ever got to see the new films.[113]

Lukin was never able to successfully obtain the budget he felt was needed, "so the reward remained measured less in orders than in pride in an unusual achievement — some fine reviews, plus turning on the few teachers who happened to be film buffs."[114] Universal's best-selling film was a title partially conceived by Lukin and directed by actor Richard Beymer, *A Very Special Day: An Adventure at Coney Island* (1966). A wonderful story of a chance meeting between a girl and a boy, the film sold approximately 600 units.[115]

The firm's name was eventually changed to Universal Education & Visual Arts, and

Franey was let go in 1971, replaced by Peter McDonald. In 1973, Universal suddenly insisted that all films in process be finished immediately, and shortly thereafter, the educational film division was closed, and responsibility was shifted to the industrial film division. At its height, Lukin suggests that perhaps 100 films were sold through Universal's catalogue, fifty or so of which were produced in-house.[116]

Weston Woods

Founded by educator Morton Schindel in 1954, Weston Woods (named after the wooded area outside his home in Weston, Connecticut) specialized in producing children's picture books on film. Schindel graduated from Columbia Teachers' College in 1947, having taken audio-visual courses on subjects ranging from projection techniques to the Margaret Mead–taught course on propaganda and mass media. In 1948, he began working on films for Teaching Films Inc., which soon would declare bankruptcy. As part of the settlement, Schindel retained the rights to six of the films on which he'd worked, and formed his own company, Key Productions. Godfey Elliott's *Young America* films then contracted with Schindel to distribute *Key* films and make new films on standard topics. By this time, Schindel had begun noticing that children who read books in libraries rarely selected "Dick and Jane," and instead gravitated toward colorful picture books. He approached Elliott with the idea of animated picture book films as a new method of teaching reading, but was rebuffed. Schindel soon left for a two-year stint with the United States Information Service in Turkey, where he made films—primarily on health and cultural issues—and traveled by jeep as part of a mobile film presentation unit, equipped with generators to power projectors in the numerous villages without electricity. Returning to the United States in 1954, Schindel produced the first Weston Woods picture book film, and in 1964 made his first animated film, *The Snowy Day*. For the next 43 years, Weston Woods would produce hundreds of titles, including works by authors such as Robert McCloskey (*Time of Wonder*, prod. Morton Schindel), Tomi Ungerer (*Beast of M. Racine*, 1971, dir. Gene Deitch), and Maurice Sendak (*Where the Wild Things Are*, 1973, dir. Gene Deitch).

Schindel's marketing approach was innovative. He hired no salespeople, feeling that teachers and librarians already knew the books, and would order the films through his catalogues. He printed 70,000 catalogues, 35,000 of which were distributed to teachers' colleges.[117]

Weston Woods' Morton Schindel c.1995 (Morton Schindel).

One of Weston Woods' most memorable films was *The Sorcerer's Apprentice* (*1962, dir. Edward English), in which artist Lisl Weil, fresh from her animation performance at Lincoln Center, drew larger-than-life characters in different colored chalks while aggressively dancing to the Paul Dukas score. Some of the strongest films produced by Schindel were those in the *Signature* series, in which the people involved in creating these books and films, from artists to directors to producers, were shown animating, reading, and discussing their works. In *Morton Schindel: From Pages to Screen* (1981, prod. Morton Schindel), the producer discusses the painstaking steps of the picture book-to-film process, from selecting artists who stylistically mirror the original artwork, to the spoken aspect, including a scene showing author/illustrator/filmmaker Gerald McDermott narrating his *Arrow to the Sun* (1973, Texture Films, dir. Gerald McDermott). The most thought-provoking title in the series was the droll interview conducted by director Gene Deitch with children's illustrator and author Tomi Ungerer (an exceptionally funny and poignant artist who worked in the adult erotic genre as well), in which the artist conveys the joy children express in being scared, and the value of occasional childhood loneliness (*Tomi Ungerer, Storyteller*, 1981).[118]

Morton Schindel sold Weston Woods Films to Scholastic Incorporated in 1996 in order to devote his time to his non-profit Weston Woods Institute, founded in 1983 to promote innovative cultural education for children.

Xerox Films

Xerox Films was formed in 1969 as part of the Xerox Education Group (XEG), working with independent producers to develop films as well as distributing films already in existence. XEG properties, included Ginn and Company textbook publishers as well as R.R. Bowker (eventual publisher, in 1978, of the Educational Film Locator, the most comprehensive directory of educational films of the era). The Films division's first president was Vincent J. Byrne, succeeded several months later by Thomas D. Anglim. Robert Braverman was soon brought into the division, and began acquiring European animation titles for distribution.[119]

In the academic film world, Xerox was perhaps best known as the distributor of the ABC produced *Multiplication Rock* series of 1974. *Multiplication Rock* was an eleven part series (# 1 and 10 were omitted), produced by illustrator/adman Tom Yohe, as part of the *Schoolhouse Rock* television series. The films were known for their humorous street-wise animation and snappy music and lyrics, written by jazz musician Bob Dorough. The tunes were sung by jazz singers Dorough, Blossom Dearie, or Grady Tate.

Yohe, along with co-creative director George Newell, had originally been asked by their boss, David McCall, to set multiplication problems to music, because McCall noticed his son could easily remember lyrics to songs by the Rolling Stones, yet couldn't remember multiplication tables. A co-worker of theirs suggested they pitch the idea to the young director of children's programming for ABC, Michael Eisner, after consulting with animation legend Chuck Jones, who bought the idea immediately.[120] Each of the *Multiplication* films (e.g., *I Got Six* and *Naughty Number Nine*, both 1974) featured visual stimuli such as balloons, jacks, and bubble gum, that appealed to young viewers, but included urban elements as well, such as billiard balls, multi-ringed hipsters, and camels bearing oil and spices. They became the genesis of *Schoolhouse Rock*, a series of 37 television segments produced between 1972 and 1980, addressing disparate subjects such as science, grammar, and ecology.

From an adult perspective, perhaps the most interesting film in the series is *The Good

Eleven (*1874), because of a well-hidden hint at a sexual escapade about to occur at 11pm. At 55 seconds into the film, the following images appear in order: the number 11, a woman troubadour serenading with a guitar against the wall of what appears to be a darkened hallway, a door suddenly opening next to her, the woman peering inside the door, a heart slowly taking up the full screen, then followed by a simple "X" which also fills the screen. Because the sequence only takes up eight seconds, this adult-themed joke might be lost to most children and many adult viewers. Nevertheless it's there, in certainly one of the few instances of good-natured adult ribaldry appearing in films made and distributed for children.

Xerox was also responsible for the airing of Perry Wolff's controversial *Of Black America* (1968) series on CBS, sponsoring it on 165 stations without commercial interruption, and contributing to the funding for Robert Geller's exceptional *American Short Story* (1977) series, distributed to schools by Perspective Films.

Network Television-Produced Series and Documentaries in the Classroom

Network produced television documentaries were an important element of the classroom film experience. To ignore the value of these films as educational materials would be a mistake, as they often provided teachers superior educational material providing perspectives on current events, and basics for understanding history in a contemporary context.

Without a doubt, the eventual proliferation of in-classroom television was one of the harbingers of the end of the academic film business. In an ironic twist, however, many of the better television documentaries of the 1960s and 1970s, timeless in terms of content and writing, can only be seen today in 16mm classroom film format, as many network executives are skeptical that they can recoup the marketing and production investment it would take to re-release them in today's popular media formats. Many of these important documentaries sit warehoused today in network archives, and can be viewed only when shown by the few film libraries that still have them in their collections.

Some of the earliest examples of television programs repurposed as educational films sold to schools were not 16mm documentaries, but instead consisted of classical music kinescopes, made by aiming a 16mm camera at a television screen to film a live program. Filmed in the late 1940s and early 1950s, they had all the resolution issues one might expect, typically including fuzzy registration, few solid blacks or whites on the gray scale, and vignetting on all four corners of the image caused by the curvature of the TV screen itself. In the early 1960s, however, documentary programs produced by network news organizations like CBS, NBC, and ABC, filmed and distributed in 16mm format, soon became the most prolific television-sponsored fare in the classroom. These were sold through educational film companies such as McGraw-Hill to school districts, with commercials removed.

The first classroom films made available to schools by television networks often were "news" or "theme" documentaries. William Bluem, in his book *Commentary in American Television*, further classifies theme documentaries:

> Within the Theme Documentary class, the subjective purposes, enhanced and affected by artistic techniques, move to the fore. The use of symbolic structures is emphasized. The poetic power of words, pictures, and music is combined with the aesthetic of cinematic structure and the dramaturgical form itself to shape the documents of reality into thematic expressions of the human condition. The control shifts from the reporter to the artist.

The work of television's theme documentarists has evolved within three basic production methods. One is in the *compilation*, involving the creative application of techniques of cinematic organization, the poetry of the spoken narrative, and the suggestive power of the musical score. In the *biographical* method the same elements are present, with the addition of elements of dramaturgical structure as distinct from the broader narrative. There is also a greater use of dialogue within the spoken narration. In the *dramatic* method the use of historical material is minimized, as the functions of dramaturgy within the more immediate records of actuality become dominant.[121]

In addition, *entertainment* documentaries, light cultural pieces that became the specialty of producers such as David Wolper, gained sudden but lasting popularity from the mid–1960s onward. Whereas the timely news documentary, appealing to the intellect of the viewer, provided students with some of the more provocative elements of contemporary culture, biographical documentaries, based on historical persons, were often essentially a collection of opinions, data, and newsreel shots. Compilation documentaries, with their reliance on music and omniscient narration, were inspired to a great extent by Henry Salomon's 1952–1953 series *Victory at Sea*, whose thundering musical score, and "voice of God" narration, provided Robert Russell Bennett and Alexander Scourby, respectively, represented something of a standard in presentation for the era.

From today's perspective, the timelessness of many of the hard-hitting social documentaries, and in particular those in the *CBS Reports* series, is remarkable. This critical genre of television documentary film was refined under CBS executive producer and former Edward R. Murrow colleague Fred W. Friendly, whose *CBS Reports*, initiated in the fall of 1959, has never been equaled in terms of courage and clarity of opinion, and quality of reporting. This series, along with those made by ABC, NBC, and National Educational Television (NET), contributed significantly to documentary films shown in classrooms in the 1960s and 1970s.

Schoolchildren of the 1980s, however, were not as fortunate as their predecessors of a decade earlier in terms of access to quality television-to-school documentaries on challenging social issues. Whereas 1970s students commonly saw *CBS Reports* and *NBC White Paper* 1960s-era documentaries in classrooms via 16mm film, prints became inexorably damaged through use, and often were not replaced. Typically, distribution companies removed older television documentary films from their catalogues if a given number of years had elapsed since the original production, regardless of the content. For the same reason, replacement footage for repair was increasingly unavailable from the original sources. The content of these early television documentaries was not, in terms of quality, being replicated by the networks either, as author Daniel Einstein notes:

> The 1970's brought about still further changes [to the documentary format]. This time, however, the trend seemed to be in a backward direction. The popularity of new magazine formats, docudramas and information/entertainment programming, the increasing reluctance of sponsors to back programs of substance and controversy, along with a decline in the public's appetite for investigative and controversial issues after the tumultuous 1960's and the Watergate experience, dramatically altered network enthusiasm for the long-form documentary. The emergence of PBS as a fourth major outlet for documentaries also engendered a cutback in commercial network production, as did the feeling among network executives that the documentary simply no longer provided enough of a monetary return on an often costly investment. The ratings game became so powerful that the low numbers garnered by most documentaries could no longer be tolerated. The threat of expensive and protracted litigation also became of great concern to the networks, especially following Gen. William Westmoreland's libel suit over the CBS REPORTS broadcast

"The Uncounted Enemy: A Vietnam Deception" (aired 1/23/82), the result being that the networks became less inclined than ever to tackle controversial subjects. This trend away from the long-form, investigative report has been coupled in recent years by the rise in lightweight magazine programs ... [which] conveniently dispose of any issue in twenty minutes or less. News and informational programming for young people has also been drastically curtailed due in part to recent deregulatory policies that have allowed the commercial networks virtual free rein. All of these factors have played a large part in the decline of the network documentary and have done so to such a degree that by the middle of the 1980's, the network documentary, compilation series, and public affairs program had virtually ceased to exist to any meaningful extent.[122]

The importance of these early television documentaries, both in terms of content and for the development of critical thinking on the part of students, is significant. As Einstein suggests, though, documentaries made by U.S. television networks had lost much of their intellectual cachet by the 1970s. In their place, educational film companies such as Films Incorporated, LCA, and Time-Life began mining the gold of exceptionally-produced overseas documentaries from British Broadcasting Company, Film Australia, and others. These two important resources for documentary classroom academic film, U.S. and foreign-produced, are noted in separate categories below.

Television Series Produced by U.S. Networks and Distributed to Classrooms: An Alphabetical List by Network

A number of series produced by network television were re-purposed for classrooms on 16mm film. Those listed below were, from a cognitive and affective perspective, among the most significant.

ABC

ABC News Close-Up!

In late 1960, ABC introduced *Bell & Howell Close-Up*, produced by John H. Secondari, who, in addition to spearheading films made by ABC personnel, oversaw the work produced by Time, Inc.'s Robert Drew, whose influential team included documentarists Richard Leacock and Gregory Shuker. The initial *Close-Up!* series was taken off the air after the 1963 season. The series resurfaced in 1973 as a monthly series of documentaries, now retitled *ABC Close-up*! The productions spanned the political spectrum, from the anti–Castro perspective in *Cuba: The Castro Generation* (1977, dir. Arthur Holch) to *West Virginia: Life, Liberty, and the Pursuit of Coal*, (1973, dir. Stephen Fleischman), which offered a sobering investigation into the excesses of coal company management.

The Saga of Western Man

ABC News producer John H. Secondari developed this eighteen-part series, aired from 1963 through 1969 (distributed to classrooms by McGraw-Hill), on events and people contributing significantly to Western civilization. The series depicted events and persons through drama, often narrated by off-screen actors depicting historical persons speaking in the first-person. Some, especially those portraying famous musicians (*Beethoven: Ordeal and Triumph*, 1966, prod. John Secondari, and Helen Jean Rogers) and great artists (*I, Leonardo da Vinci*,

1965, prod. John Secondari), seem dated by contemporary standards. Much more effective (and largely devoid of dramatic excesses) is Secondari's *The Legacy of Rome* (1966), produced with wife Helen Jean Rogers, an exceptionally good treatment of the theme. The Secondaris' non-serial academic films evolved significantly over the following five years, resulting in stellar historical films such as *Middle Ages: a Wanderer's Guide to Life and Letters* (1970, dir. Piers Jessop), and *Romanticism: Revolt of the Spirit* (1971, dir. Helen Jean Secondari), made by the Secondaris' own production company and distributed by the Learning Corporation of America.

CBS

CBS Reports

Of the total of 268 *CBS Reports* television specials made from 1959 to 1979, the argument can be made that the first 146 of them, made prior to 1967 under the guidance of conceptual developer and executive producer Fred W. Friendly, constitute one of the most significant bodies of work in the history of documentary filmmaking.[123] They broached subject matter that many educational film companies wouldn't address (e.g., abortion), giving teachers important cinematic teaching material not to be found elsewhere. CBS Reports distribution to schools in 16mm format began in 1961. Several factors contributed to the superior quality of the work, among them the early blessings of CBS chairman Bill Paley, who authorized a well-paid, intellectual reporting staff and generous production budgets.[124] With a keen eye toward sharp investigative reporting skills, Friendly hired a large number of newsmen who had formerly worked with the legendary Edward R. Murrow during World War II. Perhaps the single greatest force in driving the quality of the reporting was Fred W. Friendly himself, who cajoled, battled, and coddled CBS executive staff, sponsors, and reporters in his effort to present intellectually uncompromising and brutally honest stories to the American public. Refusing to kowtow to commercial or political interests, he presided over a documentary style that eschewed the use of music, the resulting starkness imparting greater power to the naked, spoken word. Much of the time CBS Reports didn't recoup production costs, due to the departure of advertisers wishing to distance themselves from controversial — and hence potentially offensive to consumers — material. David Lowe's exceptional *Abortion Under the Law* (1965), a shocking film about the reality of back-street abortions, was a program that today, some 40 years later, no network desirous of avoiding religion-inspired boycotts would have the bravery to tackle. *Abortion* was just one of the many CBS Reports documentaries distributed to schools in 16mm format. (Today's climate, as far as teaching about abortion in public schools, may be more volatile than it was in 1965.) This documentary is timeless, as the issues associated with the topic have not changed. With the reticence of major networks to re-release 50-year-old documentaries in their archives, perhaps the only way one will ever have an opportunity to see *Abortion Under the Law* is if the school film library nearby hasn't already de-accessioned it.

Because of the uncompromising nature of the material, commercial sponsorship was unreliable and unpredictable. *CBS Reports,* in spite of Paley's support, was continually moved to different times and days, especially as more commercially viable programs began generating higher revenues in desirable time slots.

During his tenure, Friendly eschewed using independent producers, whom, he felt, would be beholden to commercial or political interests. Instead, he cultivated talented — and often testy — producers such as David Lowe and Jay McMullen. Both had exacting standards and worked tirelessly. (Overwork, Friendly once said, killed David Lowe.)[125] Jay McMullen was one of the first reporters to enter the Dachau concentration camp at the end of World War II, and came away with the feeling that "part of the job of a journalist is to be a watchdog," determined that the focus of his career would be to expose injustices in his own country.[126] A perfectionist, he took as long as he felt necessary to complete a documentary, once refusing to even promise Friendly the year in which a work would be completed.[127]

In 1966, furious over an executive decision to schedule an *I Love Lucy* re-run instead of an important hearing in the U.S. Senate on the subject of Vietnam, Friendly tendered his resignation as president of CBS News.[128] In the post–Friendly years, both Jay McMullen and producer Perry Wolff credit CBS News President Frank Stanton with creating a "firewall" between commercial interests at CBS and the documentary staff, which allowed them to produce outstanding documentaries with a minimum of challenge from advertisers.[129] *Campaign American Style* (1968, dir. Jay McMullen), an exposé of how a local campaign machine packaged up-and-coming candidate Sol Wachtler, proved that CBS Reports still had "bite" in the immediate post–Friendly era.[130] *CBS Reports* continued to be broadcast into the 1980s, but Friendly-era programs were easily the most compelling and uncompromising. Those fortunate to stumble upon them in 16mm film libraries will discover some of the most exciting documentaries ever made, sterling examples of what can be accomplished when tough programming is unfettered in funding and uncompromised in content. From their introduction to schools in 1961, they were to constitute an important resource for teachers wishing to introduce controversial topics in classroom instruction, and to inspire critical thinking.

Of Black America

This seven-part CBS News series that aired in 1968 was intended by Executive Producer Perry Wolff to "change the language of the current racial dialogue by showing that racial trouble stems from historic attitudes — an inheritance of ignorance."[131] More than a simple presentation of facts, *OBA* was a ruthless indictment of the social and political status quo, with a style of delivery that pulled few punches. Distributed by *Bailey Film Associates (BFA)* to classrooms, OBA became an essential element to the process of educating non-black students on the causes and effects of racism, and black students on the valuable — and often hidden — contributions to a national culture by Blacks throughout history.

Perhaps *Black History: Lost, Stolen, or Strayed* (prod. Andy Rooney and Vern Diamond) had the greatest impact of any of the films in the series, as it seems to have been placed in more educational film libraries than its counterparts.[132] Written by Rooney and narrated by a very serious and somewhat cynical Bill Cosby, it presents a fascinating and scathing explanation of how historical contributions of Blacks had been ignored by newspapers, book publishers and broadcast media, thus perpetuating the myths and stereotypes that were the foundation of oppression. In Peter Davis' *Heritage of Slavery*, reporter George Foster tours the old Charleston slave market, and interviews Whites still longing for the "good old days." The viewer soon becomes fascinated with reporter Foster's ingratiating style of interviewing, and is at times incredulous that Whites would feel comfortable expressing their blatantly bigoted views to him. Another in the series, *Portrait in Black & White* (dir. Vern Diamond, prod. Jay McMullen) describes the mutual suspicion between Blacks, who fear white racism, and Whites, who fear black extremism, as reported by a biracial news team of Charles Kuralt and Hal Walker. Productions in this important series are exceptional creations of the news and documentary organization that descended from Edward R. Murrow and Fred W.

Friendly, and were among the most significant film contributions to social studies curriculum in North American classrooms.

The Twentieth Century

Airing weekly for nine years on CBS beginning in 1958, one-half-hour series, hosted by Walter Cronkite, used archival footage to describe personalities and events that shaped the century (it was superseded by the *Twenty-First Century* series in late 1966). Less provocative than Fred W. Friendly's *CBS Reports* series, this series nevertheless provided a workmanlike chronicle of the history of the century, although occasionally suffering from the excesses of orchestrated musical scores endemic to many similar programs of the era (e.g., *Nisei: Pride and the Shame*, 1965, prod. Isaac Kleinerman, music by Glen Paxton). *The Twentieth Century* was sufficiently broad in scope to cover topics as diversified as contemporary music (*Duke Ellington Swings through Japan*, 1964, prod. Isaac Kleinerman) to the co-opting of the government of Denmark by the Nazis (*Sabotage!*, 1960, prod. Burton Benjamin). Under executive producer Burton Benjamin, however, *The Twentieth Century* did effect one major innovation in television compilation documentary: the expert eye-witness, brought on-camera to discuss what he or she had seen, heard, and discussed at the time of the original action.[133]

The Twenty-First Century

In January 1967, the *Twentieth Century* series changed both title and objective, now focusing on new trends in technology and culture. One of the more fascinating of the half-hour programs was *Incredible Voyage* (1968, prod. Isaac Kleinerman), a microscopic journey through the human body utilizing optical probe photography, with music by electronic music pioneer Otto Luening. Shorter-lived than its predecessor, this series ended in 1969, but remained in distribution to schools through the 1980s.

You Are There

Begun in the early 1950s, this Walter Cronkite–hosted dramatic series featured mock broadcasts of news coverage of historical events. Going off the air by mid-decade, it was revived in the late sixties or early seventies, again hosted by the well-known news anchor, with cameos by such notable reporters as Morley Safer, Richard C. Hottelet, and Hal Walker. While directing and acting were workmanlike *(Mystery of Amelia Earhart*, 1971, dir. Burt Brinkerhoff, featuring a young Richard Dreyfuss as "Radioman Riggs"), the premise of the treatment itself was hackneyed, and, one guesses, must have been embarrassing professionally for the reporters.

NBC

NBC White Paper

In 1960, NBC hired ex–CBS producer Irving Gitlin to form a documentary production team to compete with Fred W. Friendly's *CBS Reports*. Albert Wasserman, a formerly successful documentary producer at CBS Reports (*Biography of a Cancer*, 1960) was soon hired, and Chet Huntley was selected to be the host and narrator. Although initially suffering from less support in terms of production funding than that enjoyed by competitors at CBS, the irregularly-scheduled White Paper broadcasts could be compelling nonetheless. One of the series' more controversial productions was Arthur Zegart's *The Battle of Newburgh* (1962), the story of a town in the state of New York that had recently elected a slate of politicians who ran on a platform of ridding the town of "welfare cheaters." The documentary crew reported that the vast majority receiving assistance were elderly, infirm, or incapacitated.

Overall, White Paper films were intelligently crafted, compelling productions. Films such as *Death of Stalin* (1963, dir. Len Giovannitti), which investigated the personalities and backgrounds of the four leading candidates for succession, were among the finest political films shown in North American classrooms.

No network environment was without its own internal battles, and NBC's would occasionally affect the treatment of a film distributed to classrooms. Robert M. Young, a brilliant director who refused permanent employment in his own personal quest for independence, and whose subsequent films (*Bushmen of the Kalahari*, 1975) would become staples in classroom film libraries, became embroiled in two controversies at this early stage of his career:

> It was Irv Gitlin who took out a sequence I had shot in Angola of a napalm burned village — burnt corpses, huts, etc. I brought back from Angola two nose cones from Napalm bombs. I gave one to NBC and one to a friend of mine who was Adlai Stevenson's assistant at the UN. My friend found out that the nose cones were indeed from American napalm bombs dropped by the Portuguese. I could not find out if they were NATO. Gitlin took the sequence out of my film. We had a big argument. He said that this would feed the Russian claims that US/NATO arms were being used against Africans. I should have quit and gone to the *NY Times* — but I didn't. So the program was aired without that sequence.
>
> After my film was on the air, I was approached and asked to join the CIA. I wasn't interested. My next film was about the lives of the poor in Palermo, Sicily and this film got stopped half way through the mix and the program cancelled. I think that Gitlin was either in or in direct contact with the CIA and it was decided three days before the airdate that my program should not be broadcast. This was the time of the Opening to the Left in Italy. After a big fight I was fired. The original film was destroyed by NBC, but someone inside who thought highly of the film, sneaked into the vault and made copies of the original. He returned the originals to the vault, but several years later gave me the copies — so I had the film. But it had no copyright and I was afraid it would be discovered and taken away. Anyway, a copy of the film was passed around — making its way to Henri Langlois, head of the French Cinémathèque — who loved it. Then, twenty-eight years later, Channel 4 in England and La Sept in France decided the film had to be shown — and now the people who had suppressed it were dead. They wanted me to go to Sicily and do an introduction — and miraculously I found members of the family I had filmed. Channel 4 and La Sept gave me a little money and I raised the rest to bring the old film up to date.[134]

Project 20

This NBC series was launched in 1954 by producer Henry Salomon, consisting of films on historical subjects such as Lincoln, the Nazis, and Communism. While achieving critical acclaim with the stills-to-action animation technique pioneered *in Meet Mr. Lincoln* (1959, dir. Donald Hyatt), much of the series suffered from grandiose production values, with Robert Russell Bennett's heroically lavish musical scores and Alexander Scourby's stentorian narration. *Project 20's* compilation treatment of Communism *(Nightmare in Red*, 1955, dir.

Henry Salomon) was a blatantly propagandistic film, of questionable objective merit in the American classroom, but having historical value for scholars today considering the era in which it was made.

NET (National Educational Television)

National Educational Television, the predecessor to PBS, supplied a number of made-for-television programs to schools. Production quality in the early films distributed to schools was often poor, probably due to the continual financial malaise experienced by this publicly funded institution. In contrast to that of much of the output of its successor, NET's programming, although often shaky technically, commonly addressed lofty intellectual topics, demanding that its audience rise to the standards of the material presented. The NET of 1966 was decidedly not about Lawrence Welk fundraising marathons. Some of the finer NET programs to be distributed to schools included Lane Slate's austerely produced, nine-part *USA Artists* series (e.g., *Claes Oldenburg*, 1966, dir. Mallory Slate), and occasional specials produced by individual stations, such as the Nathan Kroll–produced *Dancer's World—Martha Graham* (1967, WQED Pittsburgh), in which director John Houseman and cameraman Peter Glushanok captured exquisitely the choreography and rhythm of Graham's troupe.

NET Journal

The *NET Journal*, a series of documentary programs produced in the same decade as *CBS Reports* and the *NBC White Paper*, never quite measured up with the others in an affective sense, often suffering from inconsistent camera work, choppy editing, insufficient sound quality, and cloyingly "silly" introductory and closing music that weakened the impact of the film (e.g., *Where is Prejudice*, 1967, prod. Dick McCutchen). Jack Willis' 53-minute *Hard Times in the Country* (1970), for example, featured a series of compelling interviews of farmers being forced off their land in favor of big agribusiness. The final five minutes, though, contained incongruous, unexplained shots of urban sprawl accompanied by the pop hit *Age of Aquarius*, giving it the feel of a student film rather than a professional production. This type of inconsistency of point-of-view was common in this series, which was obviously hampered by low budget and the use of inexperienced filmmakers, apparently still struggling through the learning stages of the craft of filmmaking.

Wolper Productions

Although not formally affiliated with a particular network, Wolper's films were a network documentary staple, and many were distributed to schools in 16mm format. Former film salesman David Lloyd Wolper formed his company in 1958 after having discovered 6,000 feet of footage detailing the Soviet space program. While the networks were debating their value, Wolper made the purchase. He then convinced NASA of the value of opening its archives to him, and completed his first major production, *The Race for Space* (1960), which he sold to network television after acquiring sponsorship from the Shulton Company. Carried by 105 local television stations, it was the first non-network produced documentary to have been distributed on a comparably nationwide basis. Choosing producer Jack Haley, Jr. and composer Elmer Bernstein as mainstays, he soon hired former CBS and NBC producer Mel Stuart, CBS writer Marshall Flaum, CBS Reports' Arthur Swerdlow, NBC radio man Alan Landsburg, and contracted with Mike Wallace as occasional narrator. By 1962, Wolper had 200 employees. In 1964, Wolper Television Sales launched its first series, *Men in Crisis*, consisting of thirty-two programs fueled largely by his purchase in 1963 of 15 million feet of newsreel film from Paramount.

Judiciously eschewing public affairs documentaries that might conflict with work being done by the networks' own news teams, Wolper chose to specialize in compilation entertainment and historical documentaries. Some of Wolper's early works are of marginal educational value, due to the fact that they were produced to sell to television networks, with schools being a secondary, non-prioritized market.[135] From the well-known *Biography* series, *Ben-Gurion* (1962, dir. Alan Landsburg) is a thinly-veiled propaganda piece lacking mention of an Arab perspective, and lists a number of Zionist organizations in the production credits. *Joseph McCarthy* (1962, dir. Alan Landsburg) presents a somewhat uncritical view of the senator, made well after McCarthy's excesses were common knowledge. To the series' credit, Wallace proved to be a superb and dramatic narrator, as evidenced by his chilling account of the final dwindling dark days *of Helen Keller* (1962, dir. Jack Haley, Jr.).

Wolper was heavily influenced by Robert Flaherty, whom he considered to be the prototypical docudramatist.[136] In discussing his story of Willie Davis, a young baseball player breaking in with the Los Angeles Dodgers (*Biography of a Rookie*, 1961, dir. Mel Stuart), Wolper stated, "We call these dramatic documentaries, and we try to make them like any other drama with a hero, a villain, a conflict and a climax."[137]

Although making his reputation as a maker of docudramas and compilation documentaries, some of the more satisfying Wolper productions, such as *Story of a Writer — Ray Bradbury* (1963, dir. Terry Sanders), and *Bushmen of the Kalahari* (1975, dir. Robert M. Young) were more in the traditional vein of providing information rather than entertainment.

Television Series Produced by Foreign Networks and Distributed to Classrooms: An Alphabetical List, by Firm

British Broadcasting Corporation

As mentioned earlier, BBC titles were commonly found in American school film libraries after *Time-Life's* acquisition in approximately 1969 of the license formerly held by Peter Robeck. In 1981, this non-theatrical distribution license was acquired by *Films Inc.*, which continued providing BBC films to schools through the remainder of the 1980s. The BBC produced the following popular pre–1980 series of films, all of which were distributed to U.S. classrooms in that era by Time-Life:

America (Alistair Cooke)

Host Alistair Cooke's view of the United States consisted of thirteen programs, first shown in the U.S. in 1972–73 on NBC, and later edited to twenty-six half-hour programs shown on PBS. Cooke's ability to select and distill various cultural and historical elements of the United States is fascinating, particularly when the series is viewed in sequence. All films in the series make for compelling viewing, with themes as varying and dynamic as U.S. military history (*Arsenal*, 1972, dir. David Heycock) and racial contention (*Fireball in the Night*, 1972, dir. Michael Gill).

The Ascent of Man (Jacob Bronowski)

Hosted and written by mathematician/scientist Jacob Bronowski, this was a thirteen-part series of one-hour lectures co-produced by the BBC and Time-Life, filmed by directors such as David Kennard and Adrian Malone. Released in 1973, Bronowski's intellectually stimulating commentary on the history of science represents a landmark in documenting the exploration of science in cinema. His *Knowledge or Certainty* (dir. Mick Jackson) is a highly recommended and chilling account of the depravations of humankind in the absence of questioning, ending with a sequence filmed at Auschwitz, where several of Bronowski's family members perished.

Civilisation (Kenneth Clark)

Civilisation, Films Incorporated's Charles Benton writes, "was truly a breakthrough in dealing with the arts and culture on television. It was the first major 13-hour nonfiction mini-series that had a worldwide impact, and created a model for many similarly conceived and ambitious series to follow."[138]

The series was released in 1970. Upon viewing the films today, the paucity of information regarding the contributions of Asian cultures becomes apparent. It therefore appears that what Clark was really getting at was *Western Civilization*, which might have been a more appropriate title for the series.

The foundation for Clark's perspective is the emergence of European culture from the barbarism that followed the fall of the Roman Empire. The series, when understood in that light, is a *tour de force* in explaining the cultural concepts that make up the constructs of Western Civilization as we know it today. The contributions of Spain are a notable omission, and Charles Benton recalls *Civilisation* producer Michael Gill telling him that Clark eschewed any mention of Spain, and therefore Moorish contributions to Western culture, because he despised Francisco Franco.[139] Benton notes: "What made [the series] so interesting is not what it did not do, but what it did. Kenneth Clark was an extraordinary leader in the British arts and culture scene, including, as I remember it, being the Director of the British Museum. He grew up as a lonely child in a very aristocratic British family and the Civilization story he tells ... is in no small part the story of his personal discoveries of western European history and culture over his lifetime. Viewed as a very personal account, it is not meant to be comprehensive or encyclopedic ... but rather a fascinating story from an enormously talented and knowledgeable expert ... at its time, it was an innovative triumph.

Connections (James Burke)

Connections was a ten-part series released in 1978 and hosted by reporter James Burke. Like the earlier *Ascent of Man* and *Civilisation* series, each segment consisted of a progressive, interconnected series of ideas within the larger thematic framework. Burke, with his natural story-telling ability and chatty writing style, was better suited to communicating ideas to a broad spectrum of learners than were Bronowski and Clark, both of whom appeared to be better used to addressing academics than the average television viewer or North American high school student. In episode six in the series, *Thunder in the Sky* (1978, prod. Mick Jackson/David Kennard), for example, Burke presents a dizzying array of information, connecting from bad swamp air, to the invention of windows, to the industrial revolution, to carburetors. He describes these three links in a witty, engaging, yet logical manner, providing the viewer with more of a sense of riding a rocket through history than sitting in a cathedral-like lecture hall.

Heart of the Dragon

One of the BBC's finest contributions to the American classroom film was producer Peter Montagnon's *Heart of the Dragon* (1982–83) series, in which a crack team of documentarists (Montagnon as well as filmmakers David Kennard and Mischa Scorer, and co-producers Patrick Lui, Nigel Houghton, and Alasdair Clayre) pursues the mysteries of China, as narrated by the refreshingly mellifluous off-camera narrator, actor Anthony Quayle.

When the series was conceived in 1981, China was still officially "off limits" for Western filmmakers and, with the exception of major network news teams that were occasionally allowed to film historical spots (*Forbidden City*, 1975, prod. Lucy Jarvis, NBC News), access to people and institutions was severely limited.

The concept of *Dragon* really began when co-producer Patrick Lui met with Nigel Houghton in Hong Kong, mentioned that he had several high-level contacts in China, and wondered if it would be possible to produce a series of programs. Houghton advanced the idea to Montagnon. At the same time a new broadcasting entity, *Channel Four*, was just being launched in the U.K., and was in need of programs. Lui, Houghton, and Montagnon then formed Dromelia, a corporation set up for the production of the series, and received funding from banker Stephen Keynes (son of the economist John Maynard Keynes). At this point Montagnon brought an old friend from his Open University days, Alasdair Clayre, into the production group, and the filming began.[140]

Heart of the Dragon is one of the most fascinating documentary series ever produced on the subject of China. The director of each film in the *Dragon* series was deliberately chosen in an attempt to marry style with content, in which a lyrical theme would be matched to a director with a poetic style, whereas a director with a formal documentarist's approach would be chosen to direct a film on the subject of business or politics. The films comprise timeless vignettes that are interesting and relevant decades later, even given the tremendous changes in China which occurred in the interim. Among the most notable films of the series are *Mediating* (dir. Peter Montagnon) and *Working* (dir. David Kennard). Clayre, who would later take his own life after the failure of a later film production project, wrote an eponymous book providing wonderful historical background information to each episode.[141]

Ten Who Dared

The BBC and West Germany's Westdeutscher Rundfunk co-funded this series produced by Michael Latham. Released in 1976 and known as *The Explorers* in the U.K., it was distributed in the U.S. by Time-Life, and consisted of ten dramatized adventures of various explorers dating from Columbus to Amundsen, each approximately 50 minutes in duration. Characterized by outstanding location cinematography using hand-held cameras (e.g., the camerawork of Gary Hansen in Tony Snowdon's *Burke and Wills—1861* and Fred Hamilton in Fred Burnley's *Henry Morton Stanley—1874*), ethnographic elements, and narration based on actual diaries, the series consisted of a chronicle of travels in difficult-to-film areas on several continents.

Director David McCallum's *Charles Doughty—1877* is especially notable. Here, the noted Arabist travels in a poetic haze of colors and cultures, accompanied by singing, languages, and sounds. McCallum notes that the filming was done in the El Foud area of

Morocco due the fact that much of Arabia was engaged in military activity, and that many of the region's homeless were hired as extras.[142] The idea of utilizing McCallum, in his first directing effort, was posed to the BBC by Latham, who had noticed that the actor always took a keen interest in camera set-ups whenever he was not on-camera himself.[143]

Ten Who Dared stories rarely have happy endings, as evidenced by the death of the protagonists in the desolate and beautiful *Burke and Wills*. One may question the selection of subjects (*Francisco Pizarro* is better noted for his denigration rather than appreciation of the Inca culture he uncovered), but nevertheless, the series is far better, in both cognitive and affective senses, than many other historical academic films of the period. The series was developed for prime-time British audiences, and at a budget of roughly $10 million, and was, at its inception, the most expensive series ever produced at the BBC.

Herculean efforts were the order of the day in getting the series filmed. In Gabon, the president of the country suddenly revoked permission to film *Mary Kingsley—1893* (dir. Tony Snowdon), necessitating one full week of diplomatic bargaining. The entire crew of *Henry Morgan Stanley* was arrested in the Congo and deported just before scene one was to be filmed, for reasons that are still unknown. Tragedy struck the crew of *Alexander Von Humboldt—1799* during the three-day filming of a sequence in a cave inhabited by guacharo birds. Massive clouds of guano dust caused by the disturbed guacharos were continually inhaled in close quarters, causing everyone to experience a high degree of lung distress. Director Fred Burnley, not yet 40 years of age, returned to the U.K., and, still complaining of breathing difficulties, checked into a hospital and soon died.[144] Unsubstantiated rumors surround the circumstances of Burnley's death. While tissue samples were taken to determine cause of death, they are said to have disappeared under mysterious circumstances. Such rumors—again unsubstantiated—suggest that a reason for this occurrence could have been to prevent his survivors from being able to receive an insurance settlement after his death.

Adding to the mythic quality of the award-winning series was the presence of director Tony Snowdon—already famous as Tony Armstrong-Jones, still photographer and husband of Princess Margaret—whose films (*Kingsley* and *Burke*) were two of the finest in the series. And then, there was host Anthony Quinn. In the original British version, David Attenborough served as the host, happily ensconced in a set consisting of rich, walnut bookcases amidst leather-bound tomes. But Attenborough was, at the time, little known in the U.S., and therefore Mobil Oil, who had licensed the series for its *Mobil Showcase* television program, scouted about for a more familiar face. The luxurious library set was also discarded, Mobil feeling that Americans wouldn't take to the highbrow surroundings. Quinn, directed in the updated hosted sequences by David Hoffman and Harry Wiland, projected his larger-than-life persona in putting on a tie for "the lady" (*Mary Kingsley*) and gesticulating wildly while describing the wanderings of *Doughty*. Rather than detracting from the Latham-produced films, Quinn's introductions are an entertaining foil that essentially makes each work two films in one. Other subjects in the series include *Jedediah Smith, Christopher Columbus, Captain James Cook,* and *Roald Amundsen* (the latter, directed by David Cobham, is remarkable for its portrayal of austerity and hardship).

Film Australia

Three exceptionally well-crafted series of films made by Film Australia were distributed to North American schools by the Learning Corporation of America. Decades after their production, they remain compelling, timeless films of notable cognitive and affective value.

Human Face of China

Producer Suzanne Baker created this series of films, distributed in the U.S. in 1979. In *Something for Everyone* and *It's Always So in This World*, director Bob Kingsbury probes aspects of China, hidden from the west for decades, including startling footage of a woman undergoing a major operation using only acupuncture as an anesthetic, and her seemingly miraculous recovery minutes after the operation (Kingsbury didn't believe it either, and returned the next day to find the woman as chipper as when she'd left the operating table). Other films in the series included *Mind, Body and Spirit, One Hundred Entertainments*, and *Son of the Ocean*.

Human Face of Japan

Director Oliver Howes and producer Gil Brealey created this important series, distributed in 1982, which explored disparate elements of a country steeped in tradition, yet ever on the forefront of mechanized modernization. Films in the series include *The Career Escalator, Lifetime Employment, Raw Fish and Pickle, The Rice Ladle, Tomorrow and Yesterday*, and *A Working Couple*.

The Russians

Producers John Abbott and Tom Manefield combined with director Arch Nicholson to create this fascinating investigation into Cold War Russia, distributed to North American schools in 1979 and consisting of three titles, *People of the Country, People of Influence*, and *People of the Cities*. The films are "day in the life" views of individuals, the latter film describing the lifestyles of three families, those of a woman bus driver in Moscow, a dock foreman in Odessa, and a doctor working in a pastoral sanitarium. Filming next to Soviet overseers still wasn't all that easy in 1979. As narrator Nick Tate notes, the crew was threatened with expulsion for allegedly filming drunk people during the making of *People of the Cities*.

Survival Anglia

Survival Television was founded in London by Aubrey (later Lord) Buxton, operating under the premise that wildlife subjects could be successful as prime-time television, and soon included his son, Tim Buxton. Its first program was launched in February 1961, and the series eventually numbered over 1000 shows, made by filmmakers such as Alan Root, Simon Trevor, Hugh Miles, and Nick Gordon. Many Survival filmmakers shot under extremely dangerous conditions, and at least three lost their lives while filming. The company's films were brilliantly shot, written, and edited, generally leaning in the direction of conservation. Among their films most commonly found in North American classrooms were those of Alan and Joan Root, whose films (*Mysterious Castles of Clay*, 1978; *Balloon Safari*, 1975) continue to be distributed by Benchmark Media in the United States. In approximately 2001, Survival Anglia was absorbed into the Granada Television conglomerate, and many of their films appear to be out of international distribution as of this writing.

Looking at Filmmakers

The companies that took on the financial and organizational responsibility of making and distributing the films provided the necessary framework under which the majority of the filmmakers worked. In Chapter 5, we'll take a brief look into the life of one filmmaker, John Barnes, and investigate therein the ongoing series of conflicts and resolutions that often exemplified the relationships between filmmakers and the companies for whom they worked.

CHAPTER FIVE

Immortal Longings: The Life and Films of John Barnes

The story told in this chapter is not just the tale of a superior filmmaker. The ongoing see-saw battle between film companies and filmmakers in the academic film world was endemic. What makes this story compelling is that Barnes was a consummate documenter of his own life in film, keeping letters that tell of the conflicts, joys, and philosophies that drove the industry's aspiration to educational excellence. Reprinted and analyzed here, they carry us back to the days when academic film was a thriving business, rather than a historical era.[1]

Of the more than 100,000 classroom academic titles distributed prior to the demise of the 16mm classroom film genre, the work of John Barnes, made over a period of approximately 25 years, stands out as exceptional in its artistic quality, breadth of subject matter, and timelessness. His story not only describes a filmmaker whose work represents the apex of the genre, it also captures the milieu familiar to every filmmaker who worked in (and, as one might expect, occasionally fought to escape from) the world of 16mm educational film. Barnes exemplified the role of the *auteur* in academic film, producing, directing, writing, and often narrating his films, and fighting — sometimes vehemently — to defend his treatment and perspective with executives, film salespeople, and occasionally teachers.

Barnes crossed the threshold of the documentary film world into that of the academic, where he created a body of work consisting of many of the more compelling historical and literary films ever made. He was considered by many of his peers to the most exacting filmmaker in the genre. And he is one of the few to have prospered both artistically and professionally from educational film's dark days of the early 1950s to the denouement of the golden era in the late 1970s. Barnes' films are notable for their superior casting, as the director refused to use inferior actors, regardless of budget constraints. His directing and camera-sense are at times astonishing (e.g., *Early Victorian England and Charles Dickens*); his writing witty, ironic, and intellectually stimulating (*Shaw vs. Shakespeare*). He was a filmmaker who would have made monumental films if Hollywood had ever come calling, but one suspects his temperament would not have been symbiotic with the personalities and actions of more commercially-oriented producers. As will be seen from excerpts from Barnes' letters, this creator of radio dramas who never finished college stood his ground on an equal intellectual footing with the producers of his films as well as the greatest scholars of his day. To ask Barnes to change scripts or edits was to invite a series of often vehement letters demanding that the requestor defend his or her position before the filmmaker would consider making even the most subtle changes he perceived might diminish the value of the film.

Barnes and Frances Sternhagen on the set of *Magic Prison* (1969) (Isidore Mankofsky, A.S.C.).

Early Years and Influences

John Wadsworth Barnes was born in Belford, New Jersey, on March 25, 1920, to Edward Crosby Barnes, an insurance salesman, and Dorothy Leek Barnes, whose beauty, it was reported, was such that filmmaker D.W. Griffith had once considered her for a role (her mother wouldn't allow it). The extended Barnes family was made up of blue-collar Easterners, given to carpentry and other trades, and apparently skeptical of university training. John rarely spoke of his childhood or adolescence, but two events seemed to have influenced him above all others. At elementary school age, he was a victim of rheumatic fever, and was barely able to walk to school. In this condition, unable to excel physically, he was introduced to books by a principal who thought John's path to success should pass through the doors of the school library. There, John developed an appreciation for books and learning, something he didn't pick up at home, where, he was to say later, the only books in evidence were a history of the Boer War and "sexy novels."[2] Sometime in his adolescence he developed an aspiration to attend Robert Hutchins' University of Chicago, and sent away for a catalogue. A second telling event in John's youth was his later accidental discovery, in the household trashcan, of that much-anticipated catalogue which his mother, a deeply religious woman who distrusted intellectuals, had thrown away, hoping to keep her son close to home. A small-town Republican organizer, she had cautioned John against marrying Catholics, and refused to allow a youthful black friend of John's to enter her home, consigning the two to the back steps. It was from these events and philosophies that John developed a life-long ambivalence toward his parents, impatience with people he considered his intellectual inferiors, and anger toward those who would stand in the way of his artistic goals and professional standards. His rebellion was immediate and uncompromising. He was not a Republican (Adlai Stevenson was a favorite of his), was non-religious, and married first a Catholic, then Jeanne Weinstein, who was Jewish. Interracial themes would become an important element of his early film work, from *People Along the Mississippi* (1951) to *Equality Under The Law: The Lost Generation Of Prince Edward County* (1966).

Barnes' own intellectual emancipation was fueled by a disdain for authority that would barely be held in check in his later dealings with people to whom he nominally reported, notably EB's William Benton and Maurice Mitchell. His coping mechanisms were invented along the way, from a peripatetic international existence that would keep him away from EB headquarters for months at a time, to the formation of his own independent production company, which allowed him to commiserate with the people he enjoyed at EB, while distancing himself from those for whom he had little respect. The Barnes family had some Native American blood in its veins (the particular Nation was unknown to him, or never mentioned), and that, mixed with his plebian background, contributed to his philosophy of championing the downtrodden and disadvantaged. His groundbreaking academic films favored addressed American civil rights issues and the Bill of Rights. While enjoying the respect of the brain trust at EB, felt most comfortable with his actors and crew.

Barnes received a diploma in 1939 at Monmouth Junior College, Long Branch, New Jersey, where he edited the school paper and played the lead role in college dramas. It was the only institution of higher learning from which he would graduate. Eventually, he did attend the University of Chicago, and edited *trend*, the school's literary magazine from, 1941 to 1942. To pay a printing bill, he began working for WBBM, the CBS radio affiliate, first as a writer, then as a director/producer, resulting in a critically-acclaimed series of radio dramas which debuted in April 1945, *Michael Scott Presents* (representing a fictional character, often played by Ken Nordine). In the series, the 24-year-old producer deconstructed various books, such as Dickens' *A Tale of Two Cities*, Melville's *Moby Dick*, and Hugo's *Les Misérables*, into as many as 17 weekly episodes. Barnes would spend six hours per day writing the plays, and an additional three hours rehearsing the actors for the drama. Barnes describes his transition from radio to film:

> The program was fairly big on national radio. Broadcasting a literate daytime serial amidst (for the most part) a dreary wasteland of soap operas, it was much appreciated by thousands ... but we couldn't find a commercial sponsor. Inevitably the program came to an end, as did my radio career. Offered a ground-floor job in CBS television, I had a better idea, I thought — independent filmmaking. The next day I bought a lovely Swiss-made Bolex....[3]

By 1951, Barnes had made several amateur films, and embarked on his first film for EB, directed by John Grierson protégé Gordon Weisenborn and written and produced by Barnes. *People Along the Mississippi* (*1951) may be the first identifiable educational film portraying African-American and White children interacting as peers. In it, we see the emergence of two elements that would become common to many subsequent Barnes films: exceptional photography, and powerful sequences in which ideals of social justice are made a significant part of the overall story. The tale is a simple story of a boy in Minnesota who builds a toy boat and sends it on a journey southward along the Mississippi River. On its meandering path, the boat serves as a metaphor for the integration of the American cultures, first found by a Chippewa boy who sends it along its way now accompanied by a small totem pole. It sails along farmlands settled by Swedes, and further south, where, in the most poignant moment of the film, it falls into the hands of a young African-American boy. He shows it to his white erstwhile playmate, who has grown to the stage of avoiding playing with blacks — their friendship temporarily broken, as the film subtlety hints, by the mores of racist adults. They are brought together again through this new mutual interest, conquering, if only for a moment, the overbearing social oppression of which, willingly or not, they were now a part. This film was perhaps the earliest cinematic tool to become available to teachers in thousands of North American classrooms as a vehicle for discussions on the history of racial discord, and the viability of integration. It is memorable as Barnes' first leap into the world of classroom academic film, and one that would herald his reputation as a filmmaker whose idealistic social philosophy would guide both his subject selection and his interactions with EB executive committees for years to come.

Barnes' next venture would garner his greatest fame, and bring him, professionally, as close to Hollywood as he would ever get. *The Living City* was nominated for an Oscar as Best Documentary of 1953. Barnes, however had few delusions of grandeur as a result of the award:

> Getting nominated for an Oscar gave one a frisson of glory — dreams of riches beyond avarice — etc. But I was driving after work ... I had the award ceremonies on the radio — just in time to hear the announcer say... "And so much for the best documentaries — we now move on to the more important awards." Put me in me place, that did.[4]

The director got little opportunity to enjoy his fleeting moment of early recognition: although he was invited to attend the Oscar ceremony, William Benton, owner of Encyclopædia Britannica, "took on the chore of going (sat next to Disney)."[5]

In 1953, Maurice Mitchell became president of EB Films, coming over from Benton's Muzak company, in a move that would provide the filmmaker with one of his biggest in-company benefactors as well as his more-than-occasional *bête-noir*. In short order, Barnes convinced Mitchell to send him to make films in England, utilizing some of the money EB had in English banks that, due to post-war currency restrictions, could not be removed from the country. The filmmaker arranged to take his family to Europe by way of a business arrangement not uncommon among filmmakers, paying their passage aboard the Greek liner Olympia by making a short promotional film (*Ocean Voyage*, 1954).

He clearly enjoyed the differences in professionalism between his U.S. and England-based crews. In an internal memo to EB president Mitchell dated February 1, 1955, Barnes discussed the differences in making a film at England's Merton Studios, and "here," meaning those of EB, located in Wilmette, Illinois:

> For the first time since I left CBS years ago, I felt that I was once again working with thoroughly professional people at all levels.... Compared with shooting in a studio like Merton Park, our operation here is like the semi-monthly meeting of the Wilmette Camera Club. To be specific:
> - Never once were we delayed because someone had not attended to a detail.
> - Never once was a prop essential to a scene missing or not in hand and ready for the shooting.
> - Our studio call was for 8:30 and the crew started at 8:30 — they didn't sit around with coffee for fifteen or twenty minutes before starting half-heartedly; they started.
> - They didn't break for tea; tea was *delivered* on the set and everybody kept working while having it.

- When we were to go out on location, everybody knew when, where, how, and why.
- When we were scheduled to leave at 8:30, we left at 8:30 or so close to it that no one minded.
- We didn't wait on set, all lighted and ready to shoot, while the actors were being made up; the actors, the hair-dresser and the make-up man were *all* scheduled in early — an early as 7:00 if necessary, responsible; and that was enough.

This period also marked the beginning of Barnes' life-long practice of isolating himself from the politics and petty jealousies that he'd briefly encountered at EB Films' corporate headquarters; thereafter, Barnes would function as a quasi-independent. As a favorite of William Benton and Maurice Mitchell, Barnes was, to a great extent, protected from the politics and sales pressures that other EB filmmakers, in closer proximity to corporate headquarters, weren't able to avoid. He was also the first filmmaker at EB to successfully challenge the edict that no film should go beyond a length of approximately 10 minutes (know in the industry as a one-reeler). After *The Living City*, Barnes continued to make longer films in spite of the fact that the "one-reel" rule was still in place.[6] Eventually, EB and other film educational companies would loosen the rule. In this sense, Barnes was responsible for changing a standard practice in the industry.

Barnes' philosophical perspective (the championing of the downtrodden, pro-integration, and anti-organized religion), first apparent in *Mississippi*, now became a driving force in his historical films of the mid-through-late 1950s, which represented a clear break from all classroom academic historical films which preceded them. Other such films shunned questioning the role of religion in society and treated racism as a historical artifact rather than a contemporary challenge. In *The Pilgrims* (1954), instead of emphasizing Thanksgiving and Plymouth Rock, Barnes chose to focus on the Mayflower Compact, a document that forced the pious immigrants to live under a non-theocratic charter in the new land. Two decades later, a treatment such as this was commonplace, but in the early 1950s, it was not. Teachers in that early era had few educational materials to elucidate concepts such as separation of church and state, racial integration, or cross-cultural worldviews. Barnes' films were powerful tools that provided a mediated forum for teachers wanting to generate a discussion on important social issues. And in classrooms led by teachers, whose own ideas were less accepting of progressive social philosophy, the viewing of such films may have suggested to young learners the value of questioning what they were being taught.

As opposed to the dearth of non-educational publicity to which classroom films were relegated in the post–1960 years, academic cinema was regularly reviewed in several prestigious periodicals of the 1950s, and Barnes' work was, for the first time, being given recognition beyond the academic realm. *New York Times* film critic Howard Thompson was enamored of Barnes' early films *Captain John Smith: Founder of Virginia* (1955) and *The Pilgrims*:

> If these two superlatively alive dramatic vignettes are indicative of anything other than superior craftsmanship, then comes the revolution to the tired, assembly-line format of historical films for classroom use. That history has seldom seemed so credible and compelling is the accomplishment primarily of the brilliant young director-producer, John Barnes, whose *The Living City* was an Oscar contender two years ago.[7]

In promoting his socially progressive world view, Barnes wasn't above the use of occasional cinematic legerdemain. His *Sir Francis Drake: Rise of English Sea Power* (1957), which confounded Southern White educational film buyers in its portrayal of the mariner's black first mate as an intelligent, trusted colleague and social peer, was initially banned in the Georgia State schools. Georgian educational authorities insisted that, rather than being treated an equal by *Drake*, the historical figure in question was actually the cabin boy, and thus an inferior. History textbook in hand, Barnes testified before the state school board as to the veracity of the peer relationship between the two, and successfully won the fight to have his film placed in schools. Barnes would later admit that he had, in fact, made a willing sacrifice to historical accuracy in favor of making a point of racial equality, by showing the captain and mate together in California waters. In reality the mate, although in life regarded by Drake as a peer, had died prior to the events depicted in the film.

Increasingly, Barnes combined his passion for history with his love of the arts, and deepened his exploration into the craft of filmmaking. This was exemplified by two films, *The Renaissance: Its Beginning in Italy*, and *Leonardo Da Vinci: Giant of the Renaissance*, both released in 1957. In the former, Barnes and cameraman Michael Livesey dollied through deeply shadowed interiors, juxtaposing foreground architectural and design elements with background sculptures, niches, and high and low reliefs. Describing the contrast between the relative austerity of the art of the Middle Ages and the flowering of the Florentine Renaissance, the film was reinforced by an insightful study guide consisting of an abstract of the film, a discography of the film's music, and a complete 122-scene shooting script, listing tilts, pans, close-ups and long shots, along with the elapsed footage for each scene. Ostensibly, the shooting information was provided to assist film librarians in ordering replacement footage for damaged films; today, it has evolved as an important historical document detailing the manner in which the John Barnes of 1957 would shoot and edit a film.

In late summer of 1958, Barnes began working on his most ambitious project to date, a series of twelve films produced for the Massachusetts Council for the Humanities, which had just obtained a large amount of funding from a number of sources — the Ford Foundation among them — to make a series of films. Recognizing that filmmaking was not included in its core competencies, the Council initiated a series of meetings with various people in order to choose a filmmaking team, two of whom were John Barnes from EB, and Douglas Campbell, an actor and director associated with Canada's Stratford (Ontario) Shakespearean Festival. Upon meeting each other, Barnes and Campbell recognized their aims were complementary. Campbell (born in Glasgow, Scotland, June 11, 1922), well-known for his theatrical roles in Tyrone Guthrie's *Oedipus Rex* and Michael Langham's *Henry V*, employed a fine cast of players, but was not a film director. Barnes, the accomplished film auteur, was in search of actors with talent and professionalism reminiscent of those with whom he had worked in England. Their decision to pool their resources was, in terms of the history of the classroom academic film, to be fortuitous, producing seventeen films of exceptional power and beauty.

With the decision to select Encyclopædia Britannica Films as the distributor of choice, Barnes was appointed as executive producer of the *Humanities* series under the guidance of a committee including Robert Hutchins (now past-president of the University of Chicago), scholars Mortimer Adler and Clifton Fadiman, and John Canaday, art editor of the *New York Times*.

Initially, the Humanities project was slated to include film treatments of Shakespeare's *Hamlet*, Sophocles' *Oedipus Rex*, and Thornton Wilder's *Our Town*, resulting in four half-hour-long films for each. The program would eventually encompass over eighty individual titles, many of them "boxed" as thematic, multi-part series.

The initial series, *Hamlet* (1959), was hosted by Yale English professor Maynard Mack, with actors directed for the stage by Campbell, headlined by a riveting Peter Donat as the increasingly vicious and tormented protagonist. This film is composed of four half-hour segments, each treating a different aspect of the play, with commentary and analysis by Mack, supported by acted sequences. In 1962 and 1963, Barnes' four-part *Classical Greece* series was introduced, three episodes of which were written and hosted by noted philosopher Mortimer Adler. Adler, like his colleague Robert Hutchins, had once been an *enfant terrible* of the scholarly set, and was introduced to Western philosophy as an undergraduate while attending John Erskine's grueling Classics course at Columbia University, which included the reading of one book from classic literature each week for sixty weeks. He eventually taught the course himself, unsuccessfully attempted to replicate it later as a professor at the Hutchins' University of Chicago, and eventually ended up at St. John's College in Annapolis, Maryland, teaching the *Great Books* program. A *bon-vivant*, he attributed his good health to a rigorous regimen: "Never exercise — as for dieting, eat only the most delicious calories," and described himself as "easily intoxicated; is married to a beautiful woman; has no children, but you can never tell; is not good looking, but quite lovable; Jewish and German by ancestry, but anti-semitic and esperanto by nature."[8]

Barnes' "Dickens Quartet" of four titles was released in 1962 as another element in the *Humanities* series, and, from a directorial perspective, marks an ascendance over the relative

John Barnes (left) and John Canaday (center) discuss filming *Chartres Cathedral* (1963) (Encyclopædia Britannica, Inc.).

austerity of Adler's *Greece* films. The acting, personified by a cast that includes Old Vic actors Judi Dench, Mark Dignam and Michael Gwynn, is outstanding, and the discussion of the times of Dickens, and thematic (as opposed to chronological) exposition analysis by host Clifton Fadiman is thought-provoking. Barnes' directorial and production work was inspired and creative, and indicative that he was now a master of his craft. To close the film *Early Victorian England and Charles Dickens*, the camera dollies into a theatrical set with lighting set-ups and cables exposed, where gaffers, grips, and the director are shown making their final adjustments. Moving forward, the camera slowly closes off the wings, and non-acting personnel leave the sound stage. The clapboard is struck, and suddenly we've left Clifton Fadiman's on-screen discussion of the historical and social elements that led up to the novel, and have traveled into the cemetery setting of the opening scene, a transition that remains one of the most spectacular sequences in Barnes' work.

In the spring of 1961, Barnes made the three films in the *Art and Architecture* series (1963), which included the memorable *Chartres Cathedral*, a tour de force of architectural filmmaking. These films stand the test of time, as vibrant today as they were when released, though not all who saw them initially were pleased, as indicated in this letter of complaint addressed to the filmmaker:

> ...[T]wo English teachers who have been to France asked why you eliminated the choir screen within (Chartres) Cathedral where the chief events in the life of the Blessed Virgin are depicted in marble. They felt that this was one of the most beautiful things they had ever witnessed and wondered why you had not incorporated it into the film.[9]

For a man who refused to be bullied by the formidable brain trust at EB, the criticism of two schoolteachers proved to be an act of provocation too delectable to ignore:

> We are presenting Chartres as the greatest monument of the Middle Ages, the Romanesque and Gothic Periods. A bit of the Choir Screen (and one or two of the figures) dates from the late Gothic period, the 16th century. (The figures are by the same man who built the new Tower.)
> The rest — most of the screen, that is — was not done until the 18th century, which of course is *not* our period. And most of the figures, in the quaint words of an official guide book "are the works of several Italian sculptors, full of confidence in their chisels, but with whom faith was no longer anything but a matter of money."
> ...[T]he Choir Screen is simply not what one is impressed by at Chartres; it is the least of the wonders to be seen there.[10]

When not defending himself from schoolteachers and inhouse critics, Barnes spent a considerable amount of time writing, directing, and producing still more films in the *Humanities* series, including the remarkable *Macbeth* group (1964), comprising three short films, *The Politics of Power*, *Themes of Macbeth*, and *The Secret'st Man*. Here, each half-hour film consists of a series of separate but eventually interconnected ideas, illustrated by acted sequences, and hosted by the erudite, engaging Douglas Campbell. Continuing the elements of staging legerdemain first used in his *Dickens* films, Barnes begins the initial film with a stand-up introduction by Campbell, then pans to the soundstage, as a stagehand directs the carbon-dioxide canister toward the area that will be occupied by the three witches. Later, host Campbell walks in front of the actors, who freeze in a 38-second tableau-vivant, and delivers a prologue describing the action that will shortly occur. The action resumes, only to stop again as the camera moves in a 90-degree arc, now following the host. As Macbeth falls increasingly into despair, faces begin to appear to him as distorted specters in funhouse mirrors.

Macbeth provoked significant controversy at EB Films, best explained in excerpts from several letters that offer a fascinating glimpse into the politics and pressures faced by filmmakers working in the educational world in general, and at Encyclopædia Britannica Films in particular. They also describe in detail the processes and forces involved in creating and "selling" an academic film, and the battles fought by a creative artist against the exigencies of the corporate economic structure.

The controversy begins on June 24, 1964, exemplified by comments from a letter written by EB president Maurice Mitchell to EBF president Charles Benton:

> I think the film was ... filled with optical tricks and self-indulgences that belong on commercial television with beer sponsorship and not in a highly professional series like EBF's Series. I do not think that Douglas Campbell was addressing high school students — I feel that he missed the point of his audience entirely ... he was talking to John Barnes. To the EBF Advisory Board. To other playwrights and actors and producers — never to high school students. This, more than anything else, offended me as I watched the film.

Benton copied the above comments and sent them to Barnes, who responded to him on August 10, 1964. His letter is an intelligent and scholarly riposte to the verbal backstabbing, common at EB, that Barnes, distantly removed at his home in Italy, could not easily deflect:

> As for Mitch's comments on *Macbeth*, I can't quite see what he's driving at. I presented a case for a director's interpretation of *Macbeth* — rather than the scholar's ... on the basis that Shakespeare's plays are still living — on the stage — and that it is in this way that interesting and often profound ideas about his plays are developed.
>
> Read the best scholars on Shakespeare — Johnson, Coleridge, Chambers, Bradley, etc. — and you will find them making constant references to what this or that actor or actress did in the part of Falstaff or Lady Macbeth.... As for Campbell's ideas about *Macbeth*, they are, in my opinion, brilliant; he solves several problems — seeing the play as a director — which the scholars have never been able to solve.... I have studied all the major commentators on the play and they simply haven't got a clue to some of the play's difficulties.
>
> [T]he text of *Macbeth* is one of the most difficult of the Shakespearean plays. It is full of holes, scenes are out of order, a lot of the speeches simply aren't by Shakespeare. It is Campbell's idea that the play was not printed by a manuscript — or even a playscript — but rather was written down as dictated by a group of actors — Shakespeare's contemporaries — in whose memories alone the play lived.
>
> I come now, at length to the subject of how *Macbeth* was produced. We see the Witches as Macbeth experienced them — they appear in the room, materializing out of his black mood; he sees them now here, now there — all around him. When Lady Macbeth leaves Macbeth following the banquet — the camera draws back and high to show Macbeth alone in his vast empty castle. The camera movement and the height, in my opinion, emphasize his terrible aloneness. The results may not come off, but not because we were indulging in filming masturbation.
>
> Campbell and I may have failed, but I don't think you could find two men more seriously trying to come to terms with a difficult masterpiece or working harder at it under conditions which most qualified film-makers would consider difficult at best.

Mitchell responded to the director on September 15, 1964:

> I'll confess that I am disappointed in what I read in your August 10 letter. I do believe that the *Macbeth* film is subject to some criticism, and perhaps the day will come when we will be able to discuss this face to face.
>
> [W]e assumed that some of the students who saw the *Hamlet* films would be able to read the play with great understanding and derive much stimulation from the lectures and the dramatic sequences. Some others would be able to read the play with some difficulty but with a great

deal of understanding, and they would round out their response to the play by seeing the films. Others would not be able to read the play at all — at least with very little understanding — and would get their communication primarily through the films.

I just couldn't see where a youngster who had struggled through *Macbeth* without getting much out of it could do much more with the Campbell films.

[As] to special effects and tricks of the kind that were used to excess, in my opinion.... What troubled me in this particular film was the difficulty that I thought some students might have in understanding the use of these tricks. They are not suggested by the text. It is not always clear what you are trying to say, over and above what Mr. Shakespeare has said and what Mr. Campbell has said, when you toss them in. I think that learning is difficult, that the Humanities tend to seem overwhelming to many students, and that anything which disorients them or makes them feel that they should understand something that they don't, is detrimental to the effectiveness of the film.

I do feel that it is a proper function of the Britannica management and its screening group to raise questions of this kind.... I do not regard your insertion of material in the films as being sacred and beyond criticism and discussion, and I think it is not only reasonable but quite understandable to suggest that you do indulge yourself. What creative artist doesn't?

Barnes responded to Mitchell's letter on October 28, 1964:

Mortimer [Adler] I think, placed the trouble ... the third (and last) *Macbeth* film was shown by itself. The three *Macbeth* films build as a unit, and are closely inter-related.... I hope you will be able to see the three films in sequence.... I've always felt the after-dinner screenings for the Board not far removed from the level of a farce. I've seen many people doze through perfectly creditable films.... It seems to me that if the Board is to view films, they ought to do so when they're fairly bright and in a good screening room.

Encyclopædia Britannica Films often took its emphasis on scholarship to inquisition-like extremes, and was infamous for its high level ad-hoc review "committees" and highly critical preview screenings, attendance at which represented a generally uncomfortable experience for the director. Barnes, who typically spent two months conducting interviews, reading the literature, and engaging in research prior to writing his script, was ready, able, and willing to defend his intellectual position, to the occasional chagrin of more than one committee member.

Barnes would direct or produce — and successfully shepherd through review committees — approximately sixteen films between the years of 1964 through 1966, including *Michelangelo* (1965), the magnificent the three-part *Odyssey* series, and two important films in the *Living Bill of Rights* series, one of which was *Justice Under the Law: The Gideon Case* (1967).[11]

It was clear that John Barnes had a soft spot for convicted burglar Clarence Earl Gideon, whose landmark Supreme Court case established the right of the indigent to receive counsel. Barnes, who narrated the film, identified Gideon as "ex-convict, wanderer, a former gambler, the devoted father of three children, and a man with a deep sense of his legal rights." Many of the principals portrayed themselves in recreated court scenes, including Abe Fortas, former Supreme Court justice, who prior to that was the attorney who argued in front of the Court on Gideon's behalf. Barnes was successful in obtaining permission from prison authorities to film reenactments there. The filmmaker recalled that Gideon, upon his return to prison as a free man, was regaled by the deafening applause of his former cellmates, a scene unfortunately not included in the film. The story was one that appealed to Barnes' own sense of social justice: as a result of Gideon's success in the Supreme Court decision of August 5, 1963, 5,000 cases were re-opened, and 1,000 men were freed after having representation for the first time. Follow-up reports determined that the recidivism rate for these men was less

Clarence Earl Gideon being filmed in jail for John Barnes' *Justice Under the Law: The Gideon Case* (1966) (Isidore Mankofsky).

than for other convicts freed during the same period. The filmmaker exchanged letters with Gideon for many years after the film, occasionally sending along small sums of money. The film remains one of Barnes' most touching works, in an oeuvre replete with work championing the rights of the disadvantaged and under-represented.

In 1969, Barnes filmed his magnum opus, *Shaw vs. Shakespeare.* In terms of the melding of concept, originality, writing, directing, and acting, the three-part series must certainly be considered as one of the most important classroom academic film series ever made. They generated much controversy at EB, both because these intellectually demanding, yet wholly entertaining films were a difficult sell, and because their lavish productions raised the hackles of other EB filmmakers.

For a number of years, various filmmakers at EB had been not-so-secretly grumbling that Barnes, as an intellectual favorite of Bill Benton and Maurice Mitchell, had been given a production budget greater than theirs, an opinion not borne out, historically, through subsequent interviews with other filmmakers and a cursory perusal of production documents. What many were loath to admit was that Barnes, who operated out of similar budget constraints, was as creative in production as he was in directing. The way Barnes was able to finagle superior production assets seemingly out of thin air is dramatically illustrated by the

Richard Kiley (center), John Barnes (right) and cast discuss filming *Shaw vs. Shakespeare* (1970) (Bill Pierce).

story surrounding the underpinnings of *Shaw*, which began when the director got word that a highly touted and heavily funded Broadway musical, *Her First Roman*, starring Richard Kiley and Leslie Uggams, had failed miserably and was canceled after its initial three performances. Barnes called the show's producer, wanting to purchase the costumes:

> He said, "How much do you have to spend?" I told him a figure, and he said, "Well, the costumes are yours. Anything else you want?" And I said, "Yeah, the props, the settings, the hangings..." He asked me how much more I had in my budget, and I told him a ridiculous figure, and he said, "Come over and you can have anything you want." Well, the wreckers usually come to a show like that when it closes, knock everything down, break it into pieces and burn it up. I arrived when they arrived, and it was like presiding over the liquidation of an Egyptian dynasty. I got three moving vans and filled them with stuff and we got started immediately on our production. When we finish our film we expect to sell the stuff.[12]

Barnes paid $3000 for everything. The wigs alone had been sold to the original producers for $25,000, so a guess of up to several hundred thousand dollars for the entire set is probably not be out of line. As the *coup de grâce*, Barnes hired the Caesar of the play, a suddenly out-of-work Richard Kiley, as the protagonist. Uggams was presumably unavailable, and Suzanne Grossman, a young actress recruited from Douglas Campbell's Stratford Festival Company in Canada, was cast as Cleopatra.

Shaw vs. Shakespeare is a critique of Shakespeare's characterization of Julius Caesar, as seen from the eyes of playwright and commentator George Bernard Shaw, played by Donald Moffat, who also took on the role of Cassius.[13] In addition to exploring the character of

Caesar, Barnes wanted to emphasize the importance of George Bernard Shaw as a critic as well as a playwright. Peering backward in time (Shakespeare's *Julius Caesar* was written in 1598, and Shaw's *Caesar and Cleopatra* in 1898), the Irish critic here questions, chides, and excoriates Shakespeare for the way in which he treats the personality of Caesar. Unabashedly proclaiming his own brilliance, Barnes' Shaw provides insightful and witty examples juxtaposing the imperious character of his Caesar with the seemingly ineffectual one written by his older-by-three-centuries counterpart. Even Barnes' viewing audience is challenged by the acerbic Shaw, in the opening of the initial film: "Now, may I say that you are free to disagree with anything I say about Shakespeare; but since you undoubtedly do not know his plays as well as I, your disagreement is likely to be on very shaky ground indeed...." The *Shaw* films are alternately funny and intellectual, a brilliantly written tribute to two magnificent playwrights, with Moffat, who himself saw Shaw as his own alter-ego, as an impressively skeptical host.[14] Recognizing that they were about to distribute a unique series of films, EB's marketing department produced an 8½ × 11, glossy 26-page booklet to accompany each film, complete with the actors' script and the filmmaker's statement of purpose and production notes. The *Shaw vs. Shakespeare* series (*1970) consists of three films, *The Character of Caesar*, *The Tragedy of Julius Caesar*, and *Caesar and Cleopatra*.

Barnes' witty and often acerbic prose, so evident in the *Shaw* films, is echoed in his letters and essays of the period. In 1972, the filmmaker, back again in Italy, filmed *A Farm Family in Italy* and *Adventure in Venice*, the latter a story told through the voyage, through the canals, of young boy's toy boat. In an unpublished essay, Barnes talked of his passion and fascination for the city and its people, and his joy and frustration in making a film in that rarified atmosphere of art, culture, and decay:

> Every film producer returns from making a film with disaster stories, and the production of *Adventure in Venice* was no exception. Fortunately, the electrician swam to safety and the batteries were recovered (they had fallen into the Grand Canal and a young swimmer dove for them). Unfortunately, the still camera is still there; it fell into a canal deep in the interior of Venice where no one would think of swimming....
>
> The experienced traveler looks forward to a dry martini at Harry's Bar and then a good dinner — with Venetian specialties, squid swimming in its inky liquid, tail of flounder and after dinner, a stroll in the Piazza San Marco, and Italian coffee — very hot, very sweet — in one of the Piazza's many cafes. The waiter rips you off, of course: one coffee can't cost that much, but after all you're sitting in "Europe's most beautiful drawing room," and everywhere you look is a movable feast for your eyes....
>
> Whenever my wife and I could fit it into our schedules, we would return for a brief stopover in Venice. And each time we returned, I would sit brooding in Harry's Bar; how to return to Venice and possess her, and be possessed, for a reasonable length of time: say three weeks at the very least.
>
> How else but to make a film about Venice today? What if what if there's this little boy, the son of a gondolier, who makes this small boat — maybe a boy's loving model of the Michelangelo — he loves the sea — and this boat gets lost in the canals of the city, and goes all over, and we follow it with the camera and it gets into all sorts of adventures, people find it, it gets run over by a vaporetto, firemen on a fireboat pick it up, the film would get into the churches, the museums, show the art of Venice — a Bellini altar piece, maybe — the architecture, the fish market, the vegetable market.
>
> Then the problems. First finding a gondolier, the father of our youthful hero. I talked (along with my Venetian production manager) with several gondoliers. My Italian is pretty good, but Venetian dialect is something else again. No need for words, however note carefully the glint of avarice in that glittering Venetian eve. "What! I screamed when I heard the price. My hearing aid doesn't go that high!"

So, sitting one day brooding over my pasta on the terrace of the restaurant, I came up with a solution. Or rather a solution came up to me. In the canal opposite was a motor barge, battered, unpainted thoroughly unromantic. And on the barge, a man (the owner) and his son, a young boy. The boy, like the restaurant and the hotel, is marvelous.

I know this is what I want — a real working man, not a dressed-up nincompoop rowing spoiled tourists around! So, anyway, the problem is solved: I have my cast. The production manager approaches the barge-owner and then we all sit down over drinks (the boy gets an ice cream cone and wanders away) to discuss "details." The father is excited: "Be in a movie? Certo!" Everything seems fine: the money is right, so much per day for the man and his boat and so much for the boy. The boy! Where is he?

He's found, his face smeared with good Italian ice cream and informed of the deal. His answer: "No." "No?" "No." He doesn't wanna be in no movie. Listen, you little so-and-so, his father says (in a far-out dialect, of course), if you keep that up I'm going to... Well, the boy agrees and after a day or so of breaking him in, or perhaps breaking him down, he turns out to be as good as he looks and actually enjoys his job.

And I enjoy it: getting up at five in the morning, rain or shine, worrying about the rain and blessing the shine, going for hours without food because you don't want to lose the light, having cameras drop overboard and vice versa, struggling with the hordes of tourists who insist on looking directly at the camera (non guardare la macchine! which as you correctly translate, is "don't look at the camera").

Then negotiating with petty officials for permission to shoot where you want to, when you want to, being turned down, going back, going over their heads, going out of yours when the lab (in Rome) neglects to telephone daily reports, making take after take, each of which (except the first!) is ruined by some bit of nonsense, getting backbone-weary to your hotel, too tired to eat (with only enough energy to down those martinis at Harry's Bar)....[15]

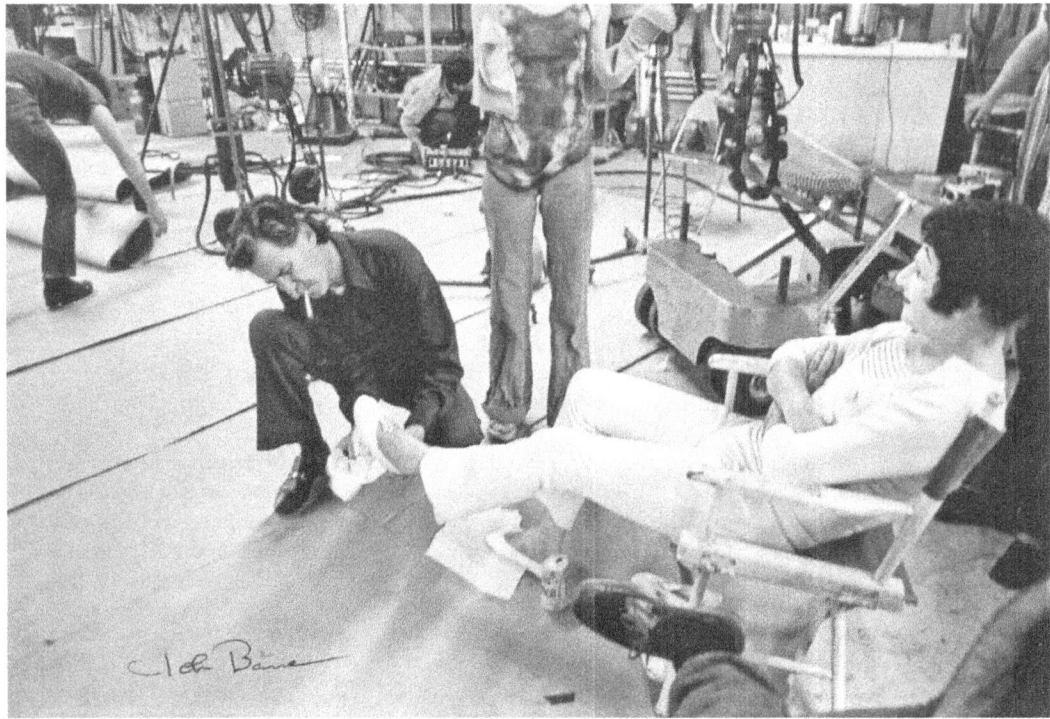

John Barnes cleans Marcel Marceau's shoes prior to shooting a film in the *Art of Silence* series (1975) (Bill Pierce).

In spite of his reputation as a wordsmith, Barnes was now ready to tackle a non-narrative project out of keeping with his previous work, the thirteen-part *Art of Silence* series with Marcel Marceau, combining the art of a superior filmmaker with that of perhaps the finest pantomime artist of his generation. The introductory film, *Pantomime: The Language of the Heart* (1975), is an explanation by Marceau of the art of pantomime, its history and its art. Subsequent films in the series, such as the sobering *Youth, Maturity, Old Age*, are introduced by a Marceau sans make-up, sitting in front of his dressing-room mirror, explaining the story of each pantomime. Barnes clearly had fun making films with the witty Marceau, as attested by the filmmaker's amusing caption to a still production photo showing Barnes washing the soles of Marceau's feet prior to the filming of a studio sequence: "Hands on again, me washing the soles of Marcel's shoes. Amused him no end — a director stooping so low? I reminded him that Jesus had washed the feet of the poor. He said that considering what I was paying him, he qualified. (Marcel never talks on stage, and never stops off-stage, in several languages.)"[16]

Final Years

Barnes' exceptional body of work in the academic film world secures his place as one of the great cinéastes of his generation. His final academic film, a treatment of Walter Van Tilburg Clark's *The Portable Phonograph* (1977), appropriately sums up the career of perhaps

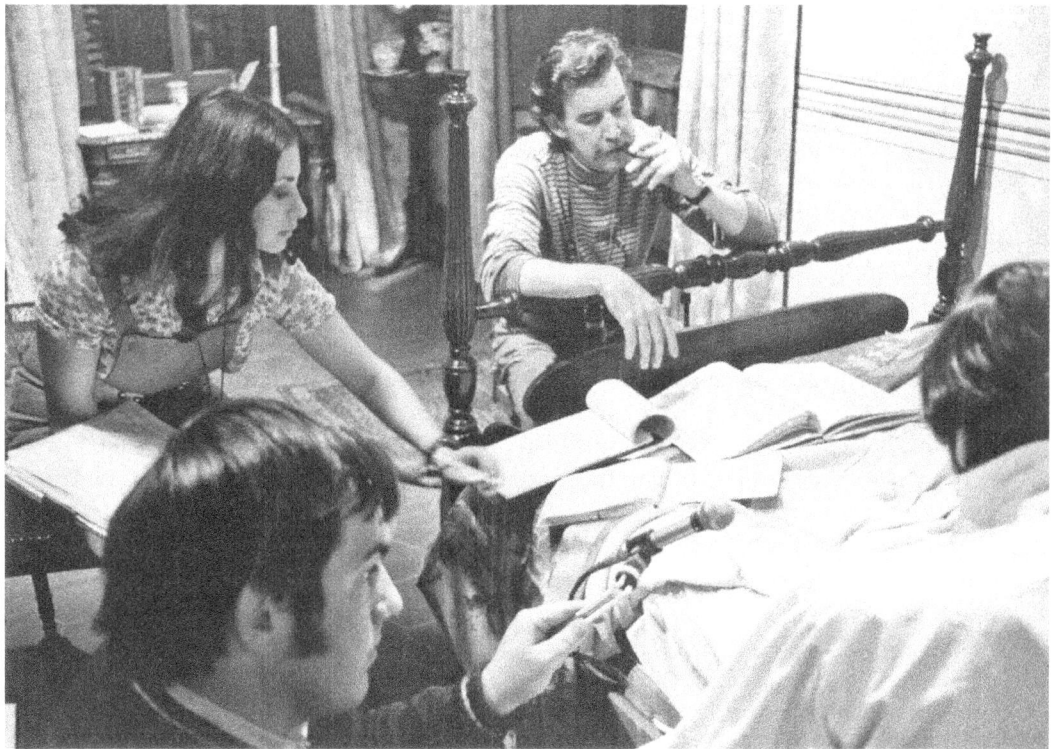

Barnes and crew discuss a scene in *John Keats: His Life and Death* (1973) (Encyclopædia Britannica, Inc.).

the genre's most intellectually stimulating filmmaker. It underscores the contribution of the arts to the human condition, introducing the viewer to a world steeped in irrevocable loss through a nightmarish future-vision, brought on by cataclysmic disaster. Here, a vintage recording of Debussy's *Nocturne* played by Walter Gieseking becomes the vehicle through which four ragged lovers of the humanities hover together to stoically celebrate and mourn, in a cold post-apocalyptic shack of sandbags. Every week at a given time, Michael Gwynn's gaunt, resigned, and vigilant professor invites his small group of tattered intellectual friends to make their way through barbed wire and rubble for an evening of painful reminiscences. Invariably, the evening ends with a choice by consensus of a rare 78 rpm recording of a famous classical piece from the past, played on a precious wind-up portable phonograph. Barnes emphatically illustrates, through flashback sequences and close-up shots, how the humanities — music, painting, literature, and theatre — are among the most enriching and ultimately unforgettable of all human endeavors. The music assists three of the men to mentally travel back in time to a point in which each was sharing an artistic experience with someone close. For one, a picnic with Debussy on the radio; another bought a used book and gave it to a companion before they attended a play; the third (the professor) painted a portrait of his disapproving daughter, accompanied by the *Nocturne,* played on the nearby phonograph. The musician, however, can picture no images, so entranced is he with the music itself. As the music dies, the men return to their dismal present, and empty, shattered lives. The music has become the most precious of commodities: instead of gold, arms, or worthless banknotes, it is the phonograph and the rare and fragile disks that the professor hides in his secret sandbag strongbox. When all friends have left, he replaces his treasure, then sits with his back to the cache, holding an iron bar as a weapon, his eyes steeling in anticipation of a potential attack. As the wind howls in the distance, a lone cough is heard just outside the hovel, and the film ends. It is one of the most powerful classroom academic films ever made.

Fortunately, a cinematic record exists of Barnes discussing on camera the intellectual challenge of bringing this powerful piece to the screen. *Story Into Film: A Discussion by John Barnes Of The Portable Phonograph* (1977) is a ten-minute short of value to filmmakers, film historians, and screenwriters alike, and one of the most introspective films ever made on the art of making academic films.

There doesn't appear to be any fixed point at which Barnes decided to formally renounce filmmaking, but *The Portable Phonograph* remains his final publicly credited film. His wife Jeanne Barnes remembers a subsequent film he shot for an insurance company, one that presumably appalled Barnes to such a degree that he apparently destroyed all records of making it or having been paid for it. There were discussions with a British feature film company, halted when John determined that "B" pictures would be the result. Supported by twenty-five years of EB film royalties and income from a family trust account, the final twenty-three years of John Barnes' life were alternately consumed by unfulfilled attempts to make films of which he could be proud, and writing plays, only some of which ever achieved public performance.

Knowing that his films were firmly established at the pinnacle of the academic film massif may have been gratifying, but the lack of recognition of his oeuvre overall was a disappointment to him. That, along with the unpredictable market for his theatrical scripts, made for a somewhat rocky denouement to Barnes' creative life. His immediate family remembers John as being more than occasionally stubborn and testy. He was often emotionally aloof. To this day, in John's Columbia Heights home overlooking New York City's East River, there remains a sizeable dent on the side of the stainless steel hood above the stove, created when the filmmaker hurled a heavy swivel chair across the room, attesting to his mercurial temper. Judging by its distance from the floor, the chair would have to have still been in the ascendancy of its arc when it made its mark.

Barnes' films have yet to receive their due, although one day, they will. His philosophy is summed up best in a quotation he delivered for a 1966 retrospective of his work in Mexico City:

> This is the important thing about educational films, I believe. Films made for the movie houses of the world — although many are made with great artistry and devotion — are essentially made to make money. Films made for television are made mostly to fill up the time between commercials. The makers of educational films are not entirely ignorant of the values of money, but essentially they have other ideas in view. But I have an idea — a faith, I suppose it really is — that some of my films — or a single film, or even a single sequence in a film or a shot in a film — will light up a young mind somewhere:— light it up so that nothing — unsympathetic teachers, lack of a decent place to live, or lack of love — can ever plunge it into darkness.[17]

One is tempted to believe that the young mind Barnes referred to is, in fact, that of the adolescent John Barnes; the filmmaker rarely divulged details about his youth or parents, and

Barnes preparing sound and lighting for *Magna Carta* (1959) (John Barnes).

much of his background will remain shrouded in mystery forever. His film legacy is perhaps his gift to other misunderstood youthful seekers who, without kindred souls in their immediate familial environs, look to books and cinematic jewels for justification and companionship.

The ultimate question, in reviewing the life and work of John Barnes, is why did this enormously talented filmmaker leave the world of film in 1977, abandoning it for the final 23 years of his life? In retrospect, Barnes was a man ideally suited to the intellectual milieu at EB. He enjoyed the clever ripostes with the Robert Hutchins, Mortimer Adlers, William Bentons, and Maurice Mitchells of the world, and, when engaged in philosophical battles, won often enough that he recognized that, in suffering the occasional defeat, he was being respected as a worthy foe and a valuable contributor. For the first fifteen years or so, he was valued as a precious commodity by those occupying EB's highest levels, who were more concerned that Hollywood would steal him away than they were at the prospect of losing him to a competitor.

By 1977, Mitchell and Charlie Benton were long gone from EB, and Senator Benton had been dead for four years. Barnes did not get along well with Ralph Wagner, who had married William Benton's daughter Louise and now ran EB's film operations. Wagner's economically stringent philosophy shunned production budgets that Barnes felt were necessary to produce a good film. Barnes' time was up, with the passing of the old guard, and there was no one left to champion the cause of this still vibrant maker of the most intellectually stimulating and visually exciting academic films of his era.

True, there were other companies with whom John might have developed a working relationship, but it's hard to imagine him proposing his intellectually challenging film projects with hat in hand. In truth, no one came calling, one guesses, because Barnes' films were never best sellers, and, as finely-crafted works of art, cost more money than the slimmed-down productions that many companies favored. Bill Deneen, then president of Columbia Pictures' Learning Corporation of America educational film division, reflected on what on one hand might have represented a resurgence of Barnes' film career, but on the other, could have produced months of acrimony:

> John called me looking for some work after EBF dried up. I demurred. Working for a company like Columbia Pictures, I couldn't subsidize a filmmaker as the Bentons and EBF had John. I also had to make films that would achieve sales of at least 500 prints, and John was much too fine a filmmaker and iconoclast to give a damn whether a film sold or not.
>
> From a manager's perspective John produced wonderful stuff, but he was trouble, imperious, and impossible to work [with], and his production costs ran way above our norm and much too high for the kind of markets we had. The equation just didn't balance. At least not for the boss at LCA, although I often thought about what great films might have been made had John contributed to our Humanities and American History series. Probably LCA's loss.[18]

John Barnes passed away on June 27, 2000, and, although in ill health for much of his final couple of years, remained a fighter up until the end, embarking on a project to document the memoirs of his radio and film career. Rather than mourn the absence of new Barnes films during his final two decades of creativity, it might be better to celebrate the fact that thrown-away university catalogues and dashed radio dreams can represent the beginning and not the end of a career, and the anger and frustration inherent in life's downturns can be repackaged. The result, glued, papered, and ribboned, can change whole industries, and lives. For nearly thirty years, John Barnes was given the gift of being able to make films, pretty much the way he wanted. He was truly the right man, at the right place, at a very special time.

Chapter Six

Profiles of 34 Significant Academic Filmmakers

The years of 1960 to 1985 represent the age of the *auteur* in academic film, as scores of filmmakers honed their craft to produce often remarkable bodies of work. While most of the filmmakers profiled here focused exclusively in academic film, several did not, instead primarily making documentary or network television films. They are included here, as their work was seen for the first time by many as a result of distribution within school film libraries.

Though this list cannot be comprehensive, the work of the filmmakers highlighted in this chapter should not be missed (John Barnes was profiled in the previous chapter). These filmmakers may not always have been the most prolific (neither Judith Bronowski nor Gerald McDermott made more than five films that were distributed the schools), nor were school films necessarily their crowning career achievements (Peter Chermayeff is better known as an architect than a filmmaker). The filmmakers described, however, produced exceptional films having the important traits of clarity of vision, precision of execution, and affective presence. Where possible, I have attempted to provide dates of birth of the filmmakers, but many are reluctant to have this information in print due to potential age discrimination issues common to the industry within which they continue to work. Filmmakers are listed alphabetically.

Johanna Alemann

Johanna Alemann is believed to be the first solo woman filmmaker specializing in making academic films in North America. Born near Berlin in Woltersdorf, Germany, on July 11, 1923, Alemann had U.S. citizenship from birth due to the fact that her father was from the United States. She had no training in filmmaking when she bought a 16mm camera for a trip to Berlin, but returned with footage that she made into her first film, *Berlin, Outpost of Freedom* (1959). She showed her film to Ann (?) Landers of *Landers Film Reviews*, and received a favorable review, which resulted in her film being acquired by school film libraries. She soon became friends with Southern California academic filmmakers Michael Hagopian and Thomas Stanton, and recalls their conversations around how many contemporary educational films were nothing more than "nuts and bolts" material, and that they wanted to make a more interesting, insightful film for students and teachers. She began her company Alemann Films in Los Angeles, and produced roughly one film per year. For a period of

A historical gathering of Encyclopædia Britannica Films alumni at Larry Yust's Los Angeles home, April, 2006. Left to Right: Bill Deneen, Geoff Alexander, Warren Everote, Milan Herzog, Bert Van Bork, Tom Smith, Larry Yust, Isidore Mankofsky, Charles Benton, Chuck Finance (Iris Shimada).

ten years, she supported her filmmaking efforts by working a 40-hour shift as an X-ray technician during weekends.

Alemann's filmmaking philosophy was to approach an idea "clearly, logically, and with good understanding" of the subject matter. She remembers taking her idea of making a film on Rococo art to one school district, who told her that the film would have limited appeal. After making the film, the same district ultimately bought ten copies of it, and it became one of her most successful films, from a financial perspective.[1] Her best selling films were in her *History Through Art* series, and *Art Portrays a Changing World: Gothic to Early Renaissance* (1963) is her personal favorite. In 1980, she wrote *The Pendulum of Choice* (1980), a book espousing her philosophy on the art of making choices in life. As of this writing, she lives in a small town in Oregon.

Norman Bean

Bean is best known for his exceptional animal life and nature films for young learners, most notably his *Backyard Science* series. He has made over 100 films, and continues to spend several months a year driving across the United States making films for Phoenix Learning Group.

Norman Bean was born in Lacrosse, Wisconsin, on November 12, 1925, grew up on a game farm, and served in the Army Air Corps in World War II. After obtaining a BA in biological science, he taught high school biology for twelve years in the L.A. County school system. Making his first film in 1953, Bean continued to teach while making short films, and began a working relationship with Paul Burnford and *Film Associates* (later *BFA*) in 1960. Bean's exceptional insect close-up cinematography involved experimenting with refrigerating insects prior to shooting, which allowed for detailed shots of moving body parts, yet slowed their metabolism so they wouldn't fly or jump away during filming (e.g., *Spiders: Backyard Science,* 2nd Ed., 1978, BFA). His slow-motion cinematography is highlighted in *Frogs: an Investigation* (1972, BFA), in which the filmmaker shows frogs catching prey with their tongues, making this a prime example of an exceptional affective film for children.

In addition to his work for BFA, Bean made films for CBS, Encyclopædia Britannica, McGraw-Hill, Aims Media, Academy, Sutherland, and Rampart. His oeuvre includes six travel films he produced and narrated on Alaska, Glacier National Park, the Bahamas, the Amazon River, Mexico and Canadian Maritimes.

Johanna Alemann, 2007 (Johanna Alemann).

Walt and Myrna Berlet

Walter and Myrna Berlet's Berlet Films, specializing in nature films, was one of the last to make academic films in the 16mm medium (*Canada Goose* was made in approximately 2000). Walter Berlet began experimenting with 8mm film while operating a dry goods store in Casper, Wyoming, and performing occasional lectures for the Audubon Society. His first film, *The Living Wilderness*, was made for the Society in 1960. While in Casper, he met Myrna, a Minot State University biology major intending on teaching as a career.[2] She soon changed career paths, and they became an inseparable film team, with Walt doing camerawork and Myrna writing most of the scripts and handling the lion's share of the editing.

One of their most memorable films is *Great Blue Heron Story* (1989), the filming of which necessitated their building a 60-foot high camera scaffold adjacent to a nest. Since most rookeries are much higher than that, they had scouted several sites before finding one located in a Lake Erie marsh subject to constant flooding, resulting in stunted tree growth. The scaffold is shown in the film, and the process of making the film is briefly discussed.

After Walt's passing in 1995, Myrna continued making nature films. Berlet closed shop in 2005, a victim of thin profit margins, constantly changing curricula, and, despite the development of a website, the difficulty of reaching film buyers.[3] From both cognitive and affective perspectives, the Berlet catalogue represents some of the finest nature films of the era.

Peter Boulton

Boulton's Boulton-Hawker Films, Ltd. was originally founded in 1946 by Gilbert Hawker and Peter Boulton, who made their first film together in Cairo for the Royal Air

Peter Boulton filming *Life Cycle of a Flowering Plant* (1975) "The time-lapse camera and flash equipment was in continuous operation in the greenhouse for several months, and the greenhouse had to be covered over at night with tarpaulins to avoid disturbing the neighbors with high-powered flashguns" (Boulton-Hawker Films, Ltd.).

Force (*Quiet Afternoon*, 1944).[4] In 1956, Hawker left amicably to concentrate on sponsored commercial films, leaving Boulton to continue with his passion for educational film, specializing in science, zoology, and botany. Boulton's family-run firm was notable for its well-written and visually arresting biology films made in England, and which were distributed in the U.S. by *Benchmark Media* and the *International Film Bureau*. Well written, beautifully photographed, and intellectually stimulating, the Boultons' films represent some of the finest examples in the sub-genre of academic science films. In this family-run enterprise, each film typically would be produced and written by son David, with exacting photography by his father, Peter, using slow-motion, time-lapse micro-photography. Additional members of the multi-dimensional (cinematography, sound, and editing) crew included son-in-law Nigel Rea, Rosemary Cizmowska, and graphic artist (and daughter) Anne Rea. A fine example of the affective techniques used by Boulton are to be found in *Fungi* (1983), which is full of attention-getters, including a close-up of a particularly virulent fungal growth on someone's large toenail, and features an exciting keyboard soundtrack by Andrew Hellaby (reminiscent of the music of Manfred Mann's Earthband of the mid–1970s). Peter Boulton passed away on March 2, 2003. In 2005, Boulton-Hawker was acquired by Cambridge Information, Ltd.

Judith Bronowski

After producing her well-received Charles and Ray Eames film *Powers of Ten: a Rough Sketch* (1968, Eames), Judith Bronowski went on to make a small but historically significant 16mm oeuvre of five titles for The Works, a company she co-owned with Robert Grant (Grant left the firm after the first three films). Four of these films depicted Mexican folk artisans at work, among them the famous woodcarver Manuel Jiménez (*Artesano de Madera*, 1977), and the exceptional maker of fantastic papier-mâché' monsters, Pedro Linares (*Artesano de Cartón*, 1975).

These important films did much to change the economic lives of their subjects and increase awareness of the significance of Mexican folk art and artisans. Bronowski's *Marcelo Ramos: Artesano Pirotécnico* (1980) is without a doubt one of the most subversive films ever distributed to classrooms. Filmed in the village of San Pedro Zumpango, renowned for its makers of elaborate fireworks, four generations of the Ramos family, from infants to grandparents, are here shown engaged in the process of mixing explosives, petroleum products, and related pyrotechnic materials. They deliver a municipal fireworks display of heroic proportions. More than a few American schoolchildren must have wanted to return home after seeing the film to dash off mad experiments with matches, gasoline, and whatever else would explode or burn, in hastily cobbled-together backyard "laboratories." Bronowski herself admits having received complaints and concerns from teachers who had shown the film. It remains today one of the most colorful and bombastic academic films ever made.

Available in both Spanish and English, Bronowski's films were often used in Spanish language classes. In addition to the value her films brought to the understanding of Mexican folk art, she also had an impact on the lives of the artists and artisans themselves. Prior to the advent of her films, Mexican artists rarely signed their work, discouraged from doing so by art distributors in order to prevent collectors from buying directly through the artist, thereby bypassing the middlemen. By bringing the individual personalities of her subjects to the foreground, Bronowski contributed to the renown of these artists, who were then able to realize fairer profits by selling directly.[5]

Unfortunately, her father, Jacob Bronowski, mathematician and host of the well-known *Ascent of Man* series produced by the BBC, died before having seen any of her films.

Peter Chermayeff

A friend of Hugo Von Lawick (married at the time to Jane Goodall), Peter Chermayeff, using their Land Rover, camera, and cook while they were away in North America, made two expeditions to Tanzania's Ngorongoro Crater (1971, 1984). He returned with difficult-to-

Peter Chermayeff surveys the set in Tanzania during the filming of his *Silent Safari* series (1969).

shoot footage of a host of fauna, and chose as sound accompaniment nothing more than a solo guitar, which, at least initially, seems somewhat out of place, fading in and out in a random pattern. What emerges, however, is a pristine, unadulterated view of the animals, the lack of narrative forcing the viewer to accept each animal on its own terms, free from scientific, cultural, or zoological context. Unlike many anthropomorphic animal films of the era, with their "mickey-mousing" musical scores, Chermayeff's films offered neither value-judgments nor socio-political statements, leaving the purpose behind their actions and interactions solely to the interpretation of the viewer. The eleven films in his *Silent Safari* series (e.g., *Lion*, 1971, and *Ostrich*, 1984), distributed by Encyclopædia Britannica Films, are among the most simple, artistically gratifying, and unique nature films ever made.

Chermayeff was born in London, England, in 1936, arriving in the United States at the age of four. As the son of noted Russian-born architect Serge Chermayeff, he was introduced at an early age to people such as Walter Gropius and Buckminster Fuller and, while studying design at Harvard, made his first film, the experimental *Orange and Blue* (1961). In 1962, the young (26 year old) architect and six associates bid for the job of constructing the New England Aquarium, surprising themselves by winning it (Chermayeff had only printed the firm's stationery the night before the initial interview). Since then, Chermayeff has become the person whom many consider to be the world's foremost designer of aquariums, having designed those in Osaka, Lisbon, Chattanooga, Genoa, and Baltimore.

Bruce and Katharine Cornwell

The Cornwells are primarily known for a series of remarkable animated films on the subject of geometry. Created on the Tektronics 4051 Graphics Terminal, they are brilliant short films, tracing geometric shapes to intriguing music, including the memorable Bach-based Third Steam jazz score in *Congruent Triangles* (*1976). Their work, distributed by the defunct International Film Bureau, is no longer available.

While in the Women's Army Corps, Katharine Cornwell was involved in investigating the ENIAC computer for bomb survey analysis, which fueled her interest in mathematics. Bruce Cornwell did graphics work for a television station in Madison, Wisconsin, where he was also engaged with the local public radio station. The Cornwells were married in 1956. Bruce has stated that his interest in math films was influenced by his seeing Disney's *Donald in Mathmagic Land* (1959, dir. Hamilton Luske), which prompted his comment, "Anyone with half a brain and one hand tied behind his back could make a better film."[6]

Like many other makers of quality academic film, the Cornwells found it made better financial sense to have additional careers. Katharine became a consultant specializing in executive compensation, while Bruce taught at Brooklyn Polytechnic. They live in Brooklyn.

Stanley Croner

Croner directed, wrote, and produced many significant academic films in the 1960s and 1970s, primarily for Encyclopædia Britannica Films. Croner's history films for EB were edgy for their time. *Santa Fe and the Trail* (1963) was perhaps the first film that utilized

Stan Croner inside an ancient well, filming in Colonial Williamsburg (Stanley Croner).

subtitled bilingual text in a historical educational film, as Croner insisted that Spanish be used for authenticity. Interracial romance and mutual respect between the cultures were dual themes that were presented a good ten years before they began appearing more frequently in films of the mid–1970s. *Gold Rush* (1965) featured naked bathers, card sharps, prostitutes, and the exhumation of corpses believed to have been buried with gold.

Stan Croner was born February 8,1927, in Baltimore, Maryland. When he was about five years old, his family moved to Charlotte, North Carolina. He grew up there, in a segregated southern society in the 1930s and early 1940s, before the Civil Rights movement got underway. He attended public schools, went camping with friends, saw films and became especially interested in still photography. His last two years of high school were spent at Riverside Military Academy in Georgia. In 1945, as World War II was winding down, he turned 18, enlisted in the U.S. Navy and became a photographer's mate.

He attended the University of North Carolina from 1946 to 1949, where he received his BA in English and American literature. In 1947, Croner and a student writer traveled to France and published picture stories in *This Week*, *Pont de Vue* and *Parade* magazines.

In 1950, he moved to New York to practice still photography. He published more picture stories, including one in *Flair* magazine about Thomas Wolfe and Asheville, North Carolina, titled *Altamont Fifty Years Later*. During this time, Croner saw and was impressed by Neo-Realist films coming out of Italy (later he would cite French New Wave films as influencing his work as well).

In 1953, Croner joined the film unit of Colonial Williamsburg in Virginia. There he worked on filmstrips and films about 18th-century life in Virginia. One of the Williamsburg films of which he was most proud was *Music of Williamsburg* (1960, dir. Sydney Meyers), written and associate-directed by Croner. This non-narrated film featured the different kinds of music — by whites and blacks — that might have been heard in Williamsburg in 1768. The film is especially noteworthy because it shows African Americans as gifted people making music in the 18th century, a concept almost unknown in academic films of the time. In making the film, Croner enlisted the help of well-known ethnologist and folk music collector Alan Lomax to choose the music and find the people who could make the music.

In 1960, he joined the filmmaking unit of Encyclopedia Britannica Films in Hollywood, as a producer and writer-director. In 1972, Croner left Britannica to freelance. He moved north to Mendocino, California, in 1977, to pursue other interests. There he wrote and produced the book *An Introduction to the World Conservation Strategy*. Stan Croner passed away on August 8, 2008.

Gene Deitch

Deitch is an Oscar-winning animation film director and scenarist. Although perhaps best known as the creator of the Tom Terrific cartoon series, Deitch is an exceptional maker of films from children's picture books, most of which he created from his Prague studio, in cooperation with his wife Zdenka. His most fascinating films would have to include *Gene Deitch: The Picture Book Animated* (1977), in which he describes graphically the painstaking process of designing a picture book, and *Tomi Ungerer Storyteller* (1981), an interview with the iconoclastic writer and illustrator, who insisted on partaking in a glass of whisky during the filming, ever-present just outside the frame.

In 1946, Deitch began working as an apprentice in the Hollywood animation studio

UPA, working as an assistant production designer on the first *Mister Magoo* cartoons for Columbia Pictures. Within five years he rose to be creative director of UPA's New York studio, where among his many gold-medal winning films were the famous Bert and Harry Piels beer commercials. His TV commercials were the first ever shown at the New York Museum of Modern Art. In 1956, CBS purchased the Terrytoons animation studio and named Deitch as its creative director. Under his supervision and direction, the studio produced eighteen CinemaScope cartoons per year for 20th Century–Fox, and won its very first Oscar nomination. He personally created and directed the *Tom Terrific* cartoon series for the CBS nationwide *Captain Kangaroo* show, the first animated serial for network television. Deitch drew Tom and wonderdog Manfred with as little ornamentation as possible, the black and white minimalist figures occasionally transparent to allow scenic images to show through their bodies. At CBS, Deitch was never able to acquire the budget needed for producing the cartoon in color, and was unceremoniously dropped from the series in 1958.

By 1959, Deitch had begun working as an independent animation director for a studio located in Prague. He was hired by Morton Schindel (who he'd met during his tenure at CBS) at Weston Woods to direct efforts utilizing Czech animators in the state-run Kratky studio, whose production manager, Zdenka Najmanová, would eventually marry Deitch. Deitch fell in love his colleague and the city and remained there, transforming over twenty picture books into film.[7] Among them were Sendak's *Where the Wild Things Are*, which took over five years to complete, and featured a *musique-concrète* score by written and performed by Deitch himself. Deitch is fond of calling this film "the Mt. Everest of picturebook films" in reference to the challenges of working with the esteemed children's author and his penchant for making changes.[8] Today, Deitch continues to make films in Prague.

William F. Deneen

A near-legendary pilot, adventurer, filmmaker, and executive, the bombastic and opinionated Bill Deneen was one of the more controversial figures in the educational film world. Born in Portland, Maine, in 1926, Deneen's film career began at the age of 10 with his mother's gift of a 16mm camera. In the 1950s he formed William Deneen Productions where he wrote, directed, produced, and shot a number of cultural/geographical films for entities including major networks, Encyclopædia Britannica Films, and National Geographic.

Deneen is perhaps today better remembered as a film executive than a filmmaker, but his films were notable, and his broadness of subject matter reflected his interest in the world around him.[9] His filmography includes 42 academic films as well as three films made for the Pontifical Institute for Foreign Missions (PIME) that include ethnographic elements.

Two of Deneen's more interesting early films were *Touch of His Hand* (1956) and *The Happy City* (1959) both funded by PIME and filmed in Burma at the leper colony founded by Father Cesare Columbo. To make each of these films, Deneen traveled as a one-man crew for two backbreaking days over jungle track to film Father Columbo's colony in Kyaingtong, Burma, using creative setups to film events such as he and Columbo walking between two rows of greeting residents. (The colony still exists today, although Columbo was forced to leave the country in the 1950s by the Burmese government.)[10]

Deneen had always been somewhat of a maverick. As a young filmmaker producing films on international subjects on a severely limited budget, Deneen thumbed his nose at censorship and export laws in foreign countries by utilizing a secret compartment in his small airplane to hide films from foreign governmental officials, thus ensuring a faster-than-normal speed to the editing table in the United States. Mexico's Department of Motion Picture Supervision, in particular, was notably thin-skinned when it came to showing anything that could be interpreted as affronting or defaming the country, including scenes of barefoot peasants or scenes of what it perceived as poverty.[11] EBF editor *par excellence* Grace Garland Janisz tells of making harrowing flights with Deneen, who would unscrew interior aircraft panels to hide exposed film, and be pursued by foreign customs officials, bribing his way out of trouble when necessary.[12] Deneen shot much of the aerial portion of *Japan: Miracle in Asia* (1963) by tilting the camera out the window of his small plane while steering the craft with his knee. When not flying his own plane, Deneen enlisted occasional confederates, such as the PanAm pilot who spirited 10,000 feet of exposed film out of an Asian country in a commercial jetliner.

Deneen's geographical films often discuss political issues sensitive to the country (*Hungary and Communism*, 1964, and *Puerto Rico: its Past, Present, and Promise*, 1965), and today represent important time-capsules of the era. His two *Arts and Crafts of Mexico* films (1961) portray historically important artisans such as potter Doña Rosa de Nieto.

Deneen made the three most lavish historical films made by any educational film company, *Claudius: Boy of Ancient Rome*, *Julius Caesar: The Rise of the Roman Empire*, and *Life in Ancient Rome* (all EB, 1964), using Samuel Bronston's extras, costumes, and sets from the epic feature film *The Fall of the Roman Empire*:

> Milan Herzog had read about the millions of dollars being poured into the making of the picture, and said, "Wouldn't it be great if we could make a film on Rome with those sets?" So I called Paul Lazarus, who worked with Bronston, and said Encyclopedia Britannica Films would love to make an educational film utilizing those sets in Spain. He thought it was a great idea because it would be great publicity for the film, and the fact that a great name like Encyclopedia Britannica would be associated

Bill Deneen in the Amazon while filming *Latitude Zero*, ca. 1960 (Bill Deneen).

with it would be a nice coup for Bronston. I ended up directing three films on that set in Spain, and they gave us access to everything, except Sophia Loren. We did get Christopher Plummer, though,[13] and the scripts were written by my high school friend Elmore Leonard.

Deneen was a serious filmmaker who wasn't afraid to occasionally tweak the brain trust at EB. His *Japanese Boy: the Story of Taro* (1963) described a day in the life of a schoolboy, narrated by Bill Deneen himself using a Japanese accent.[14]

Deneen starred his wife and three sons (all uncredited) in *Atlantic Crossing: Life on an Ocean Liner* (*1967) after he'd arranged a trade with Italian Lines for free passage for his family in return for a film about the liner *S.S. Leonardo Da Vinci*. The film is a remarkable children's film while also serving as an important document of one of the most advanced ocean liners of its day, now scrapped. This was Deneen's final title as a filmmaker. He served as an executive for the remainder of his career in academic film.

Charles L. Finance

"Chuck" Finance's career spans more than 40 years in film. Chuck was born in Klagenfurt, Austria, but grew up in Switzerland, where his father was a well-known chef. His family immigrated to the U.S. in 1952. Chuck studied film at USC, where he earned his Bachelor's degree in 1957. Following a two-year stint in the Army Signal Corps as a still and motion picture photographer, he returned to USC to complete his work for a Master's degree in cinema. Chuck's first films were made in 1961–1963 when he was brought on board as associate producer on a series of films for the Chemical Education Materials Study, sponsored by the National Science Foundation.

In 1963 he was accepted for a staff position at the West Coast Film Unit of Encyclopædia Britannica Films and became engaged in producing and directing a number of films in the legendary *AGI (American Geological Institute)* series, working alongside series advisor John Shelton and cameraman Isidore Mankofsky. After the AGI series, he began making films for EB's *Biology* and *Physics* series.

When EB decided to close its West Coast Film Unit, Chuck continued working as an independent producer/director, and for the next ten years made films for EB, the National Science Foundation, Jet Propulsion Laboratories, Churchill Films, BFA, Stanton Films, and others. He also wrote scripts, production managed, and directed non-theatrical films for other clients. Finance's academic films are engaging and, in the case of his films on the human body (*Work*

Chuck Finance on location, 1982 (Charles L. Finance).

of the Heart, 1967), are often wonderfully inventive treatments involving endoscopes and other medical devices.

Wilf Gray

The nature films of Wilf and Margaret Gray combine exceptional cinematography with efficient writing and tight editing. They pride themselves on their spirit of independence, pointing out that, of the 152 films they've made, only two were not wholly funded by themselves. Born in 1930 in the British town of South Shields, Northumberland, Wilf Gray began talking still photographs as a boy, and eventually took on the task of aerial film reconnaissance for the Royal Navy during World War II. In the mid–1950s, he helped put one of Canada's first television stations (CFCF in Montréal) on the air, and soon moved to British Columbia, where he made his first film, *Mountains to the Sea* (renamed *Northwest: Mountains to the Sea*) in 1956. His films have won numerous and well-deserved awards.

Gray was one of the first academic filmmakers to insist on using color film, and points to his feature film of 1973, *Four Seasons,* as being the first feature relying totally on natural sound. In spite of having a large library of natural sound and extraordinary footage, Gray steadfastly refused to rent these resources to other media institutions, as he felt this would dilute the value of his films. In making a film, Wilf was the cameraman and wrote the script, and his wife Margaret (also a native of Northumberland) did the research, sound recording, and handled travel and location logistics. Today, Wilf Gray's films are out of distribution. He is currently investigating the possibility of making his films available again on DVD.

Wilf Gray is a filmmaker of the old school. He writes: "You can only do a film from the heart if you finance it yourself ... to be independent, you have to make sacrifices. We are the only documentary filmmakers of note that have never gone to the government for funding." He eschews publicity ("We don't need publicity here, we're only two people"), and modern conveniences such as voicemail and email. On one hand, he's a throwback to an older, more independent era, where quality of product and insistence on personal and professional standards was paramount. On the other, his insistence on living life at his own pace, rather than one dictated by the exigencies of business, could be viewed as futuristic.

Milan Herzog (Milan Herzog).

Milan Herzog

Milan Herzog served as an executive producer on an estimated 400 academic film titles. Born in Vrbovec, Croatia, on August 23–24, 1908, Milan's greatest impact in academic film was as Encyclopædia Britannica Films' Vice President of Production, where he influenced, supported, and befriended filmmakers such as Chuck Finance, Tom Smith, Bert Van Bork, and Larry Yust. Milan has had an exceptionally rich life, and his pre-film memoirs could easily fill several volumes. Prior to his film career, he was a judge, foreign newspaper correspondent, Department Head at the U.S. Office of War Information, and commentator for the Voice of America. A citizen of the United States since 1940, Milan began his career at Encyclopædia Britannica Films in 1946 as a staff producer. Highlights of his producing career include extensive series of foreign language instruction films (the 24-title *Je Parle Français*, 1961, the 54-title *La Familia Fernández*, 1963, and the 14-title *Emilio en España*), and over 60 films on Humanities subjects.

Milan can boast several "firsts." His Medieval films from 1956 (e.g., *Medieval Manor*) were among the first academic historical films to use costumed actors, and his *Christmas Rhapsody* (1955) is the first film to include a musical score utilizing a children's orchestra and chorus. In 1958–1959, Milan served as an advisor to the fabled Physical Science Study Committee (PSSC), and produced a film (*Time and Clocks*, 1960) for them as well. He cofounded the North Shore Community Theatre in Evanston, Illinois, wrote a three-act play, and served on the board of Charles Benton's *Films Incorporated*. Milan passed away at the age of 101 on April 20, 2010. He remained a legendary raconteur until his final days (he enjoyed regaling visitors with the story of Archduke Ferdinand's assassination prior to World War I, remembering it distinctly, having discussed it at home in Sarajevo on the day it occurred). He attributed his long life to "choosing good parents and a good wife (Shanta Herzog)."

George Kaczender

A refugee from Hungary, Kaczender joined the National Film Board of Canada in 1957 as a young, experienced assistant director, where he teamed with Nicholas Balla, a producer whose parents were from Hungary as well. Challenged by a new language and culture, the filmmaker worked on over forty Film Board titles as editor or writer, and in 1964, directed the first half-hour dramatic film ever for the Board, *Phoebe*, a brilliant portrayal of a pregnant teenager. Many of Kaczender's films treat themes of transition and crisis in the adolescent (*The Game*, 1966; *You're No Good*, 1965), infant (*World of Three*), and adult (*Little White Crimes*, 1966) worlds. Influenced by Fellini, Kaczender's film world is populated with extreme camera angles, occasional forays into surrealism (*Phoebe*), superior acting, and exacting editing.

George Kaczender (Lois Siegel).

In *World of Three* (1966), we see and hear the world through the perspective of a three year old, incomprehensive as to why instructions are being given, needing to explore, and not understanding why his attempts to please his parents (Michael Learned and Peter Donat, with their real-life son Lucas) often fail, in a project for which Kaczender spent three weeks with the family during filming. In an attempt to regulate "controversial" sex education films, the Film Board was threatened with having to register as a "foreign agent," adverse to U.S. interests, and Kaczender's film *Phoebe* was temporarily withheld from U.S. distribution (eventually, in 1971, it was picked up for distribution by Bill Deneen's Learning Corporation of America). Kaczender's films on the growing pains of childhood and adolescence were not made specifically for the education market, yet became popular with educators for forceful dialogue and intelligent treatments of complex issues. As such, they are among the finest examples of affective sociodramatic educational film ever made.

Richard Leacock

Born in London, July 18, 1921, Leacock grew up on a banana plantation in the Canary Islands until shipped off to school in England. He attended Bedales then Dartington Hall schools from 1929 to 1938, where he helped form a student film unit and made his first film, the eight minute silent *Canary Bananas*. His primary contribution to classroom academic film in the United States is a series of five films made for the Physical Science Study Committee (PSSC) in the late 1950s, *A Magnet Laboratory, Frames of Reference, Electric Fields, Coulomb's Law,* and *Crystals*. Of these, Leacock recalls:

> Zach [program director Jerrold Zacharias] tended to assign the subjects that were complex, as in this case, or those where the teachers were complex as with Bitter, with whom Zach did not get along, Rogers, at Princeton who was known as a star lecturer (he had been the physics teacher at Bedales, the school I was sent to in England) I think I was the only film maker around who had majored in Physics at College so, at least I knew the language. My favorites are *Frames, Crystals*, with Allen Holden of Bell Labs (one of the group that discovered the transistor), there is an extraordinary shot in that where we melted some Saylol (spelling?) crystals under the microscope and then let them grow; they go from blobs into perfect diamond shapes. Holden was a wonderful scientist and caused me to revise my opinion of Bell Labs, an extraordinary product of the world of monopoly! *Colomb's Law* and another with Eric Rogers were more like filming a star actor doing his thing. At the end

Ricky Leacock (Richard Leacock).

Ricky Leacock utilized rotating camera rigs and stage sets while filming his often-dizzying film *Frames of Reference* (1960) in the PSSC science series. From left: host Donald Ivey (upside down), host Patterson Hume, Richard Leacock, unidentified crewman (Richard Leacock).

of the proof of the inverse square law (à la Cavendish) the young girl who we charged up with a couple of million volts to make her hair stand on end, is my eldest daughter, Elspeth. She is still mad at him because he promised to send her a Wimshurst Machine and never did.[15]

The PSSC film *A Magnet Laboratory* (*1959) featured the fabled and sartorially disheveled Dr. Francis Bitter of MIT experimenting with powerful electro-magnets, and ultimately setting one experiment on fire and quelling it with a nearby fire extinguisher.[16] Breaking nearly every rule established for academic science films up to that time, Leacock, who himself studied physics at MIT, utilized the lab as a sort of constructivist stage, at one point "breaking" a researcher at mid-torso in the upper right of the frame to linger for several minutes, rear-end to camera. Perhaps the most arresting moment of the film occurs roughly half way through when the telephone rings, an off-screen voice says, "It's for you," and Bitter, without missing a beat, responds, "Tell 'em I'll call 'em back later." Leacock gives every physicist in the lab a personality, from the droll Bitter to "Beans" Bardo, the improbable name of the technician whose responsibility it was to crank up the 12-foot high, twenty-foot long generator to nearly explosive proportions while drowning out Bitter's attempt to explain what was about to occur.[17] Assistant Dr. John Waymouth is almost as funny as Bitter, exhorting Beans to "Fire when ready, maestro!" before engaging Bitter in a duel of magnet power, culminating in the accidental calamity. The filmmaker fondly remembers working with Bitter, a constant thorn-in-the-side of the staid MIT Physics department both in the lab and at departmental parties, often accompanied by his outspoken, flamboyant, and attractive wife, renowned for needling her husband's self-important colleagues.[18]

Three other Leacock-directed PSSC films are worthy of note. *Crystals* (1958) features Bell Labs' Alan Holden's dry humor, describing his own private fun in growing crystals, diametrically opposed to the manic Princeton professor Eric Rogers hosting Leacock's *Coulomb's Law* (1959). Rogers is animated, continually removing and replacing his eyeglasses, ordering around lab assistants — he forcefully breaks a glass test tube in the hands of an assistant to demonstrate the inelasticity of water — and furiously pounds equations on a blackboard. (Leacock says the scribblings must have lasted 45 minutes, in what must be one of the more necessary cuts in the history of academic film.) Utilizing a fascinating set consisting of a rotating table and furniture occupying surprisingly unpredictable spots within the viewing area, Leacock's *Frames of Reference* (1960) features fine cinematography by Abraham Morochnik and funny narration by University of Toronto professors Donald Ivey and Patterson Hume, in a wonderful example of the fun a creative team of filmmakers can have with a subject other, less imaginative types might find pedestrian.

One of the pioneers of the *cinéma vérité* movement, Leacock' documentary work also appeared in schools, as edited versions of films made originally for U.S. television networks.

Isidore Mankofsky

Isidore Mankofsky (Isidore Mankofsky, A.S.C.).

Cinematographer Isidore Mankofsky may have been directly involved in more academic films than any other individual in his profession. His work for Encyclopædia Britannica was inventive, and more than occasionally extraordinary (note the gargantuan human hand on the beach in Warren Brown's *Beach: River of Sand* EBF, 1968). After his career in academic film, he went on to a formidable career in feature films.

Isidore Mankofsky, ASC, received his formal photographic training at the Ray Vogue School of Photography and the Brooks Institute of Photography and counts forty-three years as a cinematographer. His early career was both as a still photographer and cinematographer covering wildly eclectic assignments that included TV specials, documentaries, sports, industrials, news and nine years with Encyclopedia Britannica Films as staff cameraman. While at Encyclopedia Films he photographed over two hundred classroom films, covering a broad range of subjects. Since then, as a freelance Director of Photography his work has encompassed features, commercials, television and special venue 3-D films. Isidore's credits as Director of Photography on feature films including *Somewhere In Time* (1980, dir. Jeannot Szwarc). His telescopic shot from that film is taught as part of the curriculum in at least one film school.

Isidore's own personal history is fascinating. One of twelve children of Russian immigrants (only eight made it beyond infancy), his first name was left off his birth certificate, and his name was finally formalized upon his joining the military. While filming the massive EB *Chemistry Introductory Course* series project in 1959, he used the name "Bill Mann" on the advice of a producer who warned him of anti–Jewish bias in the state of Florida at the time. A fascinating storyteller, Mankofsky had the foresight to collect props, scripts, and other artifacts from his years at EB (1959–1968). He is in the process of finishing a book on his work as a still photographer.

Gerald McDermott

Gerald McDermott began experimenting with film as an extracurricular activity while attending Detroit's Cass Technical High School, and made his first commercial film (*Stonecutter*, *1960) at the age of 19, an extremely complex animation short featuring 2000 animation cels presented in six minutes. Influenced by Klee and Matisse, McDermott used silk-screen and traditional painting techniques in crafting ethnographic folk tale animation shorts. Traveling to Paris, he introduced himself to Henri Langlois at the Cinémathèque Française, who in turn sent him to Alexandre Alexieff, master of the *pinscreen* (a frame holding thousands of retractable pins which, when struck by perpendicular light from each side, would produce a three dimensional image based on the manner in which the pins were pushed from the opposite side of the viewer).

Returning to the U.S., McDermott attended Pratt Institute in New York. In the mid–1960s, McDermott began taking over some of the in-house animation responsibilities at the International Film Foundation (IFF), hired after Julien Bryan screened *Stonecutter*. Shortly thereafter, McDermott's life was changed dramatically by a meeting that he begrudgingly attended at the behest of Bryan, at which mythologist Joseph Campbell, heretofore unknown by the young filmmaker, viewed McDermott's film. Thus began a life-long friendship and working relationship between Campbell and McDermott, who now serves as a Fellow of the foundation bearing Campbell's name. McDermott's short but important film career consisted of some of the finest animation ever to appear in the classroom film genre.

McDermott's films have an international flavor, and several are enhanced by accented narrator Athmani Magoma and ethnic music-influenced composer Thomas Wagner. Due primarily to a career change, his filmography consists of only five films, all of which are under 12 minutes in length. After his last film, McDermott turned to illustrating children's books, for which he won the Caldecott Award as outstanding illustrator for *Anansi the Spider* and *Arrow to the Sun*, both of which McDermott turned into films. McDermott makes a brief appearance in the film *Morton Schindel: From Pages to Screen* (1981), reading in the studio for an animated version of *Arrow to the Sun*. In addition, McDermott animated several of Julien and Sam Bryan's International Film Foundation titles (e.g., *Ancient Peruvian*, 1968).

McDermott also shot film for IFF, once traveling to Russia to film that country during winter (Bryan's own Soviet footage, consisting of hundreds of hours of film, contained no winter scenes). Using a windup 16mm camera with a thirty-second limit, McDermott struggled with the camera slowing down toward the end of the wind due to the effect of the cold upon the lubrication, and after each shot he'd hastily stuff the camera into his coat to warm it up again temporarily for the next shot. His Intourist guide was a pretty young woman with whom McDermott continued to correspond after his return to the States. The traveling party also included a young blonde vacationer from the U.S. who tagged along, and had a distinct aversion to having her picture taken, an anomaly to an IFF crew, used instead to people asking to have themselves preserved on film. Years later, watching a television program, McDermott would recognize the face of the blonde woman, revealed as the CIA agent involved with the arrest of a foreign spy. By this time he had been informed that the address to which he'd been writing the young Intourist guide had been that of KGB headquarters.

McDermott today continues writing successful children's books.

Wayne Mitchell

Born in Detroit, Michigan, on April 5, 1926, the young Mitchell had set his sights on being a park ranger, eventually becoming one in Wyoming's Grand Teton National Park.

A one-family crew: Wayne Mitchell and Family in Afghanistan (Wayne Mitchell).

Soon, he embarked on a career as a successful still photographer of wildlife and nature subjects. Eventually, he pursued cinematic studies at the University of Southern California, which led to his first film, *National Park Rangers* (company unknown), in 1955. In 1959, together with sound technician Sven Walnum, he followed candidate John F. Kennedy on the campaign trail, where his footage was used for election promotional spots. He also found work as a cinematographer in the Indo-Pakistani and Viet Nam wars, taught photography for two years at Miami University, and worked briefly in the feature film world. Beginning his educational film work in 1961, Mitchell specialized in international, ethnographic, arts, and economics films, made primarily in South America, Africa, and Asia. While in Japan, he married his Japanese interpreter, Yasuko Hanada, and created fourteen films on Japan (e.g., *Japanese Mountain Family*, 1966).

Mitchell, an auteur who wrote his own narration, selected his own shots, and chose music and voiceovers, compiled an extensive library of ethnic music on ¼" reels, yet didn't shirk from occasionally beating a drum, chanting, or playing an ocarina as musical accompaniment to his films. He eschewed strict anthropological interpretations of his subject matter, and thus, knowing that elementary schools were not about to adopt films containing images of bare-breasted women, he requested the Chocó women to cover up during filming, as they did when visiting a village (*Rainforest Family*, 1971). He is opinionated as to the impact of imported Western concepts in non–Western cultures, from technology to the practices of many of the missionaries plying their trade in developing nations.

Mitchell is one of the few educational filmmakers still working in 16mm, carrying a customized portable sound and editing unit to remote locations. A multifaceted individual who now makes his home in New Zealand, Mitchell lives in a Japanese-inspired house he designed and built overlooking the Pacific Ocean.

Alan Root

Born May 12, 1937, in London, Root's family moved to Kenya while he was young. Choosing to leave school at the age of 16, he tried his hand at trapping, guiding, and flying aircraft. He learned his filmmaking craft on a Bolex 16mm camera. In approximately 1956, he began working for the father and son team of Bernard and Michael Grzimek, who were making films under the auspices of the Frankfurt Zoological Society. Tragically, Michael Grzimek's zebra-striped plane crashed into the slopes of Ngorogoro, killing him and leaving his father distraught and unable to finish the film on which they'd been working. Root was asked to finish the 35mm effort, which he did, and was distributed under the title *The Serengeti Shall Not Die* (1958).

An exceptional maker of wildlife films, Root never attended film school and considers himself a self-taught naturalist. In the mid–1970s, he, along with his wife and collaborator Joan, brought the first hot-air balloon to Africa for filming purposes, recognizing that airplanes were too fast to film animals adequately, while the noise of the slower helicopters frightened them away. A visually-stunning and amusing film is *Balloon Safari* (1976), which chronicles the arrival of the balloons, as well as the tribulations of learning to fly them. Root's films have all the characteristics of great nature documentary film: an understated — or non-existent — music track, insightful narration, and spectacular footage. Occasionally, he would use tame animals as actors, anathema to purists, but quite effective in allowing him to film often spectacular close-ups illustrating animal behavior.

A still from Alan Root's *Balloon Safari* (1975) (Alan Root).

Root's filming is often made under dangerous conditions. He had a hole ripped in his leg during an underwater hippo attack, was bitten by a leopard and a gorilla, and has suffered bouts of malaria and river blindness. He writes:

> I was bitten on the r.h. index finger when handling a very big Puff-Adder. I was in the Meru Nat Park, about seventyfive mins [sic] flight from Nairobi. I had been bitten in the past by a burrowing adder and had the antivenin, and knew I might be allergic the second time around, so held off any injections. However, halfway to Nairobi I was vomiting and fainting so I had 20ccs of antivenin intramuscularly.
>
> On arrival at the hospital I was semi-conscious — in fact from an allergic reaction to the antivenin — not because of the bite. They had been told only that I had been bitten, so gave me another 20ccs of antivenin intravenously. This triggered anaphylactic shock, which very nearly killed me. I was resuscitated but the local damage around the hand was huge, and I lost the finger and a lot of the use and mobility of that hand. I've had to move some of the buttons from the right hand control to the left so I can fly the helicopter![19]

As an ongoing project, Root has been working on a bio-diversity project in Zaire, and turned his passion for balloons into a commercial enterprise, providing rides for tourists near his home in Lake Naivasha. His ex-wife Joan, an ardent conservationist facing life threats for her work in Africa, was murdered by as-yet unidentified individuals in January 2006.

Bruce J. Russell

Bruce Russell was a former high school biology teacher who began using a camera while serving as a consultant to a Bert Van Bork–led crew making a science film for Encyclopædia Britannica. Russell soon formed BioMEDIA, an educational film company specializing in biology subjects, characterized by spectacular color close-ups of microscopic life forms, utilizing visually-arresting background colors.

Russell's first major endeavor in biological film was the fifteen-part *Inhabitants of the Planet Earth* series, made in conjunction with associate J. David Denning, and distributed in 16mm format by Ward's Natural Science.

His films for Coronet's *Biological Sciences, Cell Biology*, and *Microbiology* series are among the most significant — from both educational and cinemagraphic perspectives — ever made in the genre. Russell's films on biology are made utilizing extremely colorful backlighting for the filming of microscopic animals, and are among the most engaging photomicrographic films ever made. His *Imaging a Hidden World*—the

Bruce Russell using the DiscoveryScope, which he invented (Bruce Russell).

Light Microscope (*1984) is particularly important, as it documents the techniques he used to create his films.

In addition, Russell was the co-inventor of the *DiscoveryScope,* a hand-held microscope capable of photographing and videotaping micro subjects (over 200,000 have been sold), and was the author of a pictorial bioguide, *Guide to Microlife.* Russell died unexpectedly in a fall from the roof of his house on December 20, 2006.

Paul Saltzman

Canadian director/producer Paul Saltzman is an exceptional documenter of ethnic tradition, his films containing traditional ethnographic film elements, including the showing of processes begun and completed, and utilization of non-actors.

From 1976 through 1981, Saltzman, accompanied by wife and collaborator/scriptwriter Deepa Mehta, traveled to many developing nations to document native arts and crafts transitioning from one generation to another.[20] Saltzman's treatments focused on the adolescent learning the craft from an older practitioner, then stumbling through the initial stages of creativity to finally produce a work of art, thus guaranteeing the continuation of the craft for another generation. Saltzman unveils art forms with which we're perhaps not too not familiar: dhowmaking (shipbuilding) from Zanzibar (*Slima the Dhowmaker,* 1978), Persian mosque tiles (*Jafar's Blue Tiles,* 1979), and parasol painting from Thailand (*Lee's Parasol,* 1979). His colors are breathtaking, and the camerawork, editing and writing are exceptional.

Paul Saltzman made his first three films on a budget of $5000 each. These were eventually seen by Sheldon Sachs at Coronet who bought distribution rights and funded twenty three more films, keeping Saltzman busy through 1983 making his ethnographic films for his *World Cultures and Youth* series (known in Canada as *Spread Your Wings*).

Today, Saltzman has found new popularity as a still photographer, which began with a trip to India, where he met the Beatles, and he's published several books documenting these experiences. His latest

Paul Saltzman (left) and Fred Harris at Ras Nungwi, Zanzibar, filming *Slima the Dhowmaker* (1976) (Paul Saltzman).

documentary film, *Prom Night in Mississippi* (2008), describes the first interracial prom held at a Mississippi high school.

Bert Salzman

Born in New York City in 1931, Bert Salzman grew up in an orphanage and was a New York City high-school dropout who prided himself on becoming self-educated (he would base much of the dramatic structure he would later use in his films on Aristotle's *Poetics*). He also developed a life-long passion for painting. At the age of 17, he joined the Marines and fought in Korea. Upon his return, he worked at a number of occupations, while continuing to draw and paint. He describes his entry into the film world:

> When my G.I. Bill of Rights ran out in 1960 so did my art school tuition payments. I tried working in a frame shop for a while but the hours were long and the pay short. So, when I was approached by an ex-student friend, who offered me a "gofer" position on a low-budget industrial film, I grabbed it. He asked me if I knew a little about electricity and I said, "Yes." (I knew nothing.) "Good," he responded, "because you'll also be working with heavy movie lights." He took me to the film equipment rental company and pointed out the lighting equipment that we would be using, and rattled off some technical specs about them. I was totally confused and was about to tell my friend to hire someone else, but he already suspected that I was over my head and suggested that I spend some time familiarizing myself with the lighting equipment. When he left I stood there lost. I asked John Henry, the young man who worked there, if he could help me. From the rental contract he knew when the job began and suggested, "You've got six days and I'll be working nights when it's slow. Come in around six every evening, and in a few days I'll teach you what you need to know to get started — all for only twenty bucks." He smiled and said, "Meanwhile, go to a secondhand bookstore and buy a copy of *Electricity Made Simple* and read it through three times." For almost four hours every evening we poured through *Electricity Made Simple*. We also set up and took down just about every movie light in the shop about ten times. Later, I was to follow the same procedure with *Motion Picture Photography Made Simple*, when I was offered a job as assistant cameraman. And that is the way my

Bert Salzman, Oscar-winner for *Angel and Big Joe* (1975) (Bert Salzman).

movie career proceeded. I moved through every job on the set: Lighting, Camera, Sound, Assistant Director, and finally Writer-Director-Producer. I learned each craft on the job with the help of friends and the "made simple" books.[21]

Salzman's first film, *How Things Get Done* (1964), dealt with the subject of urban renewal, and was co-produced by George Stoney. In 1970, Linda Gottlieb of the Learning Corporation of America (LCA) asked him to choose three ethnic groups as focal points for a small series of films. The series eventually comprised eight titles, including the Oscar-winning *Angel & Big Joe* (*1975), the story of the friendship between a telephone lineman and a youth of Puerto Rican parents. Salzman infused each of these films (which he both wrote and directed) with elements essential to great film of any genre: pathos, passion, and humor. Salzman's film subjects comprised individuals the filmmaker felt had been marginalized in contemporary society, including the homeless and people of varying ethnicities. *Shopping Bag Lady* (*1975), believed to be the first academic film to address the theme of homeless people, is the story of a teenage girl who cruelly mocks an old woman she considers worthless, but changes her perspective when she views the life of the woman through an old photo album, where we see her as a baby and a young girl. Both *Matthew Aliuk: Eskimo in Two Worlds* (*1973) and *Geronimo Jones* (*1970) describe the impact on families of the clash between traditional native cultures and contemporary Western culture. In the latter, a Papago-Apache youth has been given the gift of an amulet worn by his grandfather. In buying a birthday present for the grandfather, Geronimo trades the amulet for a TV, which he places before the grandfather (played by Geronimo's great-grandson, Chief Geronimo Kuth-Li). When Geronimo turns on the TV, the two are instantly reminded or the relationship of the Native American to contemporary society.

At the age of 51, the filmmaker left the cinema world for a house in the French countryside to continue his life-long study of art and literature. "My life is my career," said Salzman to people who questioned the impact of the move on his future in film. He now lives in northern California with wife Jeanne, where he paints and teaches meditation. His book *Being a Buddha on Broadway* was released in the summer of 2004.

Georg Schimanski

Schimanski was a master of time-lapse and micro-cinematography. Working primarily for the German company FWU, his films were distributed by U.S. companies such as Benchmark and Encyclopædia Britannica. Georg Schimanski was born on the 13th of October 1919, in Allenstein/East-Prussia. In 1924 the family moved to Königsberg/East-Prussia, where, in 1936, he started an apprenticeship in the "Photographic materials and cinema special Shop — Schilling," against the wishes of his parents, who wanted him to become a Catholic priest. During his education he met Heinz Sielmann, who made his first film *Vögel über Haff und Wiesen* in 1936, and encouraged him to become a filmmaker.

In 1939 he was called up to the military service, was wounded in 1944, taken prisoner of war by the Red Army, and released in the summer of 1945. Soon thereafter, he reconnected with Heinz Sielmann and worked as his cameraman on many biological films for the FWU until 1960. In 1960 he became independent and worked as producer, cameraman and editor, and in 1965 built his own studio. He soon acquired a worldwide reputation as a specialist in photomicrography and time-lapse techniques (e.g., *Housefly*, 1982). In his famed studio he made nearly everything by himself: the shooting script, camera, sound recording, editing, text and synchronization. He invented equipment to meet his needs, shot all his films on 35mm and used Arriflex cameras as well as ARRI- cameras and very old Askanias on his microscopes and time lapse shots. The producer of nearly 100 films, many of which won national and international prizes, Schimanski passed away on March 23, 1992.

Hermann Schlenker

Schlenker is a maker of exceptional non-narrated ethnographic films, distributed in the United States during the 1960s and 1970s. His work documents social customs, arts, and crafts in mostly non–Western nations. Edited versions of his films (many of which were originally one hour or longer) were distributed in the U.S. by Julien Bryan's International Film Foundation, including fourteen Afghan, eight Venezuelan (Orinoco Indians), five Melanesian, and twelve Malian (e.g., *Building a House: Bozo People*, 1967) films.

Charles and Libby Schwartz

Two of the more remarkable filmmakers specializing in nature films were Charles W. and Elizabeth Schwartz, who made 24 films, most of which were produced for the Missouri Department of Conservation. From 1949 through 1978, Charlie and Libby Schwartz wandered through much of North America, Hawaii, and the Caribbean on arduous expeditions, carrying cumbersome camera, sound, and blind gear, filming birds, mammals, and reptiles. Typical of their fine work is the film *Bobwhite through the Year* (1953), an exceptional work that is detailed, well-shot, informative, and creative.

Charles Schwartz (b. June 2, 1914), who grew up in St. Louis, was the son of a prominent ophthalmologist, and studied biology and zoology at the University of Missouri. There, he met Elizabeth Reeder (b. September 13, 1912), originally from Columbus, Ohio, who was an instructor on the University of Missouri. faculty, and the daughter of a professor at Ohio State University. After receiving her doctorate, she taught at Sweetbriar College in Virginia, and at Stephens College, Missouri. She and Charles married in 1938. In addition to making films, Charles was a well-regarded wildlife illustrator and author, whose best known books are *Wild Mammals of Missouri* and *Wildlife Drawings*. Charles passed away in 1991, and Libby lives in retirement in Idaho. Libby Schwartz recalls their early days in film:

> [The] equipment was archaic by today's standards. For example, [the] camera speed was too slow for synchronized sound or slow motion action. The cameras were spring-driven (wound up like old fashioned alarm clocks) which meant they often stopped at an inopportune time. Sound was recorded on a microphone placed near the booming ground but this was powered by a large generator 400 feet away (because of the noise it made). Blinds of many different designs were used including some with two-way glass for observation.
>
> It would be monotonous to go into detail about each motion picture. They all consumed time because we portrayed each species throughout an entire year of its life. The best way to do this was to film one picture while we edited the picture we had filmed the year before. Thus, our life became divided into "sunny day work" (filming) and "rainy day work" (editing and other indoor projects). Each night we'd listen to the weather forecast that followed the 10 o'clock news on the radio (later TV) and then decide on our program for the next day.[22]

Charles and Libby Schwartz, Puerto Rico, 1963 (Elizabeth Schwartz).

Thomas G. Smith

In 1965, following three-years in the U.S. Air Force, Thomas G. Smith joined Encyclopædia Britannica Educational Corporation as a writer/director. In the next 12 years he made more than 60 films for EB. He also made nearly 20 films for other educational and television distributors including PBS, BFA, and Churchill Films.

One of Smith's last films for EB was *Solar System, 2nd ed.* (*1977). Through the use of visual effects, the film takes the viewer on a cinematic ride through space. The film took over a year to complete, and over 13 weeks to film. When George Lucas saw this film in 1979, he hired Smith to run Industrial Light and Magic (ILM), his visual effects facility. From 1980 to 1986, Smith oversaw the visual effects for many blockbuster features, including *Raiders of the Lost Ark* (1981), *E.T.: The Extra-Terrestrial* (1982), *Poltergeist* (1982), *Star Trek 2* and *3* (1982/83), *Return of the Jedi* (1983), *Indiana Jones and the Temple of Doom* (1984), and many others. He also wrote the best selling visual effects book *Industrial Light and Magic: The Art of Special Effects.*

The popularity of Smith's stellar feature film and television work overshadows his very good academic film work, which included the exceptional *Farm Family* series, in which Smith, visiting Red Markham's farm near Whitewater, Wisconsin, documents the life and work of the family in each of the four seasons (e.g., *Farm Family in Winter,* 1968).

Philip Stapp

Born in Madison, Indiana, on April 13, 1908, Stapp was one of the most original and creative animators ever to work in the world of academic film. After studying music and fine arts, he was awarded a traveling scholarship for European study by the Maryland Institute of Fine and Applied Arts. While in Europe, he worked briefly with designer Jules Bouy. In the 1930s, he became a painter, and exhibited his works in group shows at both the Whitney and Guggenheim museums. He taught art at the prestigious Greenwich (CT) Country Day School, where he remembers making a small, hand-drawn picture book of Chaucer's tales for a little boy who had fallen ill (that boy, future president George H.W. Bush, still has the book). In those years, Stapp also evidenced a passion for furniture design, contributing drawings for an international competition in Germany, resulting in the crafting of several pieces which were displayed as part of the exhibition.

Philip Stapp at 40 and 90 (Geoff Alexander).

In 1939, Stapp worked at Bennington College, Vermont, with dancer Martha Graham, where he designed the sets for her *Columbiad* and *Every Soul is a Circus* performances. Of those days, Stapp recalled that he "learned from her something of the time-space-pattern relationships which good choreographers understand so well. I thought, and still do, that animated film-making is a kind of choreography of graphic symbols."[23] In the early 1940s, Stapp began working at Julien Bryan's International Film Foundation, making maps and title sequences for a series of films on South America. In 1946 he made his first film, *Boundary Lines*, an abstract study of the physical and cultural limitations placed on individuals by political and social forces, then followed it two years later with *Picture in Your Mind* (*1948), a film on the theme of world peace.

Such films, with assistance from his friend Alfred Barr of New York's Museum of Modern Art, and dancer Graham, helped Stapp win a Guggenheim Fellowship in 1949. He was also invited to join the Information Division of the Marshall Plan Organization, under Stuart Schulberg, to help train animators in its film unit's animation studio in Paris. In 1953, he contributed animation to the John Halas/Joy Batchelor award-winning film version of George Orwell's *Animal Farm*. Returning to the States in 1956, he would, over the next two decades, contribute finely-crafted elements to many films in the IFF catalogue, from illustrated maps and titles to more complex animated sequences, thereby setting the standard for creativity in animating the educational film.

Stapp's importance as an animator is underestimated for two reasons. For one, his animated films were only distributed through academic or industrial film companies, and so never achieved theatrical or television distribution. Second, Stapp doggedly refused to promote himself or his work, believing that once a work was finished, it belonged to time, and merited no further discussion. Many of the films animated by Stapp do not even list him in the credits. He was influenced by interdisciplinary elements as disparate as Pointillism, Japanese Ukiyo-e "floating world" paintings, modern dance choreography, and musical counterpoint. He influenced noted filmmaker Norman McLaren, who credited Stapp's staggered image technique as having influenced his film *Pas De Deux* (1967).[24]

As opposed to the static animation style inherent in many contemporary educational films, Stapp's figures instead float, split apart, dissolve, spin, and vaporize in a constant state of metamorphosis, "a consecutive flow of drawn images calculated to be photographed in strict counterpoint to musical score."[25] This technique is perhaps best expressed in what may have been Stapp's most inventive film, the abstract-yet-geometrical *Symmetry* (*1966) distributed in by Contemporary Films. His *First Americans: Some Indians of the Southlands* (1976) is another good example of his highly stylized technique, resplendent with oriental/geometrical elements.

Stapp's animation technique was unique. To create an image, he would lay a field of solid color on the back of a piece of construction paper, placing it atop a white paper, then drawing his figures on the opposite side of the construction paper, thereby transferring a "pointillist" design to the white paper, imparting varying textures in two dimensions. Occasionally, he would create his animated pictures on a scroll (Sam Bryan of IFF remembers Stapp delivering his drawing the film *Boundary Lines* on a scroll).[26]

There are two distinct phases to Stapp's style. In the Representational phase, lasting until roughly 1960, Stapp's figures are often highly stylized, but still retain recognizable human facial characteristics. They often exist on Tanguy-like watercolor-washed plains containing surrealistic elements, changing states through shifting line, color, and shape. In his Abstract style, occurring from approximately 1960 onward, Stapp's characters are anthropomorphic dance-like figures, often pointillist, as are the seas and spaces through which they float, dance, and cavort. Unlike the figures of the earlier era, Stapp's images are now in a constant state of transformation, whether lying in a stationary plane or evolving through forward movement. Inspired by dance and music, these latter figures often climb and descend contrapuntally, often splitting into several figures to represent various voices in the musical score itself.

In his final years, Stapp was engaged in designing mammoth scrolls based on geometrical abstracts and musical structures, such as the 30-foot long scroll *Homage to Matthew Shepard*, and a 70-foot scroll displayed at New York's Cathedral of St. John. Intensely personal in nature, the scrolls are designed to be seen by one viewer at a time, the "action" unfolding, then disappearing in segments approximately 18 inches in length. Stapp designed a specialized table on which to view the scrolls, and dedicated the last several years to this vision of a very personal art which, through its slow unfolding in the hands of the viewer, can truly be experienced to its greatest extent solely by the person engaged in unrolling the artifact. Philip Stapp passed away at the age of 95 on October 2, 2003.

Gerald Thompson

Gerald Thompson was a filmmaker specializing in natural history documentaries, utilizing special effects. While his 18 films distributed to the North American market are comparatively few, his work is exceptional. Overall, Thompson contributed to over 50 educational nature films and many books on natural history.

Born in Brighton, England, in 1917, Gerald Thompson moved to Scotland with his parents and spent his early years living in inner Glasgow. It was during this time that he developed his passionate interest in natural history. He knew from an early age that he wanted to be a zoologist, and at age 20, Gerald was invited to join The Oxford University expedition to the Cayman Islands as assistant etymologist. In 1939, he volunteered at the outbreak of war and was sent to the Royal College of Science, London, to read a one year entomology course to study ways of protecting food from insect infestation. (Britain's war effort included heavy stock-piling of food; these stores were likely to be contaminated by insects.) In 1944, he began his tenure in the Colonial Forest Service in Ghana. He began teach-

Gerald Thompson of Oxford Films, 1972 (Patricia Harvey Thompson).

ing at Oxford at the Commonwealth Forestry Institute in 1950, where he taught through 1968.

In 1954 he began a detailed study of the Alder Woodwasp, Xiphydria camelus, a very local insect about which little was known. To better illustrate the story, he bought a 16mm Bolex cine camera in 1960. His next need was to develop techniques for close-up cinematography, since the insects ranged in size from two inches to one eighth of an inch, too small for conventional photographic methods, and too large to film through a microscope. The end result was his first film, *The Alder Woodwasp and its Insect Enemies*, released in the U.S. by EB under the title *Insect Parasitism: the Alder Woodwasp*. Regarding his innovative film techniques, Thompson wrote:

> I was developing my close-up cine-photographical techniques, with the able assistance of Eric Skinner, my technical officer. We had our sandwich lunches in the preparatory room of my laboratory. It was at these lunches that I began to appreciate some of the difficult and very intricate problems that faced my companions in photographing insects in their natural habitats. It was necessary to obtain high light intensities without creating high levels of temperature that would be lethal to the insects. Conventional glass heat filters were only partially effective and then only for short periods of time. The solution that I devised was both simple and effective and, as a bonus, very inexpensive. This involved large 3-litre boiling flasks of cold water interposed at several points between the light source and the glass heat filters. This system provided the exact levels of light intensity that I wanted but with no heat. I called this "cold light." The whole apparatus resembled one of Heath Robinson's inventions as it included obsolete hair-dryers obtained by Eric from ladies' hairdressers.[27]

During the next nine years, he made academic films on such subjects as stickleback behavior, tiger beetles, spiders, butterflies and moths, all of which appeared on British television. While on a visit to the United States, the Ealing Corporation, distributors of short biological films for education, told Thompson that they wished to expand their catalogue by more than eighty titles. They offered to provide the capital to enable five people, including Gerald's son David, who had worked with him for several years, to form a commercial company to make the films. The result was the founding of Oxford Scientific Films Ltd., and in 1969, custom-made buildings were erected in the old quarry in Gerald's garden. At the age of 52, Gerald resigned his university post and ventured into the world of film as a full-time professional.

In 1974, for its *Bio-Science* series, National Geographic began distributing ten exceptionally photographed films produced by Thompson to North American schools. In 2000, he became the non-executive President of World Educational Films Ltd., a company set up by his son David (himself a co-founder of Oxford Scientific Films and a renowned wildlife cameraman), his daughter Patricia, who inspired the beginnings of the new company, and Stephen Evans, a physicist with a Masters in Computer Engineering.

Gerald Thompson passed away on August 22, 2002. The rights to Gerald's films have passed to son David and daughter Patricia Harvey-Thompson, who continue to market selected Gerald Thompson films through their World Educational Films website.

Bert Van Bork

Among the most physically daring filmmakers in the 16mm academic film genre was Encyclopedia Britannica Films' Bert Van Bork, whose stunning camera shots are augmented

Bert Van Bork (on camera) and crew filming *Cave Community* (1960) (Bert Van Bork).

by his painterly eye for framing and his superior editing skills. Van Bork's story is a fascinating one, not only in terms of his own personal history, but of his multi-dimensional relationship to many different art forms as well.

Born in 1928 in Augustusburg, Germany, his art studies included stints in the Academies of Fine Arts in Berlin, Leipzig, and Dresden. The end of the war found Van Bork producing stark woodcuts of intense and terrifying beauty, often made from the pine remains of destroyed buildings and old furniture, depicting a Berlin struggling with an uncertain future. In 1954, he moved to Chicago by way of New York, working in oil on canvas as well as drypoint, displaying an influence of German Expressionism in his portrayals of the landscapes of the American Southwest and cityscapes of Chicago. By this time, Van Bork had become an accomplished still photographer as well, and received the National Award for Outstanding Photography in Germany in 1954. In 1957 Van Bork brought a film he had made, *The Seventeen Year Locust,* to Warren Everote at EB Films, who then hired him to produce mainly art and science films. Films such as *Cave Community* (1960) showcased Van Bork's evolving technical skills and eye for the dramatic, precursors to his later work which would eventually place him among the more outstanding filmmakers to work in the classroom academic genre in the 1970s and 1980s.

Van Bork's exacting standards occasionally caused run-ins with EB personnel. A confidential memo from Bill Deneen to Charles Benton, EB's VP of production, describes the former's frustrating experience working with Van Bork on the film *Life in a Vacant Lot* (1966), but also provides a glimpse into Van Bork's insistence on the importance of producing a quality product:

> When editing began on this film, Bert was told positively and daily that he was not to interfere with the editing of the picture, that this was Bill Kay's job, and that he was not to look over Bill Kay's shoulder as he worked, anymore than it would be proper for Kay to look over Bert's shoulder and constantly advise as Bert was shooting. Then both Johnny Walker and myself did try daily to police this order; it seemed impossible to keep Bert's hands off the material.... In no sense can I consider Bert a producer, since to me a producer is an individual who has the competence to take on the complete responsibility for the production of a film. Bert does not have this competence, because he has an inability to see a film as a whole. He does not understand structure and I am afraid I would have to call him a script illiterate.... Bert is an excellent cameraman, an outstanding photomicrographer. He is not a director nor a producer, in my opinion. Therefore, I do not see how I can renew Bert's contract the first of October. I am delighted to have him as a cameraman, but not as a producer. I have told Bert repeatedly that he is not a producer. He refuses to accept this. Therefore, I am left with no alternative.[28]

Benton replied that, although he agreed in principle to Deneen's opinion, Van Bork was "a man of tremendous talent and gift," and suggested that perhaps he'd be happier working with Warren Everote on an anticipated 8mm film project. Ultimately, Van Bork, who proved to be a talented producer, outlasted Deneen, who left EB in July of 1967 and founded the Learning Corporation of America shortly thereafter.

By the 1970s, Van Bork's stunning camera work in his own films increasingly became an essential part of the EB catalogue. His earlier training as a two-dimensional artist contributed to a style that is immediately recognizable as his own, defined by a superior color palette, light and shadow contrasts reminiscent of German Expressionism, and a dizzying perspective of angles and heights. Shots that would ordinarily be considered mundane, such as action shots of geological instruments in use, are often beautifully composed, balanced with other subject activity in a different plane of the same frame. Volcanism fascinated Van Bork: in his spectacular story of the eruption of Kilauhea, *Heartbeat of a Volcano* (1970), his original intention was to visit to the big island, film the sputtering Kilauhea, show the geologists using seismographs and geotometers, and maybe get a shot or two of the degassing process at the vents. Kilauhea, however, had other plans. Midway through the film, as the ground base geologist mutters into the short-wave: "She's going wild, she's going wild," the volcano trembles furiously, dramatically erupting from a threatening lava vent. The sequence which follows is perhaps unprecedented in academic film, roughly seventy seconds of non-narrated footage of a phenomenal natural event, accompanied only by natural sound. These moments are filled with spectacular night shots of a giant firefall twice as high as Niagara Falls, glowing lava streams and tremendous explosions. Van Bork burned up two pair of shoes as he hung close to the carnage to film this, one of the more spectacular volcanic films ever made. Shots were planned the day before the massive eruption, as Van Bork and assistant Ulf Backström reconnoitered the volcanic area, marking exit routes with reflective tape, and noting the location of lava vents. In one scene, geologists are shown fleeing the approaching lava, but the camera remains (Van Bork, his eye glued to the camera, was prevented from pitching forward into vents and calderas by the steady hand of Backström, holding tightly to the belt of Van Bork's pants). The influence of the AGI's John Shelton is in fine evidence here on the soundtrack, which is resplendent with time signatures from radio station

WWVH and motor sounds from seismometers to the generators powering field geometers. From an affective as well as a cognitive perspective, it is one of the finest science films ever made.

Van Bork made several other volcano films for EB, among them *Fire Mountain* (1970), *Fire in the Sea* (1973) and *Volcanoes: Exploring the Restless Earth* (1973), a riveting journey through magmatic hell on several continents. Other titles worthy of note are *Mesa Verde: Mystery of the Silent Cities* (1975, narrated by Jack Palance), featuring spectacular aerial photography obtained only after the first pilot retained by Van Bork quit, *Cave Community* (1960), *Water Cycle* (1980, 2nd ed.), and non-narrated nature films for EB, including *Daybreak* and *Falling Water* (1976).

Van Bork's film career was far from over after the EB days. His *Eyewitness,* a documentary on the sketches and paintings done secretly by men and women who lived and died inside the walls of the Nazi death camps, was nominated for an Academy Award in 1999. Van Bork's exhibitions of two-dimensional art continue to appear in international galleries, and he has released a book of his art in conjunction with an exhibition in Germany, *Bert Van Bork: Künstlerporträts.*

John Walker

John J. Walker was a transitional filmmaker at Encyclopædia Britannica films, whose science films bridged the era between the staid, didactic titles of the 1950s and the exciting new science films, made by directors such as Bert Van Bork, in the 1960s. Walker, who made over 80 films for EB, was a consummate craftsman, whose wonderful time-lapse cinematography can be appreciated in *Seed Dispersal* (1956). Many of Walker's films were made for young learners, while others were made for high school and college-level students.

EB's John Walker (Craig Walker).

Walker was born on October 24, 1908, in Clairton, Pennsylvania, and graduated from Pittsburgh's Carnegie Tech School of Drama. In 1933 he was hired by the National Park Service as a motion picture photographer to help film achievements of the Civilian Conservation Corps (CCC). He covered over 40,000 miles for the CCC, and was selected to work with ERPI films to develop a series of six films on geology. In 1937, he was hired by ERPI, which soon was absorbed under the Encyclopædia Britannica umbrella.

From 1942 through 1946, he served with the Army Air Force as a photographic officer as well as an instructor in aerial combat photography. He replaced Colonel Hal (*Our Gang*) Roach as liaison photographic officer for the 9th Bomber Command. His Army buddies included Ronald Reagan and Van Heflin, and he was discharged in 1946, having risen to the rank of major.

Walker made films on mostly science and nature subjects for EB through 1972, when he retired. In retirement, he continued with his passion for still photography, and gave lectures on his films and travels. He passed away in Fort Collins, Colorado, on August 23, 1986.[29] About Walker, fellow EB filmmaker Tom Smith writes:

> Johnnie may have produced more film at EB than any other producer/director (perhaps second only to Milan Herzog). Johnnie specialized in biology films — ants, mammals, birds etc.... When I began in at EB he was part of the older generation. He valued prompt arrival at the office, dressed in suit and tie, seeming to survey me as a young upstart. I'd roll in to the office at five past nine and he'd be standing in his office door. He'd look at me as I passed, then, glancing at his watch he'd say, "Good morning Tom." I laughed about it then and it still brings a smile. He also left promptly at 5:00 while I often worked into the night. But his contribution was substantial. Something I may not have appreciated till later. It is sad that Walker has become a forgotten name.
>
> I spoke to the two-time Academy Award winner cinematographer and filmmaker Haskell Wexler a couple years ago. We were in a social situation and he sat across from me while we had a picnic lunch. I told him that I was once a producer at EBF and had heard he too worked there. I told him Johnnie Walker once told me he taught Wexler how to load film in the Mitchell camera. (This happened a few years after World War II). I asked him if he recalled Walker and his time at EBF. Wexler beamed. He said he loved that period of film making in his life. It was an ideal place to learn the craft. He also found Walker to be a patient and considerate man, teaching Wexler the ropes. Nearly with tears in his eyes, Wexler said that it has been so many years ago at times he wonders if it really happened or if his EBF days were only an old filmmaker's dream. I assured him it was all very real.[30]

Clifford B. West

A uniquely interesting body of work was filmed by artist Clifford West, who, from 1958 to 1981, made more than 25 films on artists and aspects of art history. West developed a camera-as-brush camera technique more in keeping with the approach taken by a painter than a filmmaker. His serpentine zooms and pans emulated the non-linear way an individual looks at a work of art, as opposed to the manner in which a more traditional cinematographer first plans, then shoots. West believed in shooting as much as possible before final film ideas jelled. Many of his films on Florentine art derived from an estimated 40–50,000 feet of film shot on one trip, then later edited into films on different themes.

In addition to his Renaissance films, West made films on modern artists. Particularly notable is *Harry Bertoia's Sculpture* (1965), with its close-up hand-held pan and zoom making the sculpture seem more like a lunar landscape, its purposely out-of-focus impressionistic framing suddenly giving way to a sharper, still-abstract representational image, and its utilization of Bertoia's own musique-concrète score (it was West's idea, in fact, to invite the sculptor to bang on his work with metal objects with microphone present). Although appearing in the permanent collections of over 150 museums and having his work championed by art historian H.W. Janson, among others, West's work, ranging in subject matter from Florentine architecture to Edvard Munch, remains difficult to find, and worthy of a fresh look.

West was born in Cleveland, Ohio, on July 4, 1916, and began making films as an art instructor at Michigan's Cranbrook Academy of Art, initially due to the fact that he couldn't find appropriate film to demonstrate the concept of negative space. He continued to paint and teach in Lebanon, New Hampshire, in the non-profit AVA Gallery run by his wife Bente Torjusen, until he passed away on October 22, 2006.

Bernard Wilets

A prolific filmmaker whose subject matter included the Bill of Rights (the *Bill of Rights in Action* series), drama, music (the *Discovering Music* series), and history (the *Man and the State* series), Bernard Wilets was perhaps the greatest writer of debates in academic film. Born in Milwaukee, Wisconsin, on March 19, 1928, Wilets moved to Long Beach, California, at an early age, eventually attending UCLA and obtaining a Master's Degree in English. He began writing plays and composing music ("leaning toward atonality"). In 1964, he made his first of over eighty films.

Wilets' actors, recruited through southern California theatrical contacts, were superb, some of the finest to appear in educational films of any kind. They were never credited. Before his death, he

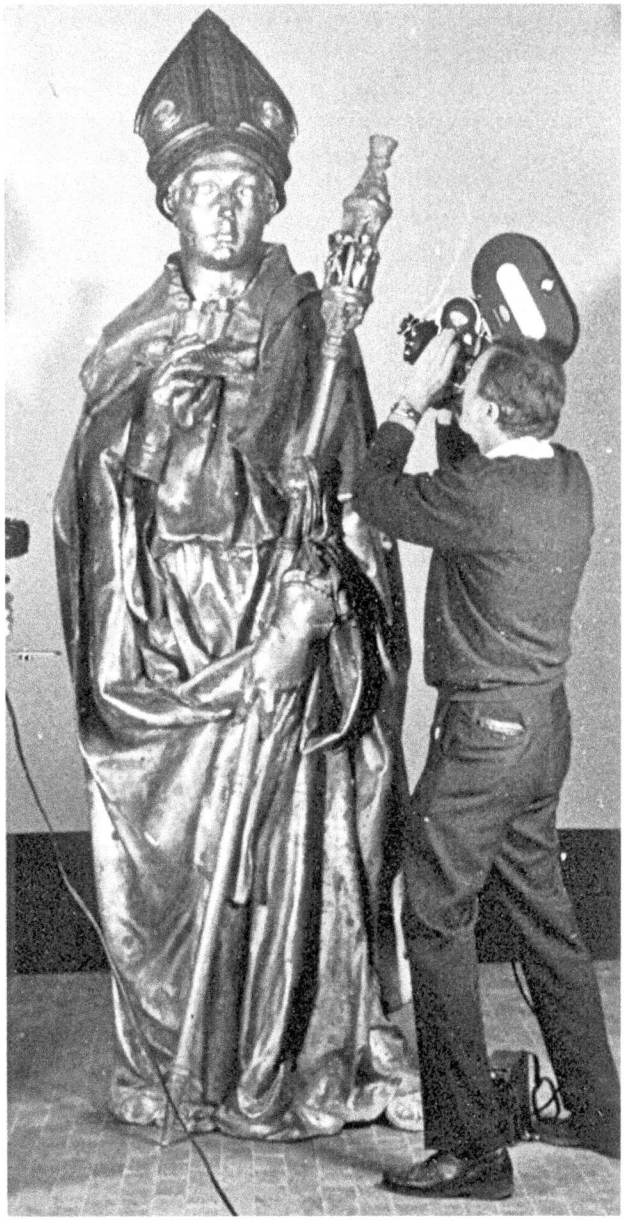

Clifford West filming *Bronze: River of Metal*, 1971 (Bente Torjusen).

revealed that he'd worked out an agreement with the Screen Actors Guild (SAG) to use certain actors at a reduced rate in return for not listing them in the credits. He asked the author not to reveal that Robert Cornthwaite, who played an exceptional role as the director in *Roosevelt & Hoover on the Economy* (1976), was one of them (the actor has since passed away). Believing the ephemera associated with his filmmaking to be of no value, Wilets destroyed most of the scripts, photos, and letters documenting his film career in the 1990s. It is believed that there no records left indicating any of the other actors hired by Wilets.

Burke & Paine on Revolution (1973) is arguably the most intriguing film in Wilets' superb *Man and the State* series, boasting fine acting, stimulating writing, and a powerfully twisted ending. This is initiated when Burke and Paine, the former a monarchist, the latter a believer in democracy, attend a dinner party at the home of playwright Richard Sheridan. In the middle of the dinner, the servants take over the house, and upon the threat of death, these friendly adversaries are forced to defend their philosophies. Their discourse is spirited, and finally Sheridan lets the guests in on his own little joke, that it was he who put the servants up to the revolt, and that the farce was a little play for his own amusement. The Sheridan element was a master stroke by Wilets in gaining the attention of the viewer, which, by placing the lives of the debaters at stake, gives the film tremendous affective value.

Wilets' *Discovering Music* series was the first introduction to world music encountered by many students, and his *Bill of Rights in Action* films featured provocative debates and questions over legal issues that eschewed didacticism. Wilets, who passed away from a heart attack in February 2007, was an exceptional writer and craftsman, whose best work is as fresh today as it was when originally released.

Donald Winkler

Donald Winkler was born in Winnipeg in 1940 and graduated from the University of Manitoba in 1961. From 1967 to 1995 he was a film director and writer at the National Film Board of Canada in Montreal, and since the 1980s, a translator of Quebecois literature. Winkler's films have dealt largely with the world of culture and the arts. His work has included short experimental films (*Doodle Film*, 1970), films on crafts and the graphic arts *(In Praise of Hands,* 1974), the theatre, and social history. Perhaps his most notable and culturally significant work consists of a

Top: **Bernard Wilets (David Nelson).** ***Bottom:*** **Larry Yust (Isidore Mankofsky, A.S.C.).**

series of films on Canadian literary figures, collected under the overall title *Poets: A Sestet,* which provide an important film record of six cultural pioneers who helped lay the foundations for modern Canadian writing. They are exceptional films on the writer's craft, one of the best of which is the riotous *Earle Birney: Portrait of a Poet* (1981).

Larry Yust

Larry Yust's most significant contributions to educational film included a series of exceptional dramas in the *Short Story Showcase* series, a finely crafted, intriguing, and intellectually stimulating group of dramatic films made for Encyclopædia Britannica from roughly 1965 to 1975. *The Lottery* (1969), Yust's treatment of the Shirley Jackson story, revealed the tragic ending sequence with such power that the EB brain

A drop-down transparency adds blood to the face of the victim and creates a dappled effect to this in-house, never-used promotional mock-up for Larry Yust's *The Lottery* (1969) (Encyclopedia Britannica, Inc.).

trust discussed not releasing the film, with the fear that it would scare young viewers. It became one of EB's best sellers. The film itself was controversial at EB prior to its release, as some considered its brutal ending to be too much for schoolchildren to endure. Ironically, EB's art department had been crafting luridly bloody still pictures to promote the film, creating a sensationalist campaign that never saw the light of day.

Yust's finest work would include the eerie *The Long Christmas Dinner* and the witty *The Well of the Saints* (both 1975). Films in the Short Story Showcase series typically had ten minute *"Discussion of"* films that could be ordered in addition to the prime film, featuring fascinating discussions by scholars such as Charles Van Doren.

Today, Yust is engaged photography projects. His latest work involves photographic elevations, "made by moving in a line parallel to the face of the subject—walking on the opposite sidewalk of a Los Angeles street, or crouching at the rail of a Vaporetto traveling down the Grand Canal in Venice and snapping overlapping shots, with the camera always aimed directly at the subject on a line perpendicular to its face. Recording the images fifteen or thirty for each elevation takes minutes. Fitting them together in the computer into a single image takes longer, typically two or three days of exacting work."[31] His book *Metro: Photographic Elevations of Selected Paris Metro Stations* was published in 2004, and each photo opens out into a three-foot wide panorama. His work was exhibited in the Louvre in 2005.

CHAPTER SEVEN

Final Takes: The Denouement of the Academic Film in Classrooms and Its Resurgence on the Internet

Learning Corporation of America's Bill Deneen tells the story of a sobering trip he once took to western New York in the early 1980s: "We arrived at one school district's media warehouse, and found a truck full of videotapes copied from our films, copies for which we would receive no profits, and filmmakers no residuals." When asked what course of action he then took, he replied, "Our hands were tied ... we had to sue one of our best customers."[1] The case, *Encyclopædia Britannica Educational Corp. v. Crooks*, 542 F. Supp. 1156 (W.D.N.Y.), concerned EBEC and co-plaintiffs Learning Corporation of America and Time-Life Films, charging that the state of New York's Board of Cooperative Educational Services (BOCES) engaged in copying videotapes for distribution to member schools without remuneration to the film companies of origin. BOCES argued that it had the right to copy any film in its possession under its interpretation of copyright and fair use law. On June 21, 1982, BOCES was found in violation of the law, and ordered, in a final decision made on March 10, 1983, to immediately cease copying, and pay damages and legal costs to the plaintiff film companies. Perhaps the most disturbing element of the case was that, more than 15 years after the halcyon days of post–Sputnik government largesse, BOCES found it financially more viable to defend a costly lawsuit than to simply buy films and tapes from film companies as it once did.

By the time the lawsuit was initiated, federal funds that school districts had traditionally used to buy films had already been drying up for some time. With the Soviet threat seemingly diminishing, politicians deemed it less important to fund school programs than to reallocate funds to pet projects, or provide short-sighted relief for taxpayers. California schools, for example, saw NDEA funds for the acquisition of mediated instruction cut from $10 million in 1959 to $1 million in fiscal year 1975–1976. ESEA funding for Library resources (Title II) dropped from $8 million in 1966 to $1,250,000 by 1976. Taxpayers, too, were increasingly reluctant to see their tax dollars allocated for what they perceived as the bottomless funding pit of public schools. The successful passage in 1978 of California's Proposition 13 was typical of the new laws, and its impact was immediate and potentially deadly for educational film companies. In one California school district, for example, the district budget allocated for mediated instruction per student was halved from $2.50 to $1.25, while Federal funds were directed away from media entirely help offset the loss of state funds.[2] The resultant dramatic reduction in purchase of films is described by many filmmakers and film company executives as the real beginning of the end of the 16mm classroom academic film business in the United States. But lack of funding wasn't the only reason for the demise of the 16mm classroom film. The somewhat fragile nature of the medium of film itself was becoming an increasing factor in the shift toward videotape.

Film: A Fragile Medium on the Edge of Disappearance

The transition from film to videotape had begun in the 1970s for a number of reasons. New teachers and their students were increasingly more familiar with videotape players, and less comfortable with expensive and often cranky projectors. As owners of home VCR equipment, many teachers found the newer technology easier to use, and less risky to the media than out-of-adjustment film projectors which could chew up a film, rendering it useless unless replacement footage had been ordered and spliced in. While state-of-the-art, easier-to-use slot load projectors — which required no threading — were now widely available, districts had for years standardized on autoload projectors such as Bell & Howell 552 or 2592 projectors, and were reluctant to replace them with slot-loaders costing $900 or so each. The ubiquitous autoloaders were originally produced as an answer to cumbersome manual-loading machines, and were outstanding pieces of equipment when they worked.

EB's Irving Rusinow films wife Kim and three uncredited children, circa 1965 (Jeff Rusinow).

When they didn't, the consequences were at the least annoying, and often expensive as well. Sometimes the tricky loop-setting mechanism would function incorrectly, various pieces of the projector would have to be taken apart, and the film threaded manually anyway. In a more egregious situation, the film would get stuck while threading into the gate as the sprocket wheel rolled merrily and destructively onward, stripping sprocket holes from the film, rendering the damaged portion virtually useless. The resulting expense of buying replacement footage for damaged film could be significant, and splicing and repair time-consuming.

Often, large chunks of film were tossed into classroom trash cans before the film was returned to the audio-visual center. This type of damage could be accelerated when the instructor or student repaired the splice with common cellophane tape or making tape found in the classroom, which glued itself to the emulsion and covered the film's sprocket holes. This prevented the sprocket mechanism from advancing the film, and, unless discovered in the AV center, many more feet of film would be shredded in the next showing. The solution to destroyed socket holes and egregious splices was to order replacement segments of the footage from the distributor by using the tiny numbers along the film edge as frame indicators. If too many years elapsed between the original order and the replacement footage order, however, the footage might not be available due to the age of the print, or might be a different hue, particularly if the new footage was of colorfast non–Eastman stock. Many restoration experts, such as Queens Borough Public Libraries' Robert Miller, would spend painstaking hours gluing white sprocket repair tape to repair an important, irreplaceable print. Others, not as meticulous or not having the time, would instead toss away damaged footage, splicing together whatever undamaged parts they had.

Overall film degradation due to age or improper storage conditions was a problem as well, most notably in the areas of color-shift and the "vinegar syndrome." In the 1970s, Mylar film stock began to replace the more fragile and less color-stable tri-acetate film. One problem that looms more important each year, as older films pass out of circulation and become increasingly difficult to find, is the reddening, over time, of Eastman color print film. Perhaps it was the instability of dyes within the stock, exacerbated by less-than-optimum temperatures, that caused hundreds of thousands of color prints made in the 1950s through late 1970s to shift to the magenta end of he color spectrum, diminishing the effect of the cyan and yellow colors, resulting in prints that were lifeless, skeletal remains of their original hues. Most companies selling educational film were affected, and although this characteristic was not apparent when the film was originally sold, decades later the damage is apparent and, in most cases, irreversible.[3] Unsubstantiated rumors persist that Eastman sold the film in spite of knowing about the instability, believing that eventually schools would be forced to order more prints to replenish faded stock. After a campaign against Eastman's print film begun in 1980 by director Martin Scorsese, Eastman finally stopped selling the troublesome film. An important task of film archivists today is to identify faded films in their collections, and attempt to replace them with unfaded contemporary prints, or, when available, later prints made from more stable stock.

Proper film storage calls for adherence to temperature and humidity controls. Many school film libraries, notably those located in hot, humid areas of the country, stored their films in environments volatile to film, resulting in what's commonly referred to as the "vinegar syndrome." In this situation, film emulsion, stressed by heat and humidity, begins feeding on itself irreversibly and acetic acid (which causes the film to smell like vinegar) is freed from its silver prison, buckling the film and leaving telltale deposits of white compounds in its wake. Films in this condition soon begin eating their metal reels and storage cans and, if not isolated or thrown away, will in short order infect adjacent unaffected film as sure as any raging parasite. Anecdotal evidence points to the efficacy of an Eastman product called Molecular Sieve, which, when inserted adjacent to the film and sealed in plastic before returning to the can, appears to stabilize, but not remediate, the process of disintegration. Several preservation advocates also suggest, after Molecular Sieve treatment, to move such films into freezers, continuing the stabilization process.[4]

In all probability, most companies welcomed the change from film to video: the profit margins were higher, as production and duplication costs for videotape were less. In addition, more prints of each title could theoretically be sold over time, considering that videotape, susceptible to random magnetism and the natural degradation of the medium itself, has a lesser shelf-life than film, which properly stored can last for decades. Schools, some opined, would in all probability have to replace videos in fewer than ten years. Profits, always high for film, could potentially be even greater for video.[5]

In terms of overall quality, film, with better resolution (especially important when projecting a larger image) and superior color depth, was inherently preferable to videotape, but the realities of funding were such that schools increasingly insisted on the less expensive medium.

Soon, an unintended but predictable consequence of this shift was becoming apparent: titles themselves were disappearing from film catalogues, never to return. Inexorably, film companies began a process of triage to remove slow sellers from the catalogue, and once existing prints were sold, the title, in any medium, would cease to exist.

The advent of videotape, cited by some as the reason for the decline of the classroom academic film in North America, may be the best technical reason, but it masks the fact that the "progressive era" of this genre of film, which lasted from roughly 1965 to 1985, was fueled by the Cold War. As the Soviet Union was perceived as less of a threat over time, so was Washington's insistence that the U.S. student be spared no expense in his or her quest for superiority over that of Soviet counterparts.[6]

Of late, suggestions have been made by experts such as Charles Benton, Bill Deneen, and Martha Gonzalez to a number of entities holding rights to these titles, to consider repackaging many of these films into current media such as the DVD, and selling them into educational and commercial markets; however, these efforts have not yet been successful. Today's corporations, with numerous projects relating to contemporary contents on their plates, seem little interested in repackaging older material, even if the content remains fresh, up to date, well produced, and visually compelling.

How Do We Save Academic Film? Some Strategies and Processes

The United States can be unforgiving when addressing preservation of past art forms if they occurred in the too-recent past. We live in a country in which progress moves so quickly that, eye fixed firmly if myopically on the future, we tend to destroy before seeking to preserve. Might it be true that the 16mm academic film is now in that uneasy purgatorial repository that lies somewhere between salvation and damnation to oblivion? As I mentioned in the *Preface*, film historians now say with a certain degree of accuracy that 80 percent of our silent film heritage has been destroyed. The films on which this book focuses, today rarely viewed as valuable contributors to the American film experience and worthy of critical investigation, may be facing their final crisis. Issues of preservation, documentation, and presentation must be addressed if we are to be truly interested in saving a cinematic art form so obviously in distress.

Before speaking of effective measures to save the *film as art*, we should address saving the *film as artifact*. Future scholars may want to consider taking a closer look at each individual film print as an artifact in itself. Splices, lines formed from foreign matter lodged in film gates, and handwritten notes on or inside film cans tell us something about the time period and locality in which it was shown. Why would a film used in schools in Ankeny, Iowa, for example, be pristine while the same title from an Oakland, California school library be practically ripped to shreds and poorly bandaged in an effort to get at least one last showing. Did Iowans have more of a respect for public property than Oaklanders? Or conversely, did Iowans let films sit on the shelves unused, while Oaklanders wore out their single poor print, loved by instructors, but not repairable due to the constraints of an already overburdened urban school budget? These are among the fascinating ruminations that may go through one's mind when opening the can and showing any new "used" film for the first time: each is in essence a time capsule, telling a fine detective story without a clear hypothesis or clever conclusion. Media archaeology is a subject area that poses fascinating questions with complex answers, and 16mm prints — and the film cans themselves — provide important clues to the scholar.

Processes for Preservation? Microcinemas and the Internet to the Rescue

At least two viable means of preservation and promotion have shown promise in keeping these films in the public eye, thereby slowing the wheels of destruction. They are public showings and Internet viewing and retrieval.

Interestingly enough, the concerned individual still holds enough power in his or her grasp to become part of a growing number of disparate groups across North America that are taking action to preserve the legacy of 16mm educational film. Our experience at the AFA is an example of the former. The *Academic Film Archive of North America (AFA)*, in San Jose, California, has developed a "cookbook" approach that can be replicated in virtually every community. After placing calls to school local school districts, the principals of the AFA, business professionals with no prior experience in film preservation or presentation, were able to purchase the film library of a nearby educational institution for less than $10,000. Wanting to show historically significant films to audiences composed of adults, and yet recognizing the financial constraints partial to paid admissions as determined by copyright laws, the AFA resolved to show films free of charge in a traditionally non-educational environment. The owner of a local bistro was found, who agreed to a no-admission policy, provided the films were shown during non-peak hours in an unused space. The AFA began showing films weekly, determining its programming thematically, and releasing weekly film notes via email. Local critics began listing programs in newspapers with the unforeseen result that educational films were shown to a wider and more sophisticated audience than they would have sitting on the shelf of an educational system whose direction had taken a marked turned toward video. Filmmakers such as Bill Deneen, Ricky Leacock, Gerald McDermott, Bert Salzman, and Larry Yust, surprised at seeing a renewed interest in their films, soon appeared at AFA retrospectives of their work. And in publishing film bios and filmographies, as well as a chronology of shows and accompanying film notes on the web, the AFA became the first nationally available resource available to those looking for information about the history and culture of the 16mm educational film.[7] Today, there are dozens of microcinemas in North America showing films in 16mm format, and many of them make a standard practice of including academic films in their repertoire.

Perhaps the best bet for the survival of academic films from the past lies with the Internet. Millions now have access to a number of academic films on sites such as YouTube and the Internet Archive. They are watching films online as well as downloading them to home computers. Parents, in particular, have begun to download films and show them to their children at night as alternatives to commercial television. The Internet has given new life to academic films that have been out of distribution for years. *Protein Synthesis: An Epic on the Cellular Level* (*1971), directed by Gabriel Weiss and produced by Robert Wilson, was a wild, fun science film that used Stanford University students choreographed to show the science of DNA in action. While never achieving widespread distribution when released, it now has over 500,000 views on YouTube.

The Internet Archive is quickly becoming a site of choice for viewers wishing to see academic films.[8] The AFA has uploaded more than 80 academic films, with a new commercial twist: film companies are starting to make money by selling clips from formerly moribund films, and thus are becoming increasingly more amenable to having their films uploaded.[9] In one such case, Encyclopaedia Britannica has licensed footage from Bill Deneen's *Japan: Miracle in Asia* (*1963) through Getty Images. It is hoped that film companies recognizing a new source for revenue will increasingly want to make older academic films available for everyone to see on the web.

Filmmakers, too, are delightedly seeing their films repurposed, through exposure on the Internet. Gerald McDermott's *Sun Flight* (*1966) was seen by a Dutch acid-jazz group on the Internet Archive, who replaced the original soundtrack with their own, and placed the film on YouTube. This prompted the filmmaker to contact them, and they began discussions for a potential new collaborative effort involving a new film.

Classroom academic films are increasingly being appreciated as this book goes to press, but to a great extent, the weight of preservation continues to rest on the efforts of the individual. At a cost of approximately $20 per film (a rough average derived from Internet collector sale lists), collecting 16mm academic films is possibly the most affordable art form extant today. Institutions such as the Academic Film Archive of North America not only educate filmgoers at large, but assist historians by proving a forum to help determine which films and filmmakers made the most significant contributions to the genre. Historically, very few movements within an art form have been hidden as profoundly as the 16mm academic classroom was within the cinematic world. Although largely undocumented, the buried world of the educational film has left hundreds of thousands, perhaps millions of films and related ephemeral artifacts. And unlike generations-old middens which so reluctantly yield yesterday's broken treasures, film historians, educators, and lovers of great film can still easily stub a toe and uncover by accident wonderful films unseen for years, waiting to be viewed with new eyes.

Appendix A

36 Films in This Book Currently Available for Free Viewing Online

Films on this page are indicated in the text of the book by an "*" sign before the year of their release (e.g., *1971).

Alphabet Conspiracy (1959, 56m., dir. Owen Crump) www.archive.org/details/alphabet_conspiracy

Angel and Big Joe (1975, 27m., dir. Bert Salzman) www.archive.org/details/angel_and_big_joe

Atlantic Crossing: Life on an Ocean Liner (1967, 21m, dir. Bill Deneen) www.archive.org/details/AtlanticCrossingLifeOnAnOceanLiner

Congruent Triangles (1977, 7m., dir. Bruce & Katharine Cornwell) www.archive.org/details/afana_congruent_triangles

Electric Eel (1954, 10m., Moody Institute of Science) www.archive.org/details/electric_eel

Fabricantes Méxicanas de Ollas (1962, 9m., dir. Stuart Roe & Richard Guttman) www.archive.org/details/fabricantes_mexicanas_ollas

Frames of Reference (1960, 26m., dir. Richard Leacock) www.archive.org/details/frames_of_reference

Gateways to the Mind (1958, 58m., dir. Owen Crump) www.archive.org/details/gateways_to_the_mind

The Good Eleven (1974, 4m, prod. Tom Yohe, music by Bob Dorough) www.youtube.com/watch?v=UxEQiI2C1WI

The Happy City (1959, 35m., dir. Bill Deneen) www.archive.org/details/happy_city

Imaging the Hidden World: The Light Microscope (1984, 20m., dir. Bruce Russell) www.archive.org/details/imaging_a_hidden_world

Iran (1971, 18m., dir. Claude Lelouch) www.archive.org/details/lelouch_iran_1971

Japan: Miracle in Asia (1963, 30m., dir. Bill Deneen) www.archive.org/details/japan_miracle_in_asia_1963

Journey to the Center of a Triangle (1977, 9m., dir. Bruce & Katharine Cornwell) www.archive.org/details/journey_to_the_center_of_a_triangle

The Loon's Necklace (1949, 10. dir. F.R. Crawley) www.youtube.com/watch?v=DfUmSFVncPk

A Magnet Laboratory (1959, 21m., dir. Richard Leacock) www.archive.org/details/magnet_laboratory_1959

Matthew Aliuk: Eskimo in Two Worlds (1973, 18m., dir. Bert Salzman) www.archive.org/details/matthew_aliuk

Mexican Village Life (1958, 18m., dir. Willard C. Hahn) www.archive.org/details/afana_mexican_village_life

People Along the Mississippi (1952, 20m., dir. Gordon Weisenborn, prod. John Barnes) www.archive.org/details/people_along_the_mississippi

Picture in Your Mind (1948, 16m., dir. Philip Stapp) www.archive.org/details/afana_picture_in_your_mind

Powers of Ten (1978 revision, 9m., dir. Charles & Ray Eames) www.youtube.com/watch?v=wm0bIuAVmOA&feature=fvsr

Protein Synthesis: An Epic on the Cellular Level (1971, 12m., dir. Robert Alan Weiss, prod. Kent Wilson) www.youtube.com/watch?v=u9dhO0iCLww

Shaw vs. Shakespeare I: The Character of Caesar (1970, 30m., dir. John Barnes) www.archive.org/details/shaw_vs_shakespeare_1

Julien and Sam Bryan in Krakow, Poland, 1974 (Sam Bryan)

From Bert Salzman's *Angel and Big Joe* (1975) (Bill Deneen, Learning Corporation of America).

Shaw vs. Shakespeare II: The Tragedy of Julius Caesar (1970, 30m., dir. John Barnes) www.archive.org/details/shaw_vs_shakespeare_2

Shaw vs. Shakespeare III: Caesar and Cleopatra (1970, 30m., dir. John Barnes) www.archive.org/details/shaw_vs_shakespeare_3

Shopping Bag Lady (1975, 21m., dir. Bert Salzman) www.archive.org/details/shopping_bag_lady

Siege (1940, 10m., dir. Julien Bryan) www.youtube.com/watch?v=M2X4GARxlH0

Silent Snow, Secret Snow (1966, 15m., dir. Gene Kearney) www.archive.org/details/silent_snow_secret_snow

Solar System, 2nd Ed. (1977, 20m., dir. Tom Smith) www.archive.org/details/solar_system_1977

The Sorcerer's Apprentice (1962, 15m., dir. Edward English) www.archive.org/details/sorcerors_apprentice_1962

The Stonecutter (1960, 6m., dir. Gerald McDermott) www.archive.org/details/afana_stonecutter

Sun Flight (1966, 7m., dir. Gerald McDermott) www.archive.org/details/sun_flight

Sun Flight (2009, Gerald McDermott's film with new soundtrack by Kilimanjaro Darkjazz ensemble) www.youtube.com/watch?v=MnrH-7URvpc

Unique Contribution (1959, 30m.) www.archive.org/details/unique_contribution

Wild Men of the Kalahari (1930, 30m., camera by Paul Hoefler) www.archive.org/details/afana_wild_men_of_the_kalahari

Appendix B

Milestones in Academic Film

1910–1919

1910: George Kleine produces what may be the world's first educational film catalogue.

1912: First use of small gauge film for educational purposes, NEA Chicago conference.

1912: Alexander F. Victor introduces spring loaded 16mm camera, and projector.

1914: Duluth's M.I. Smith presents a touring educational film show.

1917: North Carolina BOE distributes films to rural areas via roadshows.

1918: The Lynne Matcalfe-edited *Reel and Slide* becomes what may be the first journal to critically analyze educational films.

1920–1929

1922: Eastman, Victor, and Bell & Howell begin selling 16mm film, cameras, and projectors.

1928: Western Electric founds the Electrical Research Products, Incorporated (ERPI) educational film company.

1930–1939

1930: Research Council of the Academy of Motion Picture Arts and Sciences initiates cinematic training for officers of the Army Signal Corps.

1932: ERPI and the University of Chicago reach an agreement to use the University's scholars as subject matter experts.

1933: *The Educational Talking Picture,* a book written by ERPI's Frederick Devereux, discusses quantifying the educational outcomes of the use of film in classrooms.

1934: David, John, and Alfred Smart found Coronet Films.

1937: William Benton is hired as VP of the University of Chicago.

1937: International Film Bureau founded by Wesley Greene.

1939: Budge Crawley launches Crawley Films.

1939: National Film Board of Canada established, with John Grierson serving as Commissioner.

1939: Teaching Film Custodians founded to reformat major studio films, edited for educational purposes.

1940–1949

1940: *Canada Carries On* series initiated by the National Film Board of Canada.

1941: The University of Chicago acquires the Encyclopædia Britannica, to be run by William Benton.

1941: The U.S. Office of Education forms the Division of Visual Aids for War Training, chartered to develop instructional material for civilians, led by Floyde E. Brooker.

1943: William Benton of Encyclopædia Britannica acquires ERPI films from Western Electric, and changes its name to Encyclopædia Britannica Films.

1943: *Why We Fight* series directed by Frank Capra.

1943: Educational Film Library Association founded.

1944: William Benton acquires all Encyclopædia Britannica properties from the University of Chicago.

1945: International Film Foundation founded by Julien Bryan.

1946: Arthur Barr founds Barr Films.

1946: Boulton-Hawker Films is founded in the U.K. by Gilbert Hawker and Peter Boulton.

1946: McGraw-Hill Text Films founded by Albert Rosenberg.

1946: United Word Films (later Universal Education & Visual Arts) founded.

1947: Centron Films is founded.

1948: Churchill-Wexler Films is founded by Bob Churchill and Sy Wexler.

1948: Tom Daly's Unit B established by the National Film Board of Canada.

1950–1959

1950: Contemporary Films is founded.

1950: Institut für Film und Bild (FWU) is founded in Germany.

1953: Maurice Mitchell becomes president of Encyclopædia Britannica Films.

1954: Gilbert Altschul founds AGC Films.

1954: Weston Woods Films founded by Morton Schindel.

1955?: Film Associates founded by Irv Braun and Paul Burnford.

1955?: Al Bailey founds Bailey Films.

1955: Davidson Films is founded.

1956: Benjamin Bloom and colleagues introduce *Bloom's Taxonomy* describing the Domains of Learning.

1957: Sputnik launched by USSR.

1958: National Defense Education Act (NDEA) frees funds to be used for mediated instruction.

1958: Physical Science Study Committee (PSSC) films are distributed by ESI.

1959: Films for the Humanities is founded by Harold and Marianne Mantell.

1959: EB's Maurice Mitchell discusses the value of educational film on-camera in the film *Unique Contribution*.

1959: Pyramid Films founded by David and Lynn Adams.

1960–1969

1960: Walt and Myrna Berlet form Berlet Films.

1961: Fred W. Friendly's *CBS Reports* series are distributed to schools.

1962: *Man: a Course of Study* (MACOS) films are distributed by ESI.

1962: Stelios Roccos founds ACI Films.

1962: Stanton Films founded.

1963: *Project Discovery*, a joint educational venture between Encyclopædia Britannica and Bell & Howell, is created by Charles Benton, Egon Guba, and others.

1964: Civil Rights Act established.

1965: Elementary and Secondary School Act (ESEA) established.

1965: National Foundation on the Arts and Humanities Act signed.

1966: CBS creates Bailey Film Associates (BFA) via purchases of Film Associates and Bailey Films.

1968: Films Incorporated is acquired from Encyclopædia Britannica by Charles Benton.

1968: Learning Corporation of America founded.

1968: *Of Black America* series produced by Perry Wolff.

1969?: Time-Life begins marketing BBC films to classrooms.

1970–1979

1970: Environmental Education Act signed.

1970: CRM Films is founded.

1973: Bullfrog Films is founded.

1973: Phoenix Films founded by Heinz Gelles and Barbara Bryant.

1979: Perspective Films founded by Sheldon Sachs.

1980–1989

1982: AIMS Media founded.

Appendix C

Requiem

This book took over a decade to complete. Many of those interviewed were excited at the prospect of reading it, but died before it could be published. The following people all made great contributions to academic film, to this book, and to me, personally. My hope is that other researchers will want to further explore and conduct research on the academic film, and will contact those who were engaged in the process of making academic films before it's too late. The entities with whom the following departed individuals were most often affiliated are listed next to their names.

John Barnes (EB)
Peter Boulton (Boulton-Hawker)
Ralph Buchsbaum (EB)

Paul Burnford (BFA)
Stanley Croner (EB)
Clifton Fadiman (EB)

EB's Clifton "Kip" Fadiman (Encyclopaedia Britannica, Inc.).

Gene Forrell (IFF)
Virginia Garner
Leo Handel (Handel Films)
Milan Herzog (EB)
Angelika Jackson (FWU)
Grace Garland Janisz (EB)
Emily Jones (EFLA)
Ken Middleham (Stanton)
William O'Farrell (NFBC)
Jerry Olk (EB)
Tom Riha (Coronet)
Bruce Russell (BioMedia, Coronet)
Philip Stapp (IFF)
Clifford West
Bernard Wilets (AIMS, BFA, EB)

Chapter Notes

Preface

1. Jean Renoir, *My Life and My Films* (New York: Atheneum, 1974), p. 11.
2. The 1999 NICEM (National Information Center for Educational Media) database in New Mexico, which documented educational film made from the early part of this century through the latter part of the millennium, listed more than 108,000 instructional titles in 16mm format. Although some of these achieved sparse distribution, many of them remained in circulation for many years. Bowker's first educational film guide included descriptions of some 37,000 of the most commonly used titles as selected from 50 university libraries. *Educational Film Resource Locator*, 1st ed. (New York: R.R. Bowker, 1978).
3. Writer Ann Fienup-Riordan tells the all-too-typical story of distribution company Pictures Inc. After allowing its film franchise to terminate in favor of video distribution, it quietly destroyed classic Alaska features from Disney and MGM because "studio policy prohibited either donating the films to public archives or allowing them to remain intact after the franchises lapsed." Ann Fienup-Riordan, *Freeze Frame: Alaska Eskimos in the Movies* (Seattle: University of Washington Press, 1995), p. 169.
4. Penelope Houston, *Keepers of the Frame: The Film Archives* (London: British Film Institute, 1994), pp. 69, 165.

Chapter One

1. Benjamin Bloom, et al., *Taxonomy of Educational Objectives, Handbook II: Affective Domain* (New York: David McKay, 1964).
2. Re-canning films to allow for healthier archival storage is the goal of many film archives, but the unfortunate loss of important in-can documentation is often the result.
3. Paul Saettler, *A History of Instructional Technology* (New York: McGraw-Hill, 1968), p. 96.
4. *Ibid.*, p. 98.
5. *Ibid.*, p. 101.
6. "In Days Gone By: Blazing the Trail to the Schoolhouse," Chicago: KNOW, II Quarter, 1978. Encyclopædia Britannica, p. 6.
7. Saettler, p. 114.
8. The year is in dispute. Other historians claim the year was 1923.
9. ERPI's first film, the Max Fleischer-animated *Finding His Voice* (1928), explained how sound was put on film. Saettler, p. 107.
10. KNOW 78, p. 7.
11. Frederick Devereux, *The Educational Talking Picture* (Chicago: University of Chicago Press, 1933).
12. Sydney Hyman, *The Lives of William Benton* (Chicago: University of Chicago Press, 1969), p. 167.
13. As cited in the *Modern Talking Picture Service Employee Manual* of 1963. This division was bought by Frank Arlinghaus and a number of other employees, and was incorporated as Modern Talking Picture Service, with Arlinghaus eventually becoming president of the firm. In 1942, Modern's role changed from a distributor of equipment to a distributor of films. In 1960, the company initiated its Modern Learning Aids division, which distributed PSSC (Physical Science Study Committee) films, among others. MTPS was primarily engaged in distributing corporate-sponsored business and industry films to schools and other nonprofits, which large companies increasingly viewed as a valuable advertising vehicle.
14. It seems to be the case that low-budget "B" films were among those most commonly remade by TFC into educational fare, providing the studios the satisfaction of contributing to the "education" of America while at the same time profiting to some extent from what may have been otherwise useless footage. TFC, however, did make grants to organizations such as the National Council for Teachers of English to publish books like *The Motion Picture and the Teaching of English*, which used examples of 100 or so major films as a guide to teaching film literacy within the context of English Studies.
15. From an artistic and educational perspective, a better Hollywood effort would take place in the early 1970s when Learning Corporation of America's Bill Deneen, having access to Columbia's vaults, hired the editing team of Jim Hanley, Don Thompson, and Mike Mears to create the *Searching for Values* series from individual feature films.
16. A truly affective approach, as would eventually be described by Benjamin Bloom and colleagues.
17. Editors of *Look* magazine, *Movie Lot to Beach-*

head: *The Motion Picture Goes to War and Prepares for the Future* (Garden City, NY: Doubleday, Doran, 1945), pp. 40–41.

18. *Ibid.*, p. 58.
19. Saettler, p. 177.
20. *Ibid.*, p. 170.
21. EBF's *Children of Many Lands* series, initiated in the 1940s, also explored human relations themes.
22. Charles Benton believes that Brooker was also the director of the Massachusetts Council for the Humanities, which was awarded money from the Ford Foundation and others to produce the first twelve *Humanities* series of films that were done by Britannica and John Barnes in the 1960s. (Charles Benton, note to author, July 27, 2006.)
23. Saettler, p. 177.
24. D.B. Jones, Movies *and Memoranda: An Interpretive History of the National Film Board of Canada* (Ottawa: Canadian Film Institute, 1981), p. 36. Greene is perhaps best known for his acting role as Ben Cartwright in the *Bonanza* television series.
25. Charles Hoban and Edward van Ormer, *Instructional Film Research 1918–1950* (New York: Arno Press and the *New York Times*, 1970).
26. Saettler, p. 179.
27. Kenneth Kaye, *40th Anniversary of Encyclopaedia Britannica Films and Its Predecessor Companies 1928–1968* (Commissioned by Charles Benton, 1968), p. 65.
28. Hutchins' own influence on EBF would be long-lasting and significant: his 1936 book *The Higher Learning in America* decries the lack of emphasis on classical education in universities. EBF would eventually produce the most intellectually stimulating work on classical Western civilization of any film company, much of it produced and directed by John Barnes.
29. Partner Chester Bowles was an extraordinary individual in his own right. His illustrious career included tenures as governor and congressman from Connecticut, and ambassador to India. He hosted an EBF film entitled *Assignment: India* (1958).
30. Hyman, pp. 246–248.
31. The ending of "The Lottery" concerned a woman being stoned to death. In spite of EBF's reticence to distribute the film, its graphics department created a publicity photo doctored to show blood running down the face of the victim.
32. Although operating under the same corporate umbrella, the encyclopedia and film company were two separate lines of business.
33. Hyman, pp. 273–274.
34. Adler was brought to the University by Hutchins from Columbia, and later appeared on-camera as the host of John Barnes' *Classical Civilization* series of 1965.
35. Hyman, p. 293. By mid–1966, according to an internal analysis requested by Benton, EBF had paid a cumulative total of $28,717,017 to the university.
36. H.W. Wilson, New York, publisher.
37. I suspect these might have been among the works of noted artist Reginald Marsh, which Benton collected.
38. One of Colmes' projects was EB's *The Great Men* series. As Kenneth Kaye notes: "The Great Men series was not one of EBF's greatest achievements in terms of quality. But in shooting the films Walter Colmes attained a triumph of efficient production. He and his assistant, Don Hoffman (who later came with Colmes to EBF), together with EBF researcher John Bobbitt, had ten scripts prepared in advance. They hired a group of actors and set up a dozen or so sets simultaneously in the same large studio. By drawing up a schedule similar to those now used in the filming of television series, they were able to go from set to set with their actors, filming scenes for all ten films in the same two-week period. It was economical — too economical.... Colmes' actors assumed a variety of roles, and many of the Great Men and their contemporaries were confusingly familiar from other films in the series. Of course children were too involved in the action to notice the duplication, but Britannica men felt it painfully, and from that time on, low costs at the expense of quality were never again considered a virtue at EBF." Kaye, pp. 81–82.
39. Benton had bought Muzak, a company whose motto was "music that is not to be listened to," in 1939. Ironically Mitchell, the man who ran the company whose name would become synonymous with "elevator music," would be executively responsible for some of the most artistically important and intellectually stimulating educational films ever produced. Even William Benton's own mother refused her son's offer to install a Muzak outlet in her apartment. (For more on Benton's involvement with Muzak, see Hyman, pp. 211–218, and 500–502.)
40. Paul F. Healy, "They Make the Strangest Movies," *The Saturday Evening Post*, March 7, 1959, p. 29, 87.
41. *Ibid.*, p. 87.
42. Statement of Maurice Mitchell, President, Encyclopaedia Britannica Films, "Science and Education for National Defense," extract from Hearings Before the Committee on Labor and Public Welfare, United States Senate, Eighty-Fifth Congress, Second Session, 1958, p 9.
43. *Ibid.*, p. 11.
44. Baxter suggested that Mankofsky get a degree in chemistry, since he'd successfully "completed" the course. (Mankofsky, conversation with the author, February 14, 2002.)
45. Born June 14, 1902, died May 27, 1987. Eurich was also the first president of the State University of New York.
46. Born April 19, 1912, died February 25, 1999.
47. Warren Everote, conversation with the author, August 3, 2009.
48. Everote, conversation with the author, July 14, 2000.
49. Isidore Mankofsky, conversation with the author, July 8, 2000.
50. Maurice Mitchell, "A Forward Look at Communications," *Britannica Book of the Year*, 1958.
51. Everote, conversation with the author, July 14, 2000. Everote also remembers Bell & Howell, whose president was Charles Percy, entering into discussions with Benton to acquire EBF. John Barnes, in a conversation with the author on January 4, 1997, thought acquisition discussions might have occurred in the 1950s as well with Republic Films, whose Walter

Colmes had served as president of EBF prior to Mitchell.

52. Author Arnold Gingrich notes that Smart was known to carry a money roll that "would choke a horse," consisting of nine $1000 bills enveloping a number of smaller bills on the inside of the roll. Arnold Gingrich, *Nothing but People: The Early Days at Esquire* (New York: Crown, 1971), p. 2.

53. Coronet reportedly paid $300 per minute of finished film, as told by producer Hal Kopel to Bill Deneen. (Deneen, letter to the author, June 13, 2000.) By comparison, EBF's budget was reportedly $1000 per minute. (Isidore Mankofsky conversation with the author, July 8, 2000.) The 4.2 days figure is from Ken Smith, *Mental Hygiene: Classroom Films 1945–1970* (New York: Blast Books, 1999), p. 91.

54. Low budgets and unrealistic production schedules were nothing new to people working under Smart, as evidenced by the travails experienced by illustrators George Petty and Alberto Vargas. Reid Stewart Austin, *Petty* (New York: Gramercy Books, 1997). Alberto Vargas and Reid Stewart Austin, *Vargas* (New York: Harmony Books, 1978). EB eschewed credits in this early era as well. Warren Everote (conversation with the author, September 15, 2009) says this was because Maurice Mitchell didn't want to appear to be diminishing the importance of the credited scholar/subject matter experts. I cannot find an EB film with filmmaker credits prior to the John Barnes–scripted *People Along the Mississippi* (*1951, prod. Gordon Wessenborn).

55. Warren Everote, *Warren Everote's Odyssey* (unpublished memoir, 2009).

56. Bob Kohl, conversation with the author, April 21, 1998.

57. The comment about doorknobs is from Gingrich, p. 128. The "mental suicide" quote is from Smith, p. 98.

58. See Chapter Four of this book for a description of the progressive movement that occurred at Coronet in the post–1970 years.

59. Julien Bryan, *Ambulance 464* (New York: Macmillan, 1918).

60. Later, Bryan was instrumental in assisting Emily Jones, executive secretary of the Educational Film Library Association (EFLA), by providing the organization rent-free space and paying her salary in the organization's formative months.

61. D.B Jones, *Movies and Memoranda: An Interpretive History of the National Film Board of Canada* (Ottawa: Canadian Film Institute, 1981), p. 7.

62. John Grierson, *Grierson on Documentary*, cited in Jones, pp. 13–14.

63. For an overview of Grierson's early days at the Film Board and presence in M.I.6, see Gerald Pratley, *Torn Sprockets: the Uncertain Projection of the Canadian Film* (London and Toronto: Associated Universities Presses, 1987), pp. 48–57.

64. Unit A consisted of agricultural, French-speaking, foreign language films; C, theatrical, newsreels, tourist, educational, and travel, and D, international affairs and special projects. In 1951, Unit E was created for sponsored films (films for television were added in 1953). Unit F eventually was created for films in French.

65. O'Connor was murdered in 1969 while filming a documentary in Appalachia. His killer served one year on a manslaughter charge.

66. Tom Daly, quoted in D.B. Jones, *The Best Butler in Business: Tom Daly and the National Film Board of Canada* (Toronto: University of Toronto Press, 199), pp. 59–60.

67. Jones, *The Best Butler in the Business*, p. 126.

68. *Ibid.*, pp. 68–69.

69. *Ibid.*, p. 74.

70. "Cinéma vérité" is customarily differentiated from "direct cinema" by its more active presence as a cinematic *provocateur*. Each has the following characteristics: 1) real people are filmed in uncontrolled (nondirected) situations; 2) events are not re-created; 3) people are not formally interviewed; 4) there is no "point of view" narration; 5) music is used sparingly, or preferably not at all.

Chapter Two

1. Much of the congressional impetus to accelerate funding for science, math, and foreign language may have come from the momentum generated by Rickover's testimony before Congress. The "father of the nuclear navy," who would eventually go on to write several books critical of the American education system, had visited the Soviet Union as part of Vice President Richard Nixon's entourage in July, 1959, and returned to testify before the House Committee on Appropriations. Much of his testimony described the efficacy of the Soviet education system. Utilizing his popularity with politicians of both parties, the irascible admiral established a bully pulpit for the advocacy of longer school hours and better teachers. While the movement to create more federal funding for curriculum was already underway, people like Rickover kept continual pressure on Washington with the goal of establishing educational primacy over the Soviets. For more on Rickover, see Norman Polmar and Thomas B. Allen, *Rickover: Controversy and Genius* (New York: Simon & Schuster, 1982), pp. 585–600.

In addition, a fascinating film document indicative of his increasingly public stance can be found in an episode of Hearst Metrotone News' *Screen News Digest* classroom newsreel (1959, vol. 2, no. 4), in which, in addition to sounding the alarm on the necessity of increased science and math instruction, he forcefully advocated liberal arts studies and emphasized the value of educating women.

2. William Benton had visited the USSR in 1955, and wrote for the Encyclopaedia what some consider the most comprehensive Western study of the Soviet education system to date. (Hyman, pp. 513–516.) The $480 million figure is found in Polmar and Allen, p. 587. The impact on individual states and districts could be extreme: California received more than $10 million per year in the early years of the program. The Los Angeles City School system alone obtained more than $400,000 in NDEA matching funds to expand its film library. Hardy Pelham, *Chalkboard to Computer: Audiovisual Education in California* (San Francisco: Photo & Sound, 1989), pp. 72–73.

3. *Title VII-New Educational Media News and Re-

ports, U.S. Department of Health, Educational and Welfare, Office of Education, July 1960, p. 4.

4. Desegregation was eventually enforced on a national level through the Civil Rights Act of 1964.

5. Peter Dow, *Schoolhouse Politics: Lessons from the Sputnik Era* (Cambridge: Harvard University Press, 1991), p. 8.

6. Science films, in particular, were being made in numbers never before seen, with strong emphasis on space exploration (e.g., EBF's *Rockets: How They Work*, 1958, prod. Hal Kopel, with Willy Ley acting as consultant).

7. Dow, p. 48.

8. Americo Lapati, *Educational and the Federal Government: A Historical Record* (New York: Mason/Charter, 1975), p. 38.

9. EBF's Charles Benton noted that the company's revenues increased from $10 million the year previous to the passage of ESEA, to $30 million the year thereafter. One important factor in the revenue increase was the fact that, although schools traditionally earmarked the lion's share of budget for teacher salaries, there weren't enough teachers available to hire in the 1965-1966 school year, so schools had to buy curriculum materials — including mediated instruction —- to spend the money. Benton also credits the implementation of Project Discovery as an important factor in the increase in revenue. (Conversation with the author, February 10, 1998.)

10. Morton Schindel of Weston Woods Films, conversation with the author, March 3, 1998.

11. Charles Benton, note to author, July 27, 2006.

12. Charles Benton, note to author, July 19, 2006.

13. Larry Yust, producer of EBF's *Short Play Showcase* series, occasionally would have shooting ratios of 15–1, meaning that one frame might be used in a film for every 15 frames shot.

14. Textbooks of the era were equally responsible for promulgating this Euro-centric view. (Charles Benton, note to author, July 27, 2006.)

15. Smith, letter to the author, February 16, 2000. Smith went on to later fame as the visual effects director for George Lucas' Industrial Light and Magic company. Erik Barnouw recalls that Hollywood employed a similar tactic to keep alleged Communist actors from appearing in television and films. If a given actor's name appeared on a selected list, he or she would be deemed too tall, or not tall enough, and would be rejected for the role on that basis, thus forestalling legal interference from groups such as the ACLU. Erik Barnouw, *Tube of Plenty* (New York: Oxford University Press, 1990), p. 130.

16. EBF management apparently had a concern that if provoked, Barnes would leave the company, head for Hollywood, and become successful there (Warren Everote and Milan Herzog, separate conversations with the author).

17. Charles Benton, conversation with the author, September 2, 2000.

Chapter Three

1. John Hoskyns-Abrahall of Bullfrog Films, conversation with the author, July 7, 1999.

2. Morton Schindel of Weston Woods, conversation with the author, March 3, 1998.

3. EBF typically budgeted $1000 per minute for a complete film, from script to post-production (Isidore Mankofsky, conversation with the author, July 8, 2000).

4. Bill Deneen of Learning Corporation of America, conversation with the author, January 1, 1999.

5. Martha Gonzalez, EBF, conversation with the author, September 15, 1998.

6. Zelda Burnford, wife of the late filmmaker Paul Burnford, related that she was unable to obtain promised royalties from an existing company that repeatedly ignored her requests for sales data. The amount in question, while important in principle, was predictably too low to warrant her hiring an attorney (conversation with the author, February 7, 2000). In a later conversation (April 27, 2007), she disclosed she'd heard that financial improprieties at the company were responsible for the errors in her account. She further understood that she was just one of several victims.

7. Ann Fienup-Riordan, *Freeze Frame: Alaska Eskimos in the Movies* (Seattle: University of Washington Press, 1995), p. 148.

8. For example, *Farm Family in Autumn*, 1967, dir. Tom Smith, EBF.

9. Tom Smith, note to the author, June 12, 2001.

10. Coronet's creative director Mel Waskin, whose tenure at the firm lasted from 1949 to 1994, notes that scholars were always an essential element in each Coronet film (conversation with the author, September 23, 2009).

11. Matoian's study guide for the LCA film *The Seven Wishes of a Rich Kid* (1979, dir. Larry Elikann) was especially provocative, asking children to question their parents about financial decisions relating to family economics.

12. Cinematographer Isidore Mankofsky was making $9000 per year at EBF when he left in 1968. EBF refused to pay overtime, which was almost always needed to produce work of the quality for which the company was noted (conversation with the author, July 8, 2000).

13. Van Bork burned through two helicopter pilots while making *Mesa Verde*, and two pairs of Hush Puppy shoes while braving lava flows during the making *Heartbeat of a Volcano*, 1970, EBF (Van Bork, conversation with the author, November 18, 2002).

14. Leacock, conversation with the author, January 2, 2000.

15. Wilets, conversation with the author, June 9, 1999.

16. For this reason, many EBF films may never be shown in any communications medium other than 16mm film.

17. Wilets, conversation with the author, June 9, 1999. Wilets destroyed all film records some years prior to his death in 2007, making identification of actors appearing in his films virtually impossible.

18. Richard Campbell, *60 Minutes and the News: a Mythology for Middle America* (Urbana and Chicago: University of Illinois Press, 1991), p. 141.

19. Stephen Mamber, *Cinema Verite in America: Studies in Uncontrolled Documentary* (Cambridge: MIT Press, 1974), pp. 228–229.

20. As part of the film reviewer's creed, one really does have to view every part of every film, beginning to end. If I seem unfair to Davis, it's because I chose to view several of the *Exploring* films consecutively. I began asking myself what crime I had committed to subject myself to an evening of Davis' folk ditties. This, really, is the hazard of much music in film: one is forced to accept the taste of the musical director. In the case of this series, it was also self-serving and continuous, as Davis' songs continued throughout each film. I'm sure the dearth of this series in public school libraries was for the same reason that I found these films so annoying. I signed up for the history film, not the folk music concert (and I'm sure many teachers felt the same way).

21. Later, when adoption of mediated instruction was virtually complete, salespeople focused on "updating your library" with new editions of previously released films. (Charles Benton, July 27, 2006, note to author.)

22. Saettler, p. 98.

23. Of its founding, Saettler writes: "The Educational Film Library Association (EFLA) was formed in Chicago, March 17–18, 1943, for the purpose of reviewing the arrangements established by government agencies for the free distribution of their films. It was recognized by all present that unless educational institutions and agencies were given opportunity to qualify as depositories, they would not be able to meet requests for government war films from school and adult groups. The first officers of EFLA were: L.C. Larsen, chairman; Bruce A. Findlay, vice-chairman; and R. Russell Munn, secretary. Donald Slesinger, then director of the American Film Center, served as acting administrative director" (Saettler, p. 176 n.).

24. Emily S. Jones, "Remembering EFLA: 1945–1958," *Sightlines*, Fall/Winter 1983-84, pp. 6–8.

25. Jones later said her main reason for leaving EFLA was because it "never had any money," and her original intention had been to stay for only two years (conversation with the author, July 21, 1999).

26. Emily Jones, conversation with the author, January 15, 1999.

27. Covert writes: "For a few years before I left EFLA I tried to raise funds to compile a computerized catalogue of all the American Film Festival entries. It would have been a very useful reference tool for documentary film. But at the time (early 1980s), no one was interested in such a project." (Letter to the author, July 16, 2000.)

28. Smith, letter to the author, February 28, 2000.

Chapter Four

1. EFLA *Sightlines*, vol. 21, #4 (Fall 1988), p. 4.

2. The Santa Clara County (CA) Office of Education film library, for example, listed some 876 companies from which it might acquire films.

3. Phil Courter remembers that Roccos paid him $10,000 per film, plus 15 percent of the gross sales, considered generous for the time (conversation with the author, June 15, 2000).

4. Hal Weiner, conversation with the author, June 8, 2000.

5. Biff Sherman, conversation with the author, November 22, 2004.

6. Phil Courter, conversation with the author, November 14, 2007.

7. Sherman had met Siegel while at ARA, a school and charter bus transportation company.

8. Born May 4, 1896, died January 18, 1982.

9. The films were *Our Mr. Sun, Hemo the Magnificent, Strange Case of the Cosmic Rays,* and *Unchained Goddess.*

10. Frank Capra, *The Name Above the Title* (New York: Macmillan, 1971), p. 442.

11. Born December 30, 1903, died February 13, 1998.

12. Siegel's complete story can be found on the website of the California Military Museum: www.militarymuseum.org/1stmpu.html.

13. Korean War historian Resa LaRu Kirkland, conversation with the author, December 12, 2000.

14. Crump, though, did make the occasional biblical reference, including a verse ("a time to sow, a time to reap," var. Ecclesiastes 3:2) toward the end of *It's About Time* (1962).

15. Irwin Braun, d. 1994(?); Paul Burnford, b. July 19, 1914, d. March 28, 1999.

16. Paul Burnford, conversation with the author, March 12, 1998.

17. William Stevenson, *A Man Called Intrepid* (New York: Harcourt Brace Jovanovich, 1976), pp. 348–49. Stevenson discusses the British Security Coordination (BSC) and 1 Rockefeller Center on page 250. Burnford was not the only individual associated with educational film involved with these top secret programs. Scot scholar Gilbert Highet, host of John Barnes' three part *Odyssey* series of 1965 for EB, was a BSC operative prior to becoming a U.S. citizen in 1951.

18. Stevenson, conversation with the author, March 12, 1998.

19. Filmmaker Bob Stitzel, conversation with the author, July 30, 2003.

20. Holland (b. March 5, 1937) had also been serving as a freelance drama critic for the *Los Angeles Herald-Examiner*. His first task at BFA was to edit director Piers Jessop's 45-minute film *An Unworthy Scaffold* into a 14-minute version for U.S. audiences, eventually entitled *Theatre in Shakespeare's Time* (1973).

21. Pelham, *Chalkboard to Computer*, p. 133

22. Barr, conversation with the author, April 10, 1999.

23. Born 1945 in Woking, England, and 1947, San Pedro, California, respectively.

24. Hoskyns-Abrahall, conversation with the author, July 7, 1999.

25. Art Wolf b. June 11, 1917, d. November 17, 2002; Russ Mosser b. November 9, 1917.

26. An unpublished manuscript, *Centron Remembered*, written in 1999 by Russell A. Mosser, relates the fascinating history of the company. The story of Herk Harvey and the challenges of filming in South America and Mexico was related by Mosser in a conversation with the author, December 28, 2009.

27. Born 1912, died December 18, 1997.

28. EFLA *Sightlines*, vol. 21, #4 (Fall 1988), p. 4.

29. Born October 6, 1916, died March 10, 2005.

After leaving Churchill-Wexler Films, Sy Wexler founded Wexler Film Productions in 1965, specializing in medical and scientific films. He made films for many of the major pharmaceutical companies (including The House Ear Institute), hospitals and clinics, filming surgical techniques for doctors and medical instrumentation training films and videos for nurses. The firm closed in 2001.

30. EFLA *Sightlines*, vol. 21, #4 (Fall 1988), p. 4.

31. Leo Dratfield, b. July 8, 1918, d. November 22, 1986.

32. Occasionally, U.S. distribution rights were acquired for exceptional foreign-made films, such as Matsue Jinbo's creative and engaging puppet films made by Japan's Gakken company (e.g., *Moonbeam Princess*, 1967). Typical of the Coronet dictum of the era, Jinbo's name never appeared on the credits.

33. Mel Waskin, conversation with the author, July 14, 2009.

34. *Ibid.* Waskin admits that Coronet's guidance films were "kind of dumb," but recognizes that today they have some historical value in showing how people of the era "were supposed to be." Reflecting on his relationship with the many films for which he wrote scripts, he says: "I'm the ideal cocktail party guest. I can talk on any subject for 10 minutes, and then move on."

35. John Smart would die three years later, in 1982.

36. Sheldon Sachs, conversation with the author, March 2, 1998.

37. Mel Waskin, b. August 14, 1926, Chicago, Illinois.

38. "Budge" Crawley, b. November 14, 1911, d. May 13, 1987; Judith Crawley, d. September 15, 1986.

39. Barbara Wade Rose, *Budge: What Happened to Canada's King of Film* (Toronto: ECW Press, 1998), pp. 55–56.

40. *Ibid.*, p. 73.

41. *Ibid.*, pp. 73–74.

42. *Ibid.*, pp. 104–105.

43. The Film Board would occasionally turn down work, which could then legally be offered to firms such as Crawley, who, as of this writing, is credited as having co-produced of 144 films for the Film Board.

44. Budgets for half-hour films at other companies were typically capped at $50,000 during this era (Isidore Mankofsky, conversation with the author, July 8, 2000).

45. Holdner, conversation with the author, November 7, 2003.

46. Glidden, note to the author, December 12, 2009.

47. Charney, b. May 11, 1941, went on to form VideoFashion, a successful fashion media company, in 1976.

48. Warren Everote, conversation with the author, August 3, 2009.

49. A more detailed explanation of EDC's history can be found at its website: www.edc.org.

50. For more details of Leacock's PSSC films, see his entry in Chapter 6.

51. NSF granted $4.8 million to develop MACOS, and $2.16 million to implement it. Dorothy Nelkin, *The Creation Controversy* (New York: W.W. Norton, 1982), p. 34.

52. Another hunter-gatherer culture, that of the Kung bushmen of the Kalahari, was also in the running, and the Marshall family, whose research among the Kung was well-known and documented, generously agreed to make their footage available to the MACOS team. By 1967, according to project editor Peter Dow, it had become "politically unacceptable to use materials that showed partially naked, dark-skinned 'primitives' in a public school classroom," and the team regretfully chose not to include the Kung in the project. Peter Dow, *Schoolhouse Politics: Lessons from the Sputnik Era* (Cambridge: Harvard University Press, 1991), pp. 121–122.

53. *Ibid.*, p. 65.

54. *Ibid.*, p. 134.

55. Asen Balikci, *The Netsilik Eskimo* (Prospect Heights, IL: Waveland Press, 1989), p. xiii.

56. Dow, p. 161.

57. Ibid, 151.

58. Nelkin, *The Creation Controversy*, p. 25.

59. *Ibid.*, pp. 49–50.

60. Dow, p. 178–179.

61. Dorothy Nelkin, "The Science-Textbook Controversies," *Scientific American* (April 1976), p. 34.

62. Nelkin, *The Creation Controversy*, p. 41, 51.

63. Dow, p. 272. Dow's book is highly recommended for its thought-provoking discussion of MACOS, schools, and federal, state, and local politics.

64. Memories of the opinions of Mitchell, who is no longer living, are contradictory. Barnes considered Mitchell to be an advocate of his, while Bill Deneen states: "Mitch would sit in 'management screenings,' arms folded and dour, and nearly always his comments about our films were negative. He seemed to have great disdain for filmmakers. 'EBF films are made to sell. Can't sell a John Barnes film. They aren't worth a shit. Bert's [Van Bork] pictures have no imagination. Deneen's pictures are too commercial.'" (Bill Deneen, letter to the author, October 21, 2000.)

65. The former VP was much more effective in Washington for EB than in Mexico City, where his wife failed to make an expected appearance at a party given by the wife of the head of Mexico's Department of Education. Soon thereafter, EBF's Mexican distributors found that the market had inexplicably dried up for EBF films, effectively keeping the firm out of the Mexican marketplace for several years. (Martha Gonzalez, conversation with the author, June28, 2000.)

66. Charles Benton, b. February 13, 1931.

67. EB Films would, on October 1, 1966, become part of the newly formed umbrella corporation, Encyclopaedia Britannica Educational Corporation (EBEC), combining EB Films, EB Press, and EB's reference books school divisions. For continuity's sake, all post-1965 EBEC films remain classified under the acronyms "EB" or "EBF" in this book.

68. For more on Deneen and Gottlieb, see Learning Corporation of America in this chapter.

69. Letter in the collection of the author.

70. Collection of the author, March 21, 1966.

71. Collection of the author, January 15, 1967.

72. Collection of the author, January 18, 1967.

73. Unsent letter from Bill Deneen to Russell Karp, Screen Gems, March 1, 1968. Collection of the author.

74. Everote, discussion with the author, July 14, 2000.

75. Bruce Hoffman's lineage at Encyclopaedia Britannica Films included his paternal grandfather Paul Hoffman (former president of Studebaker and charter member of EB's Board of Directors) and father Don (a vice-president of EB Films).

76. Bryant later left the company to join up with Heinz Gelles to create Phoenix Films.

77. Thanks to Charles Benton for supplying the history of Films Incorporated.

78. Handel, conversation with the author, December 7, 2005.

79. More about Hoefler, Cadle, and contemporary treatment of aboriginal subjects in film can be found in Robert Gordon, *Picturing Bushmen: The Denver African Expedition of 1925* (Athens: Ohio University Press, 1997).

80. Deneen's work as a filmmaker is also notable, and is discussed under his entry in Chapter 6.

81. Deneen's efforts to recruit fellow-pilot Davidson included an incident in which Deneen put a plane containing the two into a dive, then asked his passenger for a timely answer on the possibility of joining McGraw-Hill rival LCA (Deneen, conversation with the author, August 15, 2000).

82. Deneen was used to doing a lot with somewhat limited budgets. He recalls Columbia's president Abe Schneider asking him how much *Galileo: The Challenge of Reason* (1970, dir. Dennis Azzarella) in LCA's *Western Civilization: Majesty & Madness* series cost to make. Deneen said that it was $30,000. Schneider reportedly replied "$30,000.... Columbia couldn't have made that film for $30 million!" (Deneen, conversation with the author, November 30, 2009.)

83. Salzman, letter to the author, June 8, 2000.

84. Matoian eventually left LCA to pursue a career in television, eventually becoming president of Fox Broadcasting and HBO Films.

85. Carole Hyatt and Linda Gottlieb, *When Smart People Fail* (New York: Simon & Schuster, 1987).

86. Rosenberg, b. November 25, 1909, Baltimore, Maryland.

87. Gelles eventually left McGraw to co-found Phoenix Films in 1973.

88. More about MIS history and philosophy can be found in James Gilbert, *Redeeming Culture: American Religion in an Age of Science* (Chicago: University of Chicago Press, 1997). An additional critical analysis of Moody science films was written by Marsha Orgeron and Skip Elsheimer, "Something Different in Science Films," *Moving Image: Journal of the Association of Moving Image Archivists*, vol. 7, no. 1 (Spring 2007).

89. Gilbert, pp. 142–43.

90. Gary Evans, *In the National Interest: a Chronicle of the National Film Board of Canada from 1949–1989* (Toronto: University of Toronto Press, 1991), p. 103.

91. U.S. authorities could be testy as well in determining which Canadian films would be allowed to be distributed to stateside schools. In 1969, U.S. distributors of George Kaczender's *Phoebe, The Game,* and *World of Three* were forced by the U.S. Department of Justice to register as agents of a foreign government under the little-known Foreign Agents Registration Act of 1938 in response to conservative religious pressure on the Johnson administration. Evans, pp. 283–284.

92. Borsos, the director of the well-regarded feature film *The Grey Fox* (1983), was to tragically die of leukemia in 1995 at the age of 41.

93. Evans, p. 291.

94. Born August 17, 1928. Sid Platt retired from NGEO in 1995, and continues to pursue his passion for watercolor painting.

95. Platt, conversation with the author, July 20, 1999.

96. Heinz Gelles, b. April 12, 1925.

97. Gelles, conversation with the author, August 24, 1999.

98. Bryant, conversation with the author, July 7, 1999.

99. David Adams, b. September 5, 1923, d. October 8, 2006.

100. About Mary Glasgow, Ann King writes: "Mary had a background in education — she had been a teacher of modern languages and then an HMI (Her Majesty's Inspector of Schools). During the 1939–45 war she had been a founding member of the Committee for the Encouragement of Music and the Arts (CEMA) which was established in January 1940, the result of an informal government-level conference held in December 1939. Its aim was to ensure that the Arts did not get 'lost' in wartime Britain. It consisted of the 'great and the good' in the Arts and Education worlds, and Mary Glasgow was its Secretary General. The initial objective of the committee was to give financial assistance to cultural societies finding difficulty in maintaining their activities during the war. After the war it continued as a permanent peace-time body under the name 'Arts Council of Great Britain.' Mary had launched into publishing in 1960 with the successful production of a series of magazines and recordings (on 45 rpm discs) for school learners of French and German (later, Spanish, Italian and Russian were added), embodying her conviction that language learning should engage the pupils' interest, be enjoyable, and that the voices should be authentic. Over the next few years, Mary Glasgow Publications emerged as a major player in the languages education field, broadening its range to include films, visual aids, and television courses. Mary's love of France led her to buy and restore a hilltop property in a village in Provence, and to make it the subject of *Portrait d'un Village: Entrechaux,* her first short (12–15 minutes) film for young learners, which portrays the life and culture of a southern French community. A similar film based in Normandy, *Fête à Coutances,* followed in 1973. After Mary left publishing, she founded in 1978 the Mary Glasgow Language Trust, with the aim of providing material support to enterprising language teachers. Since Mary's death in 1983, the small group of Trustees, under the chairmanship of her nephew, Edwin Glasgow QC CBE, has maintained and developed this goal." (Ann King, The Mary Glasgow Language Trust, letter to the author, December 20, 2009.)

101. Jerry Forman, b. October 28, 1928, Bronx, New York. Scott Forman, b. March 13, 1982, Manhasset, New York.

102. Scott Forman, discussing his relationship with the technology companies that sponsor Allegro's films,

notes, "We have no Nike, no Nintendo, no McDonald's." Conversation with the author, July 21, 2009.

103. Scott Forman, conversation with the author, July 21, 2009.

104. Erik Barnouw, *Tube of Plenty* (New York: Oxford University Press, 1990), p. 227. Raymond Fielding, *The American Newsreel, 1911–1967* (Norman: Oklahoma University Press, 1972), p. 186.

105. Scott Forman, conversation with the author, July 21, 2009.

106. *Ibid.*

107. Erik Barnouw, *Documentary: A History of the Non-Fiction Film* (New York: Oxford University Press, 1993), pp. 215–6.

108. Thomas Stanton, b. 1922, d. 1987.

109. Ken Middleham, b. May 12, 1927, d. May 23, 2001.

110. James M. Franey, b. 1901, d. 1993.

111. Richard Leacock, who shot the footage in *Desert Nomads* and at least one other film in the series, never saw the completed film until more than 50 years later.

112. Richard Lukin, b. May 22, 1927, New York City.

113. Lukin, conversation with the author, June 5, 2006.

114. Lukin, note to the author, September 15, 2009.

115. Lukin recalls that Beymer spent $18,000 producing *Special Day* (conversation with the author, September 24, 2007).

116. Lukin, conversation with the author, June 5, 2006.

117. Schindel, conversation with the author, March 24 and 27, 1998.

118. Deitch recalls that Ungerer's *joie de vivre* was evidenced by the ever-present glass of whiskey sipped by the author during the filming (conversation with the author, January, 1999).

119. Ann Neal, Xerox Historical Archives, letter to the author, December 21, 2009.

120. Elaine Woo, "Thomas G. Yohe, was Co-creator of 'Schoolhouse Rock,'" *Los Angeles Times* (obituary), December 23, 2000.

121. A. William Bleum, *Documentary in American Television: Form, Function, Method* (New York: Hastings House, 1965), p. 144.

122. Daniel Einstein, *Special Edition: A Guide to Network Television Documentary Series and Special News Reports, 1955–1979* (Metuchen, NJ: Scarecrow Press, 1987), p. xv.

123. Born October 30, 1915, died March 3, 1998.

124. Several *CBS Reports* reporters were making over $100,000 per year, in 1960s dollars. It was not uncommon for production costs to run over $100,000 per hourly program.

125. Fred W. Friendly, *Due to Circumstances Beyond Our Control* (New York: Random House, 1967), p. 155.

126. McMullen, conversation with the author, March 11, 2000.

127. Friendly, p. 137.

128. He immediately thereafter became an advisor to the Ford Foundation, where he was instrumental in developing funding for public television.

129. Historian Erik Barnouw wasn't as charitable toward Stanton, whom he accused of soft-pedaling on the excesses of McCarthyism. Erik Barnouw, *Media Marathon: a Twentieth-Century Memoir* (Durham: Duke University Press, 1996), pp. 175–177.

130. Wachtler eventually became chief judge of the New York State Court of Appeals, and later gained notoriety in a celebrated case when he was sentenced to prison for harassing his ex-girlfriend. Wachtler's prison memoir is a thought-provoking excoriation of the prison system: Sol Wachtler, *After the Madness: a Judge's Own Prison Memoir* (New York: Random House, 1997).

131. Wolff, conversation with the author, March 21, 2000.

132. Sales figures aren't available, but the film was resident in the vast majority of the film libraries inspected by the author during the writing of this book.

133. Bluem, p. 169.

134. Young, letter to the author, December 27, 2000. The film he is describing is *Angola: Journey to War* (1961). Young's story is also documented in Barnouw, *Documentary: A History of the Non-Fiction Film*, p. 227.

135. While the same argument could be made for all network-produced series, CBS News, especially during the Fred W. Friendly days, had an emphasis on hard news reporting that related well to educational objectives.

136. Charles Benton, note to the author, July 27, 2006.

137. Bluem, p. 90.

138. Benton, note to the author, July 27, 2006.

139. *Ibid.* In 1992, Gill produced the *Buried Mirror* series, hosted by Carlos Fuentes, which described many of the contributions made by the Moors to the Hispanic world.

140. Kennard, conversation with the author, February 12, 1998.

141. Alasdair Clayre, *The Heart of the Dragon* (Boston: Houghton Mifflin, 1985).

142. McCallum, conversation with the author, December 14, 1998.

143. Latham, conversation with the author, December 15, 1998. McCallum is better known to North American audiences for his acting role as agent Illya Kuryakin in the 1960's television series *Man from U.N.C.L.E.*

144. *Ibid.*

Chapter Five

1. Much of the material in this chapter appeared in the author's monograph entitled *An Academic Perspective: The Life and Films of John Barnes*, published in the Fall 2002 issue of *The Moving Image: the Journal of the Association of Moving Image Archivists*, published by the University of Minnesota Press, pp. 41–72.

2. As quoted by Jeanne Barnes to the author, June 26, 2001.

3. Letter to the author, March 26, 1997.

4. *Ibid.*

5. Letter to the author, December 8, 1999.

6. Warren Everote, *Warren Everote's Odyssey*.

7. *New York Times*, July 3, 1955.
8. Harry Ashmore, *Unseasonable Truths: the Life of Robert Maynard Hutchins* (Boston: Little, Brown, 1989), p. 104.
9. Letter to Barnes, written by EB's Harold McNaney, May 15, 1963 (original in the collection of Jeanne Barnes).
10. Letter from Barnes to EB's Harold McNaney, June 3, 1963 (original in the collection of Jeanne Barnes).
11. The other was *Equality Under the Law: The Lost Generation of Prince Edward County* (1965).
12. He did, to a college theatrical group, for the same $3000 he paid for it. (Conversation with the author, July 26, 1998.) This story appears in Don Heckman, 'The Endless Day of a Filmmaker,' *Boys Life* (January 1970), pp. 23–24.
13. Moffat's first career cinema role was in 1957, as the protagonist in Barnes' *Roger Williams: Founder of Rhode Island* (Moffat, conversation with the author, January 28, 2002).
14. *Ibid.*
15. From *By Venice Possessed* (1974), an unpublished essay by John Barnes, collection of the author.
16. Writer Studs Terkel offered a similar opinion of the great pantomime artist: "Only one guy ever out-talked me, Marcel Marceau. I couldn't get a word in." *San Jose Mercury*, October 13, 2001, p. 1E.
17. Delivered by Barnes in his address at *El Instituto Mexicano Norteamericano de Relaciones Culturales* in Mexico City, in June 1966, as part of a three-day retrospective of his films.
18. Deneen, letter to the author, August 7, 2001.

Chapter Six

1. Alemann, conversation with the author, December 22, 2009.
2. Walt Berlet, b. Sept. 26, 1910, d. September 6, 1995. Myrna Berlet, b. May 30, 1940.
3. Myrna Berlet, conversations with the author, December 1, 2003, and July 26, 2006.
4. Peter Boulton, b. October 25, 1920, d. March 2, 2003.
5. Bronowski, conversation with the author, March 24, 1997.
6. Bruce Cornwell, conversation with the author, January 22, 2004.
7. Deitch has written a fascinating book about his transition from New York to Prague: *For the Love of Prague* (Prague: Gene Deitch, 1995).
8. Deitch, conversation with the author, January 1999.
9. For more on Deneen's career as a film executive, see the Encyclopaedia Britannica and Learning Corporation of America entries in Chapter 4.
10. Deneen's filmmaking exploits are fascinatingly told in Jean Maddern Pitrone, *The Touch of His Hand: Colombo, a Modern Day Damien in Burma* (Staten Island, NY: Alba House, 1970).
11. Gerald Gardner, *The Censorship Papers* (New York: Dodd, Mead, 1987), p. 6.
12. Janisz Garland, *Grace* (unpublished memoir, 1999).
13. Deneen, conversation with the author, November 19, 2009. In 2008, The Miriam Collection released a Limited Collector's Edition DVD set of the film, which also contains Deneen's *Life in Ancient Rome*, along with an on-camera commentary by Deneen describing the making of his academic film.
14. Such sleight-of-voice was not all that uncommon during the days of non-synch film. BFA's Wayne Mitchell remembers contributing his own "vocalese" accompaniment to a dance in one of his American Indian films of the mid–1960s. About *Taro*, Deneen also recalls that Maurice Mitchell, in the executive screening, said that the film "had homosexuality written all over it," after viewing a sequence showing an older and younger boy sharing a bedroom in a small Japanese dwelling. To this day, Deneen still doesn't know how it ever got released (conversation with the filmmaker, November 19, 2008).
15. Leacock, letter to the author, June 29, 1998.
16. Bitter was renowned for degaussing the U.S. fleet in World War II, thus rendering German magnetic mines useless, as discussed in his book *Magnets: The Education of a Physicist*, pp. 115–128.
17. Bitter's generator had previously had powered streetcars in Pittsburgh, Pennsylvania.
18. Leacock, conversation with the author, March 1, 2001.
19. Alan Root, letter to the author, August 21, 2002.
20. Since divorced, Deepa Mehta has made a name for herself as a feature filmmaker, with films such as *Fire* (1996), *Earth* (1998), and *Water* (2005).
21. Bertram W. Salzman, *Being a Buddha on Broadway* (Carlsbad, CA: InnerDirections, 2004), pp. 9–10.
22. Elizabeth "Libby" Schwartz (unpublished memoir, 1964).
23. Philip Stapp, *Who's Who in Filmmaking*, EFLA Bulletin, vol. XXIV, no. 3 (November 1964).
24. McLaren, as quoted by Stapp in a letter addressed to Museum of Modern Art Film Librarian William Sloan on December 10, 1990. This is corroborated by an earlier letter written by filmmaker Don McWilliams on September 28, 1988, in which he refers to a conversation in which McLaren confirmed the attribution (letters in the collection of the author).
25. Stapp, conversation with the author, February 16, 1999.
26. Bryan, conversation with the author, November 5, 2009.
27. Patricia Harvey-Thompson, letter to the author, November 30, 2007.
28. Deneen, letter in the collection of the author, August 26, 1966,
29. Craig Walker, biographical information in letter to the author, June 4, 2008.
30. Tom Smith, letter to the author, May 23, 2008.
31. Yust, conversation with the author, April 2006.

Chapter Seven

1. Deneen, conversation with the author, December 20, 1996.
2. Funding figures are from Hardy Pelham, *Classroom to Computer*, pp. 72–73, 115–116.

3. Advances in digital restoration techniques have had some success in returning color close to the original in many — but not all — of the faded prints that have been digitized and preserved.

4. It should be noted that many film companies in both the theatrical and educational realms saw the need for a secure storage environment for priceless prints and negatives, and began, in the early 1960s, to store their more valuable properties in areas such as the "Salt Mine," a huge cavern located 650 feet under the terra firma of Hutchinson, Kansas. There, in the vacated bays of a still-working salt mine first breached in 1926, over 43 football fields' worth of surface area has been dedicated to the safe storage of x-rays, microfilm, data tapes, and movie film.

5. Author Gary Evans (*In the National Interest*, p. 291) cites the following statistics from the National Film Board of Canada: in 1978–77, 702 video cassettes of various titles were sold, as opposed to 10,334 prints of 16mm film. By 1985, the reverse was dramatic, with 15,744 videos sold to 1,302 16mm prints. The Film Board, which sold its one-hour films for $400 — much less than U.S. educational film companies, incidentally — now sold them in video versions for $79.

6. The National Film Board of Canada, while not dependent on concern over potential military conflict for its budget, was at the same time seeing its own funding source dry up, due to its government's preference for television in the form of the Canadian Broadcasting Corporation.

7. The AFA website is www.afana.org.

8. Founded by Brewster Kahle in 1996, the Internet Archive is a 501(c)(3) non-profit that houses a free and openly accessible online digital library. There are 15 sub-collections of films, comprising over 100,000 items.

9. The AFA's Internet Archive site is www.archive.org/details/academic_films.

Bibliography

Books, Periodicals, Press Releases, Unpublished Manuscripts, and Internet References

Alexander, Geoff. "An Academic Perspective: The Life and Films of John Barnes." *The Moving Image: The Journal of the Association of Moving Image Archivists*, vol. 2, no. 2 (Fall 2002).

Ashmore, Harry. *Unseasonable Truths: The Life of Robert Maynard Hutchins*. Boston: Little, Brown, 1989.

Austin, Reid Stewart. *Petty*. New York: Gramercy Books, 1997.

Balikci, Asen. *The Netsilik Eskimo*. Prospect Heights, IL: Waveland Press, 1989.

Barnouw, Erik. *Documentary: A History of the Non-Fiction Film*. New York: Oxford University Press, 1993.

———. *Media Marathon: a Twentieth-Century Memoir*. Durham: Duke University Press, 1996.

———. *Tube of Plenty*. New York: Oxford University Press, 1990.

Barrett, Gerald, and Thomas Erskine. *Conrad Aiken's "Silent Snow, Secret Snow."* Encino, CA: Dickenson, 1972.

Bendazzi, Giannalberto. *Cartoons: One Hundred Years of Cinema Animation*. Bloomington and Indianapolis: Indiana University Press, 1994.

Beveridge, James. *John Grierson: Film Master*. New York: Macmillan, 1978.

Bitter, Francis. *Education of a Physicist*. Garden City, NY: Doubleday Anchor, 1959.

Bleum, A. William. *Documentary in American Television: Form, Function, Method*. New York: Hastings House, 1965.

Bloom, Benjamin, et al. *Taxonomy of Educational Objectives, Handbook II: Affective Domain*. New York: David McKay, 1964.

Boddy, William. *Fifties Television: The Industry and Its Critics*. Urbana and Chicago: University of Illinois Press, 1990.

Boyer, Peter J. *Who Killed CBS?* New York: Random House, 1988.

Brenner, Anita, and George Leighton. *The Wind That Swept Mexico: The History of the Mexican Revolution of 1910–1942*. Austin: University of Texas Press, 1971.

Buchsbaum, Ralph. *Animals Without Backbones*. Chicago: University of Chicago Press, 1947.

Bryan, Julien. *Ambulance 464*. New York: Macmillan, 1918.

Cameron, Kenneth M. *Africa on Film*. New York: Continuum, 1994.

Campbell, Richard. *60 Minutes and the News: A Mythology for Middle America*. Urbana and Chicago: University of Illinois Press, 1991.

Carnes, Mark C., ed. *Past Imperfect: History According to the Movies*. New York: Henry Holt, 1995.

Capra, Frank. *The Name Above the Title*. New York: Macmillan, 1971.

"CBS Is Proud of Radio Serial Produced at Chicago Studios." *Broadcasting Magazine,* November 12, 1945, p. 48.

Clayre, Alasdair. *The Heart of the Dragon*. Boston: Houghton Mifflin, 1985.

Cook, David A. *A History of Narrative Film*. New York: W.W. Norton, 1981.

Cross, Timothy. "Clifton Fadiman '25: An Erudite Guide to the Wisdom of Others." http://www.columbia.edu/cu/college/alumni/cct/40a.html.

Day, James. *The Vanishing Vision: The Inside Story of Public Television*. Berkeley: University of California Press, 1995.

Deitch, Gene. *For the Love of Prague*. Prague: Gene Deitch, 1995.

Devereux, Frederick. *The Educational Talking Picture*. Chicago: University of Chicago Press, 1933.

Dow, Peter. *Schoolhouse Politics: Lessons from the Sputnik Era*. Cambridge: Harvard University Press, 1991.

Editors of *Look* Magazine. *Movie Lot to Beachhead: The Motion Picture Goes to War and Prepares for the Future*. Garden City, NY: Doubleday, Doran, 1945.

Einbinder, Harvey. *The Myth of the Britannica*. New York: Grove Press, 1964.

Einstein, Daniel. *Special Edition: A Guide to Network Television Documentary Series and Special News Reports, 1955–1979*. Metuchen, NJ: Scarecrow, 1987.

Elliott, Godfrey, ed. *Film and Education*. New York: Philosophical Library, 1948.

Epstein, Edward Jay. *News from Nowhere: Television and the News*. New York: Random House, 1973.

Evans, Gary. *In the National Interest: A Chronicle of the National Film Board of Canada from 1949–1989*. Toronto: University of Toronto Press, 1991.

Everote, Warren. *Warren Everote's Odyssey.* Unpublished memoir, 2009.

Fielding, Raymond. *The American Newsreel, 1911–1967.* Norman: Oklahoma University Press, 1972.

———. *The Technique of Special Effects Cinematography.* New York: Hastings, 1974.

Fienup-Riordan, Ann. *Freeze Frame: Alaska Eskimos in the Movies.* Seattle: University of Washington Press, 1995.

Friendly, Fred W. *Due to Circumstances Beyond Our Control.* New York: Random House, 1967.

Gardner, Gerald. *The Censorship Papers.* New York: Dodd, Mead, 1987.

Garland Janisz, Grace. *Grace.* Unpublished memoir, 1999.

Gates, Gary Paul. *Air Time: The Inside Story of CBS News.* New York: Harper & Row, 1978.

Gianetti, Louis. *Understanding Movies,* 5th ed. Englewood Cliffs, NJ: Prentice Hall, 1990.

Gilbert, James. *Redeeming Culture: American Religion in an Age of Science.* Chicago: University of Chicago Press, 1997.

Gingrich, Arnold. *Nothing but People: The Early Days at Esquire.* New York: Crown, 1971.

Gordon, Robert. *Picturing Bushmen: The Denver African Expedition of 1925.* Athens: Ohio University Press, 1997.

Haskins, James. *Adam Clayton Powell: Portrait of a Marching Black.* Trenton, NJ: Africa World Press, 1993.

———. *Black Dance in America.* New York: HarperCollins, 1990.

Healy, Paul F. "They Make the Strangest Movies." *The Evening Post,* March 7, 1959, p. 28.

Heider, Karl G. *Ethnographic Film.* Austin: University of Texas Press, 1976.

Heckman, Don. "The Endless Day of a Film Maker." *Boys' Life,* January 1970.

Hoban, Charles, and Edward van Ormer. *Instructional Film Research 1918–1950.* New York: Arno Press and the *New York Times,* 1970.

Holbrook, Paul. "Tom Terrific." *Big Reel,* January 15, 1998, p. 103.

Houston, Penelope. *Keepers of the Frame: The Film Archives.* London: British Film Institute, 1994.

Hovland, C.I., A.A. Lumsdaine, and F.D. Sheffield. *Experiments on Mass Communication.* Princeton: Princeton University Press, 1949.

Hutchins, Robert Maynard. *The Higher Learning in America.* New Haven: Yale University Press, 1936.

Hyatt, Carole, and Linda Gottlieb. *When Smart People Fail.* New York: Simon & Schuster, 1987.

Hyman, Sydney. *The Lives of William Benton.* Chicago: University of Chicago Press, 1969.

"In Days Gone By: Blazing the Trail to the Schoolhouse." *KNOW,* II Quarter, 1978. *Encyclopædia Britannica.*

Jacobs, Lewis. *The Documentary Tradition: From Nanook to Woodstock.* New York: Hopkinson and Blake, 1971.

Jones, D.B. *The Best Butler in the Business: Tom Daly and the National Film Board of Canada.* Toronto: University of Toronto Press, 1996.

———. *Movies and Memoranda: An Interpretive History of the National Film Board of Canada.* Ottawa: Canadian Film Institute, 1981.

Jones, Emily S. "Remembering EFLA: 1945–1958." *Sightlines* (Fall/Winter 1983–84): 6–8.

Karetnikova, Inga. *Mexico According to Eisenstein.* Albuquerque: University of New Mexico Press, 1991.

Kaye, Kenneth. *40th Anniversary of Encyclopædia Britannica Films and its Predecessor Companies 1928–1968.* Commissioned by Charles Benton, 1968.

Kirkland, Resa LaRu. *The Forgotten Warrior Project.* http://www.forgottenwarriorproject.com/.

Lapati, Americo. *Educational and the Federal Government: A Historical Record.* New York: Mason/Charter, 1975.

Lappan, Glenda. "Lessons from the Sputnik Era in Mathematics Education." Draft, prepared for the symposium "Reflecting on Sputnik: Linking the Past, Present, and Future of Educational Reform." National Academy of Sciences, Washington, D.C., October 4, 1997.

Lee, Rohama "He visualized the family of man." *Monographs on Pioneers in Sight/Sound Communications.* American Archives of the Factual Film, 2 (1975?).

Lev, Peter. *Claude Lelouch, Film Director.* East Brunswick, NJ: Associated University Presses, 1983.

Levin, G. Roy. *Documentary Explorations: 15 Interviews with Filmmakers.* Garden City, NY: Doubleday, 1971.

"Listeners' mail reflects wide popularity of great novels serialized on Columbia's 'Michael Scott Presents.'" *CBS Press Release,* February 11, 1946.

Loizos, Peter. *Innovation in Ethnographic Film: From Innocence to Self-Consciousness, 1955–1985.* Chicago: University of Chicago Press, 1993.

Mamber, Stephen. *Cinema Verite in America: Studies in Uncontrolled Documentary.* Cambridge: MIT Press, 1974.

Melcher, Richard A. "Dusting Off the Britannica." *Business Week,* October 20. 1997.

Mitchell, Maurice. "A Forward Look at Communications." *Britannica Book of the Year,* 1958.

———. "Science and Education for National Defense." Extract from Hearings Before the Committee on Labor and Public Welfare, United States Senate, Eighty-Fifth Congress, Second Session, 1958.

Monaco, James. *How to Read a Film,* rev. ed. New York: Oxford University Press, 1981.

Morris, Peter. *The Film Companion.* Toronto: Irwin, 1984.

Mosser, Russell, with Arthur Wolf. *Centron Remembered.* Unpublished manuscript, 1999.

Murray, Michael D. *The Political Performers: CBS Broadcasts in the Special Interest.* Westport, CT: Praeger, 1994.

Musser, Charles, and Carol Nelson. *High-Class Moving Pictures: Lyman H. Howe and the Forgotten Era of Traveling Exhibition, 1880–1920.* Princeton: Princeton University Press, 1991.

Nelkin, Dorothy. *The Creation Controversy.* New York, W.W. Norton, 1982.

Nelkin, Dorothy. "The Science-Textbook Controversies." *Scientific American* (April 1976): 33–39.

Orgeron, Marsha, and Skip Elsheimer. "Something Different in Science Films." *Moving Image: Journal*

of the Association of Moving Image Archivists, vol. 7, no. 1 (Spring 2007).
Owen, Harold H., Jr. *The Motion Picture and the Teaching of English.* New York: Appleton-Century-Crofts, 1965.
Peden, Charles. *Newsreel Man.* New York: Doubleday, 1932.
Pelham, Hardy. *Chalkboard to Computer: Audiovisual Education in California.* San Francisco: Photo & Sound, 1989.
Pitrone, Jean Maddern. *The Touch of His Hand: Colombo, a Modern Day Damien in Burma.* Staten Island, NY: Alba House, 1970.
Polmar, Norman, and Thomas B. Allen. *Rickover: Controversy and Genius.* New York: Simon & Shuster, 1982.
Pratley, Gerald. *Torn Sprockets: the Uncertain Projection of the Canadian Film.* London and Toronto: Associated Universities Presses, 1987.
Ravitch, Diane. *The Troubled Crusade: American Education, 1945–1980.* New York: Basic Books, 1983.
Reinhart, Mark. *Abraham Lincoln on Screen.* Jefferson, NC: McFarland, 1999.
Renoir, Jean. *My Life and My Films.* New York: Atheneum, 1974.
Rose, Barbara Wade. *Budge: What Happened to Canada's King of Film.* Toronto: ECW Press, 1998.
Russett, Robert, and Cecily Starr. *Experimental Animation.* New York: Van Nostrand Reinhold, 1976.
Saettler, Paul. *A History of Instructional Technology.* New York: McGraw-Hill, 1968.
Salzman, Bertram W. *Being a Buddha on Broadway,* Carlsbad, CA: InnerDirections, 2004.
Schickel, Richard. *The Disney Version,* rev. ed. Chicago: Ivan R. Dee, 1997.
Sevareid, Eric. *Not So Wild a Dream,* rev. ed. New York: Atheneum, 1978.
Shohat, Ella. *Israeli Cinema: East/West and the Politics of Representation.* Austin: University of Texas Press, 1989.
Siegel, George J. *Hollywood's Army—The First Motion Picture Unit, US Army Air Forces, Culver City, California.* http://www.militarymuseum.org/1stmpu.html.
Slater, Robert, *This ... Is CBS.* Englewood Cliffs, NJ: Prentice-Hall, 1988.
Smith, Ken. *Mental Hygiene: Classroom Films 1945–1970.* New York: Blast Books, 1999.
Sperber, A.M. *Murrow: His Life and Times.* New York: Freundlich, 1986.
Stapleton, Maureen, and Jane Scovell. *A Hell of a Life.* New York: Simon & Schuster, 1995.
Stevenson, William. *A Man Called Intrepid.* New York: Harcourt Brace Jovanovich, 1976.
Sussex, Elizabeth. *The Rise and Fall of the British Documentary.* Berkeley: University of California Press, 1975.
Title VII–New Educational Media News and Reports. U.S. Department of Health, Educational and Welfare, Office of Education, July, 1960, p. 4.
Townsend, Robert. *Up the Organization: How to Stop the Corporation from Stifling People and Strangling Profits, Commemorative Edition.* Hoboken, NJ: John Wiley and Sons, 2007.
Tulard, Jean. *Dictionnaire du Cinéma: Les Réalisateurs.* Paris: Robert Laffont, 1999.
Vargas, Alberto, and Reid Stewart Austin. *Vargas.* New York: Harmony Books, 1978.
Wachtler, Sol. *After the Madness: A Judge's Own Prison Memoir.* New York: Random House, 1997.
Waldron, Gloria. *The Information Film.* New York: Columbia University Press, 1949.
Wholly Communion: International Poetry Reading at the Royal Albert Hall. New York: Grove Press, 1965.
Woo, Elaine. "Thomas G. Yohe, was Co-creator of 'Schoolhouse Rock.'" *Los Angeles Times* (obituary) December 23, 2000.
Zimmerman, Patricia. *Reel Families: A Social History of Amateur Film.* Bloomington: Indiana University Press, 1995.

Annotated Film Catalogues

American Folklore Films & Videotapes. Memphis: Center for Southern Folklore, 1976.
Archaeology on Film. Boston: Archaeological Institute of America, 1983.
Catalogue de films d'interêt archeologique, ethnographique ou historique. Paris: Unesco, 1970.
Craft Films: An Index of International Films on Crafts. New York: Neal-Schuman, 1979.
Cyr, Helen. *Filmography of the Third World.* Metuchen, NJ: Scarecrow, 1976.
_____. *Filmography of the Third World, 1976–1983.* Metuchen, NJ: Scarecrow, 1985.
_____. *Third World in Film and Video, 1984–1990.* Metuchen, NJ: Scarecrow, 1991.
Educational Film Resource Locator, First Edition. New York: R.R. Bowker, 1978.
Films for Anthropological Teaching, 8th ed. Arlington, VA: American Anthropological Association, 1995.
Films on Art. New York: Watson Guptill, 1977.
Heider, Karl. *Ethnographic Film.* Austin: University of Texas Press, 1976.
Multimedia Catalogue. San Jose, CA: Santa Clara County Office of Education, 1994.
NFB Film Guide: The Productions of the National Film Board of Canada from 1939 to 1989. Montreal: National Film Board of Canada, 1991.
Weatherforf, Elizabeth, ed. *Native Americans on Film and Video, Vol. I.* New York: Museum of the American Indian, 1981.
_____. *Native Americans on Film and Video, Vol. II.* New York: Museum of the American Indian, 1988.

Index

Numbers in ***bold italics*** indicate pages with photographs.

Abbott, John 137
Abraham, Jack (Coronet) 13, 31, 77–78
ABC: *Close Up* series 127; television 116, 124–128
Abortion Under the Law 128
Academic Film Archive of North America (AFA) 5, 198–199, 218*n*7
academic films: cinematography 51–52, 80, 115, 121, 130, 144, 146–147, 154, 159–160, ***163***, 165–166, 170–172, ***171***, 172–174, 177–178, 180–181, 183, 186, 188–190; costs, distribution, profits, promotions and sales 7, 24, 47–48, 52–53, 58–60, 71, 73, 75, 82–84, 90, 92, 97, 100, 115 119–120, 149–150, 156, 166–167, 178, 194–195, 199, 211*n*53, 211*n*54, 212*n*9, 214*n*44, 214*n*65, 215*n*82; defined 5; demise 5–8, 97–98, 115, 126–127, 191, 194–199, 218*n*5; edicts against crediting filmmakers 30–31, 74, 77–78, 115, 211*n*54, 214*n*32; quality assessment 13–15, 156; teaching guides 58, 70, 73, 88, 108, 115, 135, 144, 151, 209*n*2; 212*n*11; transition to videotape and other media 194–195, 197–199, 218*n*5
Academy Films 159
Academy of Motion Picture Arts and Sciences (Academy Awards, Oscars) 18, 32, 65, 68, 75, 77, 82, 107, 118, 142, 165, ***179***, 180, 189–190, 204
ACI Films 60, 64–65, 205, 213*n*3
ACLU (American Civil Liberties Union) 111
Adler, Mortimer 23, 27–28, 55, 144–146, 148, 156, 210*n*34
Adventure in Venice 151
Africa Speaks 103
African Village series (IFF) 105
AGC Films 65–66, 205
Ahnemann, Michael 107
AIMS Mutimedia 65–66, 110–111, 159, 205

Alder Woodwasp see *Insect Parasitism*
Alemann Films (Johanna Alemann) 157–158, ***159***
Alexander Von Humboldt 136
Alexieff, Alexandre 173
Alexovich, David 98
Algar, James 86
Algebra and the Powers of Ten 26
Alk, Howard 82
Allegro Productions see Forman, Jerome
Alphabet Conspiracy 67–69, 201
Altschul, David 65, 205
Altschul, Gilbert 65, 205
Altschul, Joel 65, 205
Ama Girls 86
Amazon Family 105
Ambrose, Bill 101, 121
Ambulance 464 (book) 31
America series (PBS) 121, 133
American Association of Publishers 42
American Chronicles series (AIMS) 66
American Crayon Company 64
American Film and Video Association see EFLA
American Film Center 59, 77
American Film Festival see EFLA
American Geological Institute (AGI) series (EB) 57, 97, 167, 188–189
An American Romance 17
American Shoeshine 116
American Short Story series (Perspective) 116, 124
Americans on Everest 116
Amitai, Amiram 72
Anansi the Spider 173
Ancient Africans 105
Ancient Peruvian 173
Anderson, William A. 57
Angel and Big Joe 65, 107, 180, 201, ***202***
Anglim, Thomas D. 124
Angotee 87
Animal Families series (Barr) 73
Animal Farm 184

animated films 123–124, 164–165, 173–174, 183–185, 214*n*32
Apgar, Ellis 64
Apgar, Ethel 64
Arlinghaus, Frank 209*n*13
Armenian Film Festival and Foundation 70
Armstrong-Jones, Anthony see Snowdon, Anthony
Arnold & Porter 42
Arnspiger, Clyde (ERP) 16
Arrow to the Sun 124, 173
Arsenal 133
Art and Architecture series (EB) 146
Art and Motion 57
Art in America series (Handel) 102
Art in the Western World ***49***
The Art of Silence series (EB) ***152***, 152–153
Art Portrays a Changing World: Gothic to Early Renaissance 158
Artesano de Cartón: Pedro Linares 161
Artesano de Madera: Manuel Jiménez 161
Artesano Pirotécnico: Marcelo Ramos 161
Arts and Crafts of Mexico 166
The Ascent of Man series (BBC) 121, 134, 161
Assignment India 210*n*29
AT&T (and AT&T Bell Labs) 16, 21–22, 62, 66–69, 87, 170–172
At the Autumn River Camp 87
At the Winter Sea Ice Camp 87–88
Atlantic Crossing: Life on an Ocean Liner 167
Atlantis Films 69–70
Attenborough, David 136
Atwell, Josie 72
Audio Visual group (AVG) 66
Azzarella, Dennis 215*n*82

Background of the Declaration of Independence 55
Backström, Ulf 188
Backyard Science series (BFA) 56, 71, 158–159

223

Badgely, Frank 34
Bailey, Al 71, 205
Bailey/Film Associates (BFA) 63, 70–72, 117, 129, 159, 167, 183, 205, 213*n*20
Baker, Suzanne 137
Baliksi, Asen 86–87
Balla, Nicholas 112, 169
Balloon Safari 137, 175, **176**
Baobab: Portrait of a Tree 73
Barnes, Jeanne Weinstein 141, 154
Barnes, John **2**, 6, 21, **25**, 26, 37, 44–46, 50, 54–55 91, 97, 139–156, **140, 145, 150, 152, 153, 155**, 201, 203, 206, 210*n*22, 210*n*34, 210*n*51, 211*n*54, 212*n*16, 213*n*17, 217*n*12; camera craft: 146–147, 151–152, 157; critics and criticism 143, 146–148, 214*n*64; philosophy on constitutional issues, education, politics, racism, religion 141–144, 148–149, 155; production costs and issues 142–143, 150–152, 156
Barnouw, Erik 120, 212*n*15, 216*n*129
Barr Films (Arthur, Don, and Elaine Barr) 72–73, 111, 204
Bass, Saul 118
Bate's Car 114
The Battle of Newburgh 131
Baxter, Dr. Frank 63, 66–69, 213*n*8
Baxter, John F. 26, **27**
BBC (British Broadcasting Corporation) 62, 96, 101–102, 121–122, 127, 133–136, 205
Beach, River of Sand 172
Beacon Films 65
Bean, Norman 53, 56, 71, 158–159
Beast of M. Racine 123
Bechtel Investments 84, 110
Beckett, Marta 116
Bedales School (UK) 170
Bees: Backyard Science 56
Beethoven: Ordeal and Triumph 127
Being a Buddha on Broadway (book) 180
Bell and Howell 15–16, 43, 195, 204–205, 210*n*51
Bell and Howell Close-Up 127
Bell Labs *see* AT&T Bell Labs
Bell Science series 63, 66–69; religious messages in 66–67
Ben-Gurion 133
Benchmark Films (Mike Solin) 73, 160, 180
Bender, Ivan 101
Benjamin, Burton 130
Bennett, Robert Russell 126, 131
Benton, Charles **21**, 42, 44–46, 77, **91**, 91–102, 116, 134, 147, 156, **158**, 169, 188, 197, 205, 210*n*22
Benton, Helen 98, 156
Benton, Helen (Mrs. William) **21**
Benton, John 98, 156
Benton, Louise 98, 156

Benton, Marjorie (Mrs. Charles) 46, 91
Benton, Sen. William 13, 15, **21**, 21–24, 28, 30, 39, 46, 91, 93–96, 98, 141–143, 149, 156, 204, 210*n*35, 210*n*37, 210*n*39, 211*n*2; political persecution of 24, 210*n*37
Benton & Bowles 21, 24, 210*n*29
Benton Foundation 98, 102
Berkeley Repertory Theatre 120
Berlet Films (Walt and Myrna Berlet) 62, 159, 205, 217*n*3
Bernstein, Elmer 132
Bethune 112
Beymer, Richard 122, 216*n*115
BFA *see* Bailey/Film Associates
Big Green Caterpillar 121
Big Henry and the Polka Dot Kid 108
Bigras, Norman 112
Bill of Rights in Action series (Wilets) 71–72, 191–192
Biography series 109, 133
Biography of a Cancer 130
Biography of a Rookie 133
Biological Sciences series (Coronet) 78, 177
Biology series (EB) 97, 167
BioMEDIA 177
Bio-Science series (NGEO) 115, 186
Birch Canoe Builder 64
Bird Circus 72
Bird Community 110
Bitter, Dr. Francis 87, 170–172, 217*n*16, 217*n*17
Black, Noel 46, 108
Black Girl 120
Black History: Lost, Stolen, or Strayed 129
Blanc, Mel 67
Blinder, Abe 78
Bloom, Benjamin (Taxonomy) 13–15, 205
Bluem, William 125
Bobbitt, John 210*n*38
Bobwhite Through the Year 181
BOCES (New York Board of Cooperative Educational Services) lawsuit 194
Bochner, Lloyd 54
Boenish, Carl 117
Bon Anniversaire! 118–119
Bonnièrre, René 55, 81
Borsos, Philp 74, 114, 215*n*92
Boulton, David 160
Boulton Hawker Films (Peter Boulton) 51, 73, 159–160, **160**, 206, 217*n*4
Boundary Lines 32, 184
Bouy, Jules 183
Bowe, William 98
Bowen, Ellen 78
Bower, Joe 98
Bowker's (R.R. Bowker) *Educational Film Resource Locator* (book) 59, 124, 209*n*2
Bowles, Chester 24, 210*n*29
Boyer, Charles 93

Boyko, Eugene 114
Bracher, Werner 57
Bradbury, Ray 133
Brault, Michel 36
Braun, Irwin "Irv" 70–72, 205, 213*n*15
Braverman, Charles 117–118
Braverman, Robert 124
Brealy, Gil 137
Breeden, Bob 115
Brent, Jason 66
Brinkerhoff, Burt 130
British Military Intelligence 33
British Ministry of Information 70
British Security Coordination (BSC) 213*n* 17
Brittain, Donald **112**, 112
Britton, James 77
Broffman, Mort 101
Bronowski, Jacob 121, 134, 161
Bronowski, Judith (The Works) 55, 118, 157, 161
Bronston, Samuel 166–167
Bronze, River of Metal **191**
Brooke, Daphne 65
Brown, Quentin 87–88
Brown, Warren 172
Brown v. Board of Education 40
Bruner, Jerome S. 86
Bryan, Julian (IFF) 13, 18, **31**, 31–32, 59, 105–106, 173–174, 181, 184, **202**, 203–204, 211*n*60
Bryan, Sam 31–32, 106, 173, 184, **202**
Bryant, Barbara 100, 116–117, 205, 215*n*76
Buchanan, Robert 98
Buchbinder, Paul 58
Buchsbaum, Ralph 97, 206
Building a House (Bozo People) 105, 181
Bullfrog Films (John Hoskyns-Abrahall and Winnie Scherrer) 73–74, 205, 213*n*23
Buried Mirror series (BBC) 216*n*139
Burke, James 122, 134–135
Burke & Paine on Revolution 192
Burke and Wills 135
Burnford, Paul 55, 57, 70, **71**, 159, 205–206, 212*n*6, 213*n*15, 213*n*17
Burnley, Fred 135–136
Bush, Pres. George H.W. 183
Bushmen of the Kalahari 131, 133
Buxton, Lord Aubrey 137
Buxton, Tim 137
Byrne, Vincent J. 124

Caedmon Records 99
Caesar and Cleopatra 151, 203
Cahill, Charles and Associates 65–66
California Academy of Sciences 111
California State Board of Education 89
Callanan, Richard 58, 110
Callner, Jerry 73
Calvin Films 74

Camera Three series (CBS) 122
Campaign American Style 129
Campbell, Douglas 144–148
Campbell, Joseph 173
Campbell, Richard 54
Canada Carries On series (NFB) 19, 34, 54, 204
The Canada Goose 159
Canaday, John 144, **145**
Canadian Broadcasting Corporation (CBC) 62
Canadian International Development Administration (CIDA) films 114
Canadian-U.S. political relations relating to academic film 112–113, 170
Canaries to Clydesdales 114
Candid Eye series (NFBC) 36
Candlemaking 72
Cannell, Marrin 114
Cannon, Bobe 77
Cappel, Walter 100, 104
Capra, Frank 18–19, 66–69, 204
Captain James Cook 136
Captain John Smith: Founder of Virginia 91, 143
Captain Kangaroo 165
Carlos, Wendy 117
Carlson, Richard 67
Carnivorous Plants 121
Carrasco, Pfc. Ricardo 68
Carrièrre Marcel 36
Carter, Donald 118
Casden, Ron 72
The Case of the Elevator Duck 107
Castaway 18–19
Castle Films (Eugene Castle) 122
Catalogue of Educational Motion Pictures 58–59
Cave Community **187**, 187, 189
Caverns & Geysers 70
CBS: *CBS Reports* 109, 126–130, 132, 205, 216n124, 216n128, 216n130; news and television 64, 66, 70–72, 87, 116–117, 122, 125–126, 130, 165, 205, 216n129, 216n135
Cease Fire! 67–68
Cell Biology series (Coronet) 177
censorship and propaganda issues 44–45, 61, 131, 133–134, 144, 165–166, 170, 193, 212n15, 214n52, 215n91
Centron Films (Art Wolf and Russ Mosser) 74–76, **75**, 78, 111, 205, 213n25, n26
Chairmaker and the Boys 34
Challenge for Change series (NFBC) 113
Chang, Wah 66
Channel 4 (UK) 131, 135
The Character of Julius Caesar 151, 201
Charles Doughty 135–136
Charney, Nicolas "Nick" 82–84, 214n47
Chartres Cathedral **145**

Chemical Education Material Study (CHEM Study) series 27, 84, 167
Chemistry Introductory Course series (EB) 26–27, **27**, 92, 173
Chermayeff, Peter 157, **161**, 161–162
Chiesa, Roberto Carlo 117
Children of Many Lands series (EB) 210n21
Chile 74
The Chinese Word for Horse 58, 110
Chisholm, Shirley 120
Christmas Rhpasody 169
Christopher Columbus 136
Churchill Films (Robert "Bob" Churchill) 58, 62, 76–77, 167, 183, 205, 213n27
Churchill-Wexler Films 76, 205
CIA (Central Intelligence Agency) 120, 131, 174
Cider Maker 64
cinél6 4
Cinecitta 91
cinéma vérité 36, 172, 211n70
CinemaScope 165
Circle of the Sun 36
Circus 71
City of Gold 33, 36
Civil Rights Act of 1964 8, 41, 46, 60, 63, 205
Civilian Conservation Corps (CCC) 189
Civilisation series (BBC) 101, 121, 134
Cizmowska, Rosemary 160
Claes Oldenburg 132
Clapp, Nicholas 116
Clark, Barry 66
Clark, Kenneth 101, 121, 134
Clark, Les 67, 69
Clark, Robert 71
Classical Civilization series (EB) 210n34
Classical Greece series (EB) 145–146
Claudius: Boy of Ancient Rome 166
Clavell, James 107
Clayre, Alasdair 135
Collette, Buddy 58
Colling, Bruce 65
Colmes, Walter 24, 210n38, 210–211n51
Colomb de Daunant, Denis 66
Colombia 74
Colombo, Father Cesare 165, 217n10
Colonial Wiiliamsburg **163**, 164
Columbia Pictures 62, 76, 96, 106–108, 156, 165, 215n82
Columbia University 123, 145
Communication: the Nonverbal Agenda 84
computer animation 162
Conguent Triangles 58, 162, 201
Conlan, Sen. John B. 89–90
Connections series 121, 134–135
Conreid, Hans 67, 69
Contemporary Films 60, 77, 100, 110–111, 184, 205
Cooke, Alistair 133

Cooper, Charles 77
Cooperage 74, 114
copyright and fair use 194
Cornthwaite, Robert 191
Cornwell, Bruce 58, 104, 162, 201
Cornwell, Katherine 58, 104, 162, 201
Coronet Films 8, 13, 25, 29–31, 46, 62, 65, 76–79, 98, 116–117, 177–178, 204, 211n52, 211n53, 211n54, 211n57, 211n58; 212n10, 214n32, 214n34
Corral 36
Cosby, Bill 129
Cosmos series 101
Coulomb's Law 170, 172
Courter, Philip 64–65, 213n3
Covert, Nadine 60, 213n27
Cowan, Paul 113
Crabtree, Graham **79**, 81
Craig, Cleo F. 66–67
Cranbrook Academy of Art 191
Crawley Films (Frank Radford "Budge" and Judith) **79**, 79–82, 113, 201, 214n38, 214n43
Crichton, Michael 84
CRM Films 61, **63**, **82**, 82–84, 110, 205
Croner, Stanley 52, 98, 162–164, **163**, 206
Cronkite, Walter 130
Crump, Owen 67–69, 201, 213n11, 213n14
Crystals (PSSC) 170, 172
Crystals: Flowers of the Mineral Kingdom 121
Cuba: The Castro Generation 127
Curriculum Development Associates (CDA) 89

Daly, Tom 34–36, **35**, 113, 205
Dancer's World: Martha Graham 132
dangerous filming conditions 80, 136, 165, 177, 188–189, 212n13
Darah, Marie-Christine "Maik" 118
Davella Mills Foundation 32
David, Patricia Harvey 115, **185**, 185–186
Davidson, Dave 107, 215n81
Davidson Films (Jack and Fran Davidson) 27, 84–85, **85**, 205
Davis, Peter 129
Davis, Robert E. 64
Davis, Stan 57, 213n20
Davis, Willie 133
Dawn Flight 117
A Day in the Life of Bonnie Consolo 73
Daybreak 189
Dearie, Blossom 124
The Death of Stalin 131
Death Valley 103
Dechartre, Emmanuel 119
Definite and Multiple Proportions 87
Deitch, Gene 123, 164–165, 216n118, 217n7
Deming, W. Edwards 101

Democracy: Role of Dissent 54
Democracy on Trial: The Morgenthaler Affair 113
Demonstrations with Light 111
Dench, Judith 146
Deneen, William F. (Bill) 56, 91–92, 94–98, **106**, 106–109, 156, **158**, 165–167, **166**, 170, 188, 194, 197–199, 201, 209n15, 211n53, 214n64, 214n68, 215n80, 215n81, 215n82, 217n9, 217n10, 217n13, 217n14
Denning, J. David 177
de Rochemont, Louis 122
de Rouselière, Guy Marie 87
Desert Nomads: French Morocco 122, 216n111
The Detour 117
Devereux, Frederick (ERPI) 17, 20, 204
DeVore, Irven 86
Diamond, Vern 129
Dick, Esmé 60
Dickens, Charles series (EB) 139, 145–146
Diet for a Small Planet 74
Digard, Uschi 83
Dignam, Mark 146
Dinosaurs: Terrible Lizards 66
Dirty Dancing 109
Discovering Music series (Wilets) 71, 191–192
Discovery Communications (Education) 65–66, 76
"*Discussion of* " films (EB) 193
Discussions of Bioethics series (NFBC) 114
Disney Studios (Walt Disney) 67, 85–86, 99, 103, 142, 162, 209n3
Dixon, Matt 43
Dr. Leakey and the Dawn of Man 54
Doña Rosa de Nieto 166
Donald in Mathmagic Land 162
Donat, Lucas 145, 170
Donat, Michael Learned 145, 170
Donat, Peter 145, 170
Donenfeld, Bernard 66
Donnell Library (New York Public Library) 60
Doodle Film 192
Dorough, Bob 58, 124, 201
Douglas, Michael 109
Dow, Peter 40, 86, 88–89, 214n52, 214n63
Dratfield, Leo 60, 77, 100, 110
Dream of Wild Horses 66
Drew, Robert 127
Dreyfuss, Richard 130
Drucker, Peter 83
Dudley Pictures 122
Duke Ellington Swings Through Japan 130
Dyer, Gwynne 111
Dyhrenfurth, Norman 116
Dynamics of Male Bonding in a Baboon Troop 88

Eagle Lion 76
Ealing Corporation 186
Eames, Charles 118, 161, 201
Eames, Ray 118, 161, 201
Earhart, Amelia 120, 130
Earle, Bob 72
Earle Birney: Portrait of a Poet 113, 193
Early Victorian England and Charles Dickens 139, 149
Earth and Its Peoples series (Universal) 122
East Germany 115
Eastman Kodak 16, 22, 196, 204
Edison, Thomas 13, 15
Edison Kinetoscope Projector 15
Educational Film Resource Locator see Bowker's
Educational Research Products Inc. see ERPI
Educational Services, Inc, (ESI), Education Development Center, Inc. (EDC) 86–90, 205, 214n49
The Educational Talking Picture (book) 17, 204
Edwards, Bill 95
EFLA (Educational Film Library Association) 4, 47, 59–60, 121; American Film Festival 59, 100, 204, 211n60, 213n23, 213n25; *Bulletin, Evaluation, Sightlines* magazine and publications 59–60, 76, 213n23, 213n27
Einstein, Daniel 126–127
Eisenstein, Sergei 33, 70
Eisner, Michael 124
Electric Eel 111, 201
Electric Fields 170
The Electric Grandmother 108
Elementary and Secondary Educational Act (ESEA) 8, 27, 41–44, 46, 99, 106, 194, 205, 212n9
Elementary Mathematics for Teachers and Students series (Davidson) 85
Elikann, Larry 212n11
Elliott, Joe 98
Ellis, Perry 107
Emilio en España series (EB) 169
Emperor and Slave 55
Encyclopaedia Britannica Films (EBF, EBEC) 8, 13, 15, 17, 20–30, **21**, **23** 39, 42–46, 48, 52–53, 58, 61–62, 77, 86–87, 90–98–100, 111, 141–156, 159, 162, 164–169, 172–173, 177, 180, 183, 186–190, 193–194, **195**, 199, 204–205; 210n22, 210n28, 210n35, 210n38, 210n39, 210n42, 210n44, 210n51; 211n2; 212ch2n9, 212n13, 212n15, 212n16, 212ch3n12, 212n13, 212n16, 213n17, 214n64, 214n65, 214n67; rumors of purchase 210–211n51
Engel, Herman 87
ENIAC computer 162
Environmental Education Act of 1970 41, 205

Equality Under the Law: The Lost Generation of Prince Edward County 141, 217n11
ERPI (Educational Research Products Inc.) 8, **14**, 15, 20, 21–22, 91, 189, 204, 209n9
Erskine, John 145
espionage and smuggling 34, 70, 166, 174, 213n17
Esquire, Inc. see Coronet Films
Ethnic Heritage Program of 1972 41
Eurich, Alvin C. 26
Everote, Warren **21**, 26–27, 30, 52–53, 91–92, **92**, 96–98, 100, **158**, 187–188, 210–211n51, 211n54, 212n16
The Explorers series see *Ten Who Dared*
Exploring Our Solar System 115
Exploring the Body series (Films Inc.) 100
Exploring: The Story of America series (NBC) 57, 213n20
Eyewitness 189

Fabricantes Méxicanas de Ollas 70, 201
Faces of Man series (Screenscope) 120
Fadiman, Clifton "Kip" 23, 27, 93, 144, 146, **206**, 206
Faille, Albert 112
The Fall of the Roman Empire 166–167, 217n13
Falling Water 189
La Familia Fernández series (EB) 169
Fano, Michael 57
A Farm Family in Italy 151
Farm Family in Winter 183
Farrgher, Joe 65
feature films 15, 17, 20, 51–52, 81, 86, 98–99, 102, 107–109, 154, 166–167, 172–173, 179, 183, 209n15
Federal Communications Commission (FCC) 17, 39
Feldman, Gene 52, 65
Feldzamen, Alvin 98
Fiddle-De-Dee 34
Field, John 46
Fielding, Raymond 120
Film Australia 62, 127, 136–137
film cameras 16, 141, 160, 181, 186, 190
film catalogues, guides, journals, and catalogues 15, 17, 23, 58–60, 100, 107, 123, 124, 157
film content consultants 50, 212n10
film degradation 195–197
Film Fair 65
film projectors 15–16, 23, 34, 43, 123, 195–196, **189**
film stock and gauge 16, 188, 196
filmmaker financial compensation 48–49, 71, 212n6, 212n12, 213n3
Films for the Humanities 99, 205
Films Incorporated 77, 92, 94, 96,

99–102, 104, 111, 116–117, 127, 133, 169, 205
Films Media Group 99
Finance, Charles L. "Chuck" 97, *158, 167*, 167–169
Findlay, Seaton 82
Fire in the Sea 189
Fire Mountain 189
Fireball in the Night 133
Firefly 73
First Americans: Some Indians of the Southlands 184
Fitzpatrick, Jim 42
Fitzsimmons, Laurence *21*
Flaherty, Robert 33, 77, 133
Flaum, Marshall 132
Fleischman, Stephen 127
Fletcher, Cyril Scott 24
Flight of the Gossamer Condor 77
Floating Logging Camp 116
Flory, Elizabeth Harding "Bee" 59
Food and People 91
Food from the Sun 44–45
Forbidden City 135
Ford Foundation 26–27, 86, 144, 210n22, 216n128
foreign language academic and instruction films 48, 70, 76, 104–105, 118–119, 161–162, 164, 214n65
Forests and Conservation 29
Forman, Jerome "Jerry" (Allegro Productions) 119–120, 215n101, 215–216n102
Forman, Scott (Allegro Productions) 119–120, 215n101, 215–216n102
Forrell, Gene 207
Fortas, Abe 148
Foster, George 129
Four Apple Dishes 80
Four Seasons 168
Fox, Amanda K. 74
Fox, Burton K. 74
Fractions and Rational Numbers 85
Frames of Reference 170–172, *171*, 201
France: Fifth Republic 122
Franey, James M. 122–123, 216n110
Friendly, Fred W. 109, 126, 128–131, 205, 216n123, 216n128, 216n135
Fritsch, Gunther 76
Frogs: An Investigation 159
From Where I Sit: Foreign Policy 55
Fuentes, Carlos 216n139
Fungi 160
Furniss, Adrianne 101–102
FWU *see* Institut für Film und Bild

Gakken puppet films 214n32
Galileo: The Challenge of Reason 215n82
Gallery 117
The Game 169, 215n91
Gardner, John 42
Garland Janisz, Grace *29*, 166, 207

Garner, Virginia 207
Gateways to the Mind 67–68, 201
Geller, Robert 116, 125
Gelles, Heinz 109–110, 116–117, 205, 215n87, 215n96
gender and sexual attitudes, conflict, and themes in academic film 83, 107, 110, 113, 117, 118–120, 124–125, 128, 164, 169–170, 175, 217n14
Gene Ditch: The Picture Book Animated 164
generational attitudes, conflict, and themes in academic film 105, 107–108, 110, 169–170, 178, 180
Gerald Mc BoingBoing 77
Geronimo Jones *45*, 46, 107, 180
Getty Images 199
Gideon, Carence Earl 148–149, *149*
Gill, Michael 133–134, 216n139
Gitlin, Irv 131
Glasgow, Mary 118, 215n100
Glenn, Don 89
Glidden, Stephanie 83–84, 110
Glore, Bob 77
Glushanok, Peter 132
Goetz, Tom 98
Gold Rush 164
Gonzalez, Martha 98, 197, 214n65
Good Eleven 58, 124–125, 201
Goodall, Jane 161
Gottlieb, Carl 84
Gottlieb, Linda 92, 106–107, 109, 180, 214n68
government funding for academic film in the United States 7–8, 16, 28, 39–43, 47, 211n1, 211n2
Grady, Don 68
Graf, Rudiger 105
Graff, Sherman 64
Graham, Martha 132, 184
Granada Television 137
Grant, Robert 161
Gray, Margaret 65, 168
Gray, Wilf 65, 168
Gray Gull the Hunter 26
The Great American Student 79
The Great Blue Heron Story 159
Great Men series (EB) 210n38
Green, Al 100
Greene, Lorne 19, 54, 210n24
Greene, Roger 104–105, 204
Greene, Sparky 116
Greene, Wesley 104–105, 204
The Grey Fox 215n92
Grierson, John 33–34, 80, 100, 121, 141, 204, 211n63
Griffith, D.W. 140
Grist Miller 64
Gronowski, Bob 78–79
Grossman, Suzanne 150
Grzmek, Bernard 175
Grzmek, Michael 175
Guards of the North 19, 54
Guba, Egon 43, 205
guidance films 5, 29–31, 57–58, 77–79, 214n34
Guide to Microlife (book) 178

Gulf + Western 76, 78, 116
Guten Tag and *Guten Tag wie geht's* series (IFB) 104–105
Guthrie, Tyrone 144
Guttman, Richard 70, 201
Gwynn, Michael 146, 154

Haanstra, Bert 121
Hafeman, Bill 64
Hagopian, J. Michael *69*, 69–70, 157
Hahn, Willard *103*, 103–104, 201
Halas & Bachelor (John and Joy) 184
Haley, Jack, Jr. 132–133
Halley's Comet 56
Hamilton, Fred 135
Hamlet series (EB) 144–145
Hanada, Yasuko 53, 70–71, *174*, 174–175, 205, 217n14
Handel Film Corporation (Leo Handel) 102, *102*, 121, 207
Hanley, Jim 209n15
Hansen, Gary 135
Happy Birthday 114
The Happy City 165, 201
Happy to Be Me 110
Harry Bertoia's Sculpture 190
Hart, Bruce 83–84
Hart, Carole 83–84
Harvey, Harold A. "Herk" 74, 213n26
Hayes, Keith 69
Hearst Metrotone News 119–120; *see also* Forman, Jerome
Heart of the Dragon series (BBC) 121, 135
Heartbeat of a Volcano 188–189, 212n13
Heflin, Van 190
Hellaby, Andrew 160
Hellen Keller 133
Hemo the Magnificent 67
Henry Morton Stanley 135–136
Her First Roman 150
Heritage of Slavery 129
Herzog, Milan *49*, 52, 91, 95–96, 98, *158*, 166–167, *168*, 168–169, 207, 212n16
Heycock, David 133
Hibbs, Dr. Albert 57
Hicks, Orton *21*, 99
High School 57
Higher Fungi 26
The Higher Learning in America (book) 210n28
Highet, Gilbert 27, 213n17
Highgate Pictures 108–109
Hiseman, Jon (Colosseum) 110
History of the Drama series (Films for the Humanities) 99
History Through Art series (Alemann) 158
Hoban Charles 19
Hoedeman, Co *48*
Hoefler Productions, Paul 48, 102–104, 203, 215n79
Hoffman, Anna Rosenberg 39

Hoffman, Bruce 98, 215*n*75
Hoffman, Daniel 74
Hoffman, David 136
Hoffman, Don 210*n*38, 215*n*75
Hoffman, Paul *21*, 215*n*75
Holch, Arthur 127
Holden, Alan 87, 170–172
Holdner, Preston 66, 83–84, 110
Holdridge, Barbara 99
Holland, George 71–73, *73*, 117, 213*n*20
Holland: Hold Back the Sea 121
Holloway, Sterling 69
Hollywood Looks at Its Audience (book) 102
Hopkins, Anthony 109
Hottelet, Richard C. 130
Houghton, Nigel 135
Housefly 73, 104, 180
Houseman, John 132
Houston, James 81
How Things Get Done 180
Howe, James Wong: Cinematographer 85
Howell, Wayne 42
Howells, Barry 114
Howes, Oliver 137
Hughes, Langston 117
Human Face of China series (Film Australia) 137
Human Face of Japan series (Film Australia) 137
Humanities series (EB) 27, 144–148, 210*n*22, 210*n*34
Hume, Patterson 87, *171*, 172
Humphrey, Sen. Hubert H. 91, 214*n*65
Hungary and Communism 166
Huntley, Chet 130
Hutchins, Robert Maynard 20–23, *21*, 144, 156, 210*n*28, 210*n*34
Huxley, Sir Julian 70
H.W. Wilson Educational Film Guide 23, 59
Hyatt, Donald 131

I Got Six 124
I, Leonardo da Vinci 127
Ianzelo, Tony 114
If Japan Can, Why Can't We? 101
Ihde, Albert 74
Imaging the Hidden World: The Light Microscope 177–178, 201
IMAX 113
In Praise of Hands 113, 192
The Incredible Voyage 130
Indians of California: Food 72
India's History 30
Industrial Light and Magic (ILM) 183
Industrial Light and Magic: The Art of Special Effects (book) 183
Industrial Revolution in England 30
Information Processing 83
Inhabitants of the Planet Earth series (Ward's) 177
Insect Parasitism: the Alder Woodwasp 186

Institut für Film und Bild (FWU) 63, 73, 96, 100, 104, 180, 205
Interference of Protons 87
International Film Bureau 63, 104–105, 111, 160, 204
International Film Foundation (IFF) 13, 18, 31–32, 59, 104–106, 173–174, 181, 184, 204
international laws and challenges regarding in-country filming 74, 136–137, 142, 166
The Internet Archive 199, 218*n*8
An Introduction to the World Conservation Strategy (book) 164
Iran 117, 201
Irvin, John 109
It's About Time 67
It's Always So in This World 137
Ivey, Donald 87, *171*, 172

J. Paul Getty Trust 60
Jackson, Angelika 207
Jackson, Mick 134
Jackson, Shirley 6, 98, 193
Jackson, Stanley *33*, 34–35
Jafar's Blue Tiles 178
James, William 32
Janis 82
Japan Harvests the Sea 86
Japan: Miracle in Asia 166, 199, 201
Japanese Boy: the Story of Taro 56, 167, 217*n*14
Japanese Mountain Family 175
Jarvis, Lucy 135
Je Parle Français series (EB) 169
The Jean Richard 54, 81
Jedediah Smith 136
Jekel, Gus 65
Jenny 114
Jessop, Piers 55, 128, 213*n*20
Jet Propulsion Laboratories (JPL) 167
Jiménez, Manuel 161
Jinbo, Matsue 214*n*32
John Keats: His Life and Death **153**
Johnson, Pres. Lyndon B. 41
Johnson, Dr. T.W., Jr. 26
Jones, Carl 116
Jones, Emily 59–60, 65, 207, 213*n*25
Jones, Tommy Lee 116
Jordan, Peter 84, 110
Joseph McCarthy 133
Journal Films 65
Journey to the Center of a Triangle 201
Julius Caesar: The Rise of the Roman Empire 166
Juniper Films 65
Justice Under the Law: The Gideon Case 148–149, **149**

K-III Communications 99
Kaczender, George 6, 58, 112, *169*, 169–170, 215*n*91
Kammerling, Rudy 77
Kane, Dennis 115
Karp, Russell 214*n*73

Katten, Steve *63*, 83–84
Katz, Fred 58
Kay, Bill 188
Kaye, Arthur M. 85
Kaye, Kenneth 20, 210*n*38
Kennard, David 134–135
Kennedy, Sen. Edward 90
Kennen Sie meinen Sohn? 105
Kentucky Rifle 72
Keynes, Stephen 135
Kickels, Mary-Kay 98
Kilauea (Mt.) 188–189
Kiley, Richard **150**, 150
Kimball, Ward 85
King, MacKenzie 34
King, Dr. Martin Luther, Jr. 41, 46
Kingsbury, Bob 137
Kinney, Jack 85
Kirshner, Irvin 81
Kleine, George 15, 59, 204
Kleinerman, Isaac 130
Knowledge or Certainty 134
Knox, Bernard 27
Koenig, Wolf 34–36, 113–114
Kohl, Robert "Bob" 30, 76, 78
Konowal, Charles 55, 114
Kopel, Hal 30, 78, 211*n*53, 212*n*6
Korean War 67–68, 90, 179
Kraftwerk 74
Kroitor, Roman 33–36, **112**, 112–113
Kroll, Nathan 132
Kuehl, William 68–69
Kung Bushmen 103, 203, 214*n*52, 215*n*79
Kuralt, Charles 129

Labor Movement: Beginning & Growth in America 30
Labyrinth 113
Lai, Francis 118
Land of Immigrants 58
Land of the Long Day 34, 87
Landers Film Reviews 157
Landsburg, Alan 132
Landsburgh, Lawrence 117
Langham, Michael 144
Langlois, Henri (Cinémathèque Française) 131, 173
La Sept (France) 131
Latham, Michael 121–122, 135–136, 216*n*143
Latitude Zero **166**
lawsuits and legal issues 126–127, 194, 196
Lazarus, Paul, III 83–84, 166
Lazarus, Tom 83–84, 166
Leacock, Elspeth 171
Leacock, Richard (Ricky) 4, 6, 57, 86–87, 122, 127, **170**, *171*, 170–172, 198, 201, 214*n*50, 216*n*111
Leaf, Carolyn 114
Learned, Michael *see* Donat, Peter
Learning 84
Learning Corporation of America (LCA) 50, 58, 61, 65, 94, 101, 106–109, 111, 117–118, 127–128, 136, 156, 170, 180, 194, 205,

209n15, 212n11, 215n81, 215n82, 215n84
Learning to Be Human series (LCA) 107, 180
Lecompte, Jacqueline 57
Lee's Parasol 178
The Legacy of Rome 128
The Legend of the Raven 81
Legg, Stuart 34
Lehman, Robin 57
Leimbach, Paul 52–53
Lelouch, Claude 118, 201
Leo Beuerman 75
Leonard, Elmore 167
S.S. *Leonardo Da Vinci* 167
Leonardo Da Vinci: Giant of the Renaissance 144
Leverington, Shelby 117
Levin, Marilyn 60
Lewis, Jefferson 114
Ley, Willy 212n6
Life in a Vacant Lot 188
Life in Ancient Rome 166, 217n13
Life in the Desert 57
Lighter Than Air 120
Linares, Pedro 161
Lion 162
Little, Cleavon 116
Little White Crimes 169
Livengood, Gale 100
Livesey, Michael 144
The Living Bill of Rights series (EB) 148–149
The Living City 142–143
Living the Good Life 74
The Living Wilderness 159
Logan, Larry **63**, 83
Lomax, Alan 164
Lonely Boy 36
The Long Christmas Dinner 193
The Loom 72
Loon's Necklace **79**, 81, 201
Loren, Sopia 167
The Lottery 6, 22, 98, **193**, 193, 210n31
The Louvre: Golden Prison 93
Low, Colin 33–36, 112–113
Lowe, David 128–129
Lower Fungi 26
Lucas, George 183
Luce, Henry 22
Lucerne Media 65
The Luck of Ginger Coffey 81
Luening, Otto 130
Lui, Patrck 135
Lukin, Richard 122–123, 216n112, 216n115
Luske, Hamilton 162

Macartney-Filgate, Terence 36
MacArthur Foundation 101
Macbeth series (EB) 146–148
Mack, Maynard 27, 144–145
MACOS see *Man, a Course of Study*
Magic and Music 85
Magic Highway 85
Magic Prison **140**

Magic Tree 56
Magna Carta **25**, 26, 54, **155**
A Magnet Laboratory 57, 170–172, 201, 217n16, 217n17
Magoma, Athmani 56, 106, 173
Make Mine Metric 117–118
Malone, Adrian 134
Mamber, Stephen 57
Man: A Course of Study (MACOS) series 40, 86–90, 205, 214n51, 214n52, 214n63
Man and His World series (Films Inc.) 100
Man and the State series (Wilets) 66, 71–72, 191–192
Man: The Incredible Machine 115
The Man Who Skied Down Everest 82
Manefield, Tom 137
Mankofsky, Isidore 26, **27**, 50–53, **51, 158, 172**, 172–173, 210n44; 211n53; 212n3, 212n12, 214n44
Mantell, Harold 99
Marceau, Marcel **152**, 153, 217n16
Markoff, Steve (A-Mark Entertainment) 73
Marks, Joel 78
Marquand, Richard 108–109
Marsh, Reginald 210n37
Marshall, John 214n52
Marshall Plan 184
Marston, Winslow
Mary Kingsley 136
Maslowski, Karl 75, **76**
Maslowski, Stephen 75, **76**
Mason, Claire Crawford 101
Mason, Elaine 58, 107
Massachusetts Council for the Humanities 144, 210n22
Matoian, John 50, 108, 212n11, 215n84
Matthew Aliuk: Eskimo in Two Worlds 180, 201
Matthews, William (Bill) 97
Max, Zappy 119
Mayor **51**
McCall, David 124
McCallum, David 135–136, 216n143
McCarthy, Sen. Joseph 24, 28, 133
McCloskey, Robert 123
McCutchen, Dick 132
McDermott, Gerald 56, 106, 124, 157, 173–174, 198–199, 203
McDonald, Peter 122
McDonald, Robert 107
McGraw-Hill Text Films 26, 62, 73–74, 77, 83–84, 94, 106, 109–111, 116–117, 125, 127, 159, 204, 215n81
McIntyre, Ron 60
McLaren, Norman 34, 104, 114, 184, 217n24
McLean, Grant 100, 112–113
McMullen, Jay 128–129
McNamara, Robert 120
McQueen, Butterfly 109
McQuilkin, George 77

Mead, Margaret 123
Mears, Mike 209n15
Medak, Peter 109
Media Guild Films 66, 110
Mediating 135
Medieval Manor 169
Meet Mr. Lincoln 131
Mehta Saltzman, Deepa 178, 217n20
Memory 84
Mersey Brothers 58
Merton Stdios (UK) 142
Mesa Verde: Mystery of the Silent Cities 52, 189, 212n13
Metcalfe, Lynne 17, 204
Metro: Photographic Elevations of Selected Paris Metro Stations (book) 193
Metropolitan Museum of Art 60
Mexican Village Life 104, 201
Meyers, Sydney 164
MGM 28, 99, 102, 209n3
Michael Scott Presents 141
Michelangelo 148
Micklin Silver, Joan 107, 109
Microbiology series (Coronet) 177
microcinemas 198–199
Middle Ages: A Wanderer's Guide to Life and Letters **55**, 55, 128
Middle America Regional Geography series (McGraw) 74, 109
Middle Atlantic Region 109
Middleham, Ken 51, 121, 207, 216n109
Mideast series (BFA) 71
Miles, Hugh, 137
Miller, Robert 196
Miner, Richard 84
Minow, Newton 39
Mister Magoo 165
MIT (Massachusetts Institute of Technology) 86–87, 171–172
Mitchell, Maurice (EB) 15, **21**, 24–28, 86–87 91–98, 141–143, 147–149, 156, 210n39, 210n42, 210–211n51, 211n54, 214n64, 217n14
Mitchell, Wayne 53, 70–71, **174**, 174–175, 205, 217n14
Miura, Yuichiro 82
Mobil Oil 108, 136
Modern Biology series (Benchmark) 73
Modern Europe series (McGraw) 74, 109
Modern Learning Aids 209n13
Modern Talking Picture Service 209n13
Modoc 55
Moffat, Donald 150–151, 217n13
Mokin Films (Arthur and Bill Mokin) 110–111
Montagnon, Peter 121, 135
Montgomery, John 98
Moody Institute of Science (MIS) 62, 110–111, 201, 215n88
Moon, Irwin A. 110–111
Moonbeam Princess 214n32
Moray, Joseph 85

Morochnik, Abraham 172
Morrison, Phillip 55
Morton Schindel: From Pages to Screen 124, 173
The Motion Picture and the Teaching of English (book) 209n14
Mountain Community of the Himalayas 70
Mountain Men 72
Mozambique: Building a Future 55, 114
MTI 78
Mulholland, Donald 35
Multiplication Rock series 58, 124–125
Munch, Edvard 190
Munro, Dorothy *79*
Murrow, Edward R. 126, 128–129
Murtagh, Terence 56
Muscle: A Study of Integration 84
Museum of Modern Art (MOMA) 184, 217n24
music and soundtracks in academic film 15, 56–58, 74, 85–86, 110, 112, 117–118, 122, 126, 130–132, 154, 160, 162, 164–165, 169, 173, 175, 188–189, 190–192, 199, 213n20, 217n14
Music of Williamsburg 164
Muzak Company 24, 91, 142, 210n39
My Three Sons 68
Mysterious Castles of Clay 73, 137
Mystery of Amelia Earhart 130

Nahanni 112
Najmanová, Zdenka 123, 164–165, 216n118, 217n7
Nanook of the North 33
narration characteristics and styles in academic film 56, 103, 106, 115, 126, 131, 217n14
National Council of Teachers of Mathematics 85
National Defense Education Act of 1965 (NDEA) 28, 39–40, 42, 194, 205, 211n2
National Endowments for the Arts and the Humanities 41
National Film Board of Canada (NFBC) 8, 13, 19, 32–37, 63, 73–74, 80–81, 87, 93–94, 100, 104, 111–115, 169–170, 204, 211n63, 211n64, 211n65, 214n43, 218n5, 218n6; Unit B 34–36, 112–113; Unit C 112, 211n64
National Foundation on the Arts and Humanities Act of 1965 41, 205
National Geographic (NGEO) 93, 100, 115–116, 165, 215n94
National Park Rangers 175
National Science Foundation (NSF) 39, 86–87, 89–90, 167, 214n51
Nations of the World series (NGEO) 115
Naughty Number Nine 124
NBC: news and television 66, 93–94, 100–101, 125–126, 130–132, 135; *White Paper* series 101, 126, 130–133
Nearing, Helen 74
Nearing, Scott 74
Neighbours 34
Nelkin, Dorothy 89
NET (National Educational Television) 126, 132; *NET Journal* series 132
Netsilik Eskimo films 86–89
New World Pictures 109
New York Times 143–144
Newell, George 124
Newman, Sydney 19
NICEM (National Information Center for Educational Media) database 209n2
Nicholson, Arch 137
Nightlife 57
Nightmare in Red 131
Niko: Boy of Greece 65
Nisei: The Pride and the Shame 130
nitrate film 16
Nixon-Lodge: Champions of Freedom 65
Noble, Lorraine 59
Nordine, Ken 141
North Carolina Board of Education 16, 204
Northwest Mountains to the Sea 168
Not Far from Bolgatanga 114
NOVA series (PBS) 122
Now and Then 66
Noxon, Nicolas 54

Ocean Voyage 142
O'Connor, Hugh 34, 113; murder 211n65
Odyssey series (EB) 148, 213n17
Oedipus Rex series (EB) 144
Oertel, Curt 77
Of Black America series (BFA) 63, 71, 125, 129–130, 205, 216n132
O'Farrell, William (Bill) 207
Office of Coordinator of International Affairs (CIAA) 32
Olk, Jerry, 98, 207
One Life to Live 109
One Who Came Back 68
Orange and Blue 162
Ostrich 162
Otterman, Lloyd 71
Our Latin American Neighbors series (McGraw) 74, 109
Our Mr. Sun 66–67
Overture: Linh from Vietnam 46, 107
Owls 76
Oxford Scientific Films, Ltd. 115, 186

Pacific Island Life series 105
Page, Walter 22
Palance, Jack 189
Paley, William 128
Pantomime: The Language of the Heart 153
Paramount Pictures 29, 67–68, 99
Parton, Jim 98
Pas de Deux 114, 184
Patterson, John Henry 21
Paul Tomkowicz: Street-railway Switchman 36
PBS (Public Broadcasting Service) and CPB (Corporation for Public Broadcasting) 101, 116, 126, 132–133, 183
Pelham, Hardy 72
Pendulum of Choice (book) 158
Pennell Nicholas 55, **55**, 109
People Along the Mississippi 21, 37, 45, 141–143, 201, 211n54
People of the Cities 137
Peoples of the Soviet Union 31
Percy, Sen. Charles 210–211n51
Perspective Films (Coronet) 62, 78, 116, 125, 205
Peru 74
Phillips, Patricia 114
Phoebe 112, 169–170, 215n91
Phoenix Films (Learning Group) 72, 76–77, 79, 109, 116–117, 158, 205
Photography: Beginning of a New Art 102
Physical Science Study Committee (PSSC) series 26, 39, 57, 86–87, 92, 169–172, 205
Physics: The Complete Introductory Course series (EB) 26, 92, 167
Piaget, Jean 85
Picture in Your Mind 184, 201
The Pilgrims 26, 91, 143
PIME (Pontifical Institute for Foreign Missions) 165
Pimentel, George 84
Pinsker, Seth 46, 107
Pioneer Life series 72
Plankton 115
Platt, Sid 115, 215n94
Plummer, Christopher 167
Poets: A Sestet series (NFBC) 193
Polanski, Roman 77
The Politics of Power 146
The Portable Phonograph 44, 153–154
Portrait in Black & White 129
Post Office Film Unit (UK) 33, 70
Potemkin 33
Powers of Ten (1978) 118, 201
Powers of Ten: A Rough Sketch (1968) 55, 161
Pratt Institute 106, 173
Praying Mantis 73
Princeton University 170
Project Discovery (film and project) 42–43, 205, 212n9
Project 20 series (NBC) 131
Prom Night in Mississippi 179
Proposition 13 (California) 194
Protein Synthesis: An Epic on the Cellular Level 199
Protozoa 26
PSSC *see* Physical Science Study Committee

Psychology Today magazine and textbooks *see* CRM Films
Public Media, Inc. *see* Films Incorporated
El Pueblo 65
Un Pueblo de España 76
Pueblo Méxicano de Pescadores 70
Puerto Rico: Its Past, Present, and Promise 166
The Purple Turtle 64
Pyramid Films (David, Lynn, and Denise Adams) 111, 117–118, *118*, 205, 215*n*99

Quayle, Anthony 135
Qué Viva México 70
Quiet Afternoon 160
Quinn, Anthony 136

The Race for Space 13
Rachmil, Mike 84
racial attitudes, discrimination, and themes in academic film 44–46, 60, 103–104, 107, 109, 117–120, 129–130, 133, 142–143, 164, 212*n*14, 214*n*52
Raccoons 76
Railroad Rhythms 57
Rainforest Family 175
Rallye des Neiges 112
Ramos, Marcelo 161
Rampart Films 159
Rancho Life 72
Random House 84
Rankin, Arthur 80
Les Raquetteurs 36
Rasmussen, Knut 87
Rathbun, Eldon 35
Reagan, Pres. Ronald 190
Rediscovering Art series 64
Reeder, Elizabeth "Libby" 181–*182*
Reel and Slide (journal) 17, 204
Reflections 46
regional politics relating to academic film 60–61, 144
Reid, Don 74
Reiniger, Lotte 77
religion and academic film 62, 66–67, 88–90, 110–111, 143, 173, 175, 213*n*14, 215*n*91
The Renaissance: Its Beginning in Italy 144
Renoir, John 3
Restless Sea 67, 69
Revolution in Russia 115
Reynolds, George 82
The Rice Ladle 137
Richler, Mordecai 114
Rickover, Adm. Hyman 39, 211*n*1
Ridgway, David W. 26–27, *27*
Riha, Tom 30, 207
Rise and Decline of the Roman Empire 78
Rival World 121
Roach, Hal 190
Roald Amundsen 136
Robeck, Peter 133

Roccos, Stelios (ACI) 60, 64–65, 205, 213*n*3
Rochman, Irwin 108
Rockefeller, John D., Jr. 22
Rockefeller, Laurance 21–22
Rockefeller, Nelson 21–22, 32
Rockefeller Foundation 22, 33, 59
Rockets: How They Work 212*n*6
Rocky Mountains: Continental Divide 72
Roe, Stuart 71, 201
Roger Williams, Founder of Rhode Island 26, 45, 217*n*13
Rogers, Eric 170, 172
Rogers, Helen Jean 127–128; *see also* Secondari
Rogers, Shorty 69
Romanticism: Revolt of the Spirit 128
Roney, Marianne 99
Rooney, Andy 129
Roosevelt & Hoover on the Economy 191
Root, Alan 73, 137, 175–177, *176*
Root, Joan 73, 137, 175–177, *176*
Roots 101
Rose, Barbara Wade 80–81
Rose, Bob 74
Rosenberg, Albert 109, 204
Rosenblatt, Maurice 42
Royal Air Force 159–160
Royal Canadian Mounted Police series 81
Royal Navy 168
Rubbo, Michael 114
Ruby, Jay 50
Rudolph, Ken 117
Ruml, Beardsley 17, 20, 23
Rusinow, Irving 43, *195*
Russell, Bruce J. 15, 51, 78, *177*, 177–178, 201, 207
The Russians series 137
Ruth Stout's Garden 110

Sabotage! 130
Sachs, Sheldon 78, 116, 178, 205
Sackett, Ross 98
Safer, Morley 130
safety film 16
Safety series (Disney) 85
Safra, Jacob 98
The Saga of Western Man series 128
Sagan, Carl 101
Salomon, Henry 54, 126, 131–132
Saltzman, Paul 56, *56*, 78, 116, *178*, 178–179
Salzman, Bert 6, 45–46, 65, 107–108, *179*, 179–180, 198, 201, 203
Sampan Family 32
Sanders, Terry 133
Santa Fe and the Trail 162, 164
Saunders, Jack 95, 98
Schimanski, Georg 51, 73, 104, 180–181
Schindel, Morton (Weston Woods) 41, 58, *123*, 123–124, 165, 173, 205
Schlenker, Hermann 104, 181
Schnitzler, Peter 74

Scholastic Films 118–119, 124
Schoolhouse Rock series 124
Schutzer, Anne 77
Schwartz, Charles 181–*182*
Science Screen Report series (Allegro) 119; *see also* Forman, Jerome
Scorer, Mischa 135
Scorsese, Martin 196
Scott, Michael Presents 114
Scourby, Alexander 54, 126, 131
Screen Actors Guild 18, 53, 97, 191
Screen Directors Guild 18
Screen News Digest series (Hearst Metrotone News) 119–120, 211*n*1; *see also* Forman, Jerome
Screen Writers Guild 18
Screenscope Films 64, 120
Seaborg, Dr. Glenn 27
Seabourne, John 71
Searching for Values series 107, 209*n*15
Sears, Roebuck and Company 22
Secondari, John H. 127–128
Secret Sharer 44
The Secret'st Man 146
See 'n Tell series (Films Inc.) 100
Seed Dispersal 189
Sellstrom, Brent 83–84
Sellstrom, Brian 83–84
Selznick, David O. 102
Sendak, Maurice 123, 165
Sense Perception 111
The Sernegeti Shall Not Die 175
Sesame Street 83
Seven Wishes of a Rich Kid 212*n*11
The Seventeen Year Locust 187
Shakespeare in academic film 144–151, 201, 203, 213*n*20
Shakespeare on TV series 66
Sharpsteen, Ben 86
Shaw, George Bernard 150–151, 201, 203
Shaw vs. Shakespeare series (EB) *2*, 50, 139, 149–151, *150*, 201, 203, 217*n*12
Shearer, Harry 55
Shedd, Ben 77
Shell Film Unit 62, 121
Shelton, John 97, 188
Sheridan, Richard 192
Sherman, Dave 66, 213*n*5
Sherman, Mel 66, 213*n*5
Sherman, Wynn "Biff" 66, 213*n*5
Shopping Bag Lady 46, 180, 203
Short Play Showcase and Short Story Showcase series (EB) 97, 193, 212*n*13
Shuker, Gregory 127
Shuster, George 23
Siege 32, 203
Siegel, George 68, 213*n*12
Siegel, William 66, 213*n*7
Sielmann, Heinz 180
Signature series (Weston Woods) 124
Silent Safari series (EB) 161
Silent Snow, Secret Snow 203
Simms, Willis 71

Sinclair, Robert 67–69
Sir Francis Drake: Rise of English Sea Power 26, 45, 143–144
Sisser, Pierre 118–119
Siu Mei Wong—Who Shall I Be? 107
Sky Dive! 117
Slate, Lane 132
Slate, Mallory 132
Slater, Christian 109
Slima the Dhowmaker 56, **56, 178**, 178
Slime Molds: Plants, Animals, Or? 121
Sloan, Alfred P. Foundation 86
Sloan, Marion 58
Sluizer, George 121
Smart, Alfred (Coronet) 13, 29–30, 78, 204, 211n52, 211n54, 211n57
Smart, David (Coronet) 13, 29–30, 78, 204, 211n52, 211n54, 211n57
Smart, John (Coronet) 13, 29–30, 78, 204, 211n52, 211n54, 211n57
Smith, Ken 211n53
Smith, Kevin 87
Smith, Sen. Margaret Chase 120
Smith, M.I. 16, 204
Smith, Thomas G. (Tom) 44–45, 50, 61, 98, **158**, 169, 183, 190, 203, 212n15
Snowdon, Anthony "Tony" 136
The Snowy Day 123
Snyder, Robert 77
So ein Zufall 104
Sofaer, Anna 74
Solar System, 2nd ed. 98, 183, 203
Somewhere in Time 51, 173
The Sorcerer's Apprentice (Weston Woods) 123, 203
Sorvino, Paul 109, **202**
Soumet, Jacques 118–119
The Space Between 111
Spaces Between People 107
Spain: A Journey with Washington Irving 115
Spain: Land of Tradition and Promise 122
Spare Time in the Army 76
Spider Engineers 110–111
Spiders: Backyard Science 159
Spinello, Barry 73
Spinning Wheel 72
Spottiswoode, Raymond 19, 54
Spotton, John 36
Spread Your Wings series see *World Culture and Youth*
Sputnik and the Cold War 7–8, 38–40, 87, 90, 197, 205, 212n15
Stanton, Frank 129, 216n129
Stanton Films (Thomas and Phyllis) 121, 157, 167, 205, 216n108
Stapp, Philip 19, 32, 106, 183, 183–185, 201, 207, 217n24
Star Wars 98
Steinberg, David 83
Sterling Communications 119
Sternhagen, Frances **140**
Stevenson, Adlai 23, 39, 46, 131, 140
Stevenson, Anne 70

Stevenson, Kennedy 22
Stewart, Jimmy 68
Stockton, Philip 98
Stoddard, Ed 55
Stoddard, George **21**
Stonecutter 173, 203
Stoney, George 113, 180
Story Into Film 44
Story Into Film: A Discussion by John Barnes of the Portable Phonograph 154
Story of a Writer—Ray Bradbury 133
Story of an Immigrant 17
Strauss, Harry 55
The Street 114
Stuart, Mel 133
Sucksorff, Arne 26
Sugarman, Andrew 117
Sun Dagger 74
Sun Flight 199, 203
Supergoop 76
Survival Anglia 137
Sutherland Films 159
Suzuki, Tom 82
SVE 76
Swenson, Charles 76
Swerdlow, Arthur 132
Symington, Rep. James 90
Symmetry 184

Taleb & His Lamb 72
Tate, Grady 124
Teaching Film Custodians 17, 204, 209n14
Teaching Films, Inc. 124
television networks 63, 125–127
Ten Who Dared series 135–136
Terkel, Studs 217n16
The Terrible Twos 80
Terrytoons 165
textbook companies 42–43, 82–83, 87–88, 124, 212n14
Thames Television 110
Thank You Ma'am 117
That They May Live 117
Theatre in Shakespeare's Time 213n20
Themes of Macbeth 146
Thompson, Don 209n15
Thompson, Gerald 115, **185**, 185–186
Thompson, Francis 105
Thompson, Howard 143
Thompson, Michelle 120
Thompson, R.H. 55
Thread of Life 67–69
Three Fox Fables 58
Thunder in the Sky 134
Time and Clocks 169
Time in the Sun 70
Time-Life Films 62, 101, 119, 121–122, 127, 133–134, 194, 205
Time of Wonder 124
The Titan: Story of Michelangelo 77
To Sir with Love 107
Toast 74
Today and Yesterday: American Lifestyles series 64

Tom Terrific 165
Tomi Ungerer, Storyteller 124, 164
The Touch of His Hand 165, 217n10
Toute La Bande series (Scholastic) 118–119
Townsend, Robert 83
The Tragedy of Julius Caesar 151, 203
travelogues 103–104
Trevor, Simon 137
Tristam & Wilson 65
Trojan, Judy 60
True Life Adventures series 86
Truman, Pres. Harry S. 23
The Trusting Threes 80
TV Ontario 101
The Twentieth Century (CBS) series 130
20th Century–Fox 99, 106, 117, 165
The Twenty-First Century series (CBS) 130
Twisted Cross 54
Two Men and a Wardrobe 77
Tyler, Robert 23

UCLA 27, 191
Uggams, Leslie 150
Unchained Goddess 67
Uncounted Enemy: A Vietnam Deception 127
Undercurrents 57
Ungerer, Tomi 123–124, 164, 216n118
Unique Contribution 25–26, 203
United Nations (UNESCO, UNCEF) 65, 73, 131
U.S. Army: Army Air Force 68, 121, 158, 190; public relations 67; Signal Corps 18, 76–77, 167, 204
U.S. Department of Justice 215n91
United States Geography series 109
U.S. Information Agency (USIA) 120, 123
U.S. Military Intelligence 102
U.S. Office (Dept.) of Education 41, 43, 59; Division of Visual Aids for War Training 19, 204
U.S. Office of War Information 169
United World Films 122, 204, 216n111
Universal Education and Visual Arts (and Universal Films) 62, 122–123, 204, 216n115
Universe (NFBC) 33, 36, 112
University of California 27, 84, 175
University of Chicago 14, 17, 20–23, 33, 140–141, 144, 204, 210n35
University of Southern California (USC) 66, 167
University of Toronto 87, 172
An Unworthy Scaffold 213n20
Unzu, Klaus 115
UPA 165
USA Artists series 132

Vacances en Bretagne 118–119
Vale, Bob 65
Vale, June 65

Index

Valley Town 76
Van Bork, Bert 6, 15, 26, **49**, 51–52, 91, 97, **158**, 169, 177, 186–189, **187**, 212n13, 214n64; *Bert Van Bork: Künstlerporträts* (book) 189
Van Deusen, Pieter 77
Van Doren, Charles **44**, 44, 193
Vanguard, Wendy 84
van Ormer, Edward 19
Van Tilberg Clark, Walter 153
VD: The Hidden Epidemic (1973) 61
Verrall, Robert 34–35, 113
A Very Special Day: An Adventure at Coney Island 122, 216n115
Victor, Alexander F. (Victor Animatograph) 16, 204
Victory at Sea 126
Video Japonica 73
Vietnam Epilogue: End of the Tunnel 120
Vietnam War 120, 127, 129, 175
Viki (chimpanzee) 69
Viljoen, Tina 111
Villadsen, Kurt 84
Visco Frank 64
Vishniac, Roman 26
Visual Education Center (VEC) 100, 104
Voice of America 169
Volcanoes: Exploring the Restless Earth 189
Von Lawick, Hugo 161

Wachtler, Sol 129, 216n130
Wagner, Ralph 93, 98, 156
Wagner, Thomas 173
Walker, Bill 78
Walker, Hal 129–130
Walker, John 188–190, **189**
Wallace, Mike 133
Wallis, Hal 68
Walnum, Sven 175
Ward's Natural Science 177
Warner Bros. (Jack Warner) 67–68
Waskin, Mel 78–79, 212n10, 214n34
Wasserman, Albert 130
Water Cycle, 2nd ed. 189
Watkins, Peter 107–108
Waymouth, Dr. John 171
We Seek No Wider War 120
Webster Publishing 109, 117
Wednesday's Children series 114
Weil, Lisl 124

Weiner, Hal 64–65, 120
Weiner, Marilyn 64–65, 120
Weisenborn, Gordon 21, 37, 141, 201, 211n54
Weisman, Gay 64–65, 213n3
Weiss, Gabriel (Robert Alan) 199, 201
The Well of the Saints 193
Werrenrath, Reinald Productions 65
West, Clifford B. 190–191, **191**, 207
West Virginia: Life, Liberty, and the Pursuit of Coal 127
Western Civilization: Majesty & Madness series (LCA) 215n82
Western Electric 16–17, 22, 204
Westmoreland, Gen. William (libel suit) 126
Weston Woods Films 41, 58, 118–119, **123**, 123–124, 165, 173
Wexler, Haskell 190
Wexler Films (Sy Wexler) 27, 76, 205, 213–214n29
W.F. Hall Printing 108
WGBH 101, 122
When Smart People Fail (book) 109
Where Is Prejudice? 132
Where the Wild Things Are 123, 165
Whistling Smith 114
White, Harvey 26
White, Ruth 57
White Wilderness 86
Whitehead, Peter 109
Whitney, John 83
Wholly Communion 109
Why Man Creates 118
Why We Fight 19, 204
Wiland, Harry 136
Wild Mammals of Missouri (book) 181
Wild Men of the Kalahari 103, 203
Wilder, Donald 112
Wilder, Thornton 144
Wildlife Drawings (book) 181
Wilets, Bernard 53, 66, 70–72, 191–192, **192**, 207, 212n17
Wilkins, Roy 41
Wilkinson, Douglas 34, 87
Wilkman, John 109
Willard Pictures 18–19
Willenson, Seth 100
William Shakespeare 91
Willis, Ben 46
Willis, Jack 132
Wilson, Robert 199, 201
Wilson, Tim 34

Winkler, Donald 113, 192–193
Winning Your Wings 68
Winograd, Peter 55
Winter, Jackson 103
Wirtz, W. Willard 89
Wiseman, Frederick 57
WNET 101
Wolff, Perry 63, 125, 129, 205
Wolper Productions (David Lloyd Wolper) 63, 93, 100–101, 109, 116, 126, 132–133
Wombat Films 65, 111
Women in Politics 120
Wondering About Sound 58
Wonders in Your Own Backyard 76
Wood, Gen. Robert E. 22
Woodby, Lauren G. 85
Woods, James 109
Work of the Heart 167
Working 135
World Cultures and Youth series (Coronet) **56**, 56, 78, 116, **178**, 178
World of Three 169–170, 215n91
World War II 128–129, 162; military training films 18–20, 29, 67–68, 76, 80, 109, 160
Worsley, Wallace 87
WQED 132
Wright, Randolph (Randy) 118
Writers on Writing series (Davidson) 85

Xerox Films 124–125

Yannias, Don 98
Yemen 65
Yohe, Tom 58, 124, 201
Young, Robert M. 6, 87, 131, 133, 216n134
Young America Films 124
You're No Good 58, 169
You're Not Listening 73
Youth, Maturity, Old Age 153
YouTube 199
Yukon Territory 65
Yust, Larry 6, 22, 44, 52, 87, 91, 97–98, **158**, 169, **192–193**, 193, 198, 212n13
Yust, Walter 22

Zacharias, Dr. Jerrold 27, 86, 170
Zanuck, Darryl 18
Ziff-Davis 84, 110

www.ingramcontent.com/pod-product-compliance
Lightning Source LLC
Chambersburg PA
CBHW081551300426
44116CB00015B/2842